SHOWPIECE CITY

Stanford Studies *in* Middle Eastern
and Islamic Societies *and* Cultures

SHOWPIECE
CITY

HOW ARCHITECTURE MADE DUBAI

Todd Reisz

STANFORD UNIVERSITY PRESS

Stanford, California

STANFORD UNIVERSITY PRESS
Stanford, California

This book has been published with the assistance of the Graham Foundation for Advanced Studies in the Fine Arts, the Stimuleringsfonds Creatieve Industrie (The Netherlands), and the Netherlands Foundation for Visual Arts, Design and Architecture (FBKVB).

Printed in the United States of America on acid-free, archival-quality paper

Library of Congress Cataloging-in-Publication Data
Names: Reisz, Todd, author.
Title: Showpiece city : how architecture made Dubai / Todd Reisz.
Other titles: Stanford studies in Middle Eastern and Islamic societies and cultures.
Description: Stanford, California : Stanford University Press, 2021. | Series: Stanford studies in Middle Eastern and Islamic societies and cultures | Includes bibliographical references and index.
Identifiers: LCCN 2020004569 (print) | LCCN 2020004570 (ebook) | ISBN 9781503609884 (cloth) | ISBN 9781503613867 (ebook)
Subjects: LCSH: Harris, John R., 1919-2008. | Architecture—United Arab Emirates—Dubai—History—20th century. | City planning—United Arab Emirates—Dubai—History—20th century.
Classification: LCC NA1473.2.D83 R45 2020 (print) | LCC NA1473.2.D83 (ebook) | DDC 720.95357—dc23
LC record available at https://lccn.loc.gov/2020004569
LC ebook record available at https://lccn.loc.gov/2020004570

Cover design: Kevin Barrett Kane

Cover image: Fastened to the building by wire, construction workers install the inner layer of the Dubai World Trade Centre tower's double facade. Photograph taken from the construction crane's bucket, 1978. Photograph by Gordon Heald.

Map on pp vi and vii: The Dubai 1960 town plan. Courtesy John R. Harris Library

Text design: Kevin Barrett Kane

Typeset at Stanford University Press in 11/15 Brill

CONTENTS

SHOWPIECE CITY

HERE'S A PLAN

MANY PROLOGUES have been written for Dubai. Some of these take place at the city's *khor*, or creek: the marshy waterway that Arabs, Iranians, and South Asians made into a harbor. Others start in Haifa, Khartoum, Kochin, and Saigon. There are as many prologues as starting points for journeys to Dubai. And they can be infinitely rescripted to fit the themes at hand and to anticipate those to come. No prologue is an origin. Each is an epilogue for stories before its own. It's where one chooses to begin, for now.

This prologue opens in London in 1959, because this is where many people licensed to change landscapes stood ready to change Dubai's. It is toward the end of a summer of shimmering lawns and refreshing shade. Many recalled that summer being just warm enough that an iced drink sweat through a linen napkin. Benevolent sunlight merely added color and definition to gardens that appeared to care for themselves. Such manageable conditions can seem far away from a summer endured in Dubai, where the only reprieve from howling sands that can cut through skin and the hard, diamond-bright sun was the inside of an airless, aching souk.

The difference between the two worlds composed a common narrative—the first portrayed as pleasant and accommodating, the other as grueling and inadequate. The two settings were the stage for how ideas and modern things were dispatched from one world to improve the other—things like electric grids, asphalt roads, hospital care, and hotel lobbies. Architects had no major role in this narrative, not yet, but they were ready couriers of expertise, with calculations and measurements to rectify any apparent deficiency. They were trained to chart delivery, and therefore to guarantee it. Architecture though offers more than the assembly of itemized ingredients. On a landscape that had endured millennia without it, the building of reinforced-concrete architecture would declare urgency, its completion would announce arrival, and its advertisement, as a showpiece, would affirm that standards had been set, and met, and that more was on the way.

Cold drink in hand, the British architect John Harris was at a garden party that summer in London's plush and verdant neighborhood around Campden Hill Square. It was the right place at the right time. He had just turned forty and ran a small architectural practice. He had a reputation for courtesy and composure. Mindful of others and alert to where he stood in a room, he spoke in "clipped, gentlemanly tones" and could sense "exactly which anecdotes and insights were going to convey his thoughts."[1] He could smoothly turn party chatter into a sales pitch. Procuring projects was his strength, but getting his practice off the ground had taken longer than expected. War service had interrupted his studies and sent him to Hong Kong. Then, when the British relinquished Hong Kong to Japanese forces in 1941, his "five most dreadful years" began as a prisoner of war. Detained in dilapidated military barracks, he stayed sane by creating watercolors with paints he somehow managed to come by. Medicines smuggled in saved him from dying from diphtheria, while he witnessed fellow prisoners die from diseases and random execution. Luck, he later asserted, was the reason he survived. Freed from the barracks but still trapped in a fiercely undernourished body, John Harris returned to London in 1946.[2]

As disorienting as his last five years had been, the next three were productive and deliberate. Once he regained his health, he matriculated again at London's Architectural Association and secured his degree in 1949. He met his wife, fellow architect Jill Rowe, during their studies. In 1949 they opened their "one half of one room" office in their Marylebone home, but Britain's postwar rebuilding did not provide them much work.[3] Harris wanted to translate the trauma of his imprisonment into designing for "extreme" climates. The couple pursued commissions far away from Britain, in places endowed with the petroleum required by the recovering British economy. In 1951, the firm was hired to design a small "building research station" in Kuwait, thanks to a family connection. In 1953, the pair won an open design competition for a new hospital in Doha, a city expanding on Qatar's petroleum profits. They delivered the hospital four years later as the surrounding region's largest architectural project. Such an accomplishment should have led to an influx of clients. Instead, Harris learned that new work did not materialize on its own. That realization might have been on his mind at the garden party.

There, Harris met Donald Hawley, who at thirty-eight was Britain's ranking official in Dubai. He was in London for holiday that he timed to escape Dubai's most insufferable month. His position in Dubai was considered a "hardship post." As the political agent for the Trucial States, Hawley embodied more than a century of British control over Dubai's access to the outside world.[4] As there was no higher-ranking official within a day's travel, Hawley experienced for the first time being in charge, and it suited him. His mandate from the Foreign Office was to make the British policy in Dubai seem rational, clear, and benign to those both inside and outside the city. For a rising diplomat, social events like London garden parties led to work opportunities, and vice versa. He used his summer leave to find British "short-term expert aid" for what he called Dubai's "prelude to serious development."[5] The garden party's host, Hawley's and Harris's mutual contact, was also supplying experts: English-language teachers through the British Council for new planned schools. An architect or town planner was not on Hawley's contact list, but Harris had the skills to convince him that one should be.

As a rule, Hawley kept to telling simple stories. He was paid to portray the British intercession in Dubai's affairs as fair and constructive. Hawley later claimed he organized Harris's initial visit to Dubai so that he would produce the city's first town plan. The story may be told as matter-of-fact: Two men mindful of their respective careers forge a gentlemen's agreement to shape the future of a place 5,500 kilometers away. In actuality, Hawley was not authorized to hire Harris, much less to mastermind an outright modernization program for Dubai. Instead he was instructed to choreograph the appearance of change without the British, or any other foreign entity for that matter, seeming to dictate it.

The two men's encounter at the garden party was enmeshed in a history of British empire and colonialism. Their prologue did not supersede other prologues, but it had the political power to alter other ones for good. This chance meeting determining how one of the world's most watched cities would take shape was based on more than a century of incidents, and indecision, that accumulated to define British control over Dubai. Before Hawley ever sought his London experts, Great Britain, as early as 1820, wielded military and political power to monitor Dubai's trade and restrict its imports. In his history of Dubai and the region, Hawley noted that "there were no diplomatic representatives" from other countries, but he failed to point out that this lack was because the British government prohibited them.[6] Dubai's leaders could communicate with the outside world only through their British contacts; the city's imports were officially limited to British products. As the naval ships had done previously, Hawley as the political agent restricted entrance of American, European, and Arab visitors but gave little thought to indigent arrivals from South Asia. By cordoning off the coast, British officials envisioned a place frozen in the nineteenth century. Both Hawley and Harris eventually would witness what happens when the cordon came down.

If defined as a centralized project delivered by authority, modernization began in Dubai when it was sanctioned to begin by the British Foreign Office. That had happened by the time the first political agent, Christopher Pirie-Gordon, moved to Dubai in 1954. Before then, "watch and cruise" British officers had been stationed aboard naval ships a couple of hours off Dubai's coast.[7] At first, Pirie-Gordon's arrival did not amount to more than sporadic improvement projects like a mobile health clinic and water-drilling studies. These missions did not accumulate into a vision of a city. Dubai was rarely even referred to as a "city"—more of an unsteady node of nomadic Bedouins and fleeting boatmen.[8] The arrival of the political agent was a calculated signal, an embodiment, of a modernization program. The agency framed modernization as an installation of bureaucratic legibility on a place where there had been none before. Modernization was not to be a splendid act

FIGURE P.1 Dubai Creek from aboard an abra (small boat), November 1959. Courtesy John R. Harris Library.

of power but a managerial ordering, and, on that auspicious afternoon in London summer, Harris began working on what kind of role he could play in that endeavor.

A HARBOR ALREADY MODERN

In reality, the keepers of Dubai's port—Arab, South Asian, and Iranian traders—managed it on their own. They survived economically by exploiting the incompetency of British surveillance, thereby debunking any fictional notion of the port as a nineteenth-century relic. Dubai's merchants were already making the city modern through covertly maintaining the city's connections to the rest of the world. Mercantile persistence resulted in the city's ascendancy as a regional hub for arms sales and more, to the frustration of British surveillance efforts. Modern appliances managed to arrive, as did news and ideas from other parts of the world. Traders heard about political

FIGURE P.2 Souk in Dubai, November 1959. Courtesy John R. Harris Library.

changes happening nearby and how the larger world was responding to the collapsing forms of colonial dominance outside Dubai.

In the 1950s, Dubai's traders realized they could maintain connections with the world—as long as their onshore premises did not betray those connections. Wealth, therefore, was not revealed in improved port facilities or in the city's built surfaces. The wealthiest of the merchants still expressed their stature in the coral houses made with Iranian craftsmanship and Indian hardwood. If manufactured building materials passed through the port, they were not intended for Dubai's transformation; rather they were being re-exported to other places for the sake of profit.

Once stationed in Dubai, the political agent sought to supply more intelligence on just how successfully Dubai's traders circumvented British inspection. Ostensibly there to manage and surveil Dubai, he was evaluated by how his actions advanced the British economy. In responding to this directive, the agent tried to arrange Dubai in a way commercially beneficial for British industries. He argued that the port's resourcefulness and grit could serve a British advantage by establishing a "free port" from which British companies could secure, and profit from, the regional trade in petroleum.[9] By running illegal trade rings counter to British decree, Dubai's merchants had proved their usefulness to British interests. They were the agency's evidence that the city had the potential to create a lively commercial hub, an easier and more profitable pursuit than keeping the port shut off.

THE SHEIKH RASHID YEARS

A key figure in the hiring of John Harris also enjoyed some weeks of London's memorable 1959 summer, but he wasn't at the garden party: Sheikh Rashid bin Saeed Al Maktoum, Dubai's ruler from 1958 until his death in 1990. Any telling of the Maktoum lineage of rulers usually culminates in Sheikh Rashid's ascent as a business-savvy leader who only improved on the business formula of his predecessors. Maktoum rule is often portrayed as unhindered. More truthfully, economic and political forces frequently compelled Maktoum rulers to reconsider strategy in order to ensure Dubai's endurance. In the years prior to becoming Dubai's ruler, Sheikh Rashid faced the greatest challenges ever to his family's claim to power. At the outset of his rule, the Foreign Office even doubted whether it could make good on its promise to protect his sovereignty.

The Foreign Office framed its inexact and irresolute modernization effort as a tutorial in leadership for Sheikh Rashid. Britain's continuing protection was conditioned on his pursuing a financial and bureaucratic ordering of his urban dominion on their terms. At first his British contacts didn't trust him, but within a couple of years of his ascent, Rashid was adorned with honorifics like the "merchant prince." British experts found him "extremely charming."[10] Journalists and diplomats described him as an astute, imperturbable man with a wry smile, a pipe, and a recycled aspirin bottle filled with tobacco.

Accounts of the first years of Sheikh Rashid's rule often read like a modernist legend: the ready-mix creation of a modern city out of a proverbial "fishing village."[11] According to legend, Sheikh Rashid achieved for Dubai in a couple of decades what took a century elsewhere. It has been often reported that in the first six years of his reign, Sheikh Rashid saved Dubai Creek from commercial demise, built a modern port, provided residents with running water, and launched electricity and telephone companies. In that time span, Dubai also secured street lamps, a modern hotel, and a landing strip for airplanes. Finally, the city could be seen from an airplane at night.

The 1960s and 1970s are called the Sheikh Rashid years, when Dubai's ruler allegedly assembled this city. To tell the story as a conveyor belt fairytale is as deceptive as it is enticing. Modern comforts and the infrastructure that provide them are designed to seem simple. A town plan might express where these services could be situated, but any realization comes about through a combination of compromise and brinkmanship. Reconstructing these decades through another kind of built work, this book reveals the gambits, missteps, and bravado that added up to a city. To reassemble the Dubai of these decades pries open a two-pronged myth about Dubai: On one side is the falcon-winged tale of brave Bedouins and Arab merchants enduring desert and maritime hardships, and on the other is the extraordinary "rising from the sands" of glass-and-steel towers, amassing into a "futuristic city."[12] The two mythical states result in oversimplified praise ("Look at what they've done!") and damnation ("What else would you expect?").

Between the two extremes are bouts of toil, mistake, hesitation, and restart that generated today's Dubai. As a result, the reality was in constant need of a rewrite. Dubai had to be revealed as a place where one could find work, where one could be born, where one could eat meat from the market without getting sick. Later it needed to be shown as a place where one's bank accounts were secure, where airplanes could land safely, and where central air conditioning kept the city at a comfortable 72°F. A physical city was constructed and so was the image of one. They were equally important.

JOHN HARRIS AND A HISTORY OF EXPERTS

Months after the garden party, Harris made a nine-day visit to Dubai, where he walked the city's unpaved streets, witnessed the port halfway through an unprecedented engineering project, and met the city's ruler. In May 1960, Harris presented Dubai's first town plan. More than a plan, it was then the most accurate map of Dubai from which the city's leaders and experts could chart Dubai's growth and transformation. Hawley called it Dubai's "basis for all future town planning."[13] The town plan presented Dubai as measurable and legible, and it supplied the instructions to guide future growth "along sound lines." The plan proposed the trajectories of new roads and residential districts that reached out of the apparent disorder of existing Dubai into open areas designated for new development. Adhering to those lines, a phalanx of British consultants and salesmen would deliver a newly sanctioned modernization.

Harris was but one of the experts that the political agency brought to Dubai to promote the narrative of clarity embedded in a British-friendly modernization program. Large-scale infrastructure, eventually, was the preferred tactic. Focused on the agents who designed these projects, this book offers an introspective look at how a globalizing practice of architecture and urban development found its footing in the final years of British empire. Late British colonialism is often described as politically impotent, directionless, and disorganized. On the contrary, there was a "modified form of commercial empire" being formatted, a reformulation that emphasized establishing the British economy as a lucrative exporter to the rest of the world; it was not only an economic role but also a means to hold on to a "world-power role."[14]

This economic-political stance required not only the exported goods but also the advisors and experts who ensured that the products were inserted into foreign lands. Beginning in the mid-1950s, British engineers introduced Dubai's ruler to the political potential of infrastructure. What ensued was the quiet start of a significant project of twentieth-century architecture and planning: to make a world city out of a place that had been fenced off by British policy for more than a century. At first, Dubai offered a testing ground

FIGURE P.3 Dubai work permit for John R. Harris. Courtesy John R. Harris Library.

for receiving British design as an exportable commodity. By opening Dubai's markets once again to global trade routes, however, Dubai could no longer be beholden only to British rule.

In the 1960s and 1970s, Dubai's future was its greatest asset, but no experts were showcasing fantastical visions. Instead, they exhibited prowess through a "quick calculation on the back of an envelope" and won contracts to produce the evidence that things were getting better.[15] Until the late 1970s, borders, lines, words, coordinates—entirely invisible on Dubai's landscape—assured prospective creditors, residents, and workers that Dubai had a future. They signaled what else was possible. The collateral the city could put up was the transformation already happening.

At this time, the presence of foreign experts was justified by an apparent absence of local expertise. Foreign consultants, however, delivered a more crucial element: the appearance that Dubai's growth and expansion happened outside its politics. By being reduced to their financial transactions,

FIGURE P.4 Experts and advisors attend Sheikh Rashid bin Saeed Al Maktoum (*center*) during a site visit to Dubai's World Trade Centre, circa 1978. Courtesy John R. Harris Library.

engineers, designers, and administrative professionals were set outside Dubai's social and political reality. Whether serving a military force or an engineering firm, many experts claimed that "the last thing on my mind was interfering in local politics."[16] As the anthropologist Ahmed Kanna has made clear, this "political ingenuousness" promised by so many experts continues to drive how Dubai markets itself today.[17]

The hired experts—engineers, architects, contractors, and marketers—both built the city and composed a story about a sound investment. They even helped write Rashid's own biography, cobbled together from handed-down anecdotes and quips recorded by newspapers and magazines. Those smitten by their own part in the telling of a city's thrilling rise contributed to Dubai's global image. Their stories of profitable successes in turn lured more of their professional ilk to the city. Maxims like "What's good for the merchant is good for Dubai" were attributed to the ruler merely because countless businessmen swore they had heard him say it.

Even while these profit-minded advisors helped create the city's infra-structure and modern institutions, they regaled journalists with stories of how Dubai was free of red tape and any stultifying bureaucracy. A handshake, they claimed, was as good as a contract. They took pleasure in describing how Rashid sealed their deals by drawing literal lines in the sand to mark a future construction site. Such stories, however, did not take into account what happened after the theatrics of deal-making in the desert: A Pakistani municipal worker promptly arrived and recorded the coordinates with British-sourced surveying equipment. This worker was evidence that Dubai was mapped and modern before it might have ever looked it. Just as much as they created Dubai's mythology, experts also chipped away at it. Increasingly, the ruler relied on published contracts, ordinances, and merchant-bank loan agreements, all of them written up by hired experts. The more information that experts documented on paper, the more that could be read, and therefore scrutinized, by even more experts.

The experts proved to be excellent storytellers, but they concealed as much as they revealed. Rarely are their contracts, and even more rarely the correspondence around those contracts, found in public archives. We can still witness some of their commissions that altered Dubai's landscapes—like bridges, buildings, and deepwater ports. Beyond the built environment, we can read trade magazines, promotional brochures, and newspaper advertisements for the tales contracted service providers spun for good copy. They praised their built projects to promote themselves and, in the process, praised Dubai. Brazenly self-promoting language, correlated with profit-driven motives, makes it obvious that these claims should not be taken at face value. Perhaps an exception among his contracted peers in Dubai, John Harris was eulogized by a former colleague as "a remarkable man in the sense that he was unremarkable. A master of the understated who went about his work quietly and yet with determination."[18] Subtler experts, like John Harris, were careful with what they shared, usually relying on rehearsed crowd-pleasing anecdotes. In the 1980s and 1990s, many more British firms were finally clued in that their future profits might lie in a region Harris knew well in the 1950s. He was often invited to speak at professional organizations and even at his alma mater, in the hope that he would divulge trade secrets. He rarely veered from his talking points.

FIGURE P.5 Sheikh Rashid, a construction worker, and John Harris during a site visit to the World Trade Centre. Courtesy John R. Harris Library.

Since the issuance of Harris's town plan, millions have come to Dubai to execute it. The number of professional experts was dwarfed by the numbers of skilled and unskilled workers who arrived to realize and maintain the structures that Dubai's leaders financed. In the early years of the British-endorsed modernization project, Dubai's port was as open as its wall-less city to those who would come to build the projects. As late as the 1970s, almost anyone could land on shore in the pursuit of financial opportunity, if at their own peril. Without a reliance on formal recruitment networks, the message got out quickly that Dubai needed help in making something bigger than itself.

But unlike cities such as Bombay and Guangzhou, whose migrants largely hail from the rural areas of their respective countries, Dubai relied on transnational labor networks, many of which were already configured by a century

FIGURE P.6 Two residents of Dubai, November 1959. Courtesy John R. Harris Library.

of British imperialism. By the mid-1950s, foreigners made up the city's majority. Each new plan, building project, and engineering feat heightened Dubai's
appeal to foreign workers. Every worker who came, sometimes despite life-
threatening risk, had reason to believe this city of dusty construction sites
and expanding horizons offered new chances and opportunities. Stories of
previous workers were the prologues to their own stories.

UNRECORDED

There is no publicly accessible archive in Dubai. Many documents should be
at hand but are not to be found—for example, cadaster maps that Dubai's
municipality produced as a result of Harris's town plan and the early decrees

by which the municipality sought to maintain the city's spatial ordering. Many who agreed to talk about this recent past rely on nostalgic memories and often do not want to say anything possibly construed as negative. Stories prefaced with "You can't write this" are often not scandalous: It is understandable, for example, that a leader of a rapidly developing city being shaped by an evasive British presence, profit-hungry foreigners, and a delicate local power structure could occasionally lose his temper. What unfolds in trying to gather Dubai's urban history is a complex and ambiguous field of hints, snapshots, and occasional documents. One might expect that modernization—specifically its capacity to calibrate and to record—would leave behind an archive. In fact, the outright rejection of posterity's importance might have been a deliberate, and also modern, act. A constant cleanup of messy histories can lead to a city that suggests the modern ideal—self-willed, simple, and on-message.

That nearly every major development project in Dubai was completed without much attention to preserving a historical record can be interpreted to mean that there was no time to think of legacy. Sheikh Rashid's name adorns the city's feats of infrastructure, but aside from an unexceptional "eternal flame" commemorating Dubai's oil discovery, monuments don't have much of a role in the city. Rashid's champions often portrayed him as too busy to be thinking of memorialization.

There was, however, an early and vigorous marketing effort—found on the pages of the London *Times*, the *Financial Times*, the *Economist,* and countless professional magazines—broadcasting Dubai's stories of transformation. From the 1960s onward, Dubai's government had a press machine, a team of storytellers for Arabic- and English-language audiences, to make sure the city appeared in print. These published pages, while not so much focused on redrafting the past, aimed to reset Dubai's starting point to coincide with modernization. All the while, Dubai's history was slipping away through the revolving door of consultants. One hazard of an inaccessible history lies in what happens when people eventually want to tell that history. As there is increasing interest (and money) to preserve and publish Dubai's history, the voids are creating tempting opportunities to fill the blanks with comfortable fictions instead of awkward facts.[19]

Donald Hawley once complained that it seemed "extraordinary that so small a place as this can engender so much paper."[20] For him the paper work was the testimony for how "we do so much work" for Dubai's nascent bureaucracy. This book relies on hundreds of government files that made it into the British National Archives and the British Library. What remains ranges in quality from carefully crafted reports to brusquely sent telegrams. Dossiers from the succession of political agents provide impressions of the political and economic landscape on which modern Dubai was being built. One can begin to piece together strands and fragments of policy decisions across files to suggest the larger picture that might not have ever been fully articulated. The historian Nelida Fuccaro, however, has argued for caution in reading British records. Even after opening their office on Dubai Creek, British officials could not fully grasp the intricacies of inner- and inter-sheikhdom politics, despite the certainty projected in their reporting.[21] The British archives offer a particular, and therefore limited, perspective, but they are nevertheless valuable for understanding the motivations behind British policies in Dubai.

Even the British record can seem empty. Instead of clearly stated goals or policies, we are most often left with the minutiae of bureaucratic management. Government papers capture, for example, how one invoice needed an additional report to explain a £3 discrepancy or how an officer's acquisition of an American, instead of a British, secondhand auto could incur admonishment. On the one hand, minutiae can seem trivial and distracting, both for the historian and the poor bureaucrat too occupied with clerical duties to take in the larger picture. On the other hand, their accumulation can suggest a latent set of guidelines by which the political agency exerted its influence. A consequential policy shift might be delivered in a hasty telegram from London. We can read it closely for its implied messages, perhaps just like the political agent left to explain it to a city of skeptics. These bureaucratic micro-histories make clear that modern urbanization need obey no grand visions, even in a city sometimes referred to at times as a *city of spectacle*.

Beyond British-government documents, there is also the work of journalists, mostly Westerners, to provide a historical record, but they proved they could be hoodwinked. British advisors in the pay of Dubai's government and Sheikh Rashid were adept at planting stories and disseminating unsubstantiated statistics. In search of a good story, writers and editors accepted these fictions. Stories became facts. In addition, issues of the London *Times* and *Financial Times* in the 1960s and 1970s brazenly overlapped advertising and reporting. There are also various English trade magazines that provided regular coverage of Dubai's development progress. In many of these articles, it is difficult to differentiate praise for their subscribers' industries from the praise for Dubai. Some Arabic-language periodicals have also provided additional perspective on the city. One in particular, *Akhbar Dubai*, published by Dubai Municipality, provides insight into how the local government wanted to convey itself.

There are also the files of John Harris, kept in his home and offices in London. For this book, Harris could only be interviewed once before he died in 2008. He had suffered a number of strokes, which at times left gaps in his memory and at other times allowed a fluid exchange through time and time zones. The interviews that did not happen are among this story's holes and shadows. In many ways, however, Harris had already done his work. He speaks through buildings, photographs, drawings, and letters. He also left behind lecture notes that offer the menu of anecdotes he arranged according to the occasion.

Focused on the histories of foreign expertise, this book provides minimal elucidation on a significant aspect of Dubai's urban development, namely the wealthy merchants whose family businesses presided over Dubai's port since as early as the nineteenth century. Their financial and societal role began to change with the arrival of oil explorers in the 1950s and the local presence of British officers. As they sought new ways to sustain their businesses and maintain their influence on the city, they collaborated with and challenged both Sheikh Rashid and the present British officers.[22] Members of these families have been variously described—from profit-motivated traders to would-be political reformists. They were certainly influential local voices, and some of them contributed greatly to Dubai's urban growth. They built the earliest shopping centers, the sprawling tracts of villas, and the rows of apartment blocks that housed incoming populations.

FIGURE P.7 Sheikh Rashid (*center*) at construction site, flanked by advisors and experts including John Harris and William Duff (*foreground, second and third from left*). Courtesy John R. Harris Library.

Though the British government was committed to protecting Maktoum rule, it also realized it shared motives with the merchants. In this way, the merchants shaped British policy in Dubai. More profoundly, their trade connections ensured that the port was filled with the necessary supplies—concrete, steel, air conditioners, automobiles, and building equipment—when a building boom began. These leaders in politics and commerce—counterpoints to the dominating narratives about the Maktoums and British officers—remain frustratingly unresearched. Some of these families are mentioned in this book, but their stories need more attention.

THIS BOOK'S PLAN
This book tells a story about how experts make a pitch for projects they believe they can manage. Too often today, those contracted to design Dubai treat the city as a ludicrous playground divided up for their own pleasure.

"Every architect dreams of being given a blank canvas," wrote London's former mayor during his paid publicity stunt for Dubai.[23] It turns out, those hired to design for the city surrender restraint more often than they push boundaries. They have condoned sloppiness and shunned intelligence. At the end of a typical design process, presenting architects might step away from their office's creation, shrug their shoulders, and claim, "But it's Dubai!" Feigning self-deprecation is cover for shirking professional responsibility. Defense comes in the form of invoices and the hedging of bets to secure the next project. Belittling Dubai while proposing to build it is worse than condemning the city altogether. The joke, the wink, the distancing oneself from one's own proposal: These are all examples of deliberate obtuseness to conceal professional transgressions.

Unlike much of Dubai's more recent development proposals (including underwater resorts and Ferris wheel hotels), John Harris's work was legitimately commissioned, sincerely pursued, and, more often than not, resolutely executed. Nearly all the work Harris's firm created for Dubai has gone away with time, a testament to its prescribed role in making a city. Although street patterns in "old Dubai" still follow Harris's designs, their use, density, and build-out hardly abide by Harris's initial intentions. Reading the cleft between what Harris drew and what Dubai has become provides a great deal of perspective on the city. Dubai might be an authored city, but its contours have yielded to global strategies and economic realignments.

After a brief prelude, this book opens in 1955, four years prior to John Harris's arrival in Dubai, in the midst of early efforts by the British government to institute a modernization program. The persons involved in these initial British-led efforts were British officers, engineers, an Iraqi consultant, and a would-be monopolist contractor. The success and failures of those experts paved the way for Harris's arrival in Dubai and his town plan's influence on the city's growth. Without them, Harris's arrival would have had little effect. Once Harris enters the scene in the fourth chapter, the book employs his career in Dubai as a lens through which to observe the city's early decades of modernization. Presented in a loosely chronological structure, key designs by Harris's firm reflect Dubai's economic and political realities. In this way, examples of Harris's work reveal how such concerns as hygiene, international standards, the gold trade, global migration, and business-class comfort were addressed through designs for hospitals, banks, hotels, and Dubai's tallest office tower. This book does not cover all of Harris's work in Dubai, or elsewhere in the world for that matter, but instead focuses on the works that map out Dubai's early history of constant pitch-making and deal-brokering. It isn't a coincidence that many of these works were called *showpieces*.

A city of shiny surfaces. A shallow city. An empty shell. A fake city. These are some accusations casually directed at Dubai today, many of which carry the claim that constructed facades lack authenticity. They suggest that the city is not what it appears and that one needs to locate its "dark side" in order to know the real Dubai.[24] Dubai's urban development has certainly been motivated by appearance. In fact, it was an image problem that likely triggered the British government to formulate the first semblances of a modernization project. Early projects were described as part of a "shop window" campaign. The term "showpiece" might describe shiny structures built for banks and tourists, but in Dubai's twentieth century the term clarified the purpose of a hospital, a municipal office, and a port—to bear and express evidence of a modern city. Beyond that, a showpiece had reinforced-concrete foundations anchored in the ground. It was evidence that the city was not going to drift away. Secured to the subsurface, the city would keep growing and changing above ground.

Modern architecture made Dubai in the physical sense, but it also delivered an image easily conveyed and broadcasted. Since the summer of 1960, when Harris submitted the town plan, Dubai has enjoyed several booms and survived multiple busts thanks to the delivery of a profit-fueled imaginary. One might say a plan gets you on the map, but constant transformation keeps you there.

CHAPTER 1

BUSTLE

"WE WERE HERE BEFORE any other Power in modern times." George Curzon rehearsed his remarks prepared for the guests soon to arrive. The words
would reverberate for the duration of British intervention in the Gulf region:
"We found strife and we have created order." As viceroy and governor-general
of colonial India, Curzon stood aboard the naval ship *Argonaut*, ten kilometers off the coast of the Trucial States on November 21, 1903.

"We were here" was a figure of speech. Neither he nor any other high-
ranking British officer had come close to the Trucial States in more than
eighty years of British domination. "Here" also referred to the greater coastline
encircling the Gulf, shores that navy ships policed to prevent any challenge
to British supremacy.[1] Curzon wanted to give regional leaders memorable
"impressions from outward appearances" of British power—the same year
that Russian and French warships entered Gulf waters, the same year that
German engineers launched a railway scheme between Berlin and Baghdad.[2]
Traveling with a fleet of seven coal-fueled ships and wearing his ceremonial
dress, Curzon practiced how he would remind the coastal rulers of "the paramount political and commercial ascendancy exercised by Great Britain" over
them. His guests, though, were delayed by storms.

"No fewer than eight" truces established Curzon's authority to be there. Framed as "unselfish" peacekeeping, the truces suggested bilateralism between Great Britain and a collection of sheikhdoms on the Gulf's southern shore. They came about only after the British navy ransacked the coast in 1819. The offensive, "not long sustained" but "severe," decimated the coast's reigning maritime dynasty, the Qawassim.[3] "The old régime of lawlessness and violence at once became obsolete." Several weeks after razing forts and imprisoning regional leaders came the hastily composed "General Treaty for the Cessation of Plunder and Piracy by Land and Sea."[4] It was the first of the truces to declare British dominance.

"Perfect maritime security in the Persian Gulf" allegedly ensued, by means of military surveillance and draconian limits on trade. At least officially, exclusive agreements restricted the region's imports to British products. The Trucial States were in effect cut off from the world. The lucrative pearl industry was allowed to continue, if only because colonial subjects in India also had a hand in the business.[5] British policy, as it accrued through the buildup of truces, came to mean the preservation of the status quo: The region was dictated to remain as the British had found it, incapacitated by the 1819 attacks. British officials thereafter portrayed themselves as overseeing a people who did not need, or even want, the advancements denied to them.

The truces eventually defined and reigned over seven sheikhdoms: Dubai, Abu Dhabi, Sharjah, Umm Al Quwain, Fujairah, Ajman, and Ras Al Khaimah.[6] "Relations," not powers, supposedly defined how the British ruled over them, "based on the principle of economy of force to achieve her objectives."[7] "Economy of force" limited British surveillance to the sea, thereby assuring no British intervention in the sheikhdoms' interior affairs on land. "Economy of force" also meant the sheikhdoms were not named "colonies" or "protectorates." Use of either term would have predisposed the British to too much responsibility for a land with, at least for a while, scant profit potential.

The status of the sheikhdoms gained some clarity by 1853 when leaders signed the "perfect maritime truce," which named the sheikhdoms by a British-authored logic. The writers of the so-called truces invented a word to convene the individual sheikhdoms into a collective: "trucial." The Trucial States were designated by means of a neologism, one that defined them as a unit and by their forced relationship with the British empire. The new name, in any case, was an improvement on the previous one: the Pirate Coast.

The *Argonaut* was too large to approach the shallow shore of the Trucial States, so a smaller steam launch had been prepared to transport Curzon to land. Sparing himself from inclement weather, the viceroy ordered instead that the rulers and other dignitaries come to him. Later that afternoon, the visitors boarded the *Argonaut*, fatigued by the "heavy sea," and though "descendants . . . of pirates and buccaneers, [they] had suffered severely from sea-sickness."[8] On the ship's quarterdeck, "ablaze with rich hangings and gold-embroidered carpets," Curzon received them "enthroned" on a dais and surrounded by his officers. There were not enough chairs left over for the visitors, many of whom sat on the deck's floor.

Curzon delivered "an epitome of British history in the Arab waters of the Gulf" and reminded his guests of the truces signed by their forefathers: "It was our commerce as well as your security that was threatened and called for protection."[9] The viceroy spoke in English. Upon the conclusion of his remarks, a man in civilian clothes read the visitors an Arabic translation, not from the stage but from among them. Still perched on his throne, Curzon looked down, bored. There is no record that any of the leaders spoke while aboard the *Argonaut*. They received "handsome gifts" of golden watches, swords, and rifles. And then they boarded the small craft again to suffer the heavy sea and to wait out a foreigner's lengthy, though not permanent, stay.[10]

ON LAND

In 1953, fifty years after George Curzon did not deign to come ashore, Christopher Pirie-Gordon landed in the sheikhdom of Sharjah. He was the Foreign Office's first political agent for the Trucial States, and he instigated a project more meddlesome than any British directive since the naval attacks in 1819.

Prior to Pirie-Gordon's arrival, a military force—the Trucial Oman Levies—had been established near a British airbase in Sharjah. The force protected the terrestrial boundaries of the Trucial States from foreign encroachment, namely by Saudi Arabia. Pirie-Gordon arrived in sync with the

FIGURE 1.1 Two stevedores amid landed cargo on Dubai Creek, circa 1955. Courtesy Tripp Family Archives, PDTC.

mounting British-led explorations for oil on land the levies protected. In 1935, Bahrain-based British officials had secured the region's first oil concessions for the British-controlled Petroleum Development (Trucial Coast), or PDTC.[11] With increasing prospects in the 1950s, PDTC's exploration teams, along with six other "European employers," needed a dependable port for replenishing supplies. Whichever port provided the necessary services, the Foreign Office surmised, faced the probability of growing and profiting from that business.[12] Even though the British had maintained an agency office in Sharjah for more than a hundred years and an airport there since 1932, and even though Abu Dhabi's port was closest to the most promising searches, the British government determined by 1950 that there was "more hope" in Dubai's port. Dubai, once unworthy of even protectorate-state status, now had a role in the British pursuit of oil profits.[13]

Although the Sharjah airbase and the levies' encampment were extensions of British military interference, Pirie-Gordon's mandate was about instilling "administration" and "some social services" at the promising port.[14] He brought with him a more expansive meaning of the *order* Curzon had professed. The word now had financial and societal dimensions. Pirie-Gordon was issued a ceremonial uniform reminiscent of Curzon's, but instead of representing a looming military at sea, he prefigured a campaign to build, and control, a bureaucracy in Dubai. In a city British officials perceived as having "no administration at all" save for a "poorly trained clerk," the installation of "an inexpensive administration" under British counsel would give the British government "a much better chance of getting control of the royalties from oil the moment these begin to accrue."[15] Pirie-Gordon's arrival signaled a new approach to Dubai: With as little investment as possible and with a gathering portfolio of work for British experts, Dubai was going to grow as a city of profit along a coast that the British navy ships had worked so long to stifle.

At first based in a rented house in Sharjah, Pirie-Gordon awaited completion of a new political agency compound in Dubai. The fenced-in area of future British governance was provided by Sheikh Rashid, then Dubai's de facto ruler. Its creekside location might seem a gracious gesture, but the site was also "remote, isolated from the town by a graveyard." Many suspected that Rashid had chosen the distant location so that the political agent could not "impinge too closely on the affairs of Dubai's population." In March 1954, the political agent moved into the "not very imposing" compound made up of "long, low sheds that blended in the surrounding sand" and enclosed by a "mesh fence which seemed designed to prevent egress rather than entry." Pirie-Gordon called it "the Leper Colony."[16] From the premises, even if at a distance from the active port, Pirie-Gordon could make more specific and sustained observations about a city no longer controlled from afar.

DAGGERS AND CANALETTO

Pirie-Gordon enjoyed parties and gatherings in his new host city, reportedly to a fault. His social disposition nonetheless further boosted the agency's gathering of intelligence about just how successful Dubai's merchants were. Anything there was to know about Dubai could be witnessed at Dubai Creek,

FIGURE 1.2 Aerial of Bur Dubai around the time that the British government determined there was "more hope" in Dubai's port than elsewhere in the Trucial States. Around the waterway's curve are the infamous sandbars capable of destroying cargo-carrying ships. Courtesy John R. Harris Library.

"a natural salt water lagoon discharging into the sea through a sinuous channel passing across a drifting sandy beach."[17]

Dubai Creek, the city's harbor, was in fact a marshy estuary. Tide and weather conditions determined the harbor's depth, which could vary by more than five meters. Its shape could dramatically shift over days, even overnight. Flooding on the low-lying shores was a fact of life. The creek's masters were those who knew when its waters were navigable and where an unexposed sandbar could destroy even the strongest of ships. The creek, and therefore Dubai, was set to the rhythm of tides and the vicissitudes of weather, with boat traffic limited to a few hours a day. Low tide prevented furtive nighttime arrivals of boats trying to avoid paying the import tax. One man aboard a dinghy and only armed with a dim lantern was sufficient in guarding the harbor's entry at night.[18]

The creek's silty waters separated what were still two contentious towns: Bur Deira and Bur Dubai.[19] Access to Dubai Creek united them in certain ways and so did the British truces, which defined Maktoum rule over both of them. The distance between the two shores was a maximum of 300 meters, enough to keep the two sides apart. Today's Dubai Creek is deep and clearly delineated by training walls. In 1954, it met land in most places with the gradual slope of a beach. Beyond just a harbor, it also played an essential role in workaday life. Small boats, called abras, ferried people from one side to the other, offering a cool breeze in between landings. When the tide was out and the waters too shallow for ships, Dubai Creek was a place of publicness. As an escape from the heat, the exposed beaches made for recreation, bathing, and a public toilet. Families gathered at the water's edge to relax and wash clothes. Parts were reserved for washing down sand-ridden carts. The incoming tide washed away the waste left behind.

In the 1950s, it seemed no English-speaking observer could describe Dubai Creek without using the word "bustle." Dubai's merchants, because they were forced to, still relied on ancient traditions of trade rather than on recent technologies. British-induced stasis had created for some foreign observers an aesthetic curiosity, an "untouched" realm of antiquity long vanished elsewhere. Dubai exuded "a flavour of the unexpected, the

FIGURE 1.3 Small boats, or abras, at a station in Bur Dubai, 1959. Courtesy John R. Harris Library.

unusual, the curious or dramatic or quaint."[20] Roads from the creek led to the souks, which, according to these onlookers, were authentic, unlike those of Aleppo and Cairo by then overcome with tourism. Dubai's souks, they praised, were inaccessible to most Westerners, untainted if less grandiose. In an otherwise dry description of the region in 1954, Rupert Hay, a former British official in neighboring Bahrain, conjured up the Dubai he wanted to remember:

> [Dubai's] suqs or markets on either side of its broad creek are the most picturesque I have ever seen in the Middle East and take one back to the time of the Arabian Nights. In the narrow lanes roofed with matting, where the gloom is flecked by spots of sunlight, Arabs, Persians, and Baluchis display their multifarious and many-coloured wares. Wild-eyed tribesmen with their camel-canes and daggers haggle with shopkeepers and the wealthier Persian merchants with their long flowing robes and gold-brocaded headdresses pass to and fro, intent upon their business. Graceful dhows glide into the creek, lower their sails and cast anchor while the whole day long small craft are busy ferrying shoppers from one bank to the other. The rectangular houses of the Shaikhs and merchants with their tall wind-towers cast white reflections on the water. Conditions are no doubt primitive, but there is an air of bustle and prosperity about the place that gives it a peculiar charm.[21]

Donald Hawley, one of Pirie-Gordon's successors, filtered out Dubai's distress to discern not just the "picturesque" but even the painterly:

> The graceful abras ply to and fro. They, with the still, blue and green water reflecting the "Italianate" wind towers, cause every visitor to murmur: "Canaletto."[22]

British officials also described the city as having "a business-like air about the place," noting the "prosperous appearance of the bazaar" and "lively atmosphere of the entire town."[23] The truth was, however, that Dubai was in no condition for becoming a truly thriving port. *Bustle* signaled amusement, not vigor. As charming as it might appear to someone who did not have to work and live in it, Dubai's harbor was swampy, haphazard, and without an ounce of steel.

FIGURE 1.4 White-sailed dhow on Dubai Creek, 1960. Courtesy John R. Harris Library.

ENTREPÔT

In 1954, Dubai's port impressed no one. Still, it was Dubai's primary source of income after the pearl industry was extinguished by the rise of cultivated pearls in the 1930s. The harbor ran on just one steel crane. For the rest of the shipments, a crew of men kept cargo in motion, loading sacks from their shoulders onto smaller boats and stacked piles that defined the port's edges. Without hotels or inns, the shore offered arriving boatmen little reason to alight from their boats, which for the lucky ones also functioned as mobile homes. Others made do with cardboard and scrap materials bargained for on land. Their temporary shelters were hardly distinguishable from the wharves' waste piles that festered and reeked. No one was paid to clear the garbage out. Pirie-Gordon reported from a city without hardened roads and even basic utilities like running water and electricity. The harbor was trudging through its own waste and survived at the mercy of annual flooding.

Western diplomats and journalists often referred to Dubai as a *sleepy fishing village* or a *sultry backwater*. Both tropes are misleading. Dubai was not sleepy. There was not enough sustenance on the ground to warrant anyone's indolence. There were minimal returns on Dubai's negligible exports, dried fish, mother of pearl, and animal droppings collected as fertilizer. Merchants had to keep alert to the slightest potential of niches they could exploit.

Dubai was also no backwater: a pool of water made still because it is too far from a refreshing current, isolated and septic. British policy attempted to design Dubai into a backwater, but its geography was not remote. Despite design, the city did refresh itself; it did connect to global networks of trade, culture, and communication. People's livelihood depended on these connections.

By the 1950s, Dubai's merchants—a collection of Arab, Iranian, and South Asian family businesses—learned to profit through the cracks of a fractured British policy. The merchants managed to access the larger world and exploited the creek's geography to do so. The waterway's S-curve shape provided "coves" concealed from British binoculars and unnavigable by British ships' deep hulls. Although occasionally the British came ashore and physically enforced embargoes, many other times British officials turned a blind eye. Maybe too many imported weapons might instigate armed intervention, but British forces appreciated not having to inspect, for example, a shipment of woolen gloves from Southeast Asia. They also preferred not to get involved when shipments evaded Iranian or Indian customs. Dubai's geography not only limited British control; it also allowed British forces to claim an inability to control Dubai.

Only the souks revealed signs of prosperity, where Pirie-Gordon observed just how successfully the city's merchants circumvented British embargoes. The bulk of onshore trade concentrated in the Deira souk that cached goods from Asia, Africa, and Europe, mostly to be shipped somewhere else. By the 1950s, under half-closed British eyes, Dubai traders were able to establish substantial trade networks. They brought in rice from Burma, wheat from Iran, flour from

Australia, from where they also sourced tinned fruits. Cars came from the UK, but pickups came from the US. Coffee originated from India and Yemen, though traders implored British officials to allow them access to Brazilian markets.[24] By 1954, Dubai's turnover had likely surpassed that of ports in Iran and Oman. Like a big treasure chest, the whole souk was locked up at dusk. Without electricity, the city went dark each night, retreating into itself until daylight returned.

Running "overt smuggling" routes was a way for Dubai's population to scrape up a living in the 1950s.[25] Elsewhere along the coast of the Trucial States livelihood prospects were only worse. One British report described the coast as "the ugliest stretch of territory that God has created."[26] Another recommended in 1961 that residents of Ras Al Khaimah, which had been most devastated by the 1819 British attack, should be evacuated, as if protracted and enforced impoverishment were a sudden natural disaster.[27]

Many coastal residents did make their way to Dubai on their own. Three-ton trucks, called taxis, brought people into the city from other towns and villages and from abandoned shores where sea-bound migrants alighted. The port's economic prospects, however slim, helped Dubai accumulate a population between 20,000 and 30,000 people by the mid-1950s.[28] Population counts—and any other statistics for that matter—are mere estimations recorded by distracted British officials. Whatever actual numbers might have been, the meager population was increasingly defined by its immigrants or, more accurately, by people passing through.

At some point in the 1950s, Dubai became home to more foreign-born than native-born residents. This majority arrived from somewhere else and, when they could afford to, would eventually go somewhere else. To stay in Dubai was to dream of moving elsewhere. Itinerant workers were like the cargo they hauled: staying for a period anywhere between a tidal cycle and a lifetime. To hedge risk, even those merchants considered locals were known to depart for years at a time and to maintain other lives in distant port cities like Bombay and Karachi.[29] While people moved in and out, there were also those who could not afford to leave, like the forlorn pearl divers, getting by on handouts and meager chores. When at last optimism for Dubai's prospects generated rumors of opportunity, the city's first development projects could succeed because of this ready, if tired, workforce. The excess from one economic bust was the reservoir for the next boom.[30]

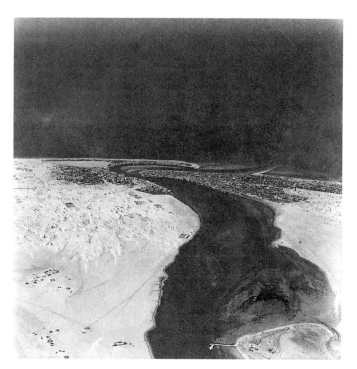

FIGURES 1.5A–1.5D Aerial photographs taken in 1944 reveal how the creek's S-curve concealed activity from shoreline views. Courtesy RAF Museum.

The British Foreign Office referred to Dubai as an *entrepôt*: a place "between ports" or, returning to the Latin base, "between *places*."[31] Dubai, the in-between, was undefined and liminal, a purposely haphazard condition open to modification. As an entrepôt, Dubai offered itself as a quick, easy, and often dubious site for profit. Dubai's trade was called "re-export," a low-overhead profit scheme that required only the space and labor to move goods from one boat to the next or to storage in the souk.

The formula was simple: Dubai attracted trade, not because it was organized but because it was not. Reigning over a clandestine station, Dubai's traders skimmed minimal profits from trade headed elsewhere. Dubai functioned as a last refuge of lawlessness in the face of increasing trade rules among nations. As British officials observed, the entrepôt business was one minimal way local residents could sustain a livelihood: Turning a blind eye was a form of British aid. Over this landscape of movement and transience, the political agency sought to establish some semblance of stability. Too much stability, though, would exceed what the British government was willing to support, financially or otherwise; it might also disrupt the very networks that made Dubai worthwhile to British interests. Too little intervention might render Dubai a less useful asset; the port could buckle under its own disorganization, and the dogged enterprise that sustained Dubai Creek could at any time drift away to the next nondescript, in-between place.

Impermanence remained a condition that British administrators found difficult to address. In 1949, a blunt attempt at applying permanence highlighted the difficulties of conducting top-down tactics on Dubai. Remote British officials introduced the ruler, Rashid's father Sheikh Saeed Al Maktoum, to a private British company that proposed constructing "permanent buildings" in Dubai, still without a concrete house. In exchange for paying rents to the ruler, the construction and civil engineering company, Holloway and Brothers, would deliver the buildings on the condition that it also secured a monopoly on all future "long-term policy and planning."[32] When the scheme was put before Dubai's ruler, he deferred a decision until after the month of Ramadan. When the delay continued beyond Ramadan, British officials did not force him to answer. Eventually Holloway and Brothers lost interest and, after completing some limited construction contracts, left town.

FIGURE 1.6 Workers at a water well, 1959. Drinking water was tapped outside city limits and then sold to Dubai residents from reused petroleum barrels. Courtesy John R. Harris Library.

In his muted way, Sheikh Saeed staved off a brazen attempt by the British government to press upon the city a simplistic real estate scheme, one that would have limited Dubai's potential to a small-minded and restrictive agreement. Holloway's conditions were the basis of a company town, not a city. The ruler was likely concerned that a private British company's indelible presence would have put a stranglehold on development, and the foreign company's demand for long-term leases would certainly have had political consequences for the ruling Maktoum family. Giving a British company exclusive development rights could have quickly incited calls that Dubai was being colonized or, maybe more threatening to local merchants, that Dubai's chances at profits were in the hands of the British, rather than locally based businesses. With Saeed's indirect rejection of Holloway, the first British attempt at spurring Dubai's development failed, but it had lasting effects.

For one, it revealed that Dubai leadership could, rather easily, resist British calls for change—and without serious repercussions. If British officials were not prepared to coerce Dubai's leadership to follow its directions, then they needed a more embedded structure that would make it appear that any British design for Dubai was a local effort. To change Dubai's port in this way would require more organization and more integrated intervention than pushing through some barracks-style buildings. Before any explicit effort at physical change, the British realized they needed a municipal bureaucracy that could manage future development. The political agent was to see to the creation of that municipality.

THE ENLIGHTENED ADMINISTRATORS

Stationed in the "Leper Colony," Christopher Pirie-Gordon was the first of eight political agents charged "to set Dubai in order."[33] He reported directly to the higher-ranking political resident in Bahrain but also kept London's Foreign Office updated. After naval officers and the failed private contractor, the political agent and a handful of deputies were commissioned to initiate schemes of administrative order and technical advancement in Dubai. Rather than deliver the schemes themselves, the political agents were expected to get local leaders to implement limited and prescribed "development programmes" designed to be as beneficial to the local welfare as to the public image of Britain.

Their earliest mandates included pursuing physical improvements, such as garbage collection; others were administrative, including instituting new court systems and urging Sheikh Rashid to systematize customs collection at the port.[34] But at nearly every step, political agents found their government balking at funding the slightest of programs. To handle such a cleft between intentions and the paltry means to enact them, there needed to be a diplomatically congenial figure to promote British directives and find the funding anywhere but from British coffers. That was the political agent. Such a figure would not only find the foreigners to run and build up the bureaucracy but also ensure that potential work contracts went to British companies. Through this setup, the British economy could gain more than just the enforced placement of a monopoly. The political agency could sow a generative idea—namely, that multiple British companies and British experts would start bringing *British quality* to a place deemed as needing it.[35] The larger, more productive the enterprise became, the more the British economy could gain from it.

Assigned to intervene in Dubai's internal affairs while not appearing to do so, the political agent was wrapped in contradiction. The local Arabic term for the British government was *ad daula*, which one political agent translated as "government power," a term that denied the political agency its behind-the-scenes mandate.[36] Still the British government kept defining the job in more congenial terms. According to one political agent, the job required "being schoolmaster, referee, counsellor, foreign minister and friend to the Ruler."[37] If, for example, the political agent could convince Sheikh Rashid to raise the commercial real estate tax, then it should happen as if by local mandate. Avoiding outright assertion of authority, the political agent understood he was nevertheless hired to exude legitimacy, stability, and predictable outcomes. The agent was not expected so much to exert British values as to embody them. According to one Foreign Office official, the agent maintained "our position as the fount of wisdom, authority, largesse and power."[38]

Further diminishing his power to act was the brevity of his stay in Dubai, rarely longer than a year or two. With each new agent, the Foreign Office could shift its priorities in the region by assigning someone with a different skill set.[39] Short-term postings hampered long-range planning. During the political agent's brief stay, he presented himself as if he occupied a timeless post, but, in reality, he supplied a stopgap between a Great Britain that ruled over lands lining the Indian Ocean and a Great Britain that sought new, private-sector ways to maintain its "world-power role."[40]

"The British might not be the greatest imperial builders of history," the writer Jan Morris once observed, "but they were unquestionably the greatest builders of imperial cities."[41] Urban histories of Hong Kong and Singapore, for example, relate how these economic powerhouses grew out of British colonialism. While comparisons to Hong Kong and Singapore are apt, the political agents looked to other precedents—specifically other development projects in the closer region—to organize a modernization program for Dubai and the other Trucial States.

British administrators could refer to a "regional blueprint," the term architectural historian Stephen Ramos uses to suggest how British officials followed precedents of petroleum-fueled urbanization in places such as Abadan, Kuwait, Manama, and Aden.[42] This blueprint was never close to an actual template for development, but the political agent often sought advice from other administrative officers in the Gulf region. Because of the agents' past experiences, Dubai's blueprint was also based on Sudanese cities. After Pirie-Gordon came at least two political agents who had been stationed with the Sudanese Political Service before Sudan's independence in 1956. They drew from their experience in organizing municipalities in Sudan and even recruited former Sudanese employees to manage Dubai's new municipality. One of these recruits described being trained by British officials "to run cities on the same concepts as British local-government laws."[43]

More than just installing systems of British-style governance, the political agent was also charged with managing the optics of British oversight. Arabic-language papers and broadcasted radio programs, especially Egyptian ones, were readily available at Dubai's port and provided moral support to Dubai's populations not directly benefiting from British rule. Policy could be shaped in response to bad press. An article in a Bahraini daily, *Al Meezan*, on October 1, 1956, exposed ruinous and unhealthy conditions that Dubai residents suffered under British control: "no school, no municipality and no electricity." British forces were present, according to the writer, "to avoid developments." The writer argued that, as an occupying force, the political agency "should open a primary school and save these people from illiteracy and establish a municipality to raise the people from dirt and diseases." The article deployed anticolonialist sentiments of the Arab nationalist movement in condemning Dubai's neglected state: "The imperialists used to look upon the Arabs as ashes but they have now discerned that the Arabs are flaming fire which would burn their dreams."[44] British observers read the article as part of a mounting campaign against British supremacy. In a matter of weeks, Great Britain would be embroiled in the Suez Crisis, which seriously destabilized its standing in the Gulf.

FIGURE 1.7 The Trucial States political agency seen from Dubai Creek, 1959. The exceptionally tall pole carrying the British flag was designed to be seen from the Deira district. Courtesy John R. Harris Library.

British officials stationed in the Gulf region acknowledged much of what the *Al Meezan* article claimed: Dubai was "innocent of all municipal services other than a rudimentary system of garbage collection"; it suffered from "disorganisation and squalor."[45] The wretched conditions that *Al Meezan* reported were handled primarily as an image problem. The article referred to the "hired press" that circulated pro-British stances throughout the region, but British officials admitted among themselves the difficulty in competing with media campaigns fueled by Arab nationalism. British mismanagement led to "an extremely bad advertisement" for the British government.[46] One official prescribed a "'shop window' type of economic aid, where assistance is not only given, but is also *seen to be given*."[47] Another argued that bringing order to the port and city "will accrue to our credit."[48] The intended result would be to "secure the continued allegiance" of the coast's leaders who otherwise "might come under the influence of other countries which might prove hostile to [British] interests."[49] Projects to be physically beheld—as opposed to literacy programs, for example—would render quick and responsive effects, the principal of which was "access to the oil on the best possible terms."[50] Managing optics on the physical landscape, the political agency concluded, offered a way "to maintain our position in the area."[51]

REFORMIST ELEMENTS

"On the whole," Donald Hawley once observed, "the merchants show very little interest . . . in anything except making money." He expressed exasperation, not veracity. Historically, merchants had been part of the "diplomatic network" by which the British governed over Gulf waters.[52] While they knew how to exploit an untended port, Dubai's merchants should have shared the political agency's interest in creating a cleaner, more organized harbor. They also knew what other great port cities looked like and how they operated. The most successful merchant families knew, for example, Kochin and Bombay in India. They knew what Muscat's and Kuwait's harbors offered in comparison to what Dubai lacked.

The merchants had once sought to enhance the city's governance. Their wealth had given them a position to "dictate their wishes" to the ruler, but that influence had waned in no small part as a result of British-government intervention.[53] That intervention had led to increasing amounts of payments for oil concessions, thereby altering Dubai's local political landscape in the Maktoums' favor—namely, because the oil concession went directly to the ruling family. As the ruler got richer, the merchants struggled to squeeze a profit from Dubai's swampy port. Bristling at their loss of wealth and therefore their loss of influence, the merchants sought ways to reset the balance of power.

In 1938, in response to changing dynamics, merchants and other local leaders successfully instituted a parliamentary advisory group, referred to as a *majlis*.[54] The majlis could potentially balance the power in that it gave merchants a say in how their customs dues were utilized; they also wanted the oil concessions to benefit the entire city, not just the Maktoum family. These efforts, however, were short-lived, as Rashid's father dissolved the majlis within a year of its formation. The British had done nothing to preserve the governmental body or to express support for the merchants' concerns. With the creation of the political agency, fifteen years later, British officers voiced government reform as a new idea. To the merchants, its sounded like an unfulfilled promise.

For so long, merchants had maintained their trade networks without governmental reforms and improvements to their port facilities. With initial organization efforts focused on systematizing customs payments, merchants would be expected to pay more, further shifting the economic, and therefore political, balance in the direction of Maktoum rule. The merchants also knew how administrative reforms and physical development had transformed nearby Iran. Reforms there had been driven by a centralized government in Tehran exacting higher fees from the southern port traders. The ports did not experience improved facilities; the money went instead to Tehran.

It would have been easy for Dubai's merchants to draw potential parallels for themselves. Many of Dubai's merchants, in fact, were descendants of the Iranian traders who had turned to Dubai to avoid paying increasing fees in the early 1900s. In the years after World War II, Iran's further physical development under Mohammad Reza Pahlavi demonstrated to Dubai's leaders what new government measures achieved: improved physical infrastructure controlled by centralized authority. The combination enabled Tehran to clamp down on Gulf ports like Bandar Abbas and claim even more of maritime profits. Iran's increased tax collection, in turn, gave rise to Dubai's profitable smuggling businesses that skirted the new tax collectors.[55] By the end of the 1950s, Dubai's port competed in trade volume with Bandar Abbas. Not only were Dubai's merchants suspicious of British-led reforms, their current formula for success depended on evading such reforms elsewhere.

In 1953, some merchants organized opposition to Maktoum rule. Called the Dubai National Front, the group found inspiration in the Lebanese Communist Party and Arab nationalist magazines and newspapers that their trade networks brought to Dubai's shore. British reports downplayed the Dubai National Front as a "loose association of reactionary individuals," not necessarily "a dangerous threat" but needing to be monitored. Their analysis disparaged them as disorganized, "hypnotized by their own slogans," and lacking "any explicit political philosophy," let alone a secretary. It further focused on the group's xenophobic tendencies revealed in pamphlets clandestinely printed, read, and circulated in the souks. Slogans like "Arabia for Arabs," the British officials often noted, referred to eradicating not only British oversight but also "the mercantile influence of the local Persians and Indians."[56]

Once the political agency opened in Dubai, British officers could track potential detractors more easily, finding them loitering in a "so called cultural club" and a politically tinted café, distributing political flyers in the souks, and plotting to destroy British property.[57] They labeled these critics as antiprogressive and indolent, noting that the café, adorned with images of Egypt's leader Gamal Abdel Nasser, also served clients of the nearby brothel area. In 1956, overly enthusiastic "handclapping" by café patrons listening to Arab nationalist radio broadcasts led Sheikh Rashid to have the premises shut down.[58] The political agent's superior summarized the growing predicament:

> We are left, as so often before, in an uneasy middle position between obscurantist Rulers attached quite deeply to us by tradition or self-interest and reformist elements with whose desire for administrative improvement we sympathise but who have no similar attachment to us.[59]

APPEARANCES

In May 1955, just at the end of his tenure in Dubai, Pirie-Gordon advised and urged Sheikh Rashid to exile some of his family members who had helped found the Dubai National Front. They had worked "as strongly against our interests as against Rashid's."[60] The political agent offered naval backup for the confrontation, but Sheikh Rashid had "asked that the ships should not spoil the effect by putting in an appearance."[61] According to the political agent, Rashid was in agreement that it should seem as if he acted on his own authority without British military support. Two ships were arranged, "available, but out of sight." More visible, the Trucial Oman Levies' land forces stationed themselves outside the city limits and were instructed to "rely upon the moral effect of their presence."

FIGURE 1.8 Peter Tripp, the second political agent in Dubai, arrives at a party in Dubai with his wife
Rosemary, circa 1957. Courtesy Tripp Family Archives.

On the designated day, Rashid's banished family members were said
to have been "much impressed" by the presence of the military squadrons.
British force had exercised only its *appearance*, thus allowing Rashid to
be the day's actor. Even the British later told themselves that "credit is
due to Shaikh Rashid who conceived and executed the operation."[62] Once
his military cohorts confirmed that the detractors had departed, Pirie-
Gordon handed over the political agency to his successor, Peter Tripp,
later that day.[63]

Within weeks of the reportedly discreet display of force, Tripp began pursuing the optics of municipal administration. "I found Shaikh Rashid enthusiastic about sanitation," Tripp wrote. "Once the inhabitants of Dubai begin
to *see* an improvement in the administration of their town, Sheikh Rashid
should be assured of their support," he wrote to his London superiors.[64]

Appearances were the driving motivation behind Curzon's seven-ship arrival on Gulf waters a half century earlier, with him sitting on a stage "ablaze with rich hangings" as dignitaries from the Trucial States sat on the floor below him. Appearances also motivated a "'shop window' type of economic aid" to counteract criticism of Britain's uncharitable handling of Dubai. As Curzon's steel fleet had once been intended to make "impressions," some gestures were made to be seen. At other times, like the naval ships on Tripp's first day, they were purposely to be kept out of sight.

Once in the position of political agent, Tripp focused on the visible. Whereas Pirie-Gordon's actual results in Dubai were limited to little more than some equipment for a medical clinic, minor irrigation projects, and drilling studies, Tripp asserted there now needed to be more than "a talking shop."[65] Profits and costs were to be made measurable. Organizational clarity would bring optical clarity. An initial list of programs included courts and a municipal bureaucracy in Dubai, more garbage collection, and a school-building project. In his first months, he founded the Trucial States Development Office (TSDO). By naming it, Tripp established an unmistakable entity around which to organize and tell the story of a regional development program.

Creating the TSDO also created a budget line at the British treasury that required funding, or at least consideration of it. He asked for £450,000 for five years, or about $12 million today. No "spectacular improvements" were to be expected. "Modest in the extreme," the TSDO was designed to focus on health care, youth and vocational education, irrigation, and agriculture. Educational programs were also proposed to teach merchants about "business efficiency" through courses in bookkeeping and letter writing.[66] Tripp expected the TSDO's limited scope to have a galvanizing effect, in not only mitigating local discontent but also neutralizing the Arab nationalist voices coming from abroad in newspapers and on radios. His advocates in London said Tripp's ideas must be pursued for "prestige reasons." Quantifiable, visible improvements, denied by British forces for a century, were now, according to Tripp, the steps toward keeping Dubai within the British political and economic orbit.

CHAPTER 2

LANDSCAPES FOR PRODUCTION

PETER TRIPP'S FIRST DAY as Political Agent Trucial States in 1955 was marked by insurgency and the British tactics to suppress it. Little changed in his first year. He had expected to spend his days improving the city's hospital, building schools, and maybe even seeing license plates issued for Dubai's increasing number of cars. His small staff focused instead on reconnaissance of National Front members. Like an ad hoc intelligence operation, his team filled out an index card for each suspected member and estimated a count. In May, the agency reported on the "outbreak of lawlessness and gang warfare."[1] Their findings led Tripp to urge London to fund a "small police force" to counter the city's "increasing lawlessness." Led by a British officer and a local "nominal head," the fledgling force was quickly "operating in a rabbit-warren of a town" and stemming "knife-fights and shop-breaking on a wide scale."[2] Had it not been for the British-led policing, Tripp reported, a customs strike in June 1956 would have been the end of Sheikh Rashid and his father's rule.[3] "Tortuous is the task," Tripp once grumbled, "of keeping Dubai on an even keel."[4]

In the days after the June strike, Tripp took advantage of the summer lull to revitalize his five-year development plan for the TSDO (Trucial States

Development Office). Other urgencies and an ambivalent Foreign Office had delayed his plans. Rather than pushing the funding through for Tripp's itemized projects, the Foreign Office had found reasons to slow it down. School construction projects were postponed because more approval processes were added. A proposed agricultural project in Ras Al Khaimah was deemed too ambitious. Part of Tripp's mandate had included establishing "a small scale and simple administration" in Dubai, but little more had come of that than "a rudimentary form of garbage collection."[5] Dubai's hospital remained unfunded. Tripp's budget for that year was halved, and then nearly quartered.[6] It is not surprising that a London official labeled Tripp's review of the agency's first years as "depressing" and "severe."[7]

The British government did not recognize the consequences of failing to fund Tripp's "prestige" programs, even in the context of Britain's mounting colonial predicament in the Arab world. Beginning with Egypt's election of Gamal Abdel Nasser in the same month as the customs strike, tensions escalated between the UK and Egypt. Those tensions came to a

FIGURE 2.1 Political agent Peter Tripp and his family with leaders of the Trucial States at the residence section of the political agency compound, 1957. Courtesy Tripp Family Archives..

head after Nasser nationalized the Suez Canal, and British troops joined French forces in a land assault in early November, a week after Israeli forces had invaded. The Suez Crisis triggered riots and demonstrations throughout the Gulf region, including Dubai. British-government documents provide little detail on what actually occurred in Dubai, except for a fire at a British property outside the agency. Once more, British forces appeared in Dubai's streets to express the maintenance of order. The agency reported no use of force, again only the display of it. Tripp and his family remained inside the political agency compound, guarded by the British military's "ostentatious re-inforcement."[8]

In the aftermath of the Suez Crisis, British supporters of Tripp's TSDO plans criticized the "niggardly amounts" the British government had been ready to provide to prevent such dissent.[9] Tripp, however, noted a deeper problem: Maktoum rule was increasingly reliant upon British displays of force, if just for "the moral effect of their presence." He was concerned that British interventions were becoming "embarrassingly obvious."[10] Military order infected any attempts at administrative order. Whether in summoning troops to break a strike or helping Sheikh Rashid collect port taxes, the more the British government upheld Sheikh Rashid's sovereignty, the more suspicious Rashid's challengers, namely the merchants, were of British motives.

In government correspondence, Tripp expressed the trouble with backing Rashid. He did not temper his opinion of the man he was instructed to support. He found him "a most confused conversationalist."[11] His reports questioned Rashid's "business acumen" and suggested that he "does not inspire a great deal of confidence. He has increasingly shown signs of weakness and irresponsibility and is easily hoodwinked by the intrigues of self-interested persons." The agency even criticized him for being too obedient to his wife.[12] "This is, perhaps, the crux of our problem in Dubai," Tripp summarized, "we have a Ruler who seems incapable of acting in defence of his own interests, thus obliging this Agency constantly to intervene, because his interests are so often also our interests."[13]

The merchants, some of whom were supportive of the Arab-nationalist Dubai National Front, had demonstrated before that they also shared some of the political agency's goals. They had tried to organize the city on their own terms. They had instituted a parallel customs-collection process so that they could monitor incoming revenue. They had tried to set up a land-deed system. They had even tried to raise capital for an electrical plant, still absent in Dubai.[14]

As much as the front's efforts mirrored the intentions of the British government, they also threatened to destabilize the political status quo. Whoever delivered improvement programs won political influence. Iranian officials, more attuned than their London counterparts, also attempted to fund modest programs as a means of influence over local leaders. They offered to build new schools and a hospital, as well as to provide the staff to run them. Rather than allow improvements funded by merchants or other governments, Tripp protected British claims to the city's future, even if the British government was not going to act on them.

Increasingly dissatisfied by local leadership's inability to steward his development ideas and rebuffed by his London superiors, Tripp remained resolute about his plans. His frustration lay in not finding the effective way to argue for them. After the peak of the Suez Crisis, he knew his role as political agent was even more compromised. For his remaining months in Dubai, Tripp attempted new tactics in arguing his case—to Sheikh Rashid, to the most powerful merchants, and to his superiors in London.

He sought strategies in two arenas. The first sought to address the tense relationship between Sheikh Rashid and the highly suspicious local merchants who kept even Rashid's most basic suggestions at an impasse. Sheikh Rashid needed the chance and ability to "explain and show the need for the improvements."[15] According to Tripp, Rashid needed a "powerful, disinterested advisor" to counter the "loudest in his majlis [who] are connected to the National Front."[16] A "disinterested advisor" was for Tripp neither British nor a merchant, but still someone sympathetic to the British agency. The second arena Tripp had to address was vaster: the regional circulation of anti-British sentiment. To counter that narrative, Tripp had to write another one. Writing a new narrative that was not true, or at least not yet true, could have another lasting impact: convincing the Foreign Office to muster the necessary funds for the Trucial States Development Office.

DISINTERESTED ADVISOR

By the end of November 1956, Tripp found reason to be hopeful. Dubai's ports and souks had returned to a semblance of normal activity after the peak of the Suez Crisis. Merchants were catching up on inventory; their boatmen were again plodding through Dubai's shallow waters to move cargo from one boat to another. The talk of the town was less about Suez and more about the Deira branch opening of the Jashanmal family's general store, after successful stores in Bahrain and Kuwait. There were rumors that Dubai would soon have its own post office. On the day before a work week was to begin, a car owned by Sheikh Rashid brought a man from Sharjah's airport to Dubai Creek. Having flown in from Baghdad, the Iraqi national stepped out of the taxi for the final leg of his journey, aboard an abra across the creek to Bur Dubai. There he was to start a three-month stay as a guest of Sheikh Rashid. Abdul Salam Er Raouf, an "Iraqi municipal expert," was Dubai's first paid consultant. Sheikh Rashid was his client.

Months earlier, Tripp had told Rashid he wanted to bring an Iraqi expert to Dubai "for the establishment of a proper 'baladiya.'"[17] (*Baladiya* is an Arabic word for municipality.) Tripp's superior agreed that an Arab expert "would do as much good locally as our financing of a British expert."[18] More than that, Tripp argued, he would perform better, and at a fraction of the cost. In such an expert, Peter Tripp found his disinterested advisor, someone who would listen to, and be respected by, the British, Sheikh Rashid, and the merchants.

Though never specifically referred to as one, Abdul Salam Er Raouf was a consultant, hired for his professed impartial knowledge gained from professional experience. It is unclear for which Iraqi local government Er Raouf worked. Also unclear is which skill set made him a municipal expert, though one British official noted that Er Raouf was "familiar with primitive town administration," and Er Raouf later claimed he was responsible for the budgets of 150 Iraqi municipalities.[19] Since 1950, the technocratic Iraq Development Board (IDB) had steered the bulk of Iraq's oil-funded infrastructural development. The IDB's members and staff included a healthy participation by British advisors and experts who subsequently hired British and other Western consultants to execute their plans.[20] It could have been that Er

FIGURE 2.2 Dubai road, perhaps Sikkat Al Khail, with early presence of electrical lines, 1960. Courtesy John R. Harris Library.

Raouf's expertise resulted from IDB training programs and that someone within the Foreign Office had provided Er Raouf as a contact. The IDB, not unlike Tripp's TSDO but many times larger, was a seemingly local governing body with British expertise embedded in it. For the purposes of the political agency, Er Raouf was "disinterested" in as much as he was an Arab working for an Arab government still under strong British oversight.

The difficulty of getting Er Raouf to Dubai underscored how unready the Foreign Office was to support Tripp's plans. Only after Er Raouf had been engaged and Rashid convinced of his usefulness did Tripp broach the topic of paying for his visit. Er Raouf's Iraqi-government employer offered to continue salary payments to his family during his three-month leave. Who would pay Raouf's modest salary for his work in Dubai became a matter of Tripp's protracted negotiations with Sheikh Rashid and his own government. Rashid was worried about the costs of the consultant and any improvements he might recommend.[21] He requested a British grant. At this stage, there was hardly any bookkeeping to measure what Rashid could afford. After first asserting that Trucial States funds could only be used to hire British consultants, the Foreign Office found 3,000 rupees, about $630, to contribute from a regional public health fund. Rashid paid the rest, including Er Raouf's expenses.

A PROPER BALADIYA

Abdul Salam Er Raouf did more than "produce a model 'baladiya.'"[22] His client, Sheikh Rashid, introduced him to Dubai's merchants at a majlis meeting. They asked how he found Dubai. A strategic consultant starts with a compliment: He was "agreeably surprised by Dubai." His first recommendation was simple and addressed the only public service the city already claimed: "to clear the streets and creek of filth and rubbish."[23] Cleanliness for Er Raouf had as much to do with public health as with outward appearance. Within a month of his arrival and with "the complete absence of any administrative machine," Er Raouf managed to get new municipal orders issued. Dubai's slaughterhouses were required to be "fly-wired" to protect meat from insects and pests.[24] "Some minor road repairs [were] set in hand."[25] New shops and houses soon required municipality-issued building permits, a timely measure since Dubai's first reinforced concrete buildings were being built, beyond those of the British compound and the hospital.[26]

Tripp observed how Er Raouf instilled enthusiasm about future development in Dubai's "rich and powerful." They were "very co-operative" with Er Raouf. The Iraqi consultant reported that the idea of a stronger and more present baladiya was even "extremely popular among the poor people."[27] The issue of taxation remained a sensitive topic, leading one meeting to end "in uproar, with two merchants tugging at each other's beards."[28]

That was the final open meeting that Er Raouf led. By then, he had already negotiated the founding of the Dubai Council, an "advisory" body approved by the ruler and "allowed" by the British secretary of state.[29] The new council included twenty-two representatives nominated by the ruler. Er Raouf stayed beyond his agreed departure date to help formulate the council. It met for the first time on March 5, 1957. When the first meeting got heated, again about taxes, it adjourned until the next scheduled meeting on March 14. Though not as "procedural" as Raouf had hoped, the second council meeting resulted in approved tax rates for leased shops and storage facilities and the hiring of a minimal staff and "sixty coolies engaged in clearing rubbish." Additionally, used trucks, "cement dust-bins," and "150 barrels for rubbish" were to be ordered. Finally, the members voted to build a public lavatory and condemn "six houses in a narrow suq."[30]

Er Raouf eventually left after nearly a year's stay. Despite assurances that Er Raouf would be back, there is no record that he ever returned.[31] Foreign Office officials determined the visit "an unqualified success."[32] Through the brief encounter with the Iraqi expert, all three parties—the political agency, the ruler, and the merchants—situated themselves into governing roles they would continue to play. Er Raouf won the confidence of Dubai's elite traders, who through the process had gained a means through which to influence taxing policies and government services. The council, not as democratic as some wished, quickly proved effective. Dubai soon operated with a tax code and some basic development regulations. For the political agency, "close co-operation" with Er Raouf brought progress at minimal cost to the British government. Physical threats continued to haunt the agency's attempts at behind-the-scenes direction, but there was now a way to see these as snags, not obstruction. Tripp could now push the "proper baladiya" to act faster and issue ordinances, probably written by him but issued by a local body. It was "vitally important . . . that Dubai citizens should *see* results for their money at an early stage, in order to convince them that the municipality is not just another 'racket' designed to line the Ruler's henchmen's pockets."[33]

Sheikh Rashid gained the most from Er Raouf's visit: Presiding over the majlis with his Iraqi consultant by his side, it was now he who instigated the making of the modern city that Tripp imagined. The framing of Sheikh Rashid as Dubai's modernizer—not the British government or any other foreign government—had begun to take form, thanks to the Iraqi expert's brief stay. Dubai, Tripp later remarked, was moving "from its mediaeval status . . . into the modern world."[34]

DIPLOMAT AS PITCHMAN

During Er Raouf's stay, other projects for optical ordering were taking shape. One in Abu Dhabi was more spectacular than anything Tripp could deliver in Dubai. On the uninhabited Das Island, a consortium led by British Petroleum (BP) prepared for Abu Dhabi's first oil exports. In preparation for upcoming publicity campaigns, BP hired a private British production company, World Wide Pictures, to film their operation.[35] After hearing of BP's film plans, the Foreign Office floated the idea that the crew could also make a film about Dubai and the other Trucial States. By not having to pay for the crew's transportation, the officials thought they could make good use of their "long term relationship" with BP.[36]

On November 15, 1957, Tripp wrote an enthusiastic "rough brief" for a propaganda film. In contrast to his frustrated attempts to get his TSDO programs funded, he proposed a film that celebrated his project as an unmitigated success—an idealization of his disheartening workdays. While in actuality London kept pulling back on its promises of development aid, the film would praise British generosity. Exploiting his usual correspondence line with London, this time he did not propose but instead *scripted* a modernization program. Far from being an original idea, the film rested in a tradition of British propaganda filmmaking, previously an effective "tool of administration" for colonial officers elsewhere in the British empire.[37] Historically the tool was wielded to convince audiences, at home or abroad in the colonies, of the well-meaning intentions of the British government.

For this film, officials in London imagined reaching audiences in Britain as well as "general Middle Eastern audiences."[38] Tripp, though, scripted for another audience. In much the same way Er Raouf had been hired as a conduit for delivering ideas to Dubai's leaders, Tripp saw the film project as a means to converse with his London superiors. Tripp wanted to show Her Majesty's Government that it had a good news story to tell—first to itself and then to the rest of the world—if the story could only be made true.

Tripp structured his film proposal around "the most photogenic" examples of his underfunded development programs, such as "anti-malar-
ial spraying, hospital and dispensary work, agricultural development and
water drilling." The leaders of the Trucial States, who Tripp claimed had not
yet become interested in British improvement projects, were transformed
through words into gracious ushers of British advice. Shots of TSDO projects,
he proposed, should be "leavened with" glimpses of the everyday: "pictures of
forts, and cannons, of Shaikhs in Majlis, of a slave being freed at the [British
political] Agency, of the Dubai suq, of a squalid barasti village, of a pearling
or fishing fleet, etc."[39] In this scripted world, the British government funded
his proposed development-aid programs, realizing just how economical the
down payment was on future oil concessions. He had already phrased it well
at the start of his posting:

> If Her Majesty's Government is to maintain their position in the Trucial States
> in the interim period, they will have to bridge the gap between the poverty of
> to-day and the plenty of to-morrow. If they fail to do this, Egypt, or some other
> Arab state, will step in and take their place.[40]

FILMMAKING THE TRUCIAL STATES

Tripp's pitch convinced the Foreign Office that a film about the Trucial States
was an "opportunity not to be missed."[41] A December 23, 1957, telegram informed Tripp that World Wide Pictures was hired.[42] The approved budget
for production was about £2,380 (or $61,000 today), a minimal price for a
film. One officer, though, found the price "really too high for a project of this
kind."[43] If one considers that the British government's total annual budget for
the Trucial States that year was capped at £100,000—which also included the
salaries of some British officials—then the film production can be measured
as a significant expense. To further control costs, Tripp was asked to write
the initial script.

Between 1957 and 1958, the camera crew of World Wide Pictures recorded
the span of Great Britain's entrenchment in the Trucial States. Hired by BP,
they filmed at Das Island—a company town of British and South Asian
men—to capture oil tankers and the huge oil industry machinery the men

FIGURE 2.3 Still from *These Are the Trucial States*. A landing at Dubai Creek. ©Imperial War Museum.

operated. Hired by the British government, they explored Dubai's port where few Westerners had been allowed entry before. In between these two focal points, the two-person team witnessed stretches of coast, which they depicted as attractively unburdened by modern life.

For its project, BP had ordered color film that made it all the easier to seduce an audience.[44] Seemingly auspicious for the British government, the crew had packed more color film than necessary for the initial project. They could use the rest to film the Trucial States in color. London officials, however, insisted on the extra expense of delivering black-and-white film to Dubai. Having already expressed that the budget was too high, the Foreign Office forced it 50 percent higher, by insisting on a black-and-white product.[45]

With color film already more affordable, and even more standard, for feature-length movies and propaganda films, black-and-white was by 1958 a machination of nostalgia.[46] BP's film was to be in Technicolor and expressive of awesome machinery and human toil. In contrast, Her Majesty's

Government insisted that their film be in black-and-white, featuring a pastoral landscape of yearning and timelessness. The project could have produced some of the region's earliest known moving images in color, clearly a missed opportunity and an intended consequence. Likely filmed in the first two weeks of February 1958, the film was titled *These are the Trucial States* in English; the Arabic title is even simpler: *The Trucial Oman States*.[47] The black-and-white film conveys an unsophisticated but self-sufficient society. Using black-and-white also achieves something else: It reduces specificity. Places and things come across as rustic but pleasantly unblemished. Black-and-white diminishes difference. It has the effect of dissolving the Trucial States' landscapes into a smooth continuum of austerity.

The black-and-white film also blurs the distinction of the region's various people—already a thriving mix of Arabs, Iranians, South Asians, and Africans—into a shared grayscale. Black-and-white unites them in a way that simplifies, if not fictionalizes, the story of the Trucial States. While the white skin of three unnamed British characters might stand out, other various tints of human skin more closely converge. The only foreigners the final script references are teachers from Kuwait and "other Arab countries."[48] (Cattle imported from India and Pakistan are also identified.) As a result, the Bedouin merge with Pakistani health care workers, Egyptian teachers, an Indian nurse, and Baluchi construction laborers. Someone with limited knowledge of the region might mistake them all as an indigenous people with a shared ethnic identity, working together to create a harmonious place.

Tripp initially proposed opening the film with orientating maps and aerial shots, common techniques in earlier propaganda films, but they likely proved beyond budget. Without the standard geographical overview, the film presents its own geography, particularly one that Tripp helped create. While in reality spread over a 1,300-kilometer coastline and "nearly the size of England," Dubai and the other sheikhdoms are arranged into a compressed microcosm. The montaged geography enables Tripp's imagined ordering of the region to come to the fore. In government documents, Tripp referred to the "Dubai model," a notion that distinguished Dubai's improvement programs from those designated for the rest of the coast. The Dubai model posited Dubai as the urban crux of the Trucial States;

FIGURE 2.4 Still from *These Are the Trucial States*. One of Dubai's first concrete buildings under construction. ©Imperial War Museum.

its "organs of development" and infrastructural improvements, once instituted, would present something to which the other Trucial States might aspire. Though they might be planned according to this model, the other sheikhdoms would never achieve Dubai's urban sophistication. Instead, they were scheduled to rely on Dubai's urbanization to sustain their more rural economies.[49] They were to be the recipients of the TSDO's small medical clinics (as opposed to hospitals), vocational education, irrigation projects, and agricultural programs.

In the film, Dubai performs as Tripp envisioned it should: the urban node around which the other trucial sheikhdoms exist. To help achieve this effect, Tripp's scriptwriting employs montage to merge distant and disparate events into a single comprehensible society. Outside Dubai, idyllic shots characterize the other Trucial States in a supporting role. A shepherd steers goats from Sharjah to Dubai's markets, as if the hinterlands, not the port, feed the city. Scenes from classrooms in Sharjah merge with schoolyards in Abu Dhabi to suggest homogenous conditions for the coast's residents. A camel caravan makes its way to the city. Water irrigation efforts in Buraimi nourish cattle fields, which in turn feed Dubai. Seeds are sown in Ras Al Khaimah so that produce eventually ends up in Dubai's souks.

Tripp's script makes Dubai the film's climax. When the camera turns to Dubai, the soundtrack abruptly changes to chanting and percussive beats, an increased tempo to match men hoisting leather buckets at a construction site, laying new roads, and building new ships. His proposed shots for the city read like the components of his idealized city:

Ruler
Dr. Majid and patient
New Buildings.
. . . donkey . . .
. . . road repairs
Filling bags with earth
Earth tipped on stones
Men levelling
Mounted Police
Policeman walking through busy market scene
Dubai creek
Boat buildings
Customs wharf
General activity
Men with Crates
Dubai creek
Boat activity in creek
Cloth merchants
Goldsmith close up hands and necklace
Case of jewellery
Group of pearl merchants
Selecting pearls
Sifting pearls
Weighing pearls.[50]

FIGURE 2.5 Still from *These Are the Trucial States*. Close-up of Dubai Municipality truck, one of the municipality's first purchases. ©Imperial War Museum.

Scenes of Dubai begin with a close-up of a truck's door emblazoned with the English words, "Dubai Municipality." As if unable to pause for the camera, the driver and his coworkers rush back to the city, perhaps after dumping a round of trash collection on the outskirts. For this shot, Tripp's initial script refers to "the cleanliness and security in the town [that] have encouraged many foreign merchants to establish themselves in Dubai."[51] The film's final Arabic lines for this shot translate to, "In the midst of all of this, there is ongoing building and construction, especially in the city of Dubai."

In addition to removed references to foreigners, the final narrator makes no mention of Tripp's terms "progress" and "cleanliness"; any suggestion of moral value has been removed in favor of work for its own sake. In this and the following shots of Dubai, work and construction need no moral association to have meaning or value. There is little being taught or instructed; there is no need for interaction with the outside. People cope with hardship through perennial, if labor-intensive, optimism.

FIGURE 2.6 Still from *These Are the Trucial States*. Men walk through the open-air souk. ©Imperial War Museum.

Outside the city, the desert also performs as labor's stage. Rather than a landscape of deprivation, it is a resource simply needing cultivation. When the film presents the desert, it is being traversed by a caravan of camels or transformed into roadways, or it is the welcoming bank for boats filled with fishermen's catch. A shot of a "dead palm stump," once scripted by Tripp to signal the region's environmental threats, is reformulated in the final script as a clue to untapped water sources.[52]

In other scenes, fallow ground is made useful by being punctured and furrowed. Similarly, water provides fish and subsistence, and it conveys cargo. There are no scenes of domesticity or recreation, as suggested by Tripp's initial treatment: "hawking, camel racing, a Baluchi wedding, recital of poems, singing of songs, dancing, mutton grab dinners, etc."[53] The hawk is reformulated as merchandise at the souk; the camels are transportation; pearls and handicrafts are items of trade. Without a hint of domesticity or indolence, every scene is about productivity. Women contribute to the

FIGURE 2.7 Still from *These Are the Trucial States*. Sheikh Rashid outside his palace. ©Imperial War Museum.

effort: selling goods in Dubai's narrow alleys, fetching water at a well, and negotiating through the market. Even children are at work, learning. The Trucial States are landscapes for production, and any applied improvements to the landscape merely extend the possibilities of a productivity already underway.

Architecture plays a significant role. It establishes that productivity renders an identifiable and self-sufficient society. Interiors are not explored, save those of the hospital, where surgery is underway, and classrooms, where children attend lessons in Arabic. There are no shots of "squalid barasti villages," as proposed by Tripp.[54] Aside from a sturdy palm-frond classroom, buildings are either solid palatial buildings for sheikhs or new concrete structures for commerce and education. Abu Dhabi's ruler, Sheikh Shakhbut bin Sultan Al Nahyan, is framed by the tower of Qasr Al Hosn. In Dubai, Sheikh Rashid stands in front of the entrance to one of his palaces with a portico of Doric columns. Sharjah's ruler delivers a public speech in front of a new large school. More than monarchical importance or modernity, architecture expresses permanence. It connotes stability and, therefore, substantiates one of the film's essential assertions: that there existed a fixed and autonomous society.

In his script, Tripp gave the British government a supporting role to this fictive society. He wanted to illustrate "the ways in which the Rulers of the Trucial States spend the money so generously provided by their old friend and benefactor—H.M.G. [Her Majesty's Government]—in order to promote the well being of their peoples."[55] No such statement makes it into the final film, which was produced in London without Tripp's further input. Instead, British officials play a largely invisible role. Only three British men appear, but they are not referred to by name or nationality: Desmond McCaully, the hospital's doctor; Robin Huntington, the agricultural expert in Ras Al Khaimah; and a ranking officer in what became named that year the Trucial Oman Scouts. Beyond that, there are only implied references to the British presence as an unattributed and vague "government" (*hukuuma*):

> [The Trucial States'] sensible leaders persevere to tend to the concerns of their subjects and put all effort in the advancement of their country, financially and morally, with the help of the government.[56]

The word "British" occurs only twice in the film's Arabic voiceover. The first occurrence associates the British government with helping found schools. The second accompanies a burnished sign of the British Bank of the Middle East that receives a close-up shot. The only other explicit mention of the British government is captured on a plaque mounted on Dubai's Al Maktoum Hospital in both English and Arabic that commemorated the "perpetual friendship" between the British government and the trucial sheikhdoms. The London officials responded to Tripp's appeal for a more organized aid program by nearly scrubbing the British government out of the final product.

The film's concluding shot begins exactly as Tripp proposed, but the accompanying message is dramatically altered. He proposed concluding with, "What of the future, in whose hands does it rest."[57] Tripp's text is a loaded

FIGURE 2.8 Still from *These Are the Trucial States*. Final scene of two boys heading toward the horizon, with God as "the source of strength." ©Imperial War Museum.

question (although without a question mark), an apparent plea for clarity to his home government. The final script avoids asking, much less answering, Tripp's question: "God brought forth their security, and God is the source of strength." Whereas Tripp intended for the film to end by demanding responsibility, the narrator recites a line that might seem borrowed from a religious proverb, deflecting ultimate determination to a higher being. The future of the Trucial States, according to the film, is left in God's hands, not the British government's and not those of the "general Middle Eastern audiences" either.

PHOTOGENIC

"The film will be a 'winner,'" predicted a London official in August 1958.[58] It was to be distributed "to all Arabic speaking posts in a very short time." In

October 1958, BP screened the film in London to "visiting Bahraini personalities," who found it "highly interesting and offered no criticism."[59] There is no record of anyone seeing the film after that.

Tripp might have never seen the film. Earlier that summer, he had completed his post in Dubai, though he would soon report to Bahrain and be "responsible for co-ordinating the development programmes" in the Trucial States and the region.[60] His successor in Dubai, Donald Hawley, hosted regular film screenings at the political agency compound. He preferred to show musicals but also projected newsreels, feature films, and his own recordings of the region; however, there is no evidence he ever showed the film (although he mentions the BP film in his published history of the Trucial States).[61] Instead of being used to promote and defend the British government's work abroad, the finished film was buried in government archives.

What made the British government lose interest in the film, especially after all the time and money invested in it and after the expressed enthusiasm for it? How could one of the coast's earliest cinematic overviews have been dismissed and forgotten?[62]

The realization that the film's message was already outdated might have led to its shelving. The original reason why a camera crew came to the region—to document the arrival of real oil wealth—could have rendered the film obsolete before it was ever completed. Portraying people getting by on ancient sources of livelihood might have seemed tone-deaf, just as the coast was on the verge of producing terrific amounts of oil and, therefore, wealth. The film was wedded to maintaining Curzon's status quo, not to preparing for inevitable change.

British experience with post-oil development in Iraq, Iran, Kuwait, and Bahrain—the "blueprints"—should have flagged the Foreign Office to patterns about to recur. The British government's attempts at framing the coast of the Trucial States as under a controlled process of minimal modernization might have become exposed for what they were: a futile fiction in light of imminent and unpreventable transformation. A film about a local people tilling their land, building wooden boats, and trading pearls would seem disingenuous, leaving the Foreign Office even more vulnerable to criticism that it was promoting denial, not sensible development.

The film's eventual abandonment also likely reveals the lack of a specific audience. Tripp originally produced a script in English intended for Foreign Office officials and a general English-speaking audience.[63] London officials chose to pursue the Arabic version first, indicating a wish to sell their vague scenario to "general Middle Eastern audiences." Propaganda films were often directed toward subjects of the British colonies, but pursuing such a broad audience, especially in places no longer colonized, was an untested strategy, and then with the dated form of a propaganda film. Perhaps before the reels could be shipped to British outposts in the Middle East someone correctly observed what the film's message turned out to be: a lax search for an argument to remain in a part of the world it claimed, with increasing difficulty, to protect.

Tripp had written a film to project a photogenic story about Great Britain's policies in Dubai. He had hoped that the optics of his development programs—changes one could see—would win over Dubai's residents and neutralize Arab-nationalist broadcasts from beyond. The visual narration of these images were supposed to coalesce into a clear British policy that would convince Tripp's own government. According to Tripp, water drilling efforts and antimalarial spraying were photogenic. There was, however, a much more photogenic project getting started on Dubai's shores, which Tripp did not mention in his original pitch. This new project was not the story of working the land, but of shaping the land. It was not the story of production, but the appearance of production. Not the fertilizing of the desert, but the sequestering of water from land for the sake of a photogenic city.

The new project is mentioned in passing toward the end of the film. Its inclusion was likely added in London, using unsteady aerial footage of Dubai Creek. Just after the film introduces the British Bank of the Middle East, the voiceover makes reference to an infrastructural project from which the British bank was profiting. The narrator mentions "a project to widen and deepen Dubai's harbor in order to allow for large ships to dock on the waterfront and to facilitate trade and the import of goods." There are no shots of the project's workers or its imported equipment.

Designed by the British engineering firm Sir William Halcrow & Partners, the dredging and reinforcement of Dubai Creek would essentially transform the creek from a natural tidal zone into an efficient waterway. The work itself was a spectacle of large machines and their thick black clouds of exhaust, neither ever seen before in Dubai's port. Halcrow's engineering of the harbor was the start of a series of lucrative development proposals designed by British industries. Engineering and architectural projects were about to be the photogenic events that framed a captivating tale of progress and development. Buildings, bridges, tunnels, roads, and ports: These things signified permanence and autonomy. Moreover, it was their ongoing construction, not just their enduring fixity, that would feed a convincing narrative. Steel and concrete—not antimalarial sprayings and husbandry—were beginning to set the stage for the unfolding and imprecise relationship between Great Britain and Dubai.

CHAPTER 3

HARDENED EDGES

IN MAY 1957, just ahead of a summer's languorous heat, an overcrowded fishing boat arrived at Dubai's port. Eighty-three people alighted. No one marked them as suspicious, but for anyone who asked, they were hajj pilgrims on their way to Mecca. They stayed in Dubai just long enough to hire a ship captain for the next leg of their journey—to Mesaieed, a Qatari town made up of little more than the workers who operated its purpose-built harbor for oil exports. Dubai's port attracted flows of people like the pilgrims, and it ran a good business in delivering them elsewhere. After they found a boatman with a couple of days to spare, the passengers pressed into another boat not designed to hold all of them.

Toward the end of the second day at sea, Qatar's coastline came into view. The captain steered his passengers to an uninhabited cove, where he set them off and assured them that they were within walking distance of Mesaieed. Maybe earning extra money corrupted the captain, or maybe he grew nervous that his absence would make the boat's owner suspicious, or maybe he worried patrols would arrest him if he came too close to the port. Whatever his reason, he left his passengers forty kilometers down the shore from Mesaieed, an impossible stretch to cover by foot without a supply of drinking water.

On land, the travelers happened upon two men who offered to take them the rest of the way in the morning, if they paid ten rupees per person in advance. It was the last of their money. Upon waking up the next day, the travelers found that their guides, a "pair of rogues from Sind," had "disappeared under cover of night." If not for a boat of Trucial Oman Scouts surveying the nearby coast, the hapless group would have died.[1] The scouts gave them water and food and then ferried them to Al Wakra, where Qatari officials denied them entry. The scouts had no other option but to bring the group back with them to Abu Dhabi, landing there on May 13, 1957. In Qatar, the travelers had numbered eighty-three. In Abu Dhabi, they were eighty-four. One person had died, and two had been born.

HAJJIS FROM NOWHERE

A British officer stationed in Abu Dhabi sought quick accommodations for the travel-weary arrivals. Abu Dhabi's ruler Sheikh Shakhbut bin Sultan Al Nahyan, still awaiting his first payments from Das Island's oil exports, agreed that the stranded pilgrims could be "encamped in and around some disused houses."[2] It was not an uncommon scenario for British officers: the rescuing of distressed people without papers, water, and money along the coast of the Trucial States. Just earlier that month, they had encountered

> parties of destitute and semi-destitute Persians, Pakistanis, Muscatis and others, who found themselves in Abu Dhabi for one reason or another. . . . [A] launch carrying some 150 Muscatis and Pakistanis, which had sprung a leak off Abu Dhabi, had to be abandoned and the Political Officer had difficulty in arranging for a fresh launch to pick them up. A few days later a group of 32 Persian tinkers and pedlars arrived, angrily demanding visas for Qatar. These were removed to Dubai, on the first stage of their homeward journey.[3]

Like these eighty-four people, many arrived wanting to get to the oil fields of Abu Dhabi, Qatar, and Saudi Arabia. And if fortune allowed, they wanted ultimately to perform the hajj in Mecca. They called themselves pilgrims, but their journey to Mecca could last a lifetime.

As much as Foreign Office officials wanted to block such arrivals, "it [was] doubtful whether much can be done . . . to stop it."[4] Dubai's port was a flushing point, where migrants both arrived in the region and departed after being labeled "undesirables." In this instance, British officers attempted to make Abu Dhabi's ruler provide for their well-being, but he exhibited a firm understanding that the situation was a foreign policy matter and therefore a British matter. As the British resident in Bahrain admitted, "These unfortunates are a British responsibility."[5] The travelers, now under British jurisdiction, found themselves trapped in a miserable, though for the time being not life-threatening, situation. Relegated to some abandoned palm-frond houses, the travelers were trapped in a place that did not want them and where they did not want to be.

The political agency calculated that this endeavor in crisis abatement was costing £12 per day (less than $250 today). The political agency could cover the expenses, but according to the Foreign Office there was a matter of principle, a "danger of setting a precedent which might encourage dumping of similar parties in the future."[6] The next step in processing these "undesirables," according to unwritten policy, was to repatriate them and try to recover expenses from their home government.

This time, however, it proved difficult to determine which government should reimburse expenses. British officials could not read, or even identify the language of, the pilgrims' documents. Eventually they confirmed that the papers were issued in Burma, and all but one of the pilgrims wanted to return there.[7] A month later, when the travel documents of five of these pilgrims were sent to London, officials confirmed they were not official travel documents but employee papers for the Burma Oil Company. Analysts suspected they were Pakistani nationals working in Burma but noted that papers for four travelers listed places of birth in the Burmese district Maungdaw.[8]

The language barrier slowed the processing, but the British also reported their frustration with the travelers' inconsistent story. Pakistani officials soon reported that the travelers were not officially registered for that year's hajj. After numerous interrogations, the pilgrims admitted they wanted to find work in the Gulf after having completed the hajj.[9] Or vice versa. Their story continued to change. Reasons for their high-risk journey alternated

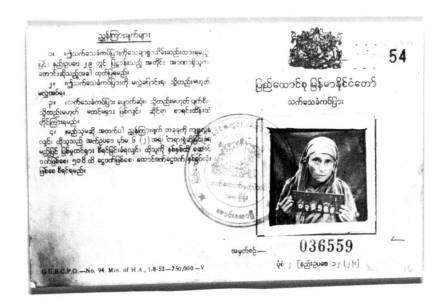

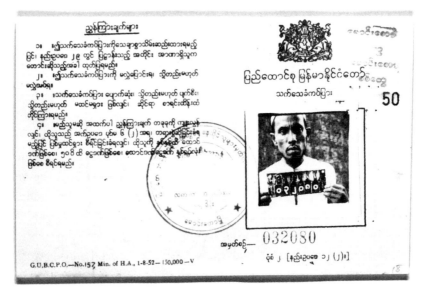

FIGURES 3.1A AND 3.1B The documents of the stateless pilgrims were sent to London for verification. Courtesy National Archives, United Kingdom.

between religious calling, economic well-being, and fleeing "persecution by communist guerrillas." Although their nationality remained unclear, the political agency found a translator among Dubai's immigrant communities, who stitched together their itinerary of the last several months. They had embarked from western Burma, crossing the border to East Pakistan (Bangladesh today). They then made their way to the port city of Chittagong, where they boarded a British-India steamship headed around the tip of India to Karachi. From Karachi they hired the boat that brought them to Dubai.

Their travels were best approximated by a British diplomat stationed in Burma's capital, Rangoon. He outlined for Foreign Office officials a history reaching back to the 1920s when what now are India, Pakistan, Bangladesh, and Myanmar (Burma) were not yet so distinctly defined by national borders. People from Chittagong (in Bangladesh today) commonly migrated to work in the rice fields of what would eventually become defined as Burma. In 1942, when Burma came under Japanese control, an "ethnologically artificial" border became more pronounced with Buddhists on the Japanese-controlled side and Muslims on the British-controlled side. By the time an international border defined Burma from East Pakistan in 1948, violence and migration had cemented an ethnic and religious divide. The diplomat in Rangoon suspected that while the travelers claimed Chittagong as their ancestral home, they had likely lived in Burma since the border creation. They could have also been born in Burma to parents from Chittagong.

His assessment of a people victimized by the hardening of nations around them, however, did not include sympathy. In his letter he warned that people from the Chittagong area were known for a "villainous appearance and propensity for lying."[10] One Foreign Office official dismissed the letter as "an interesting ethnological paper" that offered no easy solution. Another officer highlighted the remark about a "propensity for lying" as good reason to discount the travelers' story of escaping from communists. Focused on short-term problems, neither official was ready to acknowledge that they were reaping what British colonial administration had sown more than a decade before.[11]

In early 1957, when the pilgrims began their journey, they had crossed easily into East Pakistan. The decade-old Burmese government, exhibiting no affection for its Muslim minorities, would have welcomed their departure. When they had successfully boarded the boat in Karachi for Dubai, the unwanted group had successfully departed two countries, both of which could now legally deny their return. The British Embassy in Rangoon summarized the situation: "As they left Burma illegally without any definite national status, either Burmese or Pakistani, they now appear to be stateless."[12]

The days in Abu Dhabi got hotter as the deadlock continued. Ironically, the formerly colonized Pakistani officials demanded from the former colonizers, the British, more documentation of the pilgrims in order to consider the requests for repatriation. They insisted on receiving each pilgrim's name, village address, and the names of two witnesses from that village. Pressed by the British officials to provide this information, the pilgrims adjusted their stories, exchanging Burmese hometowns for East Pakistani ones. The pilgrims were now evidently more willing to go back to East Pakistan, a place where they may have never lived but that was better than being quarantined in life-threatening heat.

When the British supplied the information the Pakistanis requested, there came only more demands for more data. Entrapped in someone else's paper trail, British officials in Dubai became flustered and less focused on finding a solution. Their scheduled vacation departures grew near and daily temperatures rose. Conditions for the pilgrims only worsened. By late June, at least one more traveler had died. Soon after, those deemed capable of working were refused rations, even if there were no work opportunities in Abu Dhabi. Thirty-seven absconded "to seek work elsewhere," likely Dubai.[13] Refused rations and therefore even more desperate to find work, nine sought permission to make the several-hour journey to Dubai where work opportunities were rumored to be increasing. "We already have a large floating population in Dubai looking for work,"[14] a British official in Bahrain complained. Quarantined in Abu Dhabi, refused the most minimal of handouts, and denied a chance to work in Dubai, the travelers faced another deadly dilemma.

Just before their August holiday, officials from the political agency disbursed a final round of rations to the travelers still remaining at the designated site, leaving them "to their own devices" for the hottest, most perilous month of the year.[15] In Dubai, a single junior officer was left behind with little to do but survive the heat and send more information to Pakistani officials. One day that August, at the harbor's tranquil piers, he noticed the arrival of a boat that in a busier, cooler season would have gone unheeded. It was filled with the travelers whose faces he recognized from the headshots he had just sent to the Pakistani government. The pilgrims had used their final rations, not for water and food, but to hire a boat to Dubai. Reporting later on what happened, one British official admitted that his colleagues had turned "a blind eye," hoping to "have seen the last of them." To his chagrin, "they are back on our doorstep."[16]

In September, the travelers were corralled and taken back to Abu Dhabi as negotiations with Pakistani and Burmese officials stalled. Shortly thereafter, the agency's Arab assistant Ali Bustani went to Abu Dhabi to check on their status. He discovered they had absconded again. The political agency assumed they had returned to Dubai and "joined the existing community of stranded Far Eastern pilgrims."[17] Two weeks later, the political agency confirmed this suspicion: "Some are beggars, others coolies and at least one has died."[18]

In October, an assistant political agent "combed the town" for them again. He found one, Amir Wazzidin, pilgrim number 6 on the British list to Pakistan. Wazzidin had set up a barber shop and assured the official who found him that the others had all traveled back to Pakistan. The barber maintained that he was cutting hair until he earned enough money to afford the return travel. The officer believed "his story rang true," but it was also the story his superiors wanted to hear: that the problem had sorted itself out.

In reality, the pilgrims would never have spent their life savings in order to sneak across the border into East Pakistan, pay for passage to Karachi, and then suffer several months wandering across the Gulf only to make enough money for a return to a place that denied them. British, Pakistani, and Burmese officials had all used official channels to renounce responsibility for the fate of eighty-four pilgrims. The group had been left no other option but to disappear back into the informal networks, into "the pilgrim squatter communities in Dubai [where] there is little employment . . . and the mortality rate is high."[19]

FIGURE 3.2 Dubai residents before a pile of coral collected for constructing houses, 1959. Courtesy John
R. Harris Library.

Already by 1957 there were clear and organized systems by which petroleum companies recruited workers for the extraction operations in the
Gulf region. Histories have linked these recruitment practices not only to
earlier slave-trade networks but also to the much criticized labor recruitment
practices for cities and petroleum centers throughout the region today.[20] The
plight of these pilgrims sheds light on how, despite increasingly organized
systems of migration, many migrants were still avoiding formalized authorities to determine their own fates in light of economic hardship and ethnic
persecution. While Dubai's imminent population growth would eventually
rely on similar recruitment patterns as those for the oil fields in Abu Dhabi,

Qatar, and Kuwait, it would also result from the quiet arrival of people like these pilgrims, when mass-recruitment contracts were too great a scale for the port's small, unstable economy. These migrants' coming and going, their finding sustenance and shelter among the other migrants, would contribute to the gradual buildup of Dubai's available cheap labor force. Their immigration status would rarely be questioned.

The pilgrims' indeterminate status corresponded with Dubai's own purposefully indeterminate state—its own frontiers not yet hardened by national borders and therefore accessible to people who were refused by fixed borders elsewhere. The pilgrims' ordeal and persistence anticipated the stories of millions of others who arrived in Dubai after them, through both formal and informal networks of migration. For these

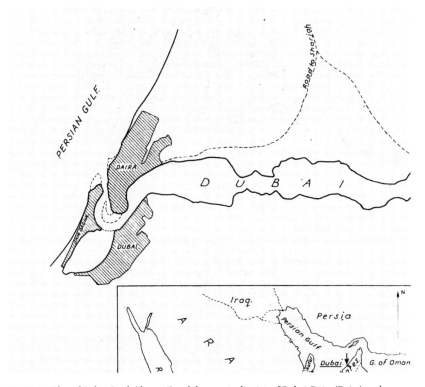

FIGURE 3.3 Plan of Dubai Creek ("lagoon") and three main districts of Dubai, Deira (Daira), and Shindagha (Shirdhaga), from Halcrow's "Report on Proposed Improvements," 1955. Courtesy National Archives, United Kingdom.

FIGURE 3.4 Dhows on Dubai Creek, 1959. Courtesy John R. Harris Library.

migrants, Dubai might not have been the ideal destination, but it was, at least for a while, the negotiated station to escape poverty and to engage economic chance.

CONCRETE ON THE CREEK

The stateless pilgrims made a living off a Dubai statistic: In 1957, the port received an estimated 10,000 tons of cement.[21] Concrete, concocted from the imported cement, was not yet a staple building material in Dubai. Most houses were predominately still made from earth, coral, and palm fronds. At this point, cement was more a profit scheme than an essential stock. When word began circulating that a project—Sir William Halcrow & Partners' harbor contract—might soon replace the creek's natural edges with steel and concrete, the merchants responded immediately by storing the necessary materials. Even if there was no short-term run on cement, there were plenty of other regional ports whose building booms the merchants could supply. When the Halcrow work began, the merchants' store would determine the market price.

These 10,000 tons of cement translated to more than 180,000 sacks burdened onto shoulders and transferred to warehouses. The pilgrims would have found the jobs of hauling the sacks or mixing the cement already taken. Instead, they took jobs cutting and making the "discarded cement sacks into paper bags," likely earning well under the port's average daily wage of eight rupees, or $1.65.[22] The pilgrims found subsistence by the pitiful grace of Dubai's market.

That is where the British record of the pilgrims' stay in Dubai ends, but their survival story had really just begun, as it folded into those of millions of others who came to Dubai. And like many others, the stateless pilgrims did not work on the most obvious construction projects but squeezed out a living at the lower rungs of commerce spun off from larger projects. Even just the rumor of Halcrow's pending engineering contract on Dubai Creek was enough to increase Dubai's port activity and its attractiveness to those desperate for work. If just the rumors of work opportunity could attract people, then the actual physical manifestation of concrete shorelines and piers—the largest development project the Trucial States had seen—was going to create an even larger pull.

SILTING UP

In the mid-1950s, Dubai's success in trade relied on geographical happenstance, even if it is usually attributed to wise leadership and shrewd businessmen. Because of the way water interacted with land along the coast, Dubai had been winning over maritime trade from Sharjah and, further north, Ras Al Khaimah, whose harbors had become clogged with silt. The same currents kept Dubai's waterway a navigable estuary but could, eventually, also fill it up like the others. According to the British development expert Ronald Griffith,

Dubai Creek's natural advantage was far from secure. Its status was instead "highly fluid," an "unstable equilibrium, with a constant battle between the sea and the land." Griffith noted that while Dubai might "for the time being" preside as the region's premier port, the Gulf's currents did not ebb and flow for the purpose of creating a "natural" harbor.[23] Regional trade was at the mercy of forces no authority had yet tried to control.

By the mid-1950s, merchants complained to the political agency that the creek was irretrievably "silting up," a fear based on knowing the fates of Sharjah and Ras Al Khaimah and little else. There were no records of past seasons to measure against and determine whether the creek was retreating into the Gulf. The political agency had reason to be wary of the merchants' entreaties. Were they truly witnessing the port's disappearance, or were they once again trying to shift the Maktoum family's income from oil concessions toward their most valuable asset?

The political agency had its own mercantile, as well as political, reasons to fear Dubai Creek's demise. If Dubai Creek's economic performance would wane, so would the livelihood for a region the British were not ready to support financially. With it would also go the conceptual narrative of the region—the "Dubai model"—in which Dubai played the central role as the region's economic anchor. In 1954, London officials carved out a budget line of £2,500 for Halcrow engineers to visit Dubai and report on whether the creek was disappearing and, if so, how it could be saved.

Sir William Halcrow & Partners enjoyed an established rapport with its home government. Its roots going back to 1866, Halcrow was founded on the realization that "acceleration in the control and exploitation of natural resources must take place." The company had reinforced the British coast against flooding and fortified the London Underground. During World War II, its activities were "almost entirely applied to the purposes of war."[24] Implementation of projects beyond the UK, including the £20 million Port of Tema under construction in British-controlled Ghana, made Halcrow a logical British candidate for work within other reaches of the British empire. The company proved it could work seamlessly with the British government, even more specifically its military, exemplifying the transformation of wartime engineering and techniques into peacetime portfolios of profit.[25]

Although Halcrow knew how to win multimillion-pound contracts, the British government lured them to Kuwait with a £106,000 "cooling water jetty" project in 1952.[26] Despite the project's simple requirements, Halcrow left Kuwaiti officials dissatisfied in terms of the results and the final cost, which far exceeded the estimates. The Kuwait government subsequently disqualified Halcrow for a larger £3 million project, which the company had expected to win. Effectively pushed out of Kuwait, Halcrow representatives blamed British officials for not protecting their claim to Kuwait's future engineering contracts, purporting they had been "short-circuited" by an American firm. There is no evidence that the Dubai project was ever framed as a conciliatory gesture by the British government, but the timing was just right to maintain a Halcrow presence in the Gulf region.[27]

In 1954, Halcrow engineers spent two summer months in Dubai for site investigations, just as the political agency was opening on Dubai Creek. In January 1955, the engineers issued their report. They premised their findings by stating that Dubai held "no records" that might "[indicate] the conditions prevailing in former times, and so it is not possible to define the extent to which the channel has deteriorated or the date at which deterioration set in."[28] Furthermore, "no records exist of any recent Civil Engineering works of any magnitude in Dubai." The report therefore claimed with unfounded certainty that the creek's "depths . . . have deteriorated seriously." It further claimed physical deterioration was triggering Dubai's economic "decline." There were several references to "local information" gathered from those who, like Halcrow, stood to profit from an improved port—local merchants and the British trading firm Gray, Mackenzie & Company.[29]

Beyond its dearth of recordkeeping, the Halcrow report concluded, Dubai had other severe shortcomings. Aside from sand and stone, Dubai was deprived of any necessary "raw materials," and its "isolated position" made it all the more difficult to acquire essential supplies. The ingredients of any proposed solution, Halcrow argued, had to be imported, including a labor force. Neither bustling nor self-sustaining, Dubai Creek could not be maintained just by hard work and good intentions. Halcrow depicted it as deficient and damaged. Its rescue would require a rational triage of engineering and development schedules. In order to last, it would need materials and

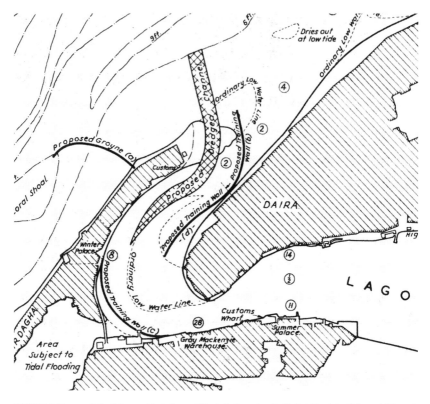

FIGURE 3.5 Proposed dredging and training-wall installation plan for Dubai Creek in Halcrow's "Report on Proposed Improvements," 1955. Courtesy National Archives, United Kingdom.

expertise beyond anything a local capacity could provide. In contrast to the murky and unstable ways of currents and storms and despite the lack of historical and demographic data, Halcrow confidently calculated the price of a predictable and compliant harbor.

Halcrow inscribed urgency into an engineering proposal, the most expensive project ever proposed for Dubai. The proposal declared efficiency, requiring only limited imported materials and relying on the manipulation of tidal movements to achieve most of the sediment removal. The scheme included dredging a course at the creek's entrance, 60 meters wide and 900 meters long. In addition, the dredgers would make the creek's bed even deeper so that it was navigable for larger boats. With the insertion of a modest amount of concrete and steel to define a narrower channel, the proposal claimed that, instead of relying on expensive machines, the natural current would provide the necessary force to keep the dug channel clear of the sediment that built up over time. The dredged channel and narrower course set by the training walls would accelerate the flow of water, thus increasing the force with which the water could sweep out silt along its way.

Although this proposal could not make Dubai Creek navigable for all ship sizes, it predicted that the harbor would accommodate boats with up to an "eight-foot draught" and remain cleared of the hull-crushing sandbars. Halcrow priced the reworking of less than a kilometer of Dubai over two years at £388,000, not including Halcrow's 5 percent fee, nearly as much as Peter Tripp proposed for the entire 1,300-kilometer coast for the coming five years.[30]

HALCROW LET LOOSE

Even though the company's portfolio included plenty of projects at similar, if not lower, prices, and even though the estimated commission was triple that of the project that had drawn them to the region, Halcrow officials treated the potential project as "comparatively small."[31] They maintained an air of indifference in communications with government officials after submitting their proposal, perhaps sensing, and taken advantage of, the fact that the British government now needed them. At this stage, it was also in the Foreign Office's interest that Halcrow did the job. Assigning the work to a British firm, and specifically one with such a history of collaborating with the British government, not only ensured that any money raised for future works was being channeled to the British economy; it also made it more likely that the government remained informed about the project. Plus, the Foreign Office had already paid for the preliminary report. It would be difficult to acquire the same funds to start over.

No government engineers reviewed the proposal. "Before we let them loose on Dubai," Peter Tripp, without an engineering background, expected explanation of how Halcrow calculated the costs of labor and materials, given the unavailability of data. "If they can make an elementary mistake … at Kuwait," Tripp observed, "they are quite likely to make the same mistake here."[32] Unlike Kuwait's government, which had petroleum profits, the Maktoum family "cannot afford such a margin of error."[33] Halcrow's representative in Kuwait used a metaphor to avoid answering: "Consulting Engineers are like doctors—they do try to give the very best advice based on their training and long experience." And then he admitted, "Even Harley Street specialists have difficult patients and can make a wrong diagnosis sometimes!"[34] Tripp reported he was "not impressed" with the response.[35]

In actuality, Halcrow was already "let loose." Having mapped and measured the creek, Halcrow had documented the present for the sake of a future history—a history that Halcrow was prepared to author and profit from. Halcrow now housed that knowledge. The creek's temperaments might have been legible to dozens of sailors and harbor workers, but Halcrow now promised to produce clinical accuracy. Such accuracy, according to Halcrow, had an accurate price. If the Foreign Office insisted on a smaller budget, then Halcrow's engineers would just recalibrate the proposal for a less effective result. Halcrow's demands could be brazen because the ball was already rolling.[36] There came more requests for cost cutting, and even the threat of a counterbid by a Danish firm. Halcrow stared down every tactic.

FINDING FUNDING

Halcrow's "Dubai Harbour Scheme" faced no real contest, just delay. Its cost estimate was "far beyond the limits of any [British] Treasury allocation."[37] By December 1956, the British treasury made clear that there would be "no financial commitments whatsoever," and the Foreign Office intended to "minimise any risk of their becoming financially committed should anything go wrong." Still, the Foreign Office expected that, "Her Majesty's Political Agent should be associated as closely as possible with the project."[38] The Foreign Office remained committed to realizing the Halcrow proposal and identified only one financial solution: to make Sheikh Rashid, not yet the ruler, a debtor. At this stage the political agency still found him to have "little idea of the finances of his State," but that was no cause for hesitation.[39]

The need to raise funding set Tripp up to approach the merchants in two seemingly contradictory ways. On the one hand, he was already handling them as political antagonists, monitoring their social networks and their funding of the Dubai National Front; on the other hand, he now had to coax them into contributing to the new "Harbour Fund." The merchants hedged their investments in Dubai's future by responding to Tripp positively. By the end of 1956, Tripp had collected about £55,000 in "subscriptions," almost equally split between the Maktoums and the merchants. It was a small, but not insignificant, fraction of the impending creek improvement costs, and it came at an advantageous time when Halcrow could pursue initial trial borings before the rest of the financing was secured.[40]

In 1956, British officials in London, Bahrain, Kuwait, and Dubai started to investigate financing options for the rest of the necessary funding. The first financing idea was that the shipping company Gray Mackenzie could extend Sheikh Rashid a line of credit. London officials argued that the loan would be a positive gesture in light of the company's long-held monopoly in handling all vessels too large to enter the creek, and the company stood to gain from the port's potential growth. According to Halcrow's preliminary study, the company's representatives had confirmed that "silting has been progressive . . . and must be considered critical."[41] However, one year later, when asked to invest in the solution, a representative was "anything but enthusiastic" about the proposed scheme. According to him, "the state of the Dubai Creek is not such as to warrant costly works of this nature." Having lorded over Dubai Creek for more than a half century and controlling the city's single steel crane, Gray Mackenzie brushed off the need for engineered plans. Contrary to the opinion recorded in the Halcrow study, a representative even denied that there was any "progressive silting" in the first place.[42] Based on its response, Gray Mackenzie seemed the only entity satisfied with its profit prospects on Dubai Creek.

The second financing idea was a loan from a British bank. The British Bank of the Middle East (BBME) had enjoyed a banking monopoly in Dubai since 1946.[43] A British-based loan, some Foreign Office officials conjectured, would enable the government to "dictate the terms" of Dubai's future urban development.[44] Since the bank had some overview of the Maktoums' earnings from port duties, government officials relied on it to confirm Sheikh Rashid's financial health when they had little other way to gauge it.[45]

The manager at the Dubai branch told Peter Tripp he was "fairly certain" Sheikh Rashid could repay the amount over ten years. However, upon being asked to supply that loan, the bank balked. It offered one possible conciliation: If the oil companies contributed, the government-protected bank might also put up some funding. British officials in Bahrain subsequently reached out to oil companies with contracts in or near Dubai. Petroleum Development (Trucial Coast), or PDTC, which held Dubai's petroleum concessions, declined, a clear indication that oil companies along the Trucial States coast had little interest in making Dubai their "normal port of entry."[46] Even if they were willing to make use of Dubai's current and future port facilities, the government-protected oil company would only invest in constructing ad hoc piers near their exploration sites.[47] With PDTC's refusal, BBME was also out as an investor.

At this point, one Foreign Office official doubted whether there was "any great future for Dubai as a port."[48] The remaining option was financing from the rulers of Kuwait, Qatar, and Bahrain, all of whom already enjoyed wealth from petroleum exports. Peter Tripp reported that Rashid was open to the idea but insisted that the British government approach the other Gulf rulers on his behalf. A British official in the Kuwait political agency approached Kuwait's emir, who agreed to extend a £400,000 loan to be administered by BBME.[49] The British bank was set to earn a handling fee on the loan it refused to extend. And likewise, British oil companies and the shipping monopoly Gray Mackenzie stood ready to financially gain from a future harbor without any risks.

As a financial impresario for the ruler it protected, the British government instigated a new role for itself in Dubai and the region. Instead of financial support and professional expertise, it used its administrative force to appoint private consultants and raise the necessary funds for the "Dubai Harbour Scheme"—all in the pursuit of embedding a role for itself in Dubai's political and economic stability.

In March 1958, three years after the initial report, BBME put papers before Sheikh Rashid for his signature, making him a debtor for the amount of £400,000, even before he was officially Dubai's ruler. Starting with the minimal salary for Abdul Salam Er Raouf in 1956, Sheikh Rashid's investment

FIGURE 3.6 Men bathing and attending to a small boat on the shore of Dubai Creek, 1959. Ongoing dredging work following Halcrow's plan is visible in the background. Courtesy John R. Harris Library.

in Dubai had now escalated to a loan surpassing Dubai's probable GDP. By signing the loan papers, Sheikh Rashid signed a survival strategy the British government had formulated for him: the debt financing of oversize infrastructure so that he, in turn, controlled it. His rule over both sides of Dubai Creek was not yet uncontested, but he now claimed what was in between them. Debt was the means by which to assert that claim.[50]

SHARJAH'S LOSS

While Halcrow's project started too late to have a major role in the film *These Are the Trucial States*, it did affirm Tripp's Dubai model—a conceptual ordering of Dubai's future development as the urban center of the Trucial States. Significantly more money was to be spent on Dubai Creek for a single two-year project than on the rest of the region in five years. Rather than being a natural center for the region, however, Dubai's port was propped up and shaped by the Foreign Office, though without British financial investment. The campaign to fortify Dubai's harbor also included the obstruction of any infrastructural project beyond Dubai that might challenge the port's position.

The usual telling of *saving* Dubai Creek depicts Sheikh Rashid leaping to do so before the competition in the neighboring sheikhdom of Sharjah could do the same. It is said to be the reason why the world today knows Dubai more than Sharjah, once "the most prosperous centre of maritime activity in the region."[51] In this telling, Rashid is portrayed as fast, farsighted, and resolute, an exemplar of Dubai's business-savvy reputation. This account is hardly accurate. First, the creek was not yet easily claimed by the Maktoums, but the contract helped Rashid claim it. Second, the account erases the British role in inviting Halcrow to Dubai and guiding Rashid toward the Kuwait loan, which could have ruined him had the project gone awry. And, third, Sharjah's ruler indeed tried to improve his city's harbor, and more actively than Sheikh Rashid. In fact, several years before such an idea was introduced to Sheikh Rashid, Sharjah's ruler, by his own motivation, had petitioned for a British loan to finance a similar project.[52]

Nine miles north of Dubai Creek, Sharjah Creek suffered more from silting and sandbars. Its winding form and shallow depths kept its shorelines deserted except for the lightest of boats. For the last twenty years, Sharjah's trade capacity had depended on a single wharf once built to supply construction materials for the British airbase.[53] By the mid-1950s, many of Sharjah's merchants had moved their businesses to Dubai, thereby forcing the city to rely on Dubai's port. Sharjah's deteriorating situation was only compounded by the Maktoums' decision to add additional tariffs on goods destined for Sharjah.[54]

As part of its initial report for the British government, Halcrow did in-spect Sharjah Creek. Its separate report for that harbor upheld Tripp's Dubai model. The Sharjah port faced "permanent decline." In order to counteract that, engineers calculated a project considerably more expensive than that for Dubai. Options included either an "uneconomical" canal or a new en-trance channel one-and-a-half times as long as that needed for Dubai. Even then, the harbor would be half the width and cost at least £600,000, almost double that if work was split into phases. To compound Sharjah's disad-vantage, Sharjah's ruler was considered a less promising debtor. A British official concluded that, "Sharjah must face the fact that its present harbour facilities must continue to decline and in due course it will cease to exist as a 'deep-sea' port."[55]

Sharjah's ruler, Sheikh Saqr bin Sultan Al Qasimi, did not accept the po-litical agency's Dubai model. While Rashid relied on the political agency to conduct his financing diplomacy, Sheikh Saqr actively sought his own solu-tions for salvaging his port. He pursued foreign investors to make "Sharjah the finest port on the Gulf," even in defiance of British-government warnings. In response to such ambition, the political agent thought it best not to offer "too much encouragement" for his unfeasible schemes.[56]

With promised concessions from the British government that remained unfulfilled, Sharjah's ruler sought business deals in West Germany and Denmark but was turned down when his sheikhdom's prospects for oil were deemed bleak.[57] In 1961, he also approached the British contracting and engineering company Costain, but a British official made known to the company his "strong views" against plans that might compete with Dubai's reinforced future.[58]

British-led plans for Dubai Creek had begun without Rashid's collabora-tion in 1954, and there is no record of him having done much work to galva-nize the project. Institutional amnesia soon settled in, however. In 1964, four years after completion of the harbor project's first phase, the political agent at the time, James Craig, recorded a revised history in his 1964 annual review:

> While Sharjah creek was allowed to silt up and the other rulers sat feckless or
> content, Shaikh Rashid borrowed money and had his creek deepened ... [to]
> prevent it [from] ever silting up.[59]

Craig assigns Sheikh Rashid—"he alone, when other Rulers sat idle, cautious and suspicious"—as the instigator of Dubai's modernization, extinguishing the British government's essential role in hiring Halcrow and arranging the funding, not to mention its role in preventing any competition from Sharjah.[60] No one offered a correction to Craig's history writing. The political agent's inaccurate account fed an oft-repeated truism, the most basic synopsis of Dubai's modern history that would be repeated in policy documents by the British government and other governments, printed as the contextual background material in international news reporting, and delivered in promotional brochures about the city's auspicious rise from anonymity.[61] The body of government that put forward the enduring myth was the same one that buried the truth.

FIGURE 3.7 Work on narrowing the creek and creating new land on Dubai Creek, January 1960. Courtesy National Archives, United Kingdom.

THREATS AND REINFORCEMENTS

On a calm, sunny morning in February 1961, Heli Allen was opening the windows of her prefabricated house that had been shipped to Dubai from Britain. Her husband had left for work. After days of torrential rains, she could finally air the house out and let the curtains wave in the breeze. Her open, aluminum-lined windows framed views of surrounding barasti houses, where she was sometimes invited for coffee with neighbors. They had made way for her house's sudden insertion. No sooner had her husband left for work that day than he was back home, stricken with panic. He pulled shut all the windows and curtains that Heli had just opened. Not knowing what had happened, Heli Allen knew that he meant to hide. He feared for his life.[62]

Heli and her two small children had moved to Dubai with Neville Allen in October 1958 so that he could oversee work on Halcrow's harbor scheme. The previous days' storms, known as the annual *shamal*, had exposed design flaws. Before Halcrow's interventions, both sides of the creek were prone to flooding, but the damage from this year's storm was wider and more severe. The flooding, though, was not the worst that had happened. The creek, reshaped according to Halcrow's design, was swollen with an unnavigable and boisterous concoction of sand and storm detritus.

Having lost days of trade due to the storm, the merchants had woken up to find the mouth of the new channel choked with sand. Dubai was cut off from the world, this time by British engineers. Prior to Halcrow's work on the creek, the annual shamal had been a feared but anticipated event. Despite the damage it caused in the short term, the shamal usually flushed the creek of a year's accumulation of silt and sandbars. Halcrow's insertions of steel and concrete, it turned out, intensified the storm's effects. Allen realized that Halcrow's design, executed so confidently, now threatened Dubai's social and economic stability.

In the days after the storm, with his composure regained, Allen attended a meeting at the political agency, where Halcrow kept its papers on the project. Those at the meeting were Donald Hawley (Tripp's successor as political agent), Sheikh Rashid, and William Duff (Rashid's British "financial expert," who had arrived the year before).[63] Duff had been catching up on Halcrow's paperwork at the British agency, where, he realized, a private company kept its papers for a project signed by Dubai's ruler and financed by yet another government. Like Halcrow, he owed his job with Sheikh Rashid to British recommendations, but he knew that his salary came from the ruler.

At the meeting, Hawley, fluent in Arabic, conveyed his grave concern about the threatening situation at the creek and attempted to mediate between the ruler and Halcrow. Also fluent in Arabic, Duff asserted himself as the new and adept mediator between Dubai's ruler and the British consultant. Less concerned than Hawley, Duff urged more engineering solutions over chastising Halcrow for miscalculations. His employer, Sheikh Rashid, agreed. Duff also arranged that Halcrow's papers would no longer be in the agency's hands but in Dubai government offices he was starting to get built.

The timing of the storm worked to Halcrow's advantage. In 1960, the first year of post-engineering port operations, customs collectors logged nearly a 25 percent increase in imports, after prior years of single-digit growth. Such a spike in profits made it easy for Dubai's traders to correlate engineering with profits.[64] A post-shamal cleanup started almost immediately, and Rashid urged Halcrow for quick recommendations for additional work. Halcrow's corrective proposal was not pursued at the company's expense but as a new, more profitable contract. More to the point, Halcrow gained financially from their initial miscalculation. The entrance canal would be dredged further out to sea, and the training walls along the Deira side would be extended. Dubai Creek was to become even more engineered.

Though he admitted no engineering background, Hawley "quizzed [Halcrow] very close," remaining hesitant to endorse their plan. Duff, in contrast, expressed that he was "quite satisfied" with Halcrow's proposal. More importantly, the merchants, far from being furious at Halcrow's errors, were enthusiastic about future profits, with one merchant offering to pay the whole price for the new works.[65] In regard to finding the financing, the political agent no longer needed to shuttle back and forth along the coast looking for lenders. Rashid, now pursuing his own fundraising, found a benefactor in his new son-in-law Sheikh Ahmad bin Ali Al Thani of Qatar, who, through what the political agency referred to as the "Secret Treaty of Doha," provided generous financing and large gifts for Rashid's key projects.[66] What made Halcrow's follow-up proposal even easier to digest was that it included an additional profit scheme specifically to Rashid's financial gain. The water in between the creek's new training walls and the sloping coast would now be filled with silt, earth, and rock scraped up from the creek's bed. In addition to saving the creek, Rashid was also gaining a new portfolio of unclaimed waterfront real estate. With this lucrative bonus built into the new plan, Halcrow's cost estimate for the next phases rose to £1,000,000 by 1964, nearly triple that of its first contract.[67] The same year that it secured the next phase of work on the creek, Halcrow also signed a £190,000 contract for the first bridge over Dubai Creek, what came to be known as Al Maktoum Bridge.

A SECOND OPINION

One person was not so enthusiastic about Halcrow's new scheme. Unlike for the first contract, Ronald Griffith, a government engineer from the Middle East Development Division (MEDD), was called in to review Halcrow's corrective measures. He was said to express "some radical criticisms" of Halcrow's proposal. Counter to Sheikh Rashid and Duff's ready stance, Griffith counseled delay and further analysis. Neville Allen's supervisor at Halcrow, Harry Ridehalgh, proved hostile to the second opinion. He challenged and attempted to discredit Griffith in the presence of other London officials, contending that the government expert was costing Dubai time and money.

In a clear demonstration of his comfort with the ranks of British government, Ridehalgh placed a call to higher-ups at the Foreign Office and said he was "fed up and annoyed with Mr. Griffith" and would not tolerate being "sniped at" by a low-rung bureaucrat. He further claimed that his staff was unable to "discover" Griffith's "qualification and record" and drew the conclusion that the development expert "appeared to be unknown in the consulting engineers' world."[68] Shaken by Ridehalgh, another British official feared that a quarrel with Halcrow could end in "unfortunate results on our relations with them in the Gulf."[69] When it was suggested that Griffith personally address Ridehalgh in Sheikh Rashid's presence, Griffith demurred, claiming such a confrontation would force him "to undermine the reputation of British engineering" when he only wanted "to raise it still higher."[70]

Caught between Halcrow and the government engineer, Hawley felt "like a nut between jaws of a nut cracker."[71] His sense of powerlessness was the price for Halcrow's ascent and Duff's new role in Dubai's development narrative. In his threatening telephone call to the Foreign Office, Ridehalgh had noted that British government concerns were irrelevant. The client, Dubai's ruler, had already approved the scheme.[72]

Halcrow was now, assuredly, "let loose." The engineering company had crafted history and defined urgency. It had then calculated solutions and supplied a blueprint for the future. Without any substantial review or regulatory process, Halcrow arose as an unchallenged voice of billed advice. Dubai was not to grow in the pursuit of a larger vision but by means of a step-by-step improvement program measured out by a single engineering company. Moreover, Halcrow established itself within Dubai's management: Neville Allen became Dubai's "resident engineer," but he reported to Halcrow. One of the municipality's earliest public orders was that all government entities, companies, and individuals needed to submit their plans for laying underground or aboveground utility lines to Halcrow's "Development and Planning Department" at the company's office in Deira.[73]

SHAPED

Before Halcrow's concrete and steel, Dubai's harbor was an auspicious accident bound to tidal patterns. The engineers' plan promised to edge out temporality and chance. In place of the "fluid" state, Halcrow's design provided a new narrative of perpetuity. Modernization is often described as a process of upheaval and change, but this work was purchased with the expectation of predictability and stable growth. No longer perceived as a capricious "sea water lagoon," the creek metamorphosed into a modern harbor facility, a concrete topography of calculation and financial prospect. Through technological might and theatrics of labor and machinery, Halcrow promised "the essential characteristic of permanence."[74]

In 1961 after Halcrow's second-phase work was well underway, a senior British official visited Dubai and wrote that he "was generally impressed"

FIGURE 3.8 New land in Deira reclaimed by Halcrow's second-phase contract for Sheikh Rashid included space for loading areas and a new shore road. The coastline further inland remained to be hardened. Courtesy John R. Harris Library.

with the roll-out of infrastructure and administrative programs initiated by the political agency. The city was "progressing on the right lines."[75] "Lines" referred literally and figuratively to the structural framework of Dubai's drafted development. Beyond the yesteryear "bustle," Dubai Creek was becoming a rational landscape of "blue prints taking shape."[76]

One morning, during Halcrow's repairs on the creek, a hired boatman ferried Heli Allen and her children around the creek so that she could take photographs of the new works overseen by Halcrow. She recalled that the water was still clear and "so rich with sea life." Fish would jump into your boat before you could catch them with a hook.[77] Meanwhile the thuds from Halcrow's mobilized dredging machinery reverberated through Deira and Bur Dubai, and coal-black diesel smoke inked the creek's skies. Within a decade, one of Donald Hawley's successors would observe that the creek was no longer clean enough for swimming.[78]

Dubai Creek once had many uses, but now it was being engineered into a single purpose: infrastructure. Any other purposes it might have served the coastal communities were being expunged. Heli Allen recalled that her husband had recommended that, further inland, the creek should keep its soft edge so that people could still access the water. The pursuit of profit squashed this idea, and Halcrow signed more contracts to line the rest of the creek with hardened edges. While limited stretches maintained their soft edges, most of the creek's shores became too deep for wading after being dredged and fortified. Dubai's families were gaining access to new houses with running water and electricity, but they were losing access to Dubai Creek. The city's residents moved inland so that the rest of the world—hajjis, workers, investors, experts, salesmen—could arrive with more ease. The promise of permanence had its price.

CHAPTER 4

TAKING MEASURES

1960 Dubai Town Plan

"MODERNITY HAD BARELY touched the Trucial States in 1958," recalled Donald Hawley about his first days in Dubai as the third political agent for the Trucial States. Observing people's "ancient way of life," Hawley approached the souks as if they were a vestige of times past.[1] The political agency did a good job of keeping European "casual visitors" out of Dubai.[2] That made the city all the more enchanting for those Europeans who could access a place with only a handful of generators and a single flushing toilet as late as 1951.[3] Hawley, though, landed very comfortably at the political agency compound, accorded air conditioning, refrigeration, and a flushing toilet. Meats, vegetables, and even drinking water were shipped from abroad to his private pier on Dubai Creek.

Hawley also discerned signs of change at the souk. And the potential for improvement. He recorded, for example, that the souk was "one of the least smelly markets in the East I have ever been in."[4] He noted improvements being made to Dubai's roads and how the first municipal workers shifted piles of festering waste to fire pits outside city limits. Ultimately, these kinds of changes, not the supposedly ancient ways, were why he was paid to observe Dubai.

FIGURE 4.1 Alley in Bastakiya, Bur Dubai, 1959. Courtesy John R. Harris Library.

Hawley credited his predecessor Peter Tripp for getting "the ball rolling" and "setting up a baladiya . . . essentially to clean the place up."[5] He used the Arabic "baladiya" instead of the English "municipality" to imply it did not yet meet British standards. From his walks through the souks, he identified what he wanted the municipality to tackle next: Cattle "still browsed on the cardboard boxes" just beyond market stalls, and he was irritated by the "enormous amount of plastic which blew everywhere."[6] He needed to install a regulatory system to tackle his checklist.

In 1958, the British government issued an order that both defined and encroached upon Dubai's autonomy. It acknowledged Dubai's "municipal regulation" but also required that all laws be translated into English and be approved by the British government.[7] Picking up where Tripp left off, Hawley framed the newly founded municipality as a government body created from scratch, as if there was no governing structure in Dubai without British intervention. Development, in this way, was the British delivery of order, specifically administrative and social order, to a location where previous British officials had found "strife" and "lawlessness." "Setting up a baladiya" required ignoring and canceling out others' attempts of political organizing, specifically by merchant groups. More than just abiding by British terms of governance, the municipality was designed British-friendly—as an effort to maintain the legitimacy of British power in Dubai and also to pave the way for British teams of expertise.

Dubai Municipality, run by experts Hawley supplied, ensured the political agency a vehicle through which it could pursue its modernization goals. As crafted by British regulation, the new government body posted ordinances seemingly of local origin but actually of British "tutelage."[8] With a vehicle for issuing new laws, Hawley could refer to directing Dubai's development as "gentle encouragement." The term acknowledged his professional hesitation to assume direct responsibility for Dubai's governance.[9] "Gentle encouragement" also minimized any risk of overreach by an underfunded and disempowered political agency. Indirect action, however, was only effective if there was that pliable municipal body. Early evidence of Hawley's success: One of Dubai Municipality's first directives addressed his earliest annoyance, the unattended cattle in public spaces.

At first Hawley targeted small and simple management projects, but they paled in comparison to the major transformations on Dubai's horizon. These oncoming changes demanded a fully functioning municipality that Hawley had not yet instituted. From the small landing at the agency compound, Hawley could estimate what was about to happen. Further down Dubai Creek toward the city, Hawley saw the thick black cloud of smoke that rested heavily over the water; he could hear the guffaws and clanking from machinery that challenged any nostalgic conjuring of a timeless port. In fact, Hawley never really experienced an "ancient" Dubai Creek without the constant din of Halcrow's harbor project. The dredgers, clamshell scoops, pile drivers, diesel generators, and pontoons all arrived before him.

The dredging and piling equipment were transforming more than the creek. Even more dramatically, they were triggering a chain of events that Hawley increasingly found to be beyond his control. The physical ordering of the port had the potential side effect of sabotaging the rest of the city. Arrivals of people and cargo increased with hardly a plan for where they would go. A real estate boom ensued. In Hawley's first year in Dubai, one property sold for 2,000 rupees; in his second year, the same property went for 200,000, or about $42,000. New buildings, sometimes made with the recent imports of concrete and steel rebar, were feverishly going up, and the municipality had no capacity to regulate their construction. There were no controls, regulatory or otherwise, set for the building boom that the British government had instigated. Dubai was at risk of collapsing in its own frenzy. Hawley was so concerned about Dubai's fate that he proposed "an immediate order by the Ruler forbidding any further building."[10]

LONDON AND SUDAN

On September 27, 1959, Hawley set off from his compound for Rashid's offices in the customs building to address such matters. Driven in a black Jaguar adorned with a British flag, the political agent made some pomp of his travel. He entered the city at a slow ceremonial pace, allowing Dubai's residents to notice. Alerted to Hawley's approach, Rashid descended from his upper-floor rooms to meet him.[11] Only if Rashid stood waiting at the car did the driver open Hawley's door.

In October 1958, just after Hawley's arrival, Sheikh Rashid officially had become Dubai's ruler upon his father's death, with British consent. There had been doubts expressed within the Foreign Office about whether it could back his ascent as ruler. Within the past year, Rashid had won the Foreign Office's favor—both because he had responded positively to British plans, including Halcrow's harbor scheme, and because the potentially violent resistance to his power seemed to have abated. Dubai's ruler welcomed Hawley as he stepped out of his car, and both ascended to a veranda where they viewed "everything going on in his busy blue green creek." From "a lovely position," Rashid could survey port activities as well as the building boom that was making him wealthier but, Hawley realized, could also bring his downfall.[12] Taking in the view, Dubai's two most powerful men discussed the city's future growth.

Both of them had just returned from travels. Sheikh Rashid had flown to London for his first time. The visit had been planned by British officials to impress upon him how a city could function. Tours and visits were specifically selected to convince Rashid how municipal coordination and functioning infrastructure promoted and conveyed an image of a city's efficiency. The visit had "opened his eyes."[13] Finally, the political agency reported, Rashid was "at least showing interest in controlling the development of his town."[14]

Hawley had also visited London that summer, using his holiday to address the municipality's imminent troubles. Staying with his parents outside London, he had made regular trips to the Foreign Office to discuss his plans for Dubai. The fact that his trip did not coincide with Rashid's visit supported the impression that Rashid came alone as an autonomous leader, but it was Hawley who came to London to recruit Dubai's future expertise. Hawley made contact with experts and consultants—the people he called "short-term expert aid"—that Dubai needed to design still-absent water, telephone, and electricity systems. From London, he flew to Sudan, his diplomatic station before Dubai. There Hawley met his former Sudanese staffers running a recently independent country. With British influence in Iraq now expunged, Hawley sought the "gradual recruitment of a few expatriate experts" from Sudan who could run the municipality the political agency had invented.[15]

Meeting Rashid on his veranda and knowing his stationing in Dubai was limited, Hawley pushed Rashid to act quickly on a next round of plans and agree to a new tranche of recruited experts. The ruler was receptive to Hawley's "ideas on a land survey and town planning."[16] Tripp had once urged Sheikh Rashid to hire a land surveyor, but now Hawley, after having been in London, encouraged something more substantial: Dubai needed a town planner. Rashid agreed.

With the ruler's verbal consent, Hawley soon after sent a telegram to London on September 23, reporting that the ruler had "asked that a survey of the town be undertaken and a development plan be drawn up as soon as possible."[17] After a week without a response from the London office, Hawley sent another telegram pressing that "this problem really is an urgent one" and that "a considerable amount of building is actually being held up" because of British delay.[18]

DUBAI LANDS

Already, Rashid was quick to negotiate with a vague roster of global businessmen, many from India, Iran, and elsewhere in the Gulf. Hawley shared Rashid's hope for a lucrative real estate market, but he wanted to make it measurable. In preparation for his meeting with Rashid, Hawley had composed a three-page document he titled "Dubai Lands," which outlined how Dubai's "development [needed] to be along sound lines."[19] "Along sound lines," was a term Hawley, like others, used to capture a bureaucratic sensibility and an abstract appreciation of organization, but with him it was becoming more literal—lines of surveying and property boundaries.

As with Halcrow's earlier report on the harbor, "Dubai Lands" laid out how additional regulations would ensure Dubai's manageable growth. The document summons the most explicit and enduring modernization efforts to characterize Dubai's growth for the coming years. It is, for example, the first major document to articulate that Dubai's economic longevity required a manageable real estate market as a necessary "prelude to serious development." Through it, Hawley not so much envisioned as directed how the city would physically grow. Municipal administration was meant to manage and encourage growth. There is no prediction of how large or how quickly Dubai would develop and no mention of necessary analyses or surveys. The document remains focused on the real estate market—on reining in Dubai's uncharted growth and making that growth a source of wealth for Dubai's new municipality.

‹ FIGURE 4.2 In 1959, electric lines and concrete blocks are already being integrated into the city's built environment. This photograph was taken by John Harris in November 1959 during his first trip to Dubai as designated town planner. Courtesy John R. Harris Library.

"Dubai Lands" defines six land uses for a future town plan: residential, commercial, industrial, "offensive spaces," open space, and "plots for mosques, clubs, Petroleum sites etc." Three "classes" of housing included a "lodging area" for "the poorer classes, who would normally build on it buildings of the 'barasti' type or other light edifices." Earlier Hawley had proposed banning these kinds of structures because they burned to the ground "in less than one minute," but moving forward he acknowledged the dangerous housing stock as a necessary means to accommodate the population flux. The other "classes" of property were restricted to more durable building materials, namely concrete block.[20] Hawley's document avoids the explicit categorization of Dubai's population into nationalities and ethnic groups. Instead, it defines demographic order through economic status and the materiality of houses.

The report also called for mapping the existing city, creating a land registry, establishing eminent domain procedures, and instituting an immediate moratorium on all new construction until a town plan and land registry were established. Hawley's real estate policies focused on the unbuilt parts of the city, specifically land not easily claimed by residents. His proposed policies foresaw a fundamental legal definition that came to characterize Dubai's urban expansion: Any land without "clearly established" ownership became the property of the "Dubai government" and therefore under the control of Sheikh Rashid and the regulations prescribed by "Dubai Lands." A "development plan" would further transform "vague and not adequately defined" practices into recognizable financial and spatial standards.[21] More instrumentally, Dubai needed a town plan in combination with a land registry that provided a way to confirm landownership claims and issue official deeds. Deeds would make owners eligible for bank loans. Hawley had once described the purpose of a town plan as "not [for] mere tidiness but certainty of title."[22] In this way, the future town plan was not intended to envision a future city; rather, it was pursued to *leverage* one.

Hawley expressed urgency about making Dubai's first town plan, but, strangely enough, he had not set out in London to find an architect or planner.[23] Had he looked, Hawley would have found a city brimming with architects and planners ready for the job. Since the final years of World War

II, London had been the epicenter of Europe's town-planning profession. The movement guided postwar redevelopment in the capital and the surrounding region, most evident in the design and development of the New Towns. During Hawley's summer visit, the first residents were moving into the early-phase New Towns, and more towns were being planned. These designed modern towns for living and working were based on decades of urban planning ideas, consolidated into a set of documents that not only redefined London but also made the city into an international source of planning advice. Beyond London, similar ideas in urban planning were taking hold in other postwar European nations and in the British colonies. If cities have been called the greatest legacy of British imperialism, then town planning was a most gainful postwar export. It had been so for planners who had drawn up proposals for Delhi, Kuwait City, Baghdad, Karachi, Colombo, Addis Ababa, and Hong Kong, but by the summer of 1959, no one in British government had considered exporting that expertise to Dubai.

A GARDEN PARTY AND SOME TELEGRAMS

During the 1959 summer in London, Hawley met John Harris at a garden party. Their time together limited to a social setting, Harris likely focused on explaining the massive hospital he had just completed in Doha. Hawley later recalled vaguely that Harris had "some experience in the Gulf," an understatement considering the scale of Harris's completed work, unrivaled by any British architect in the Gulf region.[24] Harris had recently overseen the expertise and supplies required for Qatar's first "large-framed building," held together by steel spans imported from England and outfitted with British medical technology. If Hawley had confided in Harris at the garden party about his search for a land surveyor, then it might very well have been Harris who convinced Hawley to seek out a planner instead.

In 1953, John and Jill Harris had submitted the winning proposal for a design competition, sponsored by the Royal Institute of British Architects (RIBA), for Doha's first state hospital.[25] It might have been the region's first architectural project whose design principals included a woman. The project received only minimal press coverage at a time when British media regularly covered national postwar redevelopment. It is nevertheless

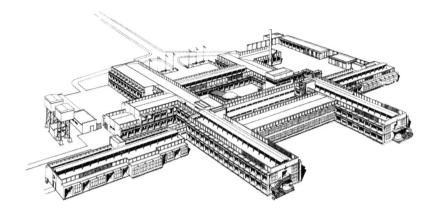

FIGURE 4.3 Doha State Hospital, designed by John and Jill Harris. Courtesy John R. Harris Library.

a surprising omission because the hospital project signaled an early postwar opportunity for British industries and consultancies to profit from foreign development projects. The Doha hospital project demanded a large, technologically intensive program and an architect capable of overseeing it. Over thirty-five British companies contributed to the hospital project, selling a range of products from concrete roof systems to laundry equipment to flagpoles. More generally, the Doha hospital offered Britain jobs, capital, and a chance at extending market reach.

Hawley later claimed it was he who subsequently brought Harris to meet Dubai's ruler, but the Foreign Office identified another candidate for the town-planning work.[26] London officials put Halcrow in touch with P. W. Macfarlane, a town planner who worked with the partnership of Anthony Minoprio and Hugh Spencely; the three of them had recently completed a planning project for Kuwait's emir and were established members of London's town-planning scene. Minoprio had been the design consultant for Crawley, one of the first completed postwar New Towns in Britain. Macfarlane had been part of Patrick Abercrombie's "small devoted staff," which had produced the consequential Greater London Plan of 1944 to guide the city's postwar redevelopment.[27]

There were then two candidates for the Dubai job: John R. Harris, the eager architect with a small firm, and the partnership of Minoprio &

Spencely, with Macfarlane, established British town planners with noteworthy projects on their résumé. In initial conversations with the Foreign Office,
Macfarlane delivered an enumeration of how a planning project begins,
including the commissioning of aerial photographs.[28] After Macfarlane's
convincing introductions, Hawley needed to remind the London office to
reach out also to Harris.[29]

Hawley sought advice from Peter Reilly, who oversaw British involvement in
development projects at the political agency in Kuwait. Reilly should have been
aware of Harris's architectural work in Kuwait, but he offered no opinion of it.
With regard to the other candidate team, Reilly should have been prepared to
offer some critical perspective. By 1952, the Minoprio team had produced Kuwait
City's first town plan. Soon after the plan's issuance, massive demolition work
began in anticipation of realizing what became known as the "Minoprio plan."
In comparison to Dubai's population of 40,000 in 1959, Kuwait's plan had been
designed for a population of 250,000.[30] The Minoprio team's work in Kuwait
seemed to have petered out around 1956, when they were last hired to "[lay]
out community centers."[31] In the previous year, their plan for Baghdad had been
discarded for a contract with Frank Lloyd Wright.[32] These disappointments,
however, did not translate into enthusiasm for the Dubai project.

Both candidates were asked to submit a proposal, which presumably
included evidence of their previous work. Harris delivered his, but Macfarlane, as the Minoprio team's contact person, did not.[33] After three weeks of
waiting, Hawley interpreted Macfarlane's silence as disinterest. Assuming
responsibility for Dubai's "mapping decisions," Hawley sent an invitation
to Harris to visit Dubai.[34] Upon hearing of Hawley's unilateral action, the
Foreign Office called John Harris to retract the invitation.[35] Harris politely
responded that, if the invitation were reissued, he could leave with ten days'
notice. London officials regained contact with Macfarlane, who expressed
that he was able to depart for Dubai just as quickly but subsequently failed
again to send his proposal to Hawley in Dubai.

London officials eventually had proposals from both candidates, but one
representative groaned, "These are no help as we are unqualified to judge between them."[36] There is no record of anyone from the British Middle East Development Division, or MEDD, which employed planners, ever being consulted

to advise on Dubai's needs. Peter Reilly, who could assess both candidate's completed work in Kuwait, provided limited input. His correspondence with the political agency in Dubai, for example, did not mention that the Minoprio team's work in Kuwait had proved contentious, after its executed prescription to entirely demolish the city center had not been followed with a rebuild.[37]

On November 4, 1959, the Foreign Office—unable or unwilling to find sufficient counsel—telegrammed that hiring Dubai's town planner had to be "the Ruler's decision," because he was the one who was going to pay the bill. The "impossible position" of selecting a planner could only be solved by hearing an architect's name uttered by Sheikh Rashid: "Even if you have to put the words into his mouth, please arrange for an expression of opinion."[38] Hawley's policy of "gentle encouragement" was replaced with induced regurgitation. "If the Ruler does not mind cost," the telegram continued, "or if he attaches special importance to having consultants who have worked on a grand scale, then he may prefer M[inoprio]."[39] With little instruction and an incomplete set of architects' proposals, Hawley was expected to report back on Rashid's decision.

Foreign Office officials knew better than anyone that Rashid had to "mind cost," and they also had the ability to assess that the "grand scale" was something an economically precarious sheikhdom should surely avoid. Still, it is peculiar that officers grasping for words to describe the work of the Minoprio team used "grand scale" in their eighty-nine-word telegram. "Grand" might bring to mind monumentalism expressed through wide, radiating boulevards and the plotting of distinctive landmarks to announce political power. The work of Minoprio & Spencely, with Macfarlane—as exemplified in Dhaka, Baghdad, and throughout Great Britain—hardly exhibited monumentality.[40] The plan for Kuwait City was not grand either, but it was extreme in that it demanded the outright erasure of the existing city. The planners called it "drastic replanning," which demanded exorbitant demolition and acquisition costs.[41] In the coming years, the "erasure of Kuwait's pre-oil past" brought lasting negative consequences for the city: It both erased any historical character and triggered a chronic inflation of real estate prices.[42]

By setting up Minoprio's team as "grand," the Foreign Office seemed to suggest a preference for Harris, but by forcing the decision on Rashid, it deflected responsibility onto an autocrat who, when previously approached on similar matters, recognized his own lack of qualifications to make the decision. During previous discussions with Hawley about a town planner, Rashid had said he deferred to Hawley's opinion. From someone who had most likely never seen a town plan and had just visited one of the largest cities in the world, Rashid's hesitation seems a reasonable reaction.

Hawley and his predecessors had worked to convince Rashid that their expertise in organization and municipality building could bring him political stability. If there was ever a moment for Rashid to rely on British expertise, this was it: the transformative decision that would shape and direct how Dubai grew. Four years prior, the Foreign Office had selected Halcrow without Rashid's input. The political agent had even kept the paper trail in its own offices, despite the fact that the project was financed by Sheikh Rashid. Since then, Hawley had named and invited other British consultants to the city, all without Rashid's approval. It remains unclear why the Foreign Office treated this decision differently. Was a town plan too consequential for the British government to take responsibility for it, or was it so inconsequential that they did not want to bother with due diligence? Or was it for some other reason altogether?

Within hours of receiving the Foreign Office's last telegram on the matter, Hawley arranged to meet Sheikh Rashid and later telegrammed back his answer:

The Ruler prefers the cheaper quotation and does not require grand scale planners.[43]

While Hawley was instructed not to make the decision, he certainly had latitude to influence the ruler's choice. It's not preserved how or whether Hawley translated "grand scale" for Rashid, but his repetition of the term in the telegram suggested he also used it during the conversation. If Hawley had pushed Harris's selection, then he likely did so with the thinking that Dubai did not need a town planner associated with major contracts. Dubai, according to "Dubai Lands," simply needed a "scheme" to enact Hawley's real estate policies.

Sheikh Rashid was forced to declare the future planner's name and expected to pay for his travels, but the British government was happy to write letters on his behalf. On November 6, 1959, the Foreign Office undersecretary informed John Harris that Dubai's ruler expected him "as soon as possible."[44] Before leaving, Harris met with representatives of Halcrow in their London offices.[45] He also quickly composed a multi-destination itinerary, with stops in Bahrain, Doha, Kuwait, and Tehran because he wanted to check in on other possible commissions. The itinerary befitted an architect who saw his firm's future beyond London. Dubai presented a great opportunity, but like everywhere else, there were no assurances. He left within twelve days of being invited to Dubai the second time.

HARRIS IN DUBAI

On November 19, 1959, Harris arrived at the Sharjah airport at 10:35 a.m. Neither Harris's prospective client, Sheikh Rashid, nor the political agent was in town to greet him. Hawley was making his way back from Bahrain that day, and then he visited Ras Al Khaimah and some inland villages. The following day, still without haste to return to greet Harris, Hawley met Sheikh Rashid outside the city to enjoy some hawking. During the two days without his two main contacts, Harris met with Halcrow's local engineer, Neville Allen. The following day he had a "long talk" with Donald Hawley, conveying a requirement advised by Allen: a 1:1000 photographic survey of Dubai and its surroundings. That evening Harris probably attended the "large and enjoyable" air-conditioned cocktail party hosted by Hawley at the political agency, along with the growing circle of British and Western expatriates congregating around Dubai's modernizing project.[46]

On his third day, Harris met Sheikh Rashid, later describing the meeting as "unusual and perhaps uncertain."[47] Donald Hawley did not attend, signaling his preferred distance from the subject matter. Instead, the political agency's "Arab assistant" Ali Bustani attended as a translator.[48] Harris likely presented his portfolio of previous work, including projects in Kuwait, Qatar, and Iran. Sheikh Rashid had visited Harris's Doha State Hospital and acknowledged it as a prime example of the region's modernization. Dubai's own Al Maktoum Hospital probably came up in the conversation. Though Harris found the meeting "tentative," Rashid summoned him along after their talk for a spontaneous call on the political agent. Hawley noted that Rashid was "deeply interested."[49] Harris was offered a £1,250 fee, or $3,500, to create the town plan, an amount he found generous.

Comfortable with how things were going, Hawley left town again, not returning until Harris's departure day. Keeping absent at a critical moment for the city's future, Hawley figured himself the "enlightened administrator."[50] The modernization processes that Dubai needed exceeded Hawley's professional capabilities and that of his limited staff. He insisted that he remain disentangled from the details attended to by the British and Sudanese experts he recruited. Off to Bahrain once more, Hawley believed he had found an ideal political position—one where he ceremoniously represented British sovereignty and was respected and listened to by the private-sector consultants he had helped find work.

Though he was not there to witness it, Donald Hawley later recalled that Harris "walked every inch of Dubai."[51] Like any visitor before him, Harris probably started at the creek. In a city with a population now estimated at around 40,000, the presence of a new Westerner was probably noticed but not newsworthy. Standing in Bur Dubai at an abra landing, Harris stood out with his suit jacket, trilby hat, and leather shoes among the Baluchi men handling crates and burlap sacks on their shoulders. Many of the stevedores were barefoot and barelegged, clothed in *lungis* that didn't impede their movement. They may have associated him with goings-on of the pontoons and clamshell scoops that interrupted their work. Harris hired a boat to take him around the creek, so that he could make sketches of the famous wind towers that moved breezes through the houses below them.

Harris was one of the first to read the city like an expert, but he was one of the last to encounter an unmapped Dubai. Protected only by the nominal shade of his hat, Harris conspicuously stood in the sun, observing, taking a note or a photograph, finishing a sketch. People watched him from the shade; dogs tracked him for novelty's sake.[52] He recorded notes at intersections of major sand roads, assessing the amount of foot and cart traffic the roads attracted. He observed how goods unloaded from ships made their way to the customs building where they were stored until merchants paid the taxes and transferred them to the souk or storage sites. He

FIGURE 4.4 John Harris's guide engages with families at a fishing settlement on Gulf waters, 1959.
Courtesy John R. Harris Library.

identified and observed the roadways that originated at the creek's wharves
and stretched toward the packed sand trails in the direction of Sharjah
and Abu Dhabi. He saw how the limited number of British accommodated
themselves mostly beyond city limits, how the wealthier Arab and Iranian
merchants still mostly lived in sturdy houses originally made of coral and
earth but now also reinforced with concrete block and steel, and how the
city's poorest maintained barastis in between.

Hawley returned to Dubai on Harris's last day and recorded in his diary
that Rashid was "delighted" with Harris. He gave Harris a copy of "Dubai

Lands." The architect promised to return in May with a town plan and to return many times after that.

PAST AND FUTURE FUSED

Harris expected that the political agency would see to the completion of the necessary aerial photography by the end of 1959, leaving him and his small staff five months to draw the plan based on the resulting detailed map. The photographs were made in January 1960, and the company, Hunting Aerosurveys, needed more time after that to complete the "aerotriangulation and mapping at 1/2000 scale by precise photogrametric methods."[53] Waiting for the essential imagery in London, Harris was introduced to "urgency" in Dubai. "Always," Harris later recalled, "there was a feeling of urgency."[54] He learned simultaneously that haste was related to another expectation: delay. This time the delay was caused by the British government making sure Sheikh Rashid, not the political agency, was financially liable for the necessary photography.

After making aerial photographs of the city and its outer reaches, Hunting Aerosurveys mapped Dubai by painstakingly tracing every house, fence, palm grove, and tree revealed in the photographs. Their map makes no distinction between tentative structures and more substantial houses. Some mosques are identified with a heavier black fill, likely so that future road reservations would avoid them. Though most of Dubai's buildings were not yet fastened to the ground with concrete and steel, Hunting's map legitimized their claim to permanence.

Hunting's aerial photograph and map defined January 6, 1960, as the starting datum from which Dubai's modernization would be measured. With Hunting's inscription of each house and Harris's subsequent preservation of those drawn lines in the plan, years of urban accumulation went from being a progression over time to a definitive legal moment. "Existing Dubai" was now a fixity, a legitimacy that extended validity to every standing house and planted palm drawn into the map. Their coordinates were now recorded, their claim worthy of a land deed and, subsequently, a mortgage.

In late March 1960 Harris received a facsimile of Dubai assembled on "fairdrawn sheets in one color." Hunting had traced a near-past Dubai. Then it was Harris's job to inscribe Dubai's future on top of, and extending from, this drawing—all based on a nine-day visit. He had little more than a month—for completing the drawing sets and sending them out for printing—to make the town plan to guide Dubai's growth for the coming decades. In early May 1960, John Harris returned to Dubai with the town plan.

During the six months that Harris had been away, Hawley further popu-lated the Dubai Municipality and established its Lands Department under the direction of his former Sudanese employee, Ahmed Adam, "an expert on land settlement and registration."[55] As Harris had been drawing the lines of the new city, Adam was preparing the deed templates to apportion land rights inside those lines. On May 16, Hawley convened a formal meeting to review Harris's plan. Invitees included British experts summoned by Hawley to a deliver a water distribution system, a telephone company, and the first power station. It was one of the first meetings for the recently arrived Wil-liam Duff. Donald Hawley was checking off the points of his "Dubai Lands" plan, realizing the political agency's vision of a delineated Dubai, ready to be measured and charted.

In his meeting notes, Harris observed that Sheikh Rashid "inspected [the plan] in detail" and "expressed agreement with the principles of the plan and approved the basic layout."[56] Unsurprisingly, everyone Hawley had brought to the table also approved the Harris plan. Hawley's water and electricity scheme designers agreed to align their services along the plan's scheduled roadways. The Dubai Telephone Company, to be officially launched in July, agreed to work with Harris's drawing to ensure that overhead wires and ser-vice stations obeyed the plan. Further, Halcrow's engineers found "nothing in the plan which would affect work" on the harbor—also unsurprising since Harris had maintained contact with Halcrow during the design process. The plan marked the exact location of Halcrow's proposed bridge, announced a few weeks before Harris arrived in Dubai. Harris's minutes from the green-light meeting end with his own question: "whose responsibility [was it] to co-ordinate all planning, architectural and engineering matters in the future"? It would be another seven months before Harris had an answer to his question.

On May 19, three days after approving the plan, Rashid "visited important areas of the Town" with Harris and his advisor Mahdi Al Tajir.[57] A folded

FIGURE 4.5 On May 19, 1960, John Harris presents Dubai's first town plan to Sheikh Rashid, ruler of Dubai. Dubai's first accurate map is also a blueprint of its future. Courtesy John R. Harris Library.

copy of his purchased plan lay by his side in the car. In between looking out over the city from the car window, Rashid scanned the map of his sheikhdom. The plan framed the two still-skirmishing towns—Bur Dubai and Bur Deira—into a single and comprehensible entity. It revealed how Halcrow's proposed bridge would stitch them together. Their union had been defined by British treaties and asserted by Maktoum rule, but now an accurately scaled drawing announced what their married form looked like. From this point on, a unified Dubai could be viewed at the ruler's desk or from the dashboard of his car. Meetings with merchants and international investors happened over the drawing, spread over his office's salon table. The city's center was on neither side of the creek; rather it lay in the waters of the creek that Rashid now controlled.

The plan's easy adoption as Dubai's new reality did not take away from how striking it must have been for Sheikh Rashid to behold the plan. At once, Rashid examined the first accurate map of Dubai's near past and a blueprint of its future. Dubai was represented on a large-format sheet of paper with established edges and channels for growth. Places he knew well from his regular walks and outings through the districts were now reproduced with definitive dark-purple lines. He could observe every existing house, barasti, and palm grove. In a glance, he could follow the S-curve of the creek and comprehend how the city's various neighborhoods related to one another. He could assess how generations of negotiations on Dubai's shores had configured assertions of ownership and profit. And now the boundaries of the two towns that he claimed were extended with lines drawn by Harris, beyond the jumble of existing housing toward a legible and ordered city.

THE BASIS FOR ALL FUTURE TOWN PLANNING

Fifty years later, Harris dismissed the plan for its simplicity. It was not mentioned in his office's publicity materials, yet it was the most essential and generative design he ever created for any city.[58] It provided the most basic outlines of a city: a portrayal of existing conditions, a comprehensive road system, a spatialization of Hawley's "three classes" of housing, and instructions for guiding future growth. Donald Hawley later called it "the basis for all future town planning."[59]

Through the plan, modernization was put forward as a set of isolated, and purchasable, options that could be arranged into a framework of order and urbanism. Established planning devices were inscribed onto Dubai's landscape: perceptible deployments like a bridge, roundabouts, a hierarchical road system, schools, a government center, neighborhood units, and broad curbsides. Development outlines emerged to be filled in with housing,

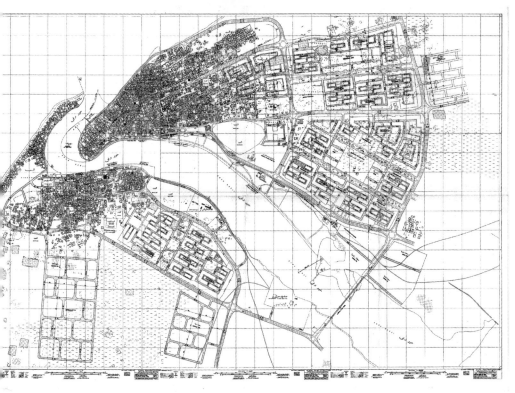

FIGURE 4.6 The Dubai 1960 town plan. Courtesy John R. Harris Library. A larger version of this plan can be found in the front matter, on pages vi-vii.

hospitals, and community and commercial centers. The result of Harris's brief week of observation was to be impressed upon Dubai for decades to come.

Donald Hawley later described Harris as being "enchanted" with Dubai, but there is no record that Harris succumbed to Orientalist ideas of untouched landscapes or ancient ways of life.[60] On the contrary, the architect was well aware that his initial walks through Dubai's streets were meant to instigate Dubai's transformation. Harris's plan nevertheless determined that some things would remain the same, at least for a while. According to the plan, the existing city was not to be razed, as the Minoprio plan had prescribed for Kuwait, and the city was not to be abandoned as obsolete.[61] Instead, the plan preserved the city's essential sites of trade and housing. The new had to integrate itself with the old. In this way, one might read the plan as a generous act of preservation.

Rushed to prepare the plan after delayed receipt of the necessary map, the printing process left no time for removing the outlines of buildings

caught in between Harris's proposed lines for road reservations.[62] The rush
meant that proposed roads in the plan appear enmeshed with the existing
urban fabric in Dubai's denser districts, as if the new coexisted with the old.
Harris's conflation of two mutually exclusive systems can also be interpreted
as professional hesitation: a rejection of the planner's blind faith in his own
drawings and an admission that he did not know all the right planning maneuvers after his one-week visit.

The 1960 plan did not necessarily ensure preservation of the city's old
houses and narrow alleyways, but it did express that it would not be the
heavy-handed act of planning that determined their fate; rather, it was
through the gradual, if uneven, process of negotiating urban development
that they would yield to more permanent structures. More effectively than
the urban planner, municipal workers would consult the town plan's contours
as much as they could when parleying with property owners and ultimately
shaping the existing city's new form.

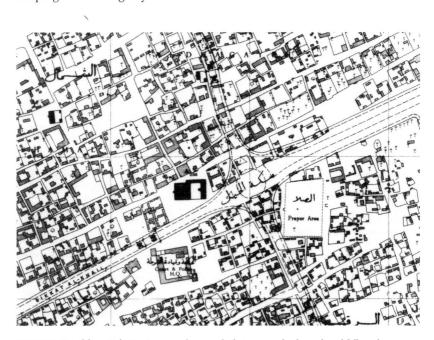

FIGURE 4.7 Detail from Dubai's 1960 town plan reveals that one newly planned road followed an
existing roadway (Sikkat Al Khail), and another would require land acquisition and demolition.
Courtesy John R. Harris Library.

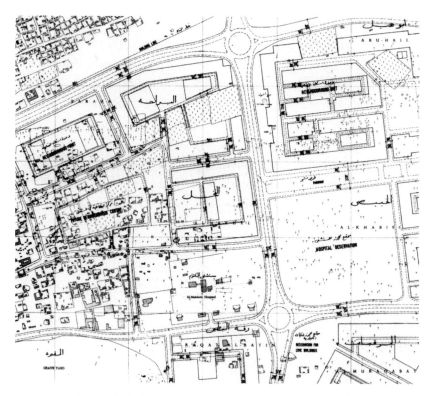

FIGURE 4.8 Detail from Dubai's 1960 town plan reveals how new districts were woven into the existing urban fabric by attaching them to existing, though not yet hardened, roads. Courtesy John R. Harris Library.

A clean-slate beginning, like the one produced for Kuwait City, was a concept the Dubai Municipality could not afford. While Kuwait's large-scale demolition and property acquisition were funded by the emir's assured oil reserves, there were not even hints of imminent oil reserves for Dubai in 1960. Beyond unaffordable, mass demolition would have been catastrophic, economically and politically, for Sheikh Rashid. The plan might have been Rashid's to implement, but he had to ensure that the merchants also saw advantages and profits in new development.

Clearing of the existing city would have demanded a halt to trading activity, which merchants were already struggling to maintain. Cutting the merchants off from their livelihood would have disrupted the delicate negotiation that was stabilizing relations between the Maktoums and the merchants. Existing souks had to be "retained in their present state" and, more importantly, continue to operate as an "important part of the character and way of life of the town."[63] The souks were perhaps unsophisticated in appearance but resilient in performance. They were Dubai's link to the rest of the world. Arriving European experts and their families were also finding the souks useful, not just "bustling." Visiting businessmen bragged of having a tailored suit ready for the next day's meetings. Western women offered cutouts from magazines, from which fabric purveyors and tailors in the souk produced London's current fashions at discount prices.[64]

If there was a part of Dubai's economy that could adjust and advance on its own, it was Dubai's trade systems that constantly sought out new networks of profit and collaboration. Better harbor conditions increased profits that the merchants knew how to translate into the necessary facilities. Similarly, the souks that stocked and sold goods from the harbor were left to modernize on their own terms and schedules. Harris also predicted the souks would eventually follow their sales market to the new outer districts. More generally, the plan argued that change in Dubai would mostly happen by means of addition, not deletion. Augmented urbanism made no assumptions that earlier development was insufficient or wrong; instead, it assumed that large-scale and technological advancement happened *beyond*. Older areas might be reconfigured in response to shifting economic factors, but then on the basis of a more gradual, and granular, decision-making process that avoided displacing, and compensating, current residents.

CRUISING NEW TOWN DUBAI, CIRCA 1965

Harris's plan proposed over 130 kilometers of roads, with the widest of them able to accommodate as many as six lanes of traffic.[65] Most of the proposed roadways were eventually built, a sign of the plan's dramatic impact. Beyond the road system, the plan put forward how Dubai was to function like a British New Town, not unlike proposals made by the Minoprio office for Britain and elsewhere in the world. But while the municipality executed Harris's road network, it all but ignored what the plan proposed in terms of land use and residential density.

Let's imagine Dubai as if it had gone according to plan. The year is 1965, five years after the plan's adoption. Here's how you would have experienced it:

FIGURE 4.9 Photograph taken during Harris's investigation of areas to be designated for Dubai's new districts, 1959 or 1960. Courtesy John R. Harris Library.

Suppose you are a medical doctor from Bangalore, recently moved to Dubai. After a day's work in Bur Dubai, you arrive by abra at Deira's Al Ras ferry station. New construction in this part of the city is not a result of the plan's instructions but rather the outcome of a thriving port economy. Deira was already the busier, more commercial district, and now the non-stop rise of new two- and three-story concrete buildings demonstrates that contrast with Bur Dubai even more prominently.

Halcrow's harbor project has attracted more cranes and other port machinery to handle increasing levels of cargo. The more active piers along the creek are now serviced by a new creekside road carved along the newly reclaimed shoreline. Increased truck traffic dominates the fresh asphalt and any space alongside it for parking. The new road reaches around the bend of Al Ras's creek frontage to the Persian Gulf shore, so that trucks can circle around and bypass Deira's dense alleys toward New Town Dubai, Sharjah, Bur Dubai, and Abu Dhabi. The shoreline road has secured Dubai Creek as the region's ascendant port, but at the expense of Deira's inland shops and businesses, which are now choked in the traffic from the road. Deira shop owners once earned their living from the creek, but now to replenish their stock they have to rely on legions of wily pushcart handlers who cross the road back and forth. Car-owning residents generally avoid driving near Deira's wharves; that is why you arrived in Deira aboard one of the abra boats from your clinic in Bur Dubai.

Braving the truck traffic, you follow the pushcarts over the new road into Deira. You start to navigate sand-packed alleyways still lined with palm-frond and mud-and-coral walls. The new concrete buildings, with leasable apartments above ground-floor shops, butt up against palm-frond houses not yet yielding to the spike in real estate values. Some of the old houses appear dilapidated and abandoned while others have been converted to demolition heaps.

Few roads in Deira are paved with asphalt; some are sealed with a mixture of petroleum and sand. Others are surfaced with slabs of *sabkha*—naturally occurring strata of sand and earth hardened by salt sediments—placed over a sublayer made of collected trash and the rubble of demolished houses.[66] A Dubai Municipality vehicle is parked where one new road was forced to end, just in front of an obstinate household. Officials have stepped out of the car and engage in a heated discussion with the homeowner over the price for his family's departure. You overhear a city representative promise "first-class" housing in one of the outer districts, but it is clear from the resident's temperament that negotiations are far from over.

Along the edge of the same new road, another resident, who once lived in a barasti compound, checks on construction progress of his two-story concrete building. In exchange for giving up half his land for a passing roadway, a municipal representative helped him secure a bank mortgage and waived the one-story height limit. Imminently a landlord, he is now an investor in the building boom.

Threading through alleys and along dusty makeshift construction sites, you sense your way toward Deira's main souk. Historically the port's most active market, its shops are now trimmed with electric signage that lights up once-shadowy passages. The artificial light burns all day in the dark souk, reflecting off the fiberglass and aluminum veneers that try to mask the stalls' construction of local mortar, straw, and mud. You stroll along the souk's main spine that brings you to the eastern entrance, which faces the alleyway once known as Sikkat Al Khail—the Alley of Horses—presumably because it was wide enough to accommodate horses. Its extension is Naif Road, Deira's widest paved street and the main artery to New Town Dubai. For the last several years, Dubai's total length of asphalt or "metalled" roads has doubled every few months.[67] Vast stretches of jet-black asphalt lie before you.

The souk's entrance is taken over by clambering Toyota vans recently operating as the city's makeshift bus service. You hail a taxi. Dubai's taxi fleet is owned by locals and driven by immigrants. A significant number of the cars, bought in bulk, are American-made Ramblers, evidence that the US automobile sector is usurping the British competition. As you get situated in a big car, the driver accelerates over the smooth asphalt surface that is still a soothing novelty for Dubai residents.

The driver has to decelerate at a large roundabout, the center of which is still sand. Soon it will be adorned with a grass base and a heaving fountain to entertain drivers. Roundabouts are an essential presence in British New Towns. And like the New Town itself, they are considered a British export (though France and the United States can claim them too). Their presence signifies a modern existence but not a booming one. They usher in traffic where there is no reliable source of electricity. Dubai still has no street lighting.

At the roundabout, your driver merges right. The roundabout's effectiveness relies upon drivers' "weaving maneuvers" and yielding to other drivers just ahead of them. Fluid traffic requires attentiveness and courtesy. Dubai's curved corners are designed to accommodate a car's turning radius and to maximize fuel efficiency. Since 1961, Dubai traffic keeps to the right, another acknowledgment that the majority of cars are now no longer British.[68]

From the roundabout, your taxi heads south toward the creek, this time on an old road whose widening required clearing away old houses to make room for cars. At the next junction, there is no roundabout or stoplight. You are lucky; there's a traffic guard on duty to help your driver make the left turn. Now you are headed east again along another new asphalt road. On either side are houses that were not in progress's way and new concrete buildings that take advantage of Dubai's roadside bonanza.

The roadway brings you to the western edge of a vast open space, known in English as Cinema Square. As Deira's largest public gathering space, it is "the only sign of social life in the long, boring nights of Dubai" and where "young men . . . roam the streets."[69] Once a vague, dusty, unspecified space— a *maidan*—defined through its uses by Deira's residents, Cinema Square is now mostly used for car parking, impromptu markets, and truck repairs. New roads and curbs have ringed the maidan into a large, oblong roundabout. The outdoor rooftop cinema that gives the square its name still occupies the opposite eastern edge, but it will soon be usurped by the new air-conditioned cinema in New Town Dubai. Before long the square will be "enhanced" with plants and a fountain, as instructed by Harris's plan. First, municipal workers will trim the square with a raised black-and-white curb to protect it from unregulated parking and markets. Then, they will install ornamental fencing and furnish the square with bolted-down park benches, some saplings, and an impossible coating of shimmering grass.

Just beyond Cinema Square was once the creek's sandy shoreline. Reclaimed land from Halcrow's harbor project has displaced the water further out, to the other side of the new shoreline road. This new land was kept outside the bounds of Harris's planning mandate. Here, developers build as high as they can, in accordance with their direct contracts with Sheikh Rashid and his chief advisors. The result has been a concentrated real estate

FIGURE 4.10 The edges of Cinema Square were defined by new asphalt roads by the mid-1960s. Deira's first cinema is at the furthest edge of the square. Courtesy John R. Harris Library.

boom within a real estate boom, the sprouting of buildings as high as nine stories that take over water views, while the rest of the city adheres, more or less, to one- and two-story height limits.

Your taxi continues along Cinema Square's perimeter, following the new road that squeezes between the cinema and the wall of Deira's main cemetery. As the road channels you along an easy curve to the right, you enter New Town Dubai. The road, known as Al Maktoum Hospital Road, widens by taking advantage of more open space. The wall of the cemetery continues on your right. On the left is a stream of palm groves and barastis, scattered rush-job concrete-block buildings, and flags and poles making claims to vacant land. The speed limit is fifty kilometers per hour, which your driver struggles to obey. You are moving along a primary road of what planners call a "three-tiered road system."[70] *Primary* roads like this one are Dubai's fastest and widest, delivering cars across the city. Going too fast on these roads is penalized with abrupt and sudden speed changes at roundabouts and exits. Traffic is never meant to stop on or along primary roads; autos converge and diverge from them like packages on an assembly line—that is, if drivers obey the speed limit.

Just beyond the fenced-in Al Maktoum Hospital, you arrive at another large roundabout. Soon its island will be topped with the famous fish-sculpture fountain that will provide the junction its name, Fish Roundabout. As your driver negotiates the roundabout, he asks for further instructions. You direct him to take the second exit after the roundabout. The car hardly has to yield at the exit's flared entry to the *secondary* road. The exit's turning radius is designed for a dynamically smooth arrival into one of New Town Dubai's neighborhood units. The secondary road is accented with landscaped islands that municipality gardeners keep green with plantings and captured sewage water. New Town Dubai promises engineered serenity.

The taxi enters the neighborhood unit where you live, Palm Village. Life here moves at a safe and steady pace. Roads are designed so that your taxi never has to stop, only yield, at turns. Right turns dominate a neighborhood unit, with left-hand U-turns at designated spots: constant, but restrained, motion. You drive by a community shopping plaza, public services, and the neighborhood swimming pool, all with ample parking.

In New Town Dubai, each neighborhood unit houses two or three hundred households, all living in one-story, walled-in garden villas. The planning term "neighborhood unit" is often credited to the American planner Clarence Perry, but the planning enthusiast Lewis Mumford also referred to "planning by neighborhoods," and, in his ideal Garden City, the British forefather of urban planning Ebenezer Howard compartmentalized residents into "wards." The main idea stays the same: A city grows by standard-size units. Each unit reproduces self-sameness and self-sufficiency with an equal supply of municipal amenities—recreation, commerce, schools—to sustain modern, happy family life. As Harris's plan predicted, the ease of life in the neighborhood units attracts shop owners to leave the old souks for the glass storefronts of New Town Dubai.

You signal your driver to take a *tertiary* road along which you have rented a villa from a local Dubai family. Here, the speed limit is a crawl. During your first few weeks, it was difficult to remember which cul-de-sac was yours, but now you know every turn it takes to get to your garden's gate. There are two property types in the new districts, just as Hawley had prescribed: first class (for houses of four or more rooms) and second class (for houses of two or more rooms). Distinguishable only in size, the houses are made of concrete block and fringed with other materials like steel, aluminum, lead-based paints, and sealants supplied by Dubai's port. Barastis are forbidden in neighborhood units.

Prior town-planning efforts for new communities in the Gulf region included explicit racially defined zoning.[71] Planning with discrete neighborhood units, or "camps," was an easy way to achieve "segregation by race or caste or income."[72] Newly planned areas often included a "British" or an "American" camp with a nearby "Arab" camp for everyone else, whether Arab, Asian, or Greek. Harris's plan, like Hawley's "Dubai Lands" document, makes no mention of race or ethnicity. Both documents refer instead to "classes" of housing, not people. Such classification does not prevent the units from being racially segregated.

By 1965, there are only a few hundred whites living in Dubai.[73] It could very well be that the plan did not anticipate that a large white population would ever need accommodating. By 1965, higher-paid Western families enjoy seaside villas outside the bounds of the town plan, as if they existed outside Dubai's cosmopolitan society. Most of Dubai's assembling middle class—immigrant Arabs and Asians—occupy the city's new neighborhood units, with informal segregation apparent through renting and marketing practices.

Your neighborhood houses mostly Indian professionals. You send your children to a Hindi- and English-language school within walking distance from your small villa. Beyond your cul-de-sac, the neighborhood center offers shops focused on their South Asian clientele, a medical clinic, a post office, and a community space that can be rented for birthdays and holidays. All houses and shops are restricted to a single story. In the center of your neighborhood is a vast lawn of glossy grass, with water supplied by your unit's water tower and water recovery system. Carved into the green are designated spaces for soccer and cricket. In the cooler months, children from the adjacent schools run around on the fields. During the hot season, the fields are glistening, shadeless voids of green.[74]

It is difficult to get a bird's eye view of the neighborhood unit from the single-story buildings. If you could climb up your neighborhood unit's water tower, you could look out toward older parts of Deira, which from here seem a world away. Deira's ostensible disarray gains some logic from above. While its houses obey no grid, they are oriented for familial proximity, solar gain, and the capture of westerly winds. In contrast, your neighborhood unit is oriented for distributive efficiency. The old is relational; the new is rational. The neighborhood unit's cul-de-sacs obey a grid optimized for telecommunications and water networks, and the electricity that keeps the houses cool now that they are no longer oriented to westerly winds. In the other neighborhood units beyond, houses are organized the same way: a sprawling and prescribed patterning of one-story villas. From the water tower, you read the city as a systematization of property ownership and spatial management. The city accommodates, and defines, daily activities (school, prayer, neighborhood shopping, neighborly interaction). Space, no longer negotiated, is regulated.

Located just a little further out is the "lodging area," Hawley's "third-class" housing for Dubai's lowest-paid residents. Housing codes and building materials are what distinguish one class from the other. The Harris plan designated this area to "cater for the needs of the migratory element in the population."[75] It uses the term "migratory element" to refer specifically to low-paid laborers, even though most of Dubai's residents are migrants, whether or not they find shelter in the lodging area. Since 1963, India has been replacing Iran as Dubai's provider of "mainstay" immigrants, a shift easily observed in your neighborhood and the lodging area.[76] Here a tightly regulated grid with wide fire lanes keeps informal housing from drifting into adjacent land kept vacant. Despite proximity to your home, the lodging area remains invisible to you on most days since it lies beyond the outer-ring road.

The neighborhood units accommodate a total of about 11,000 people; the lodging area accommodates four times as many people in a fraction of the space allotted to neighborhood units. Families, but increasingly single men, who had lived in barastis in older city districts, have been moved here, separated from their places of work and now living among Dubai's newest laborers. The British political agency already registered the barasti as a highly

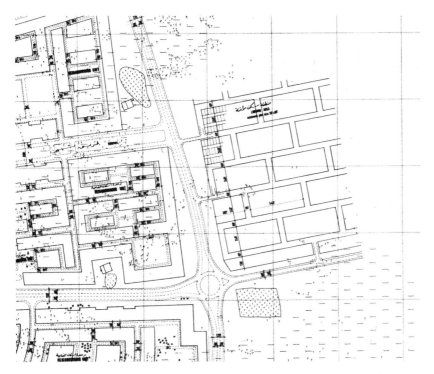

FIGURE 4.11 Detail from Harris's 1960 town plan reveals a neighborhood unit and a contained and gridded area for Dubai's "third-class" housing. The roadways were included as a firebreak and for fire trucks not yet owned by Dubai Municipality. Courtesy John R. Harris Library.

flammable housing type, but it will remain an enduring option for residents through the 1970s.

Already in 1965, New Town Dubai is nearing maximum capacity. The poorest will soon be displaced even further out to make room for another round of first- and second-class neighborhood units. Increasing housing demand means your rent next year, due in one lump payment, could rise beyond your means. The rapidly built apartments in old Dubai, much smaller than your villa, might be your alternative. Since the 1950s, Dubai has suffered from escalating housing prices, and no policy has been able to effectively keep prices stable. While Harris's plan relieved some of the shortage by charting a course for the city's expansion, it also drastically curtailed the city by limiting residential development to one-story villas. If Dubai is to maintain low-rise urbanism, New Town Dubai will need to double, if not triple, in area in the next couple of years to respond quickly enough to rising housing needs.

In some ways Dubai resembles the towns set up for petroleum industries in Dhahran (Saudi Arabia), Abadan (Iran), and Ahmadi (Kuwait). Managers of these towns, though, had more oversight of population growth since oil companies could gauge the number of workers needed to meet production targets. Not an oil town, Dubai is kept alive by its "free" port, which, dictated by the temperament of global trade, precludes such demographic determination. Looking over Dubai's sprawling homes, you might wonder: Would the massive outward unfurling of a one-story city continue as the way to accommodate growth? Could the city become stretched too thin?

But let's bring you down from the water tower. Dubai did not turn out this way. Just as the municipality could not afford mass demolition, it also could not afford to forbid multi-story development. For both the landowners and the municipality, there was too much potential profit to ignore.

LOCK, STOCK, AND BARREL

Harris's plan proved too modest for Dubai's real estate market, but not before being labeled too ambitious. For the few and overworked municipal workers, getting residents to conform to its lines was strenuous work. Even Sheikh Rashid disregarded his own plan in favor of noncompliant but irresistible business schemes.

On November 12, 1960, five months after the plan's approval, Ronald Griffith, the "engineering and industrial adviser" from MEDD who critically reviewed Halcrow's Dubai Creek scheme, arrived in Dubai. The Foreign Office had authorized Griffith's visit to review discrete development projects underway, including Halcrow's harbor scheme, the start of Dubai's water distribution system, and a new trade school.[77] Donald Hawley, away on two months' leave, was not there, a scheduling arrangement that betrayed the lack of interest in coordinating governmental planning efforts. The political agency's assistant, Ian Winchester, pulled out infrastructural and planning drawings for the expert's perusal. Halcrow officials gave him a tour of their ongoing projects. And he interviewed Eric Tulloch, who was coordinating Dubai's water supply network. While his final report commented on the discrete projects, its central and more damning point was a cumulative one: He was not charmed by the political agency's simple path to progress through discrete project contracts. He found Dubai at risk of "attack," both by its "geographical vulnerability" and by the engineers allegedly hired "to ensure that no aspect is overlooked."[78]

He reserved most of his admonishments for the town plan, an instrumental document that should have ordered the various projects into a comprehensible narrative. He called the plan "elaborate" and found it characteristic of Hawley's organizational pursuits in general: lacking oversight and preliminary analysis. The advisor felt compelled to instruct on some "fundamental facts affecting the planning," the most urgent of which was water management. Griffith attributed the port's existence to an "unstable equilibrium," "a constant battle between the sea and the land." Beyond just the built-up regions of Bur Dubai and Deira, coastal flooding threatened the vast stretch of Dubai's coastline. More than just Halcrow's minimal installations at the creek, the extensive coastline needed to be reinforced before any urban plan could even be evaluated. He stressed that the city on both sides of Dubai Creek lay "only very slightly above normal high water," with a very porous membrane protecting it from the water table below. Tulloch's new water delivery systems would compound the matter. If not in seawater, Griffith forecasted that the city was on track to drown in its own sewage, with increasing amounts of imported water combining with seawater seepage in the ground below.

Ongoing British-led projects were exacerbating, not improving, the situation. He noted the lack of an "efficient sewerage system," even the plan for one. Observing that the proposed water distribution system was already insufficient before it was completed, he asked where the 400,000 gallons of daily run-off water would go. Hawley's water engineer had no answer, but the default result was into the scattering of cesspits throughout Dubai. Griffith predicted a health epidemic. At the very least, Dubai needed a vast array of septic tanks, which would significantly affect any town planning.[79] Griffith referred to "similar conditions throughout the world" that supported his analysis of Dubai's geography and hydrography. He chastised the political agency for not having brought in the appropriate expertise to address what to him were common, and manageable, environmental threats.

Griffith was also critical of the new land being reclaimed as part of the creek improvements. First, he noted that the newly created land meant a loss of public access to the water. He seemed to be the first expert to register this social loss. Further, he questioned Halcrow's strategy to create new coastal land for a relatively small harbor city. He proposed instead that the dredged earth should be used to raise the city's overall ground level and to build "flood protection bunds." He did not mention knowing that the new land was to raise capital through land sales and rents. If anyone had mentioned such a profit scheme, he might have responded that the ruler was selling flood-prone property.

Instead of executing the plan, Griffith called for a period of "constant measurement" of the coastal condition, of road usage and travel patterns, and of "likely future trends, in trade, population, and traffic." Only after such analyses, Griffith urged, could Dubai consider a town plan. For the current moment, he deemed any effort at town planning "unrealistic," stating bluntly that the plan "should be rejected lock, stock and barrel." He warned of a "grave error to encourage the expenditure of capital on a town plan similar to that with which Kuwait has been burdened." The ruler, he recommended, should "spend his money on the more urgent matters."[80]

On November 28, 1960, three days after returning from leave but before Griffith had a chance to issue his findings, Hawley called a 100-minute meeting to discuss "the general development of Dubai with particular reference to the Town Plan." By then, Griffith had returned to his Beirut office, but the nineteen men who made up Hawley's development board were present. John Harris, whose visit was also not coordinated with Griffith's stay, was now in town for this meeting. There were no potential detractors in this group: municipal workers and private consultants Hawley had recruited. Hawley's meeting minutes reveal that the British experts did most of the talking, and Griffith's visit is not mentioned. Some of Hawley's assembled experts incorporated Griffith's concerns: for example, Eric Tulloch suggested that Dubai now needed a septic tank system. The group, nevertheless, maintained that Hawley's development program could not be stopped. Any delay was certainly not to their financial advantage. After that meeting, there is no record of Hawley's development board ever meeting again.

A few months later, after he received Griffith's final report, Hawley responded to the Foreign Office with point-by-point reactions. He suggested that some of Griffith's recommendations could be considered at a later date or that the "matter [would be given] further thought." To take any pause for Griffith's proposed "measurements," Hawley warned, would put Dubai at risk of perilous property speculation and disorderly development. The town plan and the ongoing work to realize it were at best managing the increasing incidence of land grabs and illegal building. Earlier in his stay in Dubai, Hawley himself had once proposed a ban on all new building until sufficient administrative order was in place, but now he argued that any delays in executing urban order, no matter how flawed, would cause "tremendous confusion in the town." It was "clearly too late." His only concession to Griffith was to downplay the plan as simply "a useful skeleton" and not "irrevocable" (though he later described it as "the basis for all future town planning"). Hawley claimed the support of his development board: "all the board agreed that the town planned should not be rejected."[81]

ROADS UNFURLED

One clear outcome of the development board's final meeting was an answer to Harris's question after their first meeting: Who would oversee and coordinate all the various components of Dubai's planning? Now in possession of the plan's negatives, Harry Ridehalgh gave the answer:

> [T]he job of Sir William Halcrow and Partners [is] to administer the Town Plan, to make at their discretion such minor alterations to it as local circumstances required and to refer more important ones to Mr. Harris in London.[82]

Moreover, all development proposals were to be submitted for Neville Allen's review, as stated by the 1960 municipal directive. Halcrow's engineers were now "standing in the shoes of a State Engineer" with unequaled knowledge about and influence over Dubai's urban and infrastructural development.[83]

After Hawley's experts reasserted their approval of the Harris plan, the political agency saw no reason to delay in carving Dubai up according to its specifications. Every line of new roads that Harris had drawn, however, was another that Dubai had no money to pave. Rights-of-way could be marked with "small concrete posts" to deter aberrant development, which Halcrow's employees positioned about every thirty meters along the proposed road system.[84] Soon enough, without asphalt as the more obvious deterrent, new building sites were blatantly defying these markers. According to Kamal Hamza, another municipal expert hired from Sudan, there was an almost automated process to laying asphalt: As funds came into the municipality's coffers, they were directed to Halcrow, whose engineers calculated just how much more road could be laid according to Harris's drawn lines.[85] Road-building sealed the Harris plan into Dubai's reality.

Experts at MEDD were not finished expressing their concerns. In May 1961, F. H. P. Williams, another MEDD expert, was invited to advise specifically on Halcrow's road-building processes. He backed away from rejecting the plan "lock, stock and barrel" but asserted that Dubai's road system needed to be looked at "in much more detail." More significantly, the government expert identified a lack of planning in regard to the harbor, which was being strangled by the city's ongoing growth. Williams recommended steps to direct future planning, which amounted to gathering traffic data—auto registration and ownership rates, petroleum consumption, vehicular traffic patterns, and projected budget allocations.

Williams's superior at MEDD, Paul Howell, also tried to warn the Foreign Office that "there appears to be a lack of coordination [in Dubai's planning] which may well result in an ultimate conflict of interests." Howell reminded the Foreign Office again of an essential planning principle—namely, that healthy urban development required government-led oversight: "The individual and competitive efforts of private enterprise" were not going to serve public needs.[86]

In a note to Howell, Griffith returned to his earlier misgivings. He targeted the political agents, whom the Foreign Office had termed the "architects of development." Their achievements, according to MEDD, were "not impressive." Filling in the void left by governmental incompetence, Griffith rightly observed, were private consultants who had discovered "a profitable field in the Persian Gulf." The results were not in "the best interests of the community" and threatened an "ecological unbalance which the sudden access to great wealth will create."[87] He urged that both the British government and the private sector "pause and examine not only what is happening around them but themselves as well." Dubai's urban development demanded "the highest possible form of sympathetic enlightenment," according to Griffith, but instead it was being unfurled through the self-interest of private consultants.

DISASSOCIATING HER MAJESTY'S GOVERNMENT

In the months after MEDD's final warnings, Hawley's predecessor, Peter Tripp, returned to Dubai, aware of mounting tension between government development experts and the political agency. In July 1961, Tripp delivered a report to the Foreign Office that described his visit as "both gratifying and encouraging." He measured out praise for Hawley's work by indexing his achievements that built on his own as political agent. The report played down MEDD's accumulating concerns. The subjects of water, sanitation, and more rigorous planning were projects he registered as necessary, but he now saw them as problems that the "[Dubai] Municipality and the Ruler should study." As if in response to Griffith's chilling claim that the political agency was not fulfilling its role as "the architects of development," Tripp now called for the retraction of that designation altogether. The political agency for the Trucial States had "given the necessary impetus to Dubai's development," but it now needed to embrace the "trend of dis-associating H.M.G. from direct connexion with Dubai administration and development."[88]

Donald Hawley had arrived in 1958 to make the political agency even more engaged in Dubai's affairs, and now, three years later, Tripp was re-shaping the political agent's role as pulling away. Tripp asserted that "Dubai is learning to stand on its own feet, and its independence must be seen to be a reality."[89] In those three years, Hawley had placed a significant number of experts either working in or for the municipal government. There was a process in place by which to lay new roads and assign uses to certain areas of town. There was a land-deed process by which that land could be properly claimed and financed. Tripp, however, made two false assumptions. The first was that Dubai was nearing independence. Its subjected status to Britain remained unchanged. The second assumption was that Dubai's municipal

FIGURE 4.12 A roundabout in Deira with asphalt exits leading to sand roads not yet hardened, early 1960s. Also shown is the new Deira Cinema under construction. Courtesy John R. Harris Library.

government could maintain the administrative faculties that the British had not even been able to maintain. MEDD's multiple assessments made clear this assumption was wrong.

Tripp further asserted that the level of infrastructural coordination MEDD expected was too advanced. The order and administration, which Hawley and he had been tasked to deliver, could aid Dubai only so far: "[Dubai's] pattern of trade is so complex that it defies analysis."[90] Tools and procedures of economic and urban planning, Tripp's reasoning suggests, were only so relevant in Dubai, where trade remained too complex to be controlled and improved by rational oversight. He did not acknowledge that the coordination vacuum that the British government never filled was now being handled by Halcrow. With the British government backing further away, the private British company was even more auspiciously positioned to claim a coordinating, and therefore indispensable, role.

Dubai's landscape was changing every day, with increasing amounts of steel and concrete transforming waters' edges and hardening into reinforced-concrete buildings. But in many ways, things had not changed. There was an amount of organization that the British sought to institute and control, but only so much. More organization would demand more responsibility and more knowledge about where Dubai's profits were coming from. These demands had been at the center of MEDD's expectations. Instead, the political agency fostered a reliance on "individual efforts," which afforded no chance of a "unifying aim and purpose." According to MEDD, more overarching coordination in the end would protect British interests, but it required a step too far for the Foreign Office. Dubai's development was to continue in compartmentalized steps. Telephone wires and water lines would continue chasing an unbounded and unmanaged building schedule. Development projects would order themselves, organizing their own logistical schedules, their own labor pools, and their own investigations of necessary technological innovations, all the while abiding by limited municipal regulation.

Now in the hands of Halcrow's Dubai office, the town plan served as the minimal guide that the municipal government would provide in directing the laying of utilities and the provisioning of plots of land. Beyond the bounded lines of the plan, Tripp determined that Dubai should never be read as a legible whole; the experts were left to make their own legible worlds set within their contracted lines and against a city determined to defy analysis.

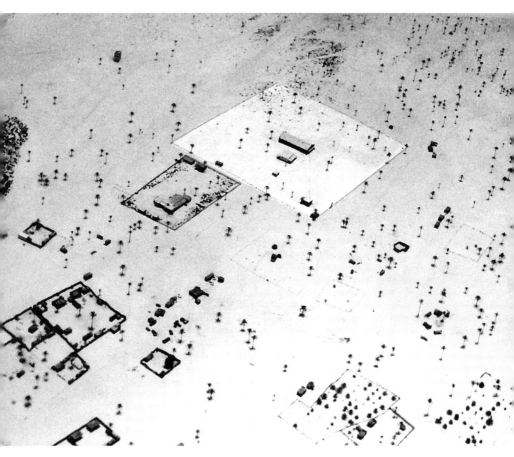

FIGURE 5.1 Aerial image of Al Maktoum Hospital fenced in among palm groves in Deira, 1959. The hospital is in the largest fenced area. An adjacent fenced-in compound contains residences for the hospital's chief doctor and other employees. Courtesy John R. Harris Library.

CHAPTER 5

PIECEMEAL

Al Maktoum Hospital

WHEN JOHN HARRIS first encountered Al Maktoum Hospital, the fence around it was worth more than its buildings. Ramparts never protected Deira from attack, but a new rigid metal fence, anchored with concrete foundations, enclosed its first hospital.[1] Erected in 1959, the fence served two purposes.[2] Most immediately, it shielded the vacant land around the buildings from others' claims. Harris recorded in field notes for the town plan that land just beyond the new fencing had been already staked out with palm-frond fences and barasti structures. Even the minimal development of an inadequate hospital had set off a land grab around it. The fence's second purpose was to designate a discrete and concentrated site for health care. One could point to Al Maktoum Hospital as distinct from the rest of the city. Whereas the hospital's buildings were deficient and underperforming, the fence enclosed the promise of future fulfillment. Harris was commissioned to design that future, by whom, though, was not clear.

An aerial photograph of the hospital was taken in 1959, the same year Harris visited it for the first time. It can be regarded with marvel—that the region's hospital, serving a 32,000-square-mile area—was surrounded by *nothing*. The photograph might betray scant evidence of buildings, but on all sides of the fenced-in hospital are signs of human activity and occupation just as Harris had observed. There are ordering systems. There are houses and fences. Points on the ground surface are date palms planted in Dubai's first grid formations. The groves did not survive without human care and therefore demonstrated cultivation and enterprise. Had the lens been tilted up a tad toward the horizon, the photographer would have also captured the durable Burj Nahar, Deira's look-out tower and a marker of the city's furthest reach. One might wonder whether the tower was cropped out to insinuate isolation. Burj Nahar, built in a similar manner as Dubai's sturdiest homes, was meant not so much to thwart outsiders as to guide arriving caravans to Sikkat Al Khail, the land entry to Deira and its souks. The tower's purpose, beyond defensive, was communicative, like an onshore lighthouse. The hospital's new fence defined, and insulated, the site from the well-trodden passage into the city.

A fence defines space, and it also limits that space. Al Maktoum Hospital's fence made it possible for the hospital to grow in the coming decade, and it also marked the limits of that growth. Knowing where to set limits mattered not just in terms of area but also in terms of how much health care the city could sustain, in terms of costs and maintenance. Harris's work on Al Maktoum Hospital filled in the fenced site with an essential expression of the political agency's modernization campaign—not only in terms of content but also process. After the political agency itself, the hospital was an introduction of a choreographed construction site: formulated schedules, negotiated budgets, computed materials costs (including imported water), and recruited labor. Within fences, experts were supposed to design closed systems of calculation and logistical coordination, defined by the clauses of a contract and within the grasp of a bounded site. There is little that is physically remarkable about Harris's design for Al Maktoum Hospital; its ordering was the spectacle.

Al Maktoum Hospital signaled Dubai as a legitimate place of welfare and safety. In Dubai, one could be born and one could be healed there, and an administrative logbook could prove it. Throughout the 1950s, however, the hospital had a reputation as a place of last resort, from where the resident doctor "sends all the broken bones and surgeries to Kuwait, Qatar, Bahrain and India."[3] The hospital's logbooks charted steady year-to-year progress away from that reputation. Staff affirmed the hospital's existence by counting every

child born, every outpatient treated, and every inpatient lodged. One hundred
forty-three people sought treatment there in 1954.[4] By 1957, no fewer than
10,000 people had been treated, and 65 Dubai residents had been born in its
barracks.[5] These statistics measured Dubai's ability to provide healthy environments and advanced medical advice. Within the clearly marked confines
of the hospital grounds, progress was meant to be within reach.

INSIDE THE FENCE

Harris's hospital design came after more than a decade of mismanaged and
frustrated attempts at building a hospital. In 1938 the British government
funded an "Indian doctor" and a "dispensary."[6] In 1950, to establish a more
substantial site for health care, Dubai's ruler secured the location and pledged
£5,000. More money came from merchants but initially none from the British government. Holloway and Brothers, the British company that had tried
to set up a development monopoly under Sheikh Rashid's father, agreed to
build a barracks-style building.

In September 1950, the building's foundations were laid, and a month
later the building was completed; it might have been another year or two
before there was a hospital in operation. "Really nothing more than a dispensary" is how one visitor described the first building, roughly twelve by thirty
meters and built out of concrete block with a pitched concrete asbestos roof.[7]
Upon completing the building, Holloway employees packed their equipment
and sent it to Bahrain. Not having secured a monopoly on Dubai's urban
development, they had no reason to stay. When the hospital's first British
doctor arrived, he brought his own refrigerator, even though there was an
inadequate source of electricity.

The Holloway building might have been Dubai's first concrete building.
The hospital's second building, completed in the early 1950s, resorted back to
a more familiar building system. With a slight and hasty injection of British-
government funding, the adjacent ward was erected and uncelebrated. Its
columns and walls were, like most other buildings in Dubai, made of mud,
straw, and coral, not the concrete blocks that had created the first building.
To conceal its means of construction, the building was stuccoed and painted
"eggshell blue," an applied effort to suggest it was clinical.[8] The second building was marked with a plaque, in English and Arabic:

THIS BUILDING IS THE GIFT OF THE BRITISH GOVERNMENT TO THE PEOPLE OF

THE TRUCIAL SHEIKDOMS AND IS A SIGN OF THEIR PERPETUAL FRIENDSHIP.

Soon afterwards, a government medical officer in 1956 deemed the hospital "sufficiently well staffed and equipped."[9] Sometime after that, John Harris discovered that the beam that bore the British plaque was structurally failing.[10]

Analogous to its mismatched buildings was the hospital's uncoordinated jumble of funding. By 1957, the British government had contributed £16,000 over three years, mostly toward salaries and capital costs (including the eggshell-blue ward). British funds were also used to purchase a secondhand truck (which, to London's chagrin, was an American Chevrolet) so that the only other truck could be repurposed as the first ambulance.[11] Dubai's ruler and merchants were paying more than 80 percent of the hospital's operational expenses, including the ten-rupee charges for patients who could not afford to pay. After having earlier refused to contribute more than fuel for the hospital's generator, British Petroleum eventually financed a four-bed ward, bringing the hospital's bed count to twenty.[12] The political agent tasked himself with fundraising, collecting money from local and Indian merchants. Old furniture was mustered together, and the Dubai Ladies' Guild raised a couple thousand pounds through charitable parties.[13]

In 1959, when Harris first visited the site, unstable funding had rendered a cobbled-together hospital with mounting deficiencies. It was easy for an observer to report that health care was "basically nonexistent" in Dubai.[14] There was no catering for patients or staff. Nurses and doctors repeatedly had to stop visitors from cooking over gas fires in the wards. Queuing patients waited outside without shade, or, if medical staff allowed, inside along the walls of the main building's dark central corridor. The main hallway's white walls showed wear and dirt where people had leaned, waiting to be treated. Eventually the lower half of the walls was painted red, purportedly to represent Dubai's flag colors, red and white. Some observed that red camouflaged not only dirt but also blood. There were staffing problems. In 1958, the sudden forced departure of a Portuguese doctor, after a social impropriety, left the hospital staff scrambling, and a Pakistani "lady doctor" had to abruptly step in when the other doctors left for the summer.[15]

‹ FIGURE 5.2 Burj Nahar, Deira, 1960. Courtesy John R. Harris Library.

FIGURE 5.3 Al Maktoum Hospital's first building by Holloway and Brothers, 1960. The hospital's second building is to the left of the central Holloway building. Courtesy John R. Harris Library.

In 1960 a "labour ward," the hospital's final addition not designed by Harris, opened. The political agent Donald Hawley had worked to grow the staff to four doctors, a radiographer (operating a secondhand X-ray machine that broke down the following year), one midwife, four orderlies, three sweepers, and one plant attendant and his assistant.[16] Most of them lived inside the fence. With the eventual hiring of two South Asian nurses to work contiguous twelve-hour shifts, the hospital could claim twenty-four-hour service (a necessary provision as accidents in the city were spiking). A British grant promised to cover the £36,000 needed to build a proper canteen, a male waiting room, a casualty room, nurse accommodations, a laboratory, and "the provision of lavatories and bathrooms, highly desirable as it is medical."[17] By then, the hospital had its own refrigerator but still no air conditioning, not even in the operating room.[18] That was all enough for a visiting medical expert to declare that "the pioneering phase in the evolution of a medical service in this region is almost over."[19]

THE MEDICAL SPHERE

A "pioneering phase" was not sufficient for the political agent. Donald Hawley recognized a powerful potential in a further improved Al Maktoum Hospital, beyond the fact that decent health care was "genuinely required on humanitarian grounds." "The medical sphere," he wrote to the political resident, "is one in which it is possible to give disinterested benefit to the local people, thereby earning their genuine gratitude, without political complications."[20] The gratitude, though, was sought for political gain, and medical care offered contact with all of Dubai's residents, more directly and more effectively than, say, harbor improvements, which could be criticized for benefiting only Dubai's wealthiest. For that reason, what he termed a "disinterested benefit" was the most visceral kind of political sphere there was. It was also priced much cheaper than the engineering scheme: When health care is "basically nonexistent," any improvement manifests large.[21]

Once again, a political agent argued for a minor contribution—in comparison to both the costs of the harbor project and the future profits from the oil fields. Modest health care was a small price to pay to protect the British government's continued intervention in the region. In this way, Hawley's reasoning was similar to Tripp's for funding the Trucial States Development Office (TSDO) as an economical transaction. Hawley's estimate for the hospital's wide-scale effects came in at around £90,000 (about $2.5 million today). Without the funding, Hawley predicted a crisis, but the insufficiency of Dubai's health care was a crisis by design. The British refusal to pay for or even lend the necessary funds was only one reason why it remained in such deficient condition. The other reason was that the political agency prevented other foreign donors from stepping in where the British government would not, for fear that they would "win prestige at our expense."[22]

The Egyptian journalist Salim Zabbal visited Dubai around the same time as Harris's first trip, at the end of 1959. In September 1960, he published an anodyne piece about life in Dubai in the Kuwait-based magazine *Al Arabi*. It was only when he discussed Al Maktoum Hospital, "a target of much complaint," that his tone rose above the matter-of-fact to near outcry: "Health departments [of the Arab world] need to act!" He reported that there was no medical staff that spoke Arabic, a result of doctors from Arab countries being prevented from opening private clinics, while Indian and Iranian medical experts could. He claimed, "The Arab countries have a responsibility to take care of the half million Arabs living without doctors."[23] Both Kuwait and Qatar expressed interest in contributing, but Kuwait demanded its funds be used outside the British development program. This was, at least for a while, not allowed.[24] In addition, the political agency caught wind of a "mysterious wooing" from Iran to fund a hospital.[25] The Foreign Office, its miserly and disorderly contributions in high contrast to others' offers, swatted away alternative funding sources with constantly deferred promises.

The British government tried to react with a plan for a complete hospital, but no more than a plan. With each new "hotch-potch addition," the political

FIGURE 5.4 Central outpatient building at Al Maktoum Hospital, designed by John Harris, with the hospital's original truck converted into the first ambulance, early 1960s. Courtesy John R. Harris Library.

resident in Bahrain observed, there was never a clear intention to create an institution.[26] A new ward or a new machine tended to express more what Dubai lacked than what it offered. In March 1960, a visiting expert criticized the hospital's structures for being "allowed to develop piecemeal." He urged for "a sketch plan of development . . . [that] would lead to an institution which is not only more imposing but more efficient."[27] If a hospital could not yet exist in actuality, then a plan, a deferral to the future, could in the meantime absorb some of the criticism.

The medical expert placed as much emphasis on optics—*imposing*—as on functionality. Much like the town plan, a site plan for a hospital conveyed that the idea existed, that there was a governing body working to realize it. Shortly after the expert's report, Harris was working on the "'ideal' hospital." Once Harris had drawn it, Hawley's strategy seemed to be, the new wings and wards could be realized as funding became available. In the meantime, the plan for the hospital would be an aspirational rehearsal of appearances.

As early as April 1960, before he had even presented Sheikh Rashid the town plan, Harris shared "very rough sketches" of a hospital with Hawley during his visit to London. Having only "a very small sum of money to play with," Harris had sought advice from the Building Research Institute in the British Colonial Office.[28] He received, as a reference, plans for a hospital building in Tanganyika, in current-day Zanzibar. Upon hearing about this interaction, Hawley stressed that Harris's design should not be for a hospital on a "shoestring" budget but should help "gauge what we might aim at here." Harris then received another, presumably more ambitious, template: "7890/66 standard African Hospital, new type admission block, Department of Town Planning and Architecture, Dar es Salaam."[29] By this time, Harris had worked on two major hospital commissions that delivered contemporary British medical standards to the Gulf; to achieve less than that, he was offered colonial templates. There is no record that the British government looked into paying Harris for his work at this stage.

In 1957, three years before Harris made a "sketch plan" and three years before the hospital had an X-ray machine or an ambulance, Desmond McCaully, the director of Al Maktoum Hospital, had described his facilities as "fully equipped." That same year, John Harris attended celebrations for the opening of the £3.7 million "splendidly equipped" Doha State Hospital, which he had designed and which was fully paid for with the Qatari government's petroleum profits. For the British economy, there was not a cent of risk in the Qatari hospital; it was a windfall for British suppliers of medical equipment and building materials, a return channel of British purchases of Qatar's petroleum.[30] While the Doha hospital collected British top-grade medical equipment and exhibited Qatari's modern advancement and welfare, Al Maktoum Hospital was being held together by haphazard fundraising, a limited number of cement blocks, and a stock of secondhand furniture and machines.

Harris's work on the Doha hospital, as relevant as it should have been, is not referred to in British governmental correspondence about Dubai's modernization.[31] But news of the hospital had certainly traveled to Dubai. Within six months of its opening, Sheikh Rashid visited Doha's hospital, which attracted people from his sheikhdom with its free medical care. Rashid had also visited hospitals in Kuwait, Bahrain, and Iran and allegedly found Doha's "the finest"; he kept a press pamphlet from the opening.[32]

In obvious contrast to Hawley's assertion that the "medical sphere" was "without political complications," Sheikh Rashid found Qatar's hospital to be a political threat. It was a sign that Qatar's ruling family provided better health care for Dubai's citizens than the city's own ruler. For this reason, Rashid regularly complained that his contributions to Al Maktoum Hospital did not result in visible improvements. The ruler sensed that the hospital's chronic stasis was causing an "increasing loss of local confidence."[33] Sheikh Rashid's nervousness and dissatisfaction also signaled that he knew that properly functioning infrastructure could "enhance Dubai's name outside the region."[34]

After the success of the Doha hospital, Harris had procured work elsewhere, more lucrative than the simple plan he made for Dubai. In contrast to the Doha hospital's £3 million construction budget, Harris's initial budget for Al Maktoum Hospital improvements was £15,000. By mid-1961, the goal was a 126-bed campus on a £90,000 budget, still a fraction of Harris's Doha contract.[35] Despite the price difference, Harris remained committed to the Dubai project. In 1961, the same year when he was laying out Al Maktoum Hospital's new women's ward with a dozen beds, he secured a commission for a 362-bed hospital in Kuwait with a £3 million budget. Kuwait too was competing with Qatar in the "medical sphere."[36]

It is a lingering question why Harris continued to pursue meager and frustrating work opportunities in Dubai, when Kuwait and Doha offered more profitable, more straightforward commissions.[37] These projects amplified Harris's global reputation as a designer of large-scale health care institutions. Why then bother with a project whose budget covered little more than enhanced barracks? Beyond just the small price tag, the development schedule for Al Maktoum Hospital offered no promise of moving forward, its finances constantly an enigma.

One reason Harris remained committed might be that his firm, like the much larger Halcrow, saw a potential future in Dubai. There was still no talk of pending oil wealth for Dubai, but if it ever came, he would have proved his staying power, ready to secure an essential role in more ambitious construction projects. A less mercantile response to the question might be that Harris found fulfillment in the work. By drawing a city's first town plan, by figuring out how the city worked and how it could expand, and then by giving shape to its most basic assertions of safety and hygiene, Harris engaged himself in one of the most foundational aspects of modern architecture: its deployment of obtainable technologies in order to transform cities into beneficial and healthy places.

URBAN HYGIENE

While the fencing of Al Maktoum Hospital offered a concentrated and delineated site for modern health, the municipality delivered a more dispersive campaign for urban hygiene. One way people began to know about the hospital was through the increasing appearance of bright white bandages worn by discharged patients in the city—more visual evidence, like garbage collection and pest control, of a sanitary city. British-mandated public health precautions reached back to as early as 1957, when Peter Tripp recruited Pakistani workers for the antimalarial spraying campaign. That project literally infused health care into people's homes. It was not just the fumes that were effective; according to Tripp, the operation was also "photogenic."[38] People witnessed the TSDO doing something on their behalf. Additionally,

FIGURE 5.5 Grocery market, circa 1965. Courtesy John R. Harris Library.

increasing numbers of Dubai's residents, old and new, were being vaccinated. McCaully, the hospital's director, credited Dubai's avoidance of the 1960 cholera outbreak that struck Pakistan and India to the forced vaccination of arriving migrants at the port.[39] Vaccinations—demonstratively carried out at stations at Dubai's busiest location—alerted newcomers that Dubai was regulated and therefore safe.

In 1960, McCaully identified "great strides" in sanitizing Dubai, a task he oversaw as Dubai's highest-ranking medical officer. "Still," he admitted, there was "a great deal to be done, especially cleaning up some of the narrow pathways." McCaully approved of the gradual erasure of Dubai's confined passageways in exchange for wider roadways. Cleared avenues for cars were his evidence of Dubai's continuing improvement. By 1961, there was a "Sanitary Inspector" directing the "fly proofing of most of the hotels and coffee shops," four years after Abdul Salam Er Raouf's initial food-safety ordinance. The success of such measures, according to McCaully, relied on the "good carpentry" ensured by the municipality building permits.[40]

The annual shamal, which had wrecked Halcrow's work in 1961, also destroyed shops and homes, leaving people unsheltered and stricken with colds and pneumonia. The storm, Tripp once observed, was traditionally followed by many burials.[41] In 1962, the current political agent James Craig remarked that the growing construction sector's "standards of workmanship are steadily improving," which would consequently mean that buildings were being completed according to institutionalized standards of health and safety.[42] Construction standards, and the enforcement of those standards, were associated with health. By this time, Spinney's supermarket had already opened in Deira and offered the optical assurance of hygienic packaging, though the store still could not offer fresh milk. That same year, the political agent noted that the city's modern means of transportation—its cars, roadways, and even its "aerodromes"—were "making life here a good deal healthier and more comfortable."[43]

Dubai Municipality, like the hospital, issued statistics to express its advancements in sanitation. In 1963, it published a publicity pamphlet, which indexed the city's public health campaigns and foretold the "future of a healthy society." The municipality's director framed how sanitation measures benefited Dubai:

In this city that God loves, in this strategic trading location, and in its natural beauty, there lacked images of improvement and development. The city was neglected in many aspects, in road and street planning, paving of the streets, and was not taken care of in terms public health and other aspects of daily life.[44]

In its combined concerns for development, image, and health, the municipality shared the hospital director's fixation on flies and narrow streets. "Images of improvement" were just as necessary as actual improvements. In fact, they were one in the same. According to the pamphlet, residents witnessed their roadways being cleaned twice a day. Municipal workers were dedicated to draining cesspools and "fighting sewage odors." The municipality counted 167 garbage collectors who conducted 10,000 annual truck trips to collect the city's garbage and burn it on the city's outskirts.

In addition to a "tree-planting experiment" to make the streets less dusty, the municipality installed the city's first public toilets to counter another public nuisance. "This addition to the city proved to be a successful solution to the problem," the pamphlet reported: "People stopped urinating in the streets where these public toilets were constructed." Public signage about fines for public urination and other offenses were being posted. Orchestrated messages announced that Dubai's public health was also paired with a police force.[45]

The municipality's director was now Kamal Hamza, another of Hawley's recruits from Sudan. In 1961 he issued Local Order No. 3 pertaining to the "cleanliness and orderly use of public roads and streets, public squares and open spaces," probably the first law to regulate the city's public spaces. No person or business could leave behind "waste paper, dirt or other refuse, solid or liquid" at "any public space." Further, "no person shall leave any Camel, Horse, or Cow, Donkey or Mule unattended within the built area of the town."[46]

On the same day that Rashid signed the order, he approved regulations for hotels, "places of entertainment," and restaurants. Hotels and cinemas were instructed to display plans of their premises that identified mandatory fire exits and public restrooms. Restaurants and cafés were required to cover the lower 120 centimeters of every wall with glazed tiles. Exhaust chimneys were made compulsory in kitchens. Other orders addressed the cleanliness of people. Workers in restaurants were required to be bathed and "adequately clothed" (with "BLUE APRONS") and to be screened for communicable diseases as part of the hiring process. Amid the health and safety regulations for hotels was inserted another kind of sanitation: no gambling.[47] Dubai might have been a free port, but the municipality was increasingly regulating daily life.

ANY GREAT GAIN

In late 1960, Harris returned to Dubai to consult Halcrow and McCaully about his expanded hospital proposal.[48] Had it been pursued in one phase, it would have been the city's largest construction project. Donald Hawley appeared to have finally secured enough British-government funding for at least the first phase. As aspirational as it was supposed to be, Harris's proposal did not resemble his designs for Doha or Kuwait. Whereas the Doha State Hospital was a monolithic, interiorized mini-city of controlled climates, Al Maktoum Hospital, modeled on colonial templates, comprised eight discrete barracks-like buildings. Harris's proposed campus preserved the Holloway building as the central north-south axis from which the new wards were diagonally flanked. The eggshell-blue building was the first on the western side and scheduled for demolition and replacement as soon as possible. The women's ward, Harris's first building for Dubai, established the plan's near symmetry by fulfilling the first wing on the eastern side. At the head of the axis, Harris proposed a new building: the outpatient clinic and waiting rooms.

Before Harris's "ideal" plan could become the hospital's blueprint for the future, the project faced further financial trouble. In July 1961, Donald Hawley's final month in Dubai, the British government dramatically cut its promised contributions to the Trucial States, including to the hospital's capital improvements. Although the Foreign Office official who made the decision conceded that John Harris's hospital plan was not extravagant, he assumed that new buildings, no matter how simple, would only result in subsequent requests for operational funding, estimated at an annual £15,000. Other sources of funding were suggested, including the United Nations, Kuwait, and the Gulbenkian Foundation. All declined. Hawley turned to Dubai's merchants for support, but he vacated his post before the problem was resolved.

Al Maktoum Hospital faced other problems too. Work on Harris's first-phase designs could in principle move forward because they were funded by the Maktoum family and locally based merchants, but there was a six-month delay. As 1961 came to a close, Peter Tripp, the former political agent in Dubai now posted in Bahrain, intervened. In a letter to Hawley's successor, James Craig, he expressed being "considerably surprised" by the delays in completing the women's ward and that work had not even started on the outpatient building. Tripp assumed the architect's "cumbersome arrangements" were to blame, warning that an architect "exposes you to the risk of receiving the wrong-sized doors from the U.K." He questioned whether an architect's presence was "justified" considering "the restrictions on our development effort" in the Trucial States. In place of an architect, why couldn't a "local contractor under local supervision" complete the work?[49]

In the months before he left Dubai, Hawley had campaigned for the hospital to move beyond its "pioneering" phase toward something more recognizable as a modern hospital. Now Tripp questioned altogether whether Dubai's hospital needed anything more than "pioneering" barracks and a structurally failing ward. Tripp's comments refer to protecting "British

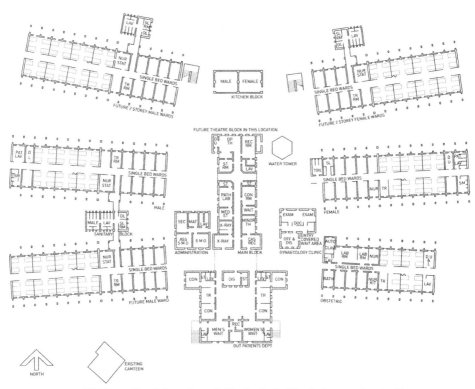

FIGURE 5.6 Al Maktoum Hospital site plan, 1961. The slender building in the center housing X-ray equipment was the original structure built by Holloway. The ward at bottom left replaced the second eggshell-blue barracks. Redrawn by Azza Aboualam. Courtesy John R. Harris Library.

financing," but the British government had already reneged on the funding. Still, British representatives believed they could, or should, determine the hospital's future.

Contrary to his predecessor's advice, Craig responded to Tripp that he could not "justify the extra expense" of an architect, even though Harris could not be blamed for the delay or the escalating costs.[50] Donald Hawley was no longer there to defend the architect's role in providing a unifying and legible process, and Craig didn't seem apprised of this reasoning. Further, Craig added some aesthetic criticism of Harris's designs, doubting whether there would be "any great gain architecturally" from the women's ward and outpatient clinic. He conceded that the buildings would be "more solid than a locally constructed one" but found the design for the ward "drab and clumsy." The hospital's expansion was being criticized for the severe parameters that were put on it in the first place. Craig suggested mild cost-saving measures, but in the end he recommended that "we should stick to the present horse" and "think very carefully before we use it again."[51] The political agency was not yet stepping away from managing a project its own government refused to fund.

As minimal as the design was for the women's ward, it was not going up easily. The project's weightiest problems had nothing to do with a remote architect. Halcrow, contracted as the project's engineer, was distracted. According to Craig, they had "far too much on their plate."[52] Further, they were carrying on "acrimonious exchanges" with the contractors. There was no clear client and no clear project manager on site to referee the various parties.

Halcrow's engineers abandoned the project. In the absence of a designated client, it fell to Craig, who scrambled to find a replacement as he managed the project's budget.[53] Beyond relational problems, the project's financial troubles were worse than Tripp imagined. The hospital was a victim of a citywide building boom. Construction costs in Dubai had surged by 50 percent in one year. Once stored in surplus, building materials were now in demand, and merchants could therefore charge a high price for them. Labor was in demand too. Craig later noted that overall costs in Dubai had already surpassed those in Qatar, one statistic that Dubai's leadership did not want to exceed.

By July 1962, the situation had not improved, and the simple ward was still not completed. Craig expected even further delays and increased costs.

FIGURE 5.7 Construction of one of the wards reveals that the hospital was built of cement blocks and concrete components cast on site, late 1960s. Courtesy John R. Harris Library.

Harris's first-phase design work had once been estimated to cost £15,000. Current material supply rates more than doubled that estimate, with no additional funding identified. Craig reported Al Maktoum Hospital was still a "pretty wretched place." "We <u>must</u> get on with the improvements," he wrote, taking the time to add the underlining on his typewritten dispatch to the Foreign Office.[54] He estimated an additional £15,000 was needed to execute the most basic component of Harris's plan—the renovation of the Holloway building—so that it could continue functioning as it had in 1959. But Dubai was not the same city it had been in 1959: The population had grown by 25 percent, according to the agency, and the increasing number of cars and construction sites brought more injuries to treat. By 1960, the political agency reported significant escalations in incidences of malaria and alcohol and drug-related accidents.[55]

There was no particular day when anyone solved Al Maktoum Hospital's funding problems. Some funding most likely came from the same sources as before—Sheikh Rashid, wealthy Dubai merchants (local and foreign), the municipality's port revenue (1962 proved to be a profitable year), and Qatar's emir, Rashid's son-in-law. One particular person's arrival on the coast might have accelerated Rashid's commitment to Al Maktoum Hospital.

In October 1962, Craig reported on the visit of a wealthy Iraqi physician named Abdussalam Mohamed Said. He was said to have made a fortune as the private physician for both Iraq's King Faisal II and Prime Minister Nouri Al Said before their deaths in the 1958 coup. Access to Iraq's power had also given him access to Iraq's petroleum wealth. According to Craig, he sought a welfare project and had read about the plight of Sharjah in an Arabic-language magazine, likely one of two 1960 *Al Arabi* articles about the Trucial States. The doctor had already hired "two Swiss engineers" who were swiftly "laying out the site" of a 186-bed hospital in the neighboring emirate. Apparently unable to stop the project, Craig reported on the swift rate at which the work was being completed, especially in contrast to Al Maktoum Hospital's inertia. He remarked that the new hospital would have a "very great effect on the present Al Maktoum Hospital and [make] it even harder to plan the future development of our hospital."[56]

Sharjah's ruler Sheikh Saqr bin Sultan Al Qasimi had petitioned the political agency as early as 1958 for a hospital like Dubai's, but without success. Just as he fought the political agency's intransigence about Sharjah's port, he threatened to fund a hospital with sources beyond the British government.[57] Countering British policy that focused urban development in Dubai, Saqr's ambitions were also set against Sheikh Rashid, who had already pursued a number of protectionist strategies against Sharjah, including inducing its traders to move to Dubai. Especially with the financial results of the Dubai harbor scheme, both rulers grasped the potential messaging power of infrastructure. In more direct competition with Sharjah than Qatar or Kuwait, Sheikh Rashid must have taken the threat of a second and better hospital seriously. Although there is no evidence that Sheikh Rashid arranged for Al Maktoum Hospital's funding as a direct response to the arrival of Sharjah's benefactor, it was soon thereafter that the hospital's funding became less a concern for the political agency. Later phases were no longer dependent on a charity drive of various donors, as Sheikh Rashid became the acknowledged owner, and benefactor, of Al Maktoum Hospital. John Harris now knew who his client was.

THE CAMPUS

Like the roads Halcrow laid in sync with municipal funds, Harris's proposed wards for the hospital broke ground as the money became available for them. Almost the whole "ideal" plan was eventually constructed.[58] Craig's initial verdict of "drab" architecture is not altogether inaccurate. Far from imposing, the hospital was a modest expression of what the political agency hoped to achieve. The involved parties were aware of the financial constraints on Al Maktoum Hospital and knew from the start that the result would not be "any great gain architecturally." More essential to Dubai's needs at hand was translating the limited funds into a straightforward place for health care.

Harris delivered seven new barracks-like wards constructed out of concrete block with some cast-concrete forms, all of which were produced on site. The result was not "clumsy," as Craig had predicted, but revealed a controlled level of detailing and an economical means of construction. Not unlike American highway motels of the 1950s, new wards were constructed of repeating six-meter-wide bays, each defined with simple concrete block columns, pointed cast-concrete arches, and screen-door entrances under covered verandas. Paint helped conceal the buildings' simple concrete-block construction, which differed minimally in construction from that of the Holloway building. Application of cost-efficient trimmings, like a brise-soleil, hid pitched roofs and conveyed smooth, continuous surfaces while also providing shade. Modernist architecture for modern medicine. Though minimal, architectural ornament provided a more welcoming institutional appearance, as if to suggest that medicine was no longer a military-style utility but a municipal concern. Painted light beige, the buildings hardly stood out on the landscape, but they were just noticeable enough to suggest their added benefit to the city's welfare.

Once Sheikh Rashid took over the confused funding campaign, the hospital gained the institutional clarity that the political agency could not provide. Harris's work in Qatar and Kuwait offered more monumental expressions of governmental largesse, hospitals seemingly purchased as a whole by petroleum-wealthy clients. In contrast, Harris's design for Al Maktoum Hospital created a narrative of step-by-step progression, but one according

FIGURE 5.8 A later-constructed ward building of Al Maktoum Hospital, 1971. Courtesy John R. Harris Library and Henk Snoek / RIBA Collections.

to an agreed-to plan. Within the larger realm of achievable results, improvements were not as transformative as they were accumulative. Deliverables were nevertheless negotiable and calculable, prescribed in technical specification drawings and itemized purchases. Outside the fence, new asphalt roads that Halcrow guided attached the hospital to Dubai's other new sites of perceptible progress: schools, apartment blocks, subdivisions, an airport, and of course the port at Dubai Creek.

The hospital was economically scaled for the city it served. Evocative of a brief era before increased wealth enabled more confident building projects, it had a thrifty beauty. This was not Dubai's first campus architecture, but it was the first campus architecture that most Dubai residents could visit or even see. It was also architecture that expressed a face to the public, one designed as accessible to the entirety of the population, which the hospital never categorized by ethnicity or provenance.

One of the earliest, and most important, phases was the central outpatient building that became the hospital's frontage. It accessed the existing Holloway building as the campus's central axis, but it blocked it from view, disapproving of its associations with a military-issue dispensary. Deep-set windows and an exterior shading installation were among the few specifications the design could afford. The seemingly austere building had other adornments. Two blind walls extended from its rear corners with the sole purpose of further concealing the Holloway building. The front was lifted about a meter off the ground to resolve the site's slope but also to exaggerate the building's height. A one-and-a-half-meter parapet further enhanced height. And then it was finished with an applied pattern, neither British nor Arabic, but maybe Greek, positing the neutrality once professed by Donald Hawley.

In 1969, Dubai Municipality declared the hospital "fully operational," with a neat count of 100 beds, "a modern operating suite," an X-ray department, a laboratory, an outpatients' clinic, an eye clinic, and a "casualty department."[59] By then, the hospital had also served its purpose in terms of offering "images of improvement and development." Harris's proposed final phase for multi-story wings, which would have doubled the hospital's bed capacity, was canceled in favor of moving on. Sheikh Rashid approved plans for another larger, more photogenic, hospital.

Up through the early 2000s, Al Maktoum Hospital remained a functioning, if surpassed, health care facility. Its premises offered a quiet and verdant-walled garden, its wards still accessible by the aluminum screen doors specified by Harris's design. The walls sequestered the complex from the noise and rush of Deira. One could find registered patients resting in the gardens or in the shade of open terraces. By this time, Al Maktoum Hospital had been demoted in importance, only serving expatriates who needed health tests for their visa renewals and the poorest of residents who required long-term care. Until it was demolished to make way for a commercial center, Al Maktoum Hospital was less an active institution than the tranquil evidence of the city's earliest efforts to stay healthy.[60] The city for which Harris had designed it was no longer.

FIGURE 5.9 Al Maktoum Hospital outpatient clinic and waiting room for women, mid-1960s. The rear wall of the outpatient building further concealed the original building from view. Courtesy John R. Harris Library.

LESSONS LEARNED

By 1969 Al Maktoum Hospital performed as had been required: to present Dubai as a place where one could live comfortably. Medical care—with its dual needs of refrigeration and heating, its demands for antiseptic surfaces, and its aura of serenity delivered by assured technology—also exhibited Dubai's capacity for technological advancement. Later promotional photographs focused more on interior scenes that revealed technology being activated for human care: a maternity ward where newborns were tended to by an unflustered nurse. Shiny floors, neatly sealed surfaces, humming fans, and artificial lighting sheathed a space for healing and nurturing. One staged photo reveals two nurses placing caring hands on a sheeted patient and her newborn, with two large air conditioning units plugged in above them. Beyond the patient's inner ring of human care is an outer expanse of modern medical equipment ready to be applied.

The photography, commissioned by Harris, captured a serenity that had to overcome the inconstancy and confusion of Al Maktoum Hospital's early development. The British government's incompetence and reneged funding had been filled in by not only Dubai's leadership but also British consultancies, including the "cumbersome engagement" of the architect. In the end, however, it was not the architect that muddled Dubai's storyline, but the British government that could not maintain a financial promise and eventually distanced itself from any on-site responsibility. Harris stood ready to orchestrate a calculated plan. There would be no risk of the wrong door being ordered, as Tripp had feared, because there would be a perfected, seamless delivery system in place. Instead of a stuttering political agency, confident private consultants, initially almost entirely British, stepped forward to present themselves as the harbingers of conceptual clarity and calculated efficiency.

Like other British consultants in Dubai at the time, John Harris had the British government, and specifically Donald Hawley, to thank for his introduction to Dubai and Sheikh Rashid. Ultimately, like the other consultants, he achieved a lasting presence in Dubai, not by being appointed by his government but by being contracted by Sheikh Rashid. While the political agency intended, at least initially, to instruct Dubai's leadership on how to run a modern city, it more effectively revealed how government could be outsourced to the private sector. After a first few years of mismanagement, the Al Maktoum Hospital project was completed to the letter of a project-management contract, similar to the ones Harris had already executed in Qatar and Kuwait. The Doha State Hospital project had demanded that Harris design a logistical system in addition to a hospital. Harris had conducted a team of surveyors, engineers, and purveyors in order to manage the hospital design as a concise logistical package delivered from Great Britain to Qatar. The experience would serve him moving forward in Dubai.

Al Maktoum Hospital's initial reliance on the "piecemeal" aggregation of materials proved an inconsistent and inefficient way to materialize a medical complex. Without the economy of scale that a larger project offered and without the ability to secure prices outside the day-to-day fluctuations of port prices, Al Maktoum Hospital's irregular progress proved wasteful at

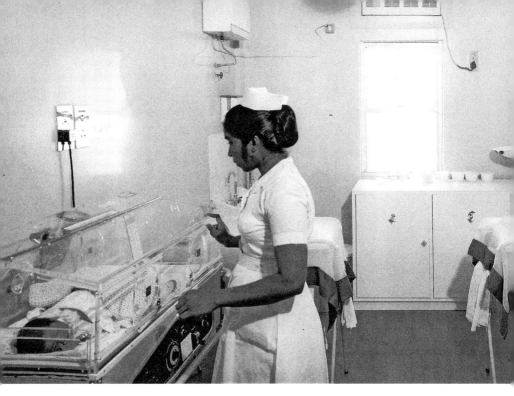

FIGURE 5.10 Interior of Al Maktoum Hospital's maternity ward, 1971. Courtesy John R. Harris Library and Henk Snoek / RIBA Collections.

nearly every step. As James Craig chronicled, cement and other necessary building materials could escalate in price as a result of high demand, either due to increased construction in Dubai or by merchants' stockpiling imports to manipulate prices. In this way Al Maktoum Hospital was built on the successes, but also at the mercy, of the port.

Larger-scale projects with defined ambitions and extensive limits could counteract the whims of the port's market and still take advantage of Dubai's resilient, resourceful local trade network. Deals could be cut between large-scale projects and the port's traders. The fence around Al Maktoum Hospital, which once protected it for future expansion, portended other delineations to come. Harris's subsequent projects for Dubai, commissioned by a ruler with more access to wealth and credit, reveal how an architect could work successfully within a defined site—cordoned off physically, financially, and logistically. A construction site's clear outlines—which differentiated internal rules from those outside it—rested in the hands of a private consultant under the bidding of a single client, and for Harris this was the ruler. The site was an area that could be designed, that could be brought to the logistical order that a commissioned team of experts could handle. Within its boundaries were schedules, deadlines, and projected numbers; outside them was an administrative "lawlessness" that called for the next project.

CHAPTER 6

CRISPNESS

National Bank of Dubai

AROUND THE TIME that the financial troubles of Al Maktoum Hospital dissipated, Dubai gained a new champion: the US government.

> A year ago the town had no black-top roads, no modern hotel or apartment buildings, a dwindling gold trade, a sand-strip airport, one bank and rather poor prospects. Today, besides her spreading roads, . . . two new banks have been established and appear to be thriving, a high-rise ultra-modern apartment building with surprisingly fine workmanship has been completed, a jet-age airport is half-finished, a fine library building is open and a new municipal building is almost completed.[1]

In the diplomatic report that reads more like a marketing pamphlet, the US consulate in Dhahran, Saudi Arabia, tells a magical, uncomplicated tale of the "one short year," from 1963 to 1964, when a seemingly automated assembly of parts induced a city. "The Boom in Dubai" originated in a "once unruly pirate town" brought to order by a "no-nonsense" ruler.[2] His pragmatism generated an idealized landscape of engineered opportunity. From the report's index of manufactured accomplishments, one might guess that

Al Maktoum Hospital's troubles got resolved in the swirl of a city under construction. A US State Department official responded to the "excellent report" with enthusiasm and inquired about the untapped opportunities for "the American business community." With fifteen kilometers of asphalt roads in 1964 "spreading" to thirty-six by 1965, Dubai made a ready market for American cars.

The report credited "eternal Arab optimism" and Rashid's "clever financial manipulation" as equal contributors to the financial bonanza, alongside the recent entry of American investments in Dubai's oil business. In 1963, the US-based Continental Oil Company secured a significant percentage of Dubai's available oil concessions, leading an international effort that further diluted British control of Dubai's oil potential. After years of suspicion that British companies created deliberate delays in Dubai's entry to petroleum wealth, the American company rejuvenated local speculation. More talk about Dubai as an oil state brought more talk about Dubai as an investment opportunity. Rashid-led investments like a "jet-age" airport and hardened roads both triggered and responded to local and foreign investments in real estate. In the footsteps of Continental came other American companies, including banks, to wager that Dubai was the next oil-rich locale. Within a year of the Americans' arrival, Dubai's real estate "skyrocketed."[3]

The American consulate admired Dubai's "boot-strap" ability to make a city without oil wealth, with not a mention of the British role in creating the city's spectacle of development. It did question, with all the apparent prosperity, how Dubai nevertheless suffered "one of the lower [per capita] incomes in the Middle East." Reports from the American consulate captured the two contradictory ways of assessing Dubai. On the one hand, Dubai's advancement could be celebrated by counting clear and quantifiable steps in creating recognizable components of a modern city. On the other hand, the consulate admitted that "the economic phenomenon that is Dubai" was "largely based on optimism."

The consulate learned or chose to believe that Dubai, to use Peter Tripp's words, "defies analysis." Officers estimated that the oil exploration contracts led by Continental could be contributing no more than 15 percent of the apparent capital available in the city. It also estimated that almost 75 percent of trade profits went unrecorded (and untaxed). The city's actual wealth could not "be entirely reckoned because of a large hidden service factor."[4] The "hidden service factor" was a euphemism for Dubai's gold trade, the port's lifeline to increased profitability in the 1960s.

By 1964, the fresh concrete of Halcrow's harbor project already showed signs of wear, revealing the cracks and barnacled patina of yesteryear. Save for a few new cranes, the port still looked old, getting by with the same patterns it had followed for decades. The wooden ships that came and went from Iran, Pakistan, and India were the same ones as decades ago. The larger ships still had to be unloaded more than a kilometer out at sea. Harbor workers no longer waded out into shallow creek waters, but they still hauled freight on their shoulders from boats to loosely guarded piles on the water's edge. Port facilities were in full demand, with 600 tons of imports coming in every day. Sheikh Rashid was prepared to spend another $1.26 million of borrowed money for Halcrow contracts to harden more of the creek's edges and to dredge more of the creek's floor. Another $100,000 was earmarked for a rush of new creekside warehouses, four of which were quickly filled only with cement.[5] Halcrow's promised delivery of a transformative project had become less a spectacle of Dubai's advancement and more a formulaic repetition of the steps that already made Dubai's port run.

In between the port and Deira's inland souks were bright swaths of sandy new land, the results of Halcrow's reclamation proposal. These vast and empty lands were the promise of what was to come. Explicitly kept outside the mandate of Harris's plan, construction projects on this new land went as high as credit lines and available elevator technology allowed. There was a seven-story building, and then a nine-story hotel. Their rise embodied Dubai's undeterred development. By the mid-1960s, Sheikh Rashid's uncontested claim to the land earned him an annual $250,000 in rents with which he could do as he pleased. The new towers were the justification for Halcrow's confidence in engineering more hard edges along the creek and the evidence that additional contracts would only make their client wealthier. On this new land between the port and Deira, on unobstructed land, Rashid designated a site for the new National Bank of Dubai, or NBD. Presumably at Rashid's direction, the new bank's British executive commissioned John Harris as the architect.

FIGURE 6.1 The original National Bank of Dubai in a refurbished building in Bur Dubai, early 1970s. Hal Smith, running Harris's office in Dubai, would design a new branch office on the location in the years following completion of the headquarters. Courtesy John R. Harris Library.

The NBD's establishment is often portrayed as resistance to British financial control. Its new quarters were supposedly meant to challenge the physical presence of the British Bank of the Middle East (BBME). The NBD in effect broke the monopoly BBME had held in Dubai, but it was no departure from British influence. Like other aspects of the bank, its founding required multiple entities. There was not enough liquidity in Dubai to start a bank; the NBD's investors came from Kuwait, Qatar, and the Lebanon-based Intra Bank.[6] Funding also came from the British Grindlays Bank, which through the 1970s considered NBD an "associated bank."[7] The NBD might have had a local name, but in reality, it was yet another example of Dubai's necessary global reach and Great Britain's part in it. Another early bank, Eastern Bank, also ran on British reserves. The NBD and Eastern Bank were now just as much of the agency's commercial mandate as BBME. As the political agent at the time remarked, "the more British banks . . . the better," especially with the arrival of US-based First National Bank as Dubai's third bank in January 1964.[8]

Besides its local name belying its global stakes, the NBD was founded on contradictions that neither the British Foreign Office nor the US State Department seemed to mind: It represented the pursuit of both accurate logbooks and hush-toned trade deals; a commitment to both measurability and immeasurability; and the delivery of convincing statistics but also lasting impressions. The design and development of the ostensibly local bank, atop Rashid's land bank, were not based on a rational estimation of needed space. The building was a vanity project. It was essential, but only in the sense that Sheikh Rashid and his advisors felt it necessary to project an image of a city open for banking, a place where briefcases clicked open and major deals were sealed. The bank was meant to express order—the order of wealth and stature. For this reason, the building's shell was inflated to be bigger than it needed to be. The bank was an expression of that optimism the US consulate described. Its upper floors remained largely unoccupied, except for when empty offices stored surplus currency.[9]

The NBD building Harris designed—in contrast to the disheveled port—stood for the surety and predictability a bank seeks to convey. This bank, however, was not opened to service most of Dubai's general public, as it focused on neither small personal accounts nor the construction loans that fueled the real estate boom. Officially, it issued and represented the currency that for a decade Dubai had shared with Qatar.[10] The NBD aspired to foster and express the city's agile and recognized participation in global networks of finance.

Almost a decade after the headquarters' completion, the *Times* architecture correspondent Charles McKean conveyed a common reading of the building. He praised Harris's design for its "crispness against the muddled waterfront."[11] One former British government official recalled the NBD as a "four-square with an air of self-assured stability."[12] Most photographs and postcards of the building captured these oft-heard sentiments, framing the rectilinear bank as a neat backdrop against the comings and goings of ships whose provenance was never clear.

"Crispness" alluded to the bank's gridded lattice of clear-cut lines made of metal and concrete. The composition evoked the lines of an actuary's financial charts that promulgated Dubai's growth rate. More than just an orderly foil to the port's "bustle" and antiquated ships, it also concealed disorder, like a curtain that hid the untidiness of Deira's ongoing transformation behind it—the sweeping away of forsaken barastis, the dust of construction digs, the road-building, and the armatures of hasty concrete construction. In their place, one witnessed a clear, simplified sign of organized finances. While Halcrow's new harbor was folding into the traditional ways of the creek's trade practices, the bank building's pristine surfaces announced there were new ways to make a profit.

In actuality, however, the two apparent opposites were not separated. The "crisp" bank was very much involved in profiting from the surrounding apparent confusion; it still depended on the vagaries of the port, on the goods and people it brought to Dubai. The NBD's business focused on commercial loans, which tied the bank to the gold trade. And just across the street on Dubai Creek is where the gold trade started and ended. Gold created Dubai's links to money reserves in Europe and beyond, and it cultivated links to people in South Asia, on whom the city also relied for a readily available, and therefore inexpensive, labor force. Gold moved as quickly and quietly as people in boats across waters of the Gulf and Indian Ocean. Construction of the NBD, like other large projects, relied on the same boats to convey stories of opportunity. New arrivals at Dubai Creek were witnesses who shared their tales of a "boom in Dubai" so that more people might also come. And the gold trade gave an enticing sheen to each telling.

Dubai's building projects provided their own alluring storylines, made true by incurred debt. Along with the NBD headquarters, their rise helped pitch a new city of "ultra-modern" buildings to convince global capital, whether in cash or in labor, to invest in the city. "One short year" was enough time, according to the American consulate in Saudi Arabia, to make something spectacular out of "poor prospects." Dubai was now something to report on and to marvel at, thanks to an easy supply of visible, quantifiable improvements. One former diplomat wrote of the NBD building: "This is Dubai's waterside show-piece, and the meeting-place of its two ways of life."[13]

MEASURING DUBAI

Even more than its finances, Dubai's demographics defied analysis. And as with funding sources, the political agency had conflicting approaches to Dubai's transformation into a populous city. The agency often looked the other away so as not to disturb the unrecorded flow of people needed to build Dubai. They knew all too well "that the economy of Dubai . . . depends on a supply of cheap labour, and . . . the logic of taking this labour in the form of illegal immigrants, especially from India, Pakistan, and Iran."[14]

After 1947, the new states of India and Pakistan looked for the means to monitor and control emigration flows to the Gulf, already the second-most desirable location for migrating workers.[15] In 1952 there were 670 registered recruiting agents in Bombay serving the Gulf region. By the early 1970s, Karachi had more than a hundred agencies sending workers to the Gulf at a cost of $100 to $300 per person.[16] These ostensibly legal operations supplied larger-scale projects with labor, focusing on, for example, oil companies that had forecastable labor demands. As the story of the stateless pilgrims highlighted, though, Dubai's labor demands were not so easily calculated.

In the later 1960s, British officials started to urge Sheikh Rashid to regulate immigration. British officials feared that a completely unmanaged situation might threaten Dubai's physical and economic health. One reason for controlling immigration was to exclude migrants from Iraq and Syria potentially entering as "subversive elements."[17] The political agency fined some of the boatmen and arrivals, but only erratically. Though having charged itself for almost a century with securing the Trucial States' shores, the political agency sought Sheikh Rashid's buy-in to further regulate immigration. Scare tactics—like the threats of political upheaval and epidemics—rarely convinced the ruler to agree to new security measures. Sometimes, by high-lighting the inhumanity of migrant smugglers, the agency could convince the ruler to cover repatriation costs, even though these were officially not his responsibility.

There was also an image problem: The number of people dying on their way to Dubai was a liability to Great Britain. There were stories of "killer whirlpools" and sharks. Boats were found with passengers who had been deprived of food and water for weeks. In 1964, a British naval ship encountered a "Pakistani trawler with 503 passengers, huddled together in unspeakable conditions."[18] Four died, and the British government sentenced the boatmen to a year in jail.

The prison sentence was meant to spread word that subsequent smugglers would be punished. Stories of gold and transforming landscapes though were more captivating. Additional policing only caused increasingly dangerous landings. Not unlike the deathly situation for the pilgrims on Qatar's shore, boatmen were known to regularly dump their human cargo further than a day's walk away from Dubai; sometimes travelers were left on a deceptive shoal from which a current could wipe them away.[19] Sometimes boats stopped a mile or two offshore, and captains ordered passengers to swim the rest of the way. If they made it to land, they were dehydrated, vomiting, and at the mercy of whomever they might meet.[20] Those who did make it to shore relied on passing truck drivers who risked punishment by taking an extra fare and filling empty truck beds after a port delivery. Even neighboring Sharjah's ruler had a stake in the arrival of immigrants en route to Dubai; they had to pay him a three-rupee landing fee.[21] There were many ways to profit from Dubai's flourishing.

THE 1968 CENSUS

In 1967, the political agency convinced Sheikh Rashid and leaders of the other Trucial States to prepare for their first official census.[22] Seven years after it had chastised its British colleagues for pursuing a town plan without a census, the Beirut-based British agency Middle East Development Division provided counsel, and Sheikh Zayed of Abu Dhabi funded the project. The census was prepared to record data on:

age, sex, marital status, nationality, tribe where appropriate, religion, school attendance, educational attainment, literacy and economic status, occupation and industry, of each member of the household, together with details on the type of construction of the dwelling, the number of rooms and whether there were mains water and electricity supplies.[23]

For the organizers, Dubai proved to be a "complex urban centre" to measure. In November 1967, "house numberers" fanned out through the city to paint numbers on houses. First, "house" had to be defined: It might be a stone house, a barasti, or "temporary dwellings of wood, hardboard, tents, caves and ships." Al Maktoum Hospital—filled with doctors, nurses, employees, and of course bedded patients—was also considered a house, as were any of the existing hotels. Each house numberer was issued metal stencils, brushes, paint, and a "labourer" who did the painting. Relying on reproductions of the town plan, they marked every dwelling in Dubai with a unique number in the designated color of its district. A house numberer and laborer registered on average seventy-five houses a day, except during the weeks of Ramadan. If only for a matter of weeks, a system of spatial organization was applied to Dubai.

FIGURE 6.2 Boatmen reload livestock onto a ship at Dubai Creek; the National Bank of Dubai building is in the background. Courtesy John R. Harris Library.

On March 21, 1968, at 6:00 p.m., Dubai's census-taking began when 340 "enumerators" went out with "torches, ballpoint pens, and identity cards" as well as books of questionnaire forms that they were trained to help residents complete. They worked three hours every evening until April 12.[24] In the months since the numbering, some of the marked houses disappeared while other houses were newly constructed. One might also wonder what happened to the ships, considered houses, that had been numbered but which could very well have been at sea and replaced by new ones.

Before starting a specific questionnaire, the enumerator had to determine the head of the household and whether there was more than one household in a given house. Enumerators took down the names of each house's residents, if the household head permitted him to do so. But if the head did not want to divulge the names of, for example, the household's women, or even admit that there were women in the household, then the enumerator was to accept the answers provided. Daily results were tallied for basic demographic information in Sharjah, and completed questionnaires were sent to Bahrain, where they were translated into punch cards for further calculations.

Foreigners who had entered Dubai through official channels were treated no differently than those who had not. The "Enumerators' Handbook" made clear that, under no circumstances, should the census takers request a subject's proof of identity. People had to be taken at their word, lest they suspect the census takers to be immigration officers or tax collectors. The handbook further advised enumerators to count anyone "who resided in the country for at least six months or who expected to do so." That meant someone who had just arrived and intended to stay was counted. It also meant that the thousands of Iranian workers who still considered themselves Iranian and who went back to Iran during the summer months were also counted, just before their annual return home.

The census established a population of 58,971, a number below recent estimates but well over twice the population of either Abu Dhabi or Sharjah.[25] It revealed that Deira accommodated nearly three times as many people as Bur Dubai (37,359 and 13,092, respectively). Jumeirah—which included the "highly modern bungalows . . . of the European population" as well as the worker settlements of Satwa and the scattering of date farms—counted 7,018 residents. The city's housing stock was almost evenly split between permanent and temporary structures, about 6,000 of each. Forty-two percent of the population identified as Dubai nationals; the rest, 58 percent, identified as Indian and Pakistani (28 percent), Iranian (21 percent), other Arabs (7 percent), American and European (less than 1 percent), and several hundred people unattributed.[26]

The results also revealed that Dubai was a city of workers, with almost 40 percent registered as "economically active" (including 640 "unpaid family workers"), and similarly almost 40 percent were between the ages of twenty-one and forty. The city's male–female ratio was already highly uneven at 65–35, though that might have been a result of an underreporting of women. Well over half of the economically active population was employed in industries directly related to Dubai's trade and urban development. The number of those employed in construction likely spiked just after the census recording, when construction work began on new hospitals, the National Bank of Dubai, the airport, and, most significantly, Port Rashid. The latter project started out employing 630 people, and the port's labor numbers would quickly surge to the thousands.[27] Most significantly, the population was more foreign than local, even when including the bulk of the Iranian population as local. And Port Rashid, which only employed twenty local men at the time, would be a project that dramatically influenced that statistic.

In 1964, the political agency counted about 200 Britons and 100 Europeans in Dubai.[28] That figure had almost doubled in four years and was about to double again, reaching 1,000, the following year.[29] Almost half of the foreign population originated from India and Pakistan. British officials were correct to estimate in 1964 that South Asians were replacing Iranians as the city's "mainstay" immigrants.[30] The Iranians who did not consider themselves local still made up the second largest group of foreigners. The report explains how long-term resident Iranians were differentiated from what the census referred to as a "Dubai national":

> For census purposes a foreigner was a person who did not regard himself as a native of Dubai, even though he might hold a Dubai passport. Conversely, a man with an Iranian passport but long resident in Dubai may have stated that he was a Dubai national.[31]

By allowing residents to define themselves, the census exposed the persistent fluidity of city residents' identities. Even with a lenient standard for determining who was local, the local population was decisively a minority. And, in terms of its population, Dubai could hardly be called Arab, but it was overwhelmingly Islamic: 94 percent of respondents identified as Muslim.

In 1969, with the census completed, the political agent approached Sheikh Rashid about restricting Dubai to a "maximum percentage of immigrants, especially non-Arab immigrants."[32] A far-fetched rumor seemed to help the British cause: 12,000 Indians and Pakistanis—a fifth of Dubai's population according to the census—awaited passage to the shore of the Trucial States from the Iranian port city Bandar Abbas. British forces could not confirm the gossip, and they did not deny it. The image of 12,000 people arriving at once stoked fear among the coast's sheikhs, with even Sheikh Rashid having to "pause for thought."[33]

Swiftly exploiting the public reaction to the rumor, British authorities drafted new legislation that increased penalties for smugglers and unregistered arrivals.[34] The flotilla carrying 12,000 people never arrived, but the British-written regulations had the unintended effect of generating another fear-stoking rumor, this time of imminent mass deportations of the city's South Asians. Citywide panic threatened to destabilize a significant part of the population, a jolt that was then felt by the city's wealthier residents who relied on their presence at the port and on construction sites. Sheikh Rashid issued a public announcement, apparently without the political agent's approval:

> We would like to assure our guests who are working in Dubai that, there is nothing of this sort. The government's intention is to continue its present policy which welcomes those guests whose intentions are to serve and make honest living. And may God bless all![35]

Rashid's public announcement assured this key demographic that their status was safe. As dispensable as they were in perilous boats on the Gulf waters, they were also the essential component for ongoing development projects. Both Rashid and the political agency had crafted Dubai into a "paradise" for the large foreign contractors, who profited from cheap pools of labor.[36] The political agency might have wanted controls on immigrants, but they also realized that British firms enjoyed "virtually no controls on the engagement and discharge of labour" and "no restrictions as regards nationality."[37] Acceding to Sheikh Rashid's renouncement of their own proclamation therefore supported a more direct British interest. Having weighed in on the side of clarity and control before the census, the agency swung back to willed negligence after it. The census was never published; knowledge of it, as with the dubious gold trade, was deferred.

GOLD FLOWS

"You want to know about gold? I will tell you about gold," began Margaret Bullard about her years in Dubai. In 1968 she arrived with her husband Julian Bullard, Dubai's seventh and penultimate political agent:

> In Dubai, gold was everywhere. When we landed at the airport, the first thing that struck me was—You know those trolleys at railways for luggage? They were used for piles of boxes stamped "Johnson Matthey," the gold bullion dealers—those gold tola bars. They were just lying around the airport. No one was guarding them.[38]

Bullard recalled how the enterprise worked: In Deira's alleys, souk merchants announced the selling of shares for an upcoming gold run. Days after a shipment had left port, one could tell how it had gone just by reading the faces in the souk. Long faces meant that a coded message had been received, something like "Mother ill [stop] Situation not hopeless." Mother was gold. Long faces were widespread because the risks were spread wide. When asked if she ever invested, Bullard was surprised by the question.[39]

The *Los Angeles Times* in 1971 observed "the sense of gold is everywhere."[40] Everyone knew who the gold dealers were because "every business entrepreneur in Dubai was in on the game."[41] More than once Dubai has been referred to as the smugglers' supermarket. As cargo that offset a flight's unpurchased seats, gold accompanied British arrivals from London. It was impossible to keep one's money separate from the gold trade if you deposited your money in a local bank branch. BBME, like the other banks, stored the gold trolleyed through its front doors.

One branch representative downplayed his bank's involvement as merely "a service to regular customers," but handling gold was more than a customer perk.[42] When US-based First National City Bank weighed Sheikh Rashid's invitation to open a branch in Dubai, there were two reasons to accept: to be in Dubai early before oil was struck and to participate in the gold trade. The US Consulate in Saudi Arabia realized that "the bank's real profitability may depend on … permission to transship gold from parties in Europe to unknown onward destinations."[43] The US State Department offices helped the bank overcome American legal restrictions pertaining to handling gold bullion.

The British government, at all levels, condoned the gold trade.[44] In 1959, Sheikh Rashid, during his first visit to London, told the Foreign Office that he was "terrified" of how Abu Dhabi's new petroleum wealth might vanquish Dubai's prosperity. In order to survive, he petitioned, Dubai's port needed the gold trade.[45] In 1961, a British official summarized Dubai for American officials as "nothing but a creek and gold smuggling to base it on."[46]

Well into the 1970s, American and British newspapers continued to refer to Dubai as addicted to shadow markets; reporting on this trade sometimes reads like a thriller novel. In fact, the popular writer Robin Moore published one titled *Dubai* in 1977. In the same year that Margaret Bullard arrived, the journalist Ray Vicker wrote in the *Wall Street Journal* that he quickly "picked up two offers to go into [the gold] business" in Dubai. But he also portrayed the gold trade as a furtive undertow:

> The Dubai dealers are hard to find; they tend to operate behind facades such as appliance distributorships, food retailing shops and construction firms, and they are close-mouthed about gold.[47]

In his reporting, Vicker described a familiar characteristic of Dubai—that it defied easy analysis: The gold trade was ubiquitous, and at the same time it was covert. For his article, he interviewed Rashid's financial advisor William Duff, who organized Dubai's finances into transparent-seeming government reports. Gold and the profits it brought were kept off his ledgers, however.

Despite his official detachment from the gold trade, he answered Vicker's questions about the element:

> We buy gold and we sell it. It is imported legally and exported legally. What happens to the gold after it leaves here isn't our affair.[48]

Duff "grins wryly" when he states that the silver used to pay for the gold "just appears here from the silver mines at the end of the creek." A humorless joke was doubly beneficial. First, it made for a great story in international papers that portrayed Dubai's gold trade as more adventurous than criminal. Second, Duff's reported grin buffed Dubai's financial vigor. For Duff to deny the undocumented gold trade would have been to deny that Dubai's economy was even stronger than it appeared.

In cartoons and heist movies, gold bullion usually takes the shape of 438.9-ounce bars, or ingots. More prevalent in Dubai were the tinier 10-tola bars Bullard referred to, specifically designed for sales through Dubai and other non-Western entrepôts. A tola bar, also endearingly referred to as a "biscuit," weighed 3.75 ounces and in 1961 was priced at about £47, or $132. Its rounded corners made it more amenable for transport on the body and in luggage. Its petite size supplied gold in purchasable bits and was more easily melted down for jewelry.[49] A single biscuit could be purchased through shares owned by a village. Even Pakistan's and India's most destitute populations stored wealth in the smallest of gold bangles—not because of an alleged "traditional love for gold ornaments" but as a hedge against unstable currencies. It seemed a harmless trade, but the purchases were illegal according to Indian and Pakistani law: The more gold citizens bought, the less stable Indian and Pakistani currencies became, as wealth left the states in exchange for the hoarded element.[50]

In 1962, when the British Treasury Department expressed concern about how Dubai's gold trade might undermine relations with India and Pakistan, the political agency issued a five-page report on smuggling. "There are two kinds of smuggling from Dubai," the report began, "gold smuggling and the smuggling of anything else."[51] The report found that—while the greater incidents of tariff-defying re-exports out of Dubai involved articles like sugar, tea, textiles, and cigarettes to Iran and the rest of the Gulf—the gold, primarily destined for India and Pakistan, was the high profit-margin cargo.

Upon receiving the report, Foreign Office officials concluded that it was "neither practicable nor desirable to take direct action to prevent the smuggling."[52] They wanted the report quickly buried so that "the sleeping dog will be allowed to lie."[53] Direct action was not practical because monitoring every small fishing boat just at the moment before crossing into Indian waters would have burdened the limited British naval presence. And it was not desirable because the trade kept Dubai's society economically afloat. The effect would have been "almost disastrous in Dubai," likely leading to a merchant-led revolt.[54] Although British relations with India and Pakistan were put at risk, British officials noted that moving to quash the trade "might well lead to [Sheikh Rashid] denying us the various facilities we require and to increased demands in economic assistance."[55] Purposely looking the other way was, once again, framed as financial aid. Further, there would have been little change to South Asia's problems: "We should merely have ruined the economy of [Dubai] in order to shift the centre of smuggling elsewhere."[56]

As the political agency was completing its report on gold, Sheikh Rashid pursued a significant piece of infrastructure to boost the gold trade—an airport. Dubai's airport was often described as a vanity project "to enhance Dubai's name."[57] In one hagiographic biography of Sheikh Rashid, the airport project is described as Rashid's resistance to British plans.[58] British officials might have been concerned about the economic consequences for Sharjah, which at the time hosted the coast's only airport. However, they had long before determined Dubai, not Sharjah, as the economic nucleus of the region. For years, Sheikh Rashid had been pursuing a campaign to lure business and traders away from Sharjah and other parts of the Trucial States.[59] And building an airport not far from Sharjah's was just one tactical move of that larger campaign.

A second airport's real threat to Sharjah's economic health was not the airport itself, but the gold trade that came with an airstrip. Gold was Sharjah's last major source of trade revenue. In 1961, Dubai began building its airport, at first nothing more than a hardened runway surface, a squat control tower, and a garage. That year, Sharjah still held a 50 percent lead on Dubai in the

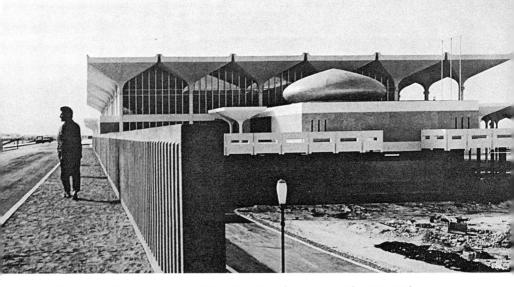

FIGURE 6.3 Dubai Airport, early 1970s. Architect, Page & Broughton. Courtesy John R. Harris Library and Henk Snoek / RIBA Collections.

gold trade.[60] By 1962, when Dubai's runway was in operation, its gold imports reached $20 million, nearly doubling in a year's time, providing as much as $8 million in profits.[61]

PRYSUMEEN, OR HOW IT WORKED

On nearly every workday, suited men from various banks convened in the same oak-paneled room at London's Rothschild Bank. With direct telephone lines to their respective banks, they conversed in hushed tones and came to agreement on gold's daily price. Most often, journalistic coverage portrayed these men as astute and upright. As historian and economist R. T. Naylor states in his investigation of the gold trade, however, the bankers must have realized "the ease with which ever-rising production [of gold] gets absorbed . . . [into] a global underground economy."[62] By 1970, 20 percent of gold trade from the "free world," or about $300 million worth, was moving through Dubai.[63] Soon after agreement in the Rothschild gold room, crates of gold arrived aboard

FIGURE 6.4 First National City Bank's completed headquarters in Bur Dubai. Architects, Tony Irving and Gordon Jones. Courtesy John R. Harris Library.

flights from London and Zurich at Dubai's airport. A Land Rover usually picked up the small individual crates of gold directly from the tarmac. The car then made its way, unguarded, to the banks lining Dubai Creek, including BBME, NBD, and First National City Bank.

Once a gold run grew near, crates of tola bars were transferred to dhows on Dubai Creek, designed to "blend into the Indian seascape."[64] A decrepit appearance was the shell for "hefty diesel engines," British-made and sometimes even Rolls-Royce, that gifted the ancient hulls a propulsion insurmountable by Indian authorities.[65] Each dhow was manned by seven or eight South

Asian men dressed as indigent fishermen. The gold was either kept in the ship's hull under a catch of fish or sown into eight-pound vests worn underneath the men's fishing garb.[66] If Indian customs managed to overcome a boat, the men would throw the vests into the water. An attached buoy would mark the location for a follow-up recovery attempt, hence the coded message "Situation not hopeless" that Margaret Bullard recalled.

In 1969, US Senator Abraham Ribicoff learned that Dubai existed. His assistant informed him about "the Shiekdom of Dubal [sic]," "a Persian Gulf gold smuggling centre."[67] Ribicoff convened hearings to probe mishandled federal funds for development and contracting companies in Vietnam. Those led to other hearings that uncovered how dubious American business deals fed Dubai's gold trade.

One person summoned to testify was "architectural consultant" Brandon H. Backlund, who described how his joint venture—called Worldwide Consultants—won a federally funded contract in Saigon and subsequently got involved in a black market money exchange. Upon arriving in Saigon, Backlund wanted to exchange American Express traveler's checks for local piasters. He claimed to need the equivalent of $40,000 (today about $270,000) for his office's petty cash. Backlund explained how he exchanged the first $20,000: Another development contractor directed him to a small, nondescript bookstore whose attendant told him to deposit the checks in a US bank account named "Prysumeen." Once receipt was confirmed, the bookstore prepared a cardboard box tied with twine and filled with piasters at almost twice the official rate for Backlund's traveler's checks. Backlund described the rest of his time in Saigon as "an awful pain," as he was forced to keep his "briefcase in hand at all times, awake or asleep."[68] The congressional members praised the architect for his willingness to cooperate, but no one asked him why he needed so much cash.

They did pursue the enigmatic Prysumeen account, eventually learning it was managed by B. S. A. Rahman, an Indian businessman. Ribicoff's chief investigator described Rahman as "a very wealthy Indian with interests in many firms across the world."[69] Rahman, according to the investigation, ran a money scheme that made his clients wealthier at the expense of national currencies' stability, including Vietnam's.[70] A lawyer representing Rahman claimed his client was "solely in the business of precious stones

and diamonds, based in Hong Kong."[71] Senate investigators discovered that
Rahman also made money in movies, rope, and wire and tracked down his
business address in Hong Kong: "It was just a small office with a desk . . . and
there was no indication openly that they were dealing in precious stones."[72]

The hearings exposed how the piaster racket worked: Once the contractor's money was in the Prysumeen account, the payment, in tandem with
others, was transferred to First National City Bank in Dubai. Those US dollars
landed in accounts owned by Dubai gold merchants. Rahman's trade ring
then picked up the gold in Dubai and delivered it to either India or China,
from where fishermen made deliveries aboard rafts to the Vietnamese coast.
From there, the gold was used to purchase piasters from wealthy Vietnamese. And then those piasters could be used to lure the more valuable dollars
once again out of the hands of the next US contractors. As one investigator
explained, "The cycle goes on and on."[73]

When the investigators asked New York-based First National City Bank to
disclose information about the Prysumeen account, the bank handed over a
memorandum signed by Sheikh Rashid stating that such disclosures violated
Dubai law. Because of the risk of prison sentences, the bank's representatives
claimed, they were forced to decline the Senate request. Still the investigators
were able to find out that more than $40 million, 82 percent of the Prysumeen
account at a given moment, had been transferred to three banks in Dubai.
American participants in the scheme were "criticized," but the panel found
that no American laws had been broken, just laws in Vietnam (and, though
not mentioned, India).

Emboldened by US dollar reserves wired to the banks along Dubai
Creek—and their hulls no longer weighed down by payments in silver—
the gold-trade dhows could return filled with valuable imports like textiles,
foods, artworks, and people.[74] Undocumented migrant workers would pay
between $100 and $300 to be stowaways on these return journeys.[75] Gold was
also linked to the *hawala* system, which enabled migrant workers to send
money abroad by paying Dubai's local currency to the gold traders. In turn,
the importers on the Indian side, instead of paying the traders, would pay
the remittance to the migrant workers' families (or their agents) in India. No

currency would have to cross borders, only gold. And the gold trade made a further profit skimmed off laborers' earning.

It was not just migrant workers who helped fuel the gold trade. The city's increasing number of banks implicated Dubai's residents in the scheme. Besides trafficking in dollars gained on the black market, banks provided the opportunity for wage earners to make quick returns on their paychecks. While there might have been men in the souk hawking available shares for a gold run, it was also possible to invest more discreetly. Dubai's growing banking industry was not known for its deposit reserves, part of the reason why many of them relied on reserves in foreign countries.[76] Therefore, any chance of attracting local deposits was welcome.

For this reason, banks in Dubai through the 1960s and 1970s offered something beyond the standard savings account: a high-interest plan for "short-term money" discreetly made from the gold trade.[77] The rates on the brief six-month deposits could have only been guaranteed through investing the funds in multiple gold runs.[78] Gold, in more ways than one, kept the electric lights burning in the city's new banks.

FIGURE 6.5 Early design for the new National Bank of Dubai building; the design proposed a smaller building but a more integrated brise-soleil structure to protect interiors from solar exposure. Courtesy John R. Harris Library.

FIGURE 6.6 The National Bank of Dubai on Dubai Creek, opened in 1970. Courtesy John R. Harris Library and Henk Snoek / RIBA Collections.

ARCHITECTURAL RESTRAINT

Gold was bringing Dubai wealth, but the National Bank of Dubai expressed a wealth the city did not yet have. It was an orchestration of limited, if not borrowed, funds. By the time the bank building was commissioned in 1967, Dubai had confirmed oil reserves, but the first, and modest, oil payments would not arrive until 1969. Work on the new building began on October 10, 1967, when David Mack, the bank's British general manager, wrote John Harris to officially commission the design of a building with a budget of £250,000.[79] At that time, the NBD occupied a retrofitted one-story building along the Bur Dubai creek frontage. Even if its banking requirements did not demand expanded premises, the bank's desired impression did.

Mack's proposed budget was not based on measured specifications for required floor areas, or the number of employees, or even how big the building should be. His commissioning letter stated little more than that the building should look like a bank headquarters. He wrote that the bank expected a "first-class building, marble flooring, etc." Beyond "marble flooring," there is no further indication of what defined "first-class, etc." "Etc." suggests that both Mack and Harris could agree on a list of expected ingredients of a first-class building: an expansive lobby, air conditioning, polished and shiny finishes, diffused lighting, vacuumed cleanliness, and electric signage, all of which Harris's design incorporated. By then, trips to London had also exposed Rashid to what a bank headquarters should look like. In subsequent correspondence, Harris assured Mack that the building would be one of Dubai's first with an elevator, another "first-class" signifier.[80]

Harris used the NBD design to establish general guidelines for subsequent buildings on the creek. As outlined in a building code Harris later delivered to the municipality, the ground floor was set back so that the above floor's overhang provided a shaded entrance during the day and an artificially lit gallery at night. The ground floor and mezzanine levels produced a double-height ground-floor massing. Above the ground floor and mezzanine were four stories of apportioned offices cloaked behind a latticed facade. At the top, set back from the midsection, was a full-floor penthouse apartment, for the bank's manager and his guests. Though the building was designed to be

FIGURES 6.7A AND 6.7B Scenes of construction at the site of the National Bank of Dubai, late 1960s. Before construction began, a spanned concrete and steel raft foundation had to be installed on the shallow land reclaimed during Halcrow's harbor project. Courtesy John R. Harris Library.

a commercial building (plus the penthouse apartment), its massing served as a model for subsequent buildings that also accommodated upper-floor residential units.[81]

Beyond massing controls, Harris employed other restraints. As with all his work in Dubai, the NBD design grappled with how to incorporate glass. Fenestration was obviously a necessity, but Harris did not exaggerate its presence for the sake of a symbolic expression of modernity. Glass was becoming a favored architectural feature in Dubai, most prominently found in the new airport terminal, whose facades were mostly glazed. But glass proved to be a troublesome material in Dubai's climate. The airport's inauguration in 1971, for example, would be remembered for the attending dignitaries' sweating brows as they endured the interior's greenhouse effect.[82] For the NBD, Harris resisted glazing as anything more than a necessary source of daylight. Not featured prominently, it was set back from the outer facade to reduce interior solar gain.

Now that Dubai had a functioning electricity grid, air conditioning units were as omnipresent as the new concrete walls and aluminum window frames that they punctured. To keep interiors chilled, the external halves of air conditioning units hung out over Dubai's streets. Inside, they provided environmental comfort, but outside, they proved a menace for designing a coherent architectural facade. Harris's proposal for the bank prescribed a brise-soleil, which wrapped around and shielded three of the building's four facades. Chiefly devised to reduce a building's solar gain by keeping direct sunlight from interiors, the brise-soleil had another purpose in Harris's bank building: to conceal the clutter of necessities, including the air conditioning units and the mechanics of operable windows. The screen also provided the building an expressive and more unified identity. Though an early proposal suggested a concrete screen hung onto the facade, the more economical final design was a repetition of metal railings and louvers fastened onto the building's columns and beams in a way that conveyed a continuous screen. The protruding facade transformed the building from a grid of selfsame office spaces into a meshwork of ordered abstraction.[83]

While the metal louvers and concrete columns defined the upper floors, the street-level base, tucked underneath the floors above, drew clients in

FIGURE 6.8 The National Bank of Dubai headquarters, early 1970s. Courtesy John R. Harris Library and Henk Snoek / RIBA Collections.

with its marble cladding, as prescribed by the bank's manager. The street-level arcade led one to a Dubai novelty: a revolving door, which had been an architectural assertion of modern financing in the region ever since a bank in Kuwait installed one twenty years earlier.[84]

Delivered by the sweep of the revolving doors, an arriving customer entered an open-plan lobby where marble paneling continued over floors and walls. Early visitors to the bank witnessed the largest interior open space in Dubai until the opening of the new airport terminal. The public area, a barely double-height space with a low-hanging mezzanine, was unified and cooled by centralized air conditioning. A long marble-clad reception desk separated the lobby's reception from the rear service desks.

Between the entry and the reception, interior surfaces were cool and understated, with details left to large gestures in marble, tile, aluminum, and glass. There was a signature stair leading to the mezzanine. Long hard benches pressed into tiled recesses. There were no chairs, no plants, no

FIGURE 6.9 Ground-level arcade at the National Bank of Dubai's entrance on Dubai Creek. Courtesy John R. Harris Library and Henk Snoek / RIBA Collections.

ashtrays. Expansive, unobstructed surfaces were austere but, for this time in Dubai, also splendid. They were easy to clean, hygienic. Clients arrived at the long counter, over which they could see the back lobby. The counter was clear, save for the teller's glass panel, the only outward sign of a security measure.[85] Customers were served at the open counter or waited to be called to a service desk in the back.

The rear and larger part of the ground floor was where the bank's humming originated—an open banking floor servicing the cosmopolitan trading elite of Dubai. In contrast to the entry's marble surfaces, this large back area operated on top of linoleum tiling that reverberated with the pecking of typewriters and the babel of voices: Arabic, Urdu, Hindi, Farsi, and English when necessary. Here there were no lavish marble work surfaces, only a grid of industrial-issue metal tables at which each banker manned a typewriter, a set of drawers, and desk chair. His customers were offered a wooden folding chair.

FIGURE 6.10 Interior lobby of the National Bank of Dubai, Dubai Creek, early 1970s. Courtesy John R. Harris Library and Henk Snoek / RIBA Collections.

NEW BUILDERS

By 1968, an infusion of new banks and easy money had helped increase Dubai's imports to £67 million, up from £27 million the previous year. In 1970, however, when the NBD headquarters opened, Dubai's gold trade had peaked, and that was not the only problem.[86] The optimism around Continental Oil Company was waning, and an oil bonanza seemed less likely. Sheikh Rashid had mobilized the visible changes to Dubai's landscape, but in the years prior to the bank's opening, British documents reported that the private sector was "exhausted" in terms of any boom.[87] The arrival of banks was supposed to appease the merchants' "uneasiness about the future without oil."

The mounting number of banks came in time to compensate for gold's diminishing returns, just as earnings from gold had to be directed elsewhere. Rising gold prices decreased demand from South Asia, necessitating that merchants find a new business. A merchant-led real estate boom began. Established families like Galadari and Ghurair, enriched by gold-led trading, easily secured financing to deliver residential and commercial projects that complemented and competed with Sheikh Rashid's projects. Their earnings from the gold trade, "a secure base of prosperity," transformed them into crucial actors in Dubai's urban development.[88] They even opened their own banks, if at their own peril. In the years after the opening of the NBD headquarters, Dubai's merchant families pursued so much development that the municipality was wealthy just from the building and licensing fees.[89]

FIGURE 6.11 Interior of the National Bank of Dubai. Behind the service desk, the lobby floor was a constant buzz of Dubai's many languages. Courtesy John R. Harris Library and Henk Snoek / RIBA Collections.

The career trajectory of piaster-exchanging B. S. A. Rahman exemplified the graduation from gold. Though never having admitted to participating in the gold trade, Rahman was well ensconced in Dubai's trade scene and, subsequently, its urban development. His 2015 obituary in a Chennai-based newspaper described him as a "trader-turned-builder-turned-entrepreneur-turned-philanthropist," the second step of which, "builder," referred to his role with the construction company, ETA-ASCON, still active today in Dubai's urban development.[90] Like Rahman, gold traders invested in Dubai, enriching other kinds of trade and industry. They kept Dubai residents fed, clothed, and accessorized with the latest homeware technologies. Gold traders could offer

FIGURE 6.12 Under Hal Smith's direction in Dubai, Harris's firm also designed a smaller branch for the National Bank of Dubai on the Bur Dubai side of the creek in the early 1970s, to replace the original building. It has been demolished. The bank's location was adjacent to Bur Dubai's main abra station for boats arriving from the Deira side. Courtesy John R. Harris Library.

newcomers apartment rentals, automobiles, and air conditioners. By 1969, at least one of Dubai's four cinemas was built with gold profits. By 1975, when the dhows reportedly had nothing left to carry, the *Times* reported that the

> the banking families are finding better returns nowadays in the hotels, apartment blocks and importing agencies for cars, electrical goods and cranes that Dubai's burgeoning business community needs.[91]

The *Times*, though, was too quick with that conclusion. Gold trade continues today.[92]

OBSOLESCENCE

Money, the theory seemed to be, infused place with longevity. Founding the National Bank of Dubai was part of a campaign to pull more banks, and therefore credit, to Dubai. The campaign worked. Between the time when Harris was hired and when he completed the bank building, Dubai's total number of banks increased from three to eighteen. In 1971, the *Financial Times* expressed concern for Dubai's banking situation, from once a "stampede" to then a "free-for-all."[93] Easy credit—like the empty upper floors of the NBD—were expressions of wealth without the surety of the actual prosperity. Banks clambering for a boom-time loan market configured a city that could not yet function in the way it declared that it could. The NBD's rise was set within an index of projects that composed a narrative of a new city built out of that financial optimism the US consulate described in 1964.

While the NBD building was an empty monument to itself, the port was running at full capacity, delivering the goods and people to make more buildings like it. The NBD and the other banks attested to new financial networks, but the port maintained more established relations with the rest of the Gulf, South Asia, and beyond. The port, with its gold trade, was the reason the foreign banks were there in the first place. It supplied both a resilient network of interdependencies and a tentative web of relations that needed constant cultivation. A wrong move, whether an overplayed or underplayed hand, could disrupt an ecosystem that profited as much from ambiguity as it did from clarity.

FIGURE 6.13 The National Bank of Dubai at night, revealing Harris's choreographed brise-soleil. Courtesy John R. Harris Library and Henk Snoek / RIBA Collections.

However justified, bank buildings evoked the appearance of permanence and security that the port couldn't project, but they also further escalated Dubai's tentative status. A completed item, like a bank headquarters, on Dubai's development index meant that its former place on the wish list had to be restocked with new ideas. The NBD building announced permanence, but it also portended its own demolition, its replacement by the next stalwart symbol of financial success.

The merchants' building boom happened inland from the creek, beyond the reclaimed land that Rashid controlled. There finally did come a neighboring building that pressed against the NBD's western side in the late 1970s. Far from adhering to Harris's building code, the new neighbor defied any possible contextual building codes. Moreover, the new building's presence transformed the NBD from an elegant modern building into a squat and timid relic of another era.

Since the new building's first several floors were reserved for offices of Sheikh Rashid, it presumably had the ruler's blessing to break any massing regulations prescribed by Harris. Designed by the British firm Fitzroy Robinson and Partners, the new tower was to house a branch of the recently established Bank of Credit and Commerce International (BCCI), founded by a Pakistani businessman and backed by Bank of America and Abu Dhabi's ruler, Sheikh Zayed bin Sultan Al Nahyan. The bank claimed to focus on investments in non-Western countries but was later shut down and labeled "the biggest bank fraud in history."[94]

The BCCI building rose more than twice as high as the NBD building. In addition to its height, the building also boldly expressed itself with glass, the material the NBD building had suppressed, asserting the material as the building's most apparent feature. In contrast to the NBD's lattice of layers that intimated transparency, the BCCI building employed glazing to project a smear of reflective gloss—that is, if it were not always powdered over in dust. John Harris regularly warned developers and other architects about specifying glass for buildings in the region. Its exposure to sun increased interior heat gains, and its constant need for cleaning added cost and stress on limited water supplies. Built almost a decade after the NBD headquarters, the BCCI building incorporated centralized cooling equipment that freed it from

FIGURE 6.14 The Bank of Credit and Commerce International's Dubai branch building, to the left of the National Bank of Dubai. Architect, Fitzroy Robinson and Partners. Courtesy Dr. Naman Al-Jalili Archives Collection.

having to conceal individual air conditioning units. The BCCI's vitreous form announced to the viewer that central air conditioning enabled confidently smooth and continuous surfaces that could endure southern exposure. Harris's building had been an expression of how architecture could work with the climate; its new neighbor was an expression of how architecture could defy it.

By the close of the 1980s, executives were again searching for how to express the NBD's "first-class" ambitions. They wanted architecture that conveyed that the bank was no longer just a new arrival, but also a venerated competitor in the global banking scene. After a design competition for a new headquarters in the early 1990s, the bank's leadership selected a concept with even more exuberant glazing. The winning architect, Carlos Ott, compared his design's protruding copper-colored glazing to a wind-filled sail, as if the glass-and-steel construction seemed to lift the building upward.[95] Glass—reflective, not transparent—no longer evoked concern or liability but instead the facile relationship between technological whimsy and global banking. The old bank headquarters, once the modern backdrop to the port's ramshackle ways, was now relegated to the very setting it had been set apart from. Banks cannot leave behind relics of earlier, less-splendid ambitions. The old headquarters was therefore unceremoniously demolished. Materialized to demonstrate Dubai's banking potential, Harris's design for the National Bank of Dubai turned out to be as fleeting as the wooden trade ships in front of it.

CHAPTER 7

HEALTH CITY

Rashid Hospital

"FUN," READ THE HEADLINE for the *Daily Mirror*'s coverage of Sheikh Rashid's 1961 visit to London. The unnamed writer followed the ruler amid the bright lights and carnival tunes, "between sideshows," at Battersea Funfair. Rashid indulged in leisurely walking and people watching, there "to see the sights," not to get "tips on how to run a power station." That was a reference to the Battersea's iconic power plant nearby. Rashid might not have met with the station's operators that evening, but two years earlier British engineering consultants had produced an "electrification scheme" for Dubai's first power station and grid. The new Dubai Electric Company had then raised well over £200,000 (today nearly $5 million) in shares so that the first installations were underway while the ruler was being interviewed. "I love the place. We don't have anything like this on the Persian Gulf," Rashid confessed, admiring how the funfair lit up London's night sky.[1] His remarks alluded to Dubai's deficiency, and nearly every aspect of London was presented to him as a showroom sample to address such deficits. As many people were ready to sell him the blueprints for a power station as there were to sell him blueprints for a funfair.

Beginning with his first visit in 1959, Rashid's trips to London were organized fusions of fun and sales pitches. Brief exchanges with a cabinet minister were often followed by catered daytrips. One of the first outings was to Birmingham, where he toured the Rover car factory, home of the Land Rovers that compacted Dubai's sands into passable trails.[2] Also on the itinerary that year was a visit to the British New Town Stevenage, an appropriate stop just before hiring a town planner, but that visit was canceled. In London, he had a private tour of Buckingham Palace's throne room, the one reproduced at Madame Tussauds. He saw the Crown Jewels and visited the Royal Crown Jewellers for a pearl-setting demonstration. Rashid also visited a doctor to inquire about recurring chest pains and to experience what was so great about British health care.[3] The British oil company holding Dubai's concessions at the time extended his stay by one week so that it and other companies "connected with Dubai" could entertain him.[4] Halcrow held a lunch in his honor so that he would hire them again for their next proposed contract after the harbor project: Al Maktoum Bridge.

Rashid's hosts noted that he liked to "see simple things and watch the daily life of people."[5] For example, he enjoyed riding the London Underground, a pleasure government officials were quick to observe. They arranged a photo op on the Underground's Piccadilly line and the press copy to go with it:

> For most British schoolboys, here is the dream that remains a dream! But when the Ruler of Dubai . . . wished to drive a "Tube" train on London's famous Underground Railway, the dream became a fact.
>
> Accompanied by his two sons, Sheikh Maktoum and Sheikh Hamdan, the Ruler travelled—as a passenger—by Tube train from Piccadilly Underground Station to Earls Court, where he inspected a signal box.
>
> Then the train thundered on to Hammersmith—but this time driven by the Ruler himself, who was quick to grasp the technique and thoroughly enjoyed this novel experience.[6]

The government-issued copy compares Rashid's pleasures to a boy's dreams, but, like the *Daily Mirror*'s funfair coverage, it overlooks the fact that the ruler was weighing infrastructure contracts peddled by British engineering companies.

FIGURE 7.1 Sheikh Rashid stands at the helm of a London Underground train during his first stay in London, 1959. Courtesy National Archives, United Kingdom.

After a few days into a visit, Rashid usually grew weary of official meetings and business lunches. Ingratiating salesmen made Rashid uncomfortable. He preferred "a cup of tea and a talk to a formal reception" and "hates speeches, whether delivered by himself or by others."[7] He sometimes turned down sightseeing options because, it was smugly observed, he "wished to do some shopping."[8] Shopping, though, was the purpose of all his programmed time in London. The visits introduced Rashid to the pace of an escalator, the felicity of a theme park, the spectacle of a high street, the propulsion of an underground metro, and the comforts of a hotel suite. London, as a whole, was no template for Dubai, but it was presented to the ruler as a sales catalogue of discrete parts and experiences.

One July morning during his stay in 1969, Rashid met his tour guides not far from the Battersea Funfair, this time to take a helicopter to the town of Farnborough. It was a crisp, high-visibility day for a flight over London and its countryside. Farnborough was the home to the Royal Aircraft Establishment, a well-guarded compound outside town where British and French engineers refined the supersonic Concorde jet airliner. There, in a hangar, Rashid witnessed a salient example of how British public and private sectors intersected—more specifically, how defense technologies were adapted for commercial opportunity. Ten years after this visit, the Concorde would go on sale to Gulf leaders. For now, Rashid and his son Mohammed, soon a pilot himself, were granted a glimpse of future sales pitches.

On another day during that visit, the Windsor Group Hospital Management Company organized a tour for Rashid of Wexham Park Hospital, a large health care complex outside central London. Opened in 1966, it was one of London's most advanced assemblages of health care technologies. Endowed with a 100-acre parcel of land, the hospital sprawled out according to "an expansive plan" of mostly single-story buildings. "Not a building but a miniature town," Wexham Park was designed as its own independent colony.[9] Medical staff lived on site in single-person and family-size housing. There were tennis courts, and the complex had its own plant systems.

The vastness of the site allowed for architects to base hospital interiors on traffic and programmatic efficiency studies. Laboratories and wards were to foster innovation and expansion.[10] In anticipation of Rashid's visit, organizers designed a tour around his particular interests: X-ray equipment and facilities for newborns and children.[11]

As the ruler visited the Wexham campus, a site in Dubai was being excavated for a new hospital there. Rashid would shortly thereafter sign contracts totaling £6.5 million for what would become known as Rashid Hospital, to be designed by John Harris and financed by a British commercial loan. The

Wexham tour was to show him both what he was purchasing and what he might anticipate buying in future phases. Like Wexham, Rashid Hospital was to be its own city of low-rise buildings focused in on themselves. It was sometimes called Rashid's Health City.

A FAMILIAR SCRIPT, DEPARTED

The pursuit of Dubai's new hospital originated on an auspicious date three years earlier, June 6, 1966. American oilmen allegedly entered Sheikh Rashid's majlis hall that day to declare what had been anticipated for years: They had discovered enough offshore oil reserves to make Dubai wealthy.[12] Among other consultants and merchants in attendance was John Harris, who later re-called, "Sheikh Rashid immediately rose and put his arms around everybody present. . . . His Highness turned to me and without a moment's hesitation said, 'We will now build a fine hospital. You start tomorrow.'"[13] The oilmen's arrival may be recalled as a jubilant surprise, but rumors had been rampant and the message impatiently awaited. Days earlier a "tipsy banker" from BBME had disclosed to the political agency that a bank transfer confirmed the discovery. Regardless of how surprised Rashid and company were, the confirmation did set off Dubai's most ambitious years of infrastructural ex-pansion and, arguably, its most rapid years of population growth.[14]

After the discovery of oil, Dubai's plans were not, in themselves, unusual when compared to how other regional states had converted oil profits into large-scale development programs. In fact, projects in Kuwait and Qatar were aspirations for Rashid, including their large expensive hospitals designed by John Harris's firm. As development pursuits at Dubai Creek and Al Mak-toum Hospital had reinforced his authority, this next round of development projects was set to further author a city around his personality. The risks as Dubai's largest debtor had brought with them unmatched political power. Oil wealth gave Rashid the opportunity to scale up the same strategy.

Following Dubai's oil confirmation came a roll call of large-scale infrastruc-tural projects that totaled almost £40 million (today more than $750 million): a new deep-sea port, an international-standard airport, and a new hospital campus.[15] All of these projects were ripe for British financing, British consul-tants, and "boosting Britain's export performance."[16] Within a year of the oil announcement, Halcrow secured the design contract for the new port, set apart from Dubai Creek. The £9 million contract, for what would be called Port Rashid, soon more than doubled in size. Page & Broughton, a small architectural partnership based in London and Beirut, caught word of Rashid's interest in an airport terminal and quickly pitched, and then secured, the design contract for a £4.1 million project.[17] The British engineering and construction firm Costain was enlisted for both projects. Like Port Rashid, the "fine hospital" that Harris was instructed to design was also to be built on credit with future oil profits as the guarantee. It was to be the largest, most expensive architectural project ever pursued in Dubai. Not exactly "tomorrow" as the ruler had insisted, work began on Rashid Hospital in 1969, three years after the oil announcement and three weeks after the first oil shipments actually departed.

Dubai's project announcements garnered coverage in the international press, especially in the reporting on foreign, largely British, firms who racked up high-price contracts. Their gains were often covered as if they were sporting events, with references to high-stakes "wins" and "awards." British dailies promoted building-sector firms, who were promoting themselves by chronicling Dubai's accomplishments. Reporting on their windfalls embellished Dubai's portrayal as a locale of unhindered development and wealth. In addition to the hired consultants who nurtured this press coverage, Rashid employed, by the late 1960s, a small circle of advisors—Dubaian, Bahraini, British, and Sudanese—who stood ready to shape Dubai's narrative around those contracts.

Marketing efforts extended beyond just the British press. In 1968, the director of Dubai Municipality Kamal Hamza produced an Arabic-language booklet titled "Dubai: Pearl of the Arabian Coast" that was addressed to "the Arab Nation."[18] The publication announced Dubai as a functioning city and a sound investment for Arabs abroad—whether as investors, store owners, traders, or possible employees to reside in the city. The booklet includes the first and only known publication of Harris's 1960 town plan in the years after its issuance. By publishing the plan, Hamza's booklet presents the city as more potential than actuality. The plan signifies the progressing municipal order, which, as Donald Hawley intended, encouraged sound investments, its outlined voids ready to be filled in with the reader's profit-driven imagination.

Hamza later acknowledged that the booklet was meant "to sell Dubai to Arabs abroad," as many locals felt the city was "flooded with Persians and Indians."[19] While the political agency had worked to hinder the Arab-nationalist reach within Dubai, Hamza made a small appeal to it. The pamphlet opens with a statement about Dubai's "Arab democracy," a positioning perhaps in light of democratic reforms in Egypt, Iraq, and Syria.[20] The term suggests that Dubai's government is representative, even if led by an unelected autocrat and an appointed, advisory council. More emphatically, Hamza argues, Dubai's "Arab democracy" is embedded in the economic opportunity that the town plan lays out. Democracy, it suggests, is channeled through a comprehensible and level playing field staged for commercial enterprise. In the pages of Hamza's scenario, Dubai is an idea, a scheme, still more a sales pitch than a reality. Seemingly unformed and unburdened by history, his Dubai appeals to investors who imagine a city shaped by individual aspirations, not the other way around.

In 1969, an English-language version of the book was rushed to print for Rashid's upcoming visit to London.[21] He would present the booklet to potential investors, consultants, and manufacturers for the port, airport, and hospital projects. In anticipation of Rashid's prior visits, the Foreign Office routinely produced crib sheets as digestible summaries of Dubai and its ruler for government and corporate officials. Not unlike the British press, which probably also accessed these sheets, the brief sketches of Sheikh Rashid usually repeated keywords like "shrewd," "agreeable," "considerable charm," "a Bedouin," and "uneducated."[22]

The English-language version of Hamza's booklet flipped the representation game, even if it substantiated some of the impressions already in circulation. It makes no reference to an Arab democracy, instead focusing directly on Dubai's economic vigor. From there, the English version delivers an uncomplicated history of Dubai and an outline of the municipality's major pursuits, like public hygiene, firefighting, and gardens. Harris's town plan is replaced with a recent aerial photograph, revealing the extensive progress made in one year of roadbuilding.

Beyond tarmac, Dubai as a concept is verified by evidence of administrative organization, including municipality telephone numbers, a guide to financing regulations, a climate overview, and selected trade statistics. There is no reference to Dubai's smuggling trade; gold is only mentioned as a tariff-free product. Dubai is presented as a land with laws and clear regulations, though kept to a minimum to encourage entrepreneurship. There are banks where wealth can be stored and protected. Streets offer shopping and even entertainment. There are hotels and a zoo. And, of course, there is a hospital. Life in Dubai is secure because it can be indexed, just as the reader's future earnings.

Rashid's advisors expanded their messaging strategy by hiring "external development services" that arranged for full-page "advertorials" in British papers. They presented Dubai as "the fastest growing trade centre in the Gulf" without factual basis.[23] Nevertheless, one installment in the London *Times*, titled "Welcome to Dubai," asserted that the "best advertisements" for Dubai were not purchased in dailies but the "hard facts quoted below from the preface of the Dubai Trade Review for 1968." The annual report and the ad copy made their way into subsequent journalistic reporting.

Beyond just the focus on quantifiable, even if not verifiable, advancements, these efforts put forward a narrative that "departs from the familiar script" of large-scale investments by petroleum-rich states like Qatar and Kuwait.[24] Once oil profits were booked, Dubai was going to be different; its champions envisioned that new wealth was not for making a few people rich but instead was scheduled for the city's large-scale infrastructure projects. As the *Times* described it, "All [were] to share port boon."[25] These projects in turn would lubricate the act of doing business in the city. Petroleum profits would keep Dubai advanced and tax-free. Advancement would be read in trade statistics, GDP numbers, and the buildup of urban matter to attract even more people and more money: a virtuous circle of profits.

Rashid's advisors angled stories to foreign media and investors along these lines, portraying a highly rational city committed to an uncomplicated business model. Rashid and his advisors were supplanting a simplistic story of extraction and exploitation with a sensible one about investment. Investment opportunity implied order and organization, Dubai's version of equal opportunity. According to the *Times*, Dubai would be "better off than fabulously rich."[26]

In regard to a city as a tax-free engine of industry, there is not much recorded analysis to substantiate it, beyond the Dubai government's own pronouncements and the British papers that published those pronouncements. The eventual sale of Dubai's oil was said to come after "long years of planning and preparation." There is little evident preparation beyond the index of fast-pace development projects in the 1964 "boom" report from the US State Department.[27] Except for William Duff's appointment, there is no further evidence of Dubai's hiring economists or financial planners to formulate an economic policy. In specific regard to the hospital, there is also no evidence of any analysis that determined a new hospital was necessary or a good investment.

When the political agency, once Dubai's self-appointed provider of order and stability, was asked in 1967 whether the city was prepared to incur so much debt for the giant port project, the hospital, and the rest of the £40 million in investments, the political agent at the time, David Roberts, responded:

> Sheikh Rashid has of course never embarked on anything of this magnitude before but he has never done anything on the development side or, as far as I can discover, any commercial enterprise which has not been successful. He is to a certain extent an adventurer and he is prepared to take risks. He does not however embark on these ventures without very careful consideration and listening to, on the whole good advice, and it has generally paid off.[28]

Roberts finds evidence of Dubai's economic health in Sheikh Rashid's personal character—his apparent Midas touch—not in the legitimacy of the projects. Rashid might *listen* to a few advisors, but there is no further mention of existing analysis of regional and global trade patterns and expectations.

The reason for not being concerned about Sheikh Rashid's imminently massive debt was simply that he hadn't got it wrong before. Rashid's character as a businessman—his "business acumen" (once highly questioned by the political agency)—was now beyond question. With £40 million worth of investments aiding the British economy, Rashid's character was at once served by British business interests and serving British business interests.

FIGURE 7.2 A small boat still finds an accessible shore along Dubai Creek, next to Al Maktoum Bridge, designed by Halcrow, early 1970s. Courtesy John R. Harris Library and Henk Snoek / RIBA Collections.

CONSULTANT DOMAINS

Besides their vastness—their combined surface areas outsized the existing city—Sheikh Rashid's post-oil projects had something else in common: They all took cues from Al Maktoum Hospital. They were all fenced-in enclaves. The sites could be protected from encroachment and others' ownership claims; they were circumscribed to signify their delivery of something not present outside their bounds and to define a realm activated by a hired suite of expertise. Each new major project was its own domain, following the formulas and systems written for it by its experts. There was no coordination among them, except by those hired to maximize the storytelling of their speedy and undeterred realization.

Unlike Al Maktoum Hospital, they were all projects that took place outside Harris's town plan. In this way, the port, the airport, and the new hospital complex also departed from the real estate frenzy in the existing city around the creek. As isolated development sites, each of these projects did less to enrich and densify Dubai's existing urban experience than to provide the decipherable components of a city ready to be assessed by global verdicts.

The development expert Peter Griffith had once criticized the British government's lack of coordination and forethought in ushering Dubai's urban development. By the time of Rashid Hospital's construction, the political agency was clearly no longer offering its "gentle encouragement" in terms of financial and administrative "tutelage." Once the political agency had been advised by Peter Tripp to withdraw from Dubai's daily administration, the job had been largely left to the people that the British government had placed around Sheikh Rashid, either as civil servants or private-sector consultants. The compartmentalization of Dubai's largest projects into discrete and manageable tasks was becoming the way of administering Dubai. In place of municipal governance, once the main goal of the political agency, was the cadre of experts who reported directly to Sheikh Rashid and his close advisors.

For Dubai, there were obvious financial risks, potentially devastating ones, in relying on private consultants. That being said, British government oversight at Al Maktoum Hospital had failed in supporting appropriate oversight for the project and collecting the necessary funds for a successful execution. Little, therefore, seemed lost in this configuration. Unchecked by government regulators in Dubai or in Great Britain, the British private sector delivered results only as good as they made them. British companies, trusted by both the Dubai and British governments, were expected to produce physical results out of smooth and tested methods. Rashid Hospital, for example, was to meet "British standards," but those standards were determined by those looking to profit directly from the process. Accountability lay in the companies' hopes to gain the next and larger project.

THE REMIT

By 1968, Sheikh Rashid had established a healthy credit history through payments for the harbor scheme and others development projects, thanks in large part to grants from his son-in-law, the emir of Qatar. Confirmed oil reserves ballooned his lending capacity. American companies reaped most of the direct profits from Dubai's oil, but there were plenty of ways British industry could help spend new debt. A British development expert stationed in Abu Dhabi once complained of an "invasion of expertise," but such an invasion was by 1968 only encouraged by the official's own government.[29]

Dubai's petroleum earnings boosted Britain's industries, with British exports to Dubai surging from £27 million in 1967 to £67 million in 1968.[30] Large machinery for construction sites and industrial plants made up the bulk of the exports, which also included cigarettes, medicine, food, stationery, and electronics.[31] Despite 1968's gains, Britain was said to be losing "pride of place"—first to Switzerland and then to Japan—as Dubai's primary exporter. Following 1968's numbers, Great Britain could not supersede Japan as Dubai's main exporter, but the years of the Rashid Hospital's construction and other contemporaneous projects were described in the *Financial Times* as the "U.K.'s come-back."[32]

Alongside Harris, there was a spectrum of British experts and purveyors who produced Rashid Hospital. Architecture resulted from the expertise that marshaled materials and labor into the complex's final form. Any critical evaluation of the campus's architecture—some found it "elegant," others "severe"—remains incomplete without considering the economic restraints and ambitions its makers were contracted to heed. In this way, architecture is as much about built form as about the definition and management of a supply system designed around boosting the British economy. The British Hospitals Export Council announced in 1972 that health-related companies earned £3.5 million in foreign sales.[33] With a budget of £6 million pounds just for building materials and equipment, Rashid Hospital was a significant contributor to that statistic.[34] After years of the British government denying aid for it, British industry now stood ready to profit greatly from Dubai's health care. Rashid Hospital, like Harris's other health campuses in the region, was a "useful advertisement" for how "British design and skills" could further advance the national economy.[35] Dubai, once feared as an economic burden to Great Britain, was now a boost.

The concept of a campus—with its delineated perimeter—allowed for the hospital to be handled like a product, as something that was purchased, not built. "Truly," a British medical journal declared, Rashid Hospital "must

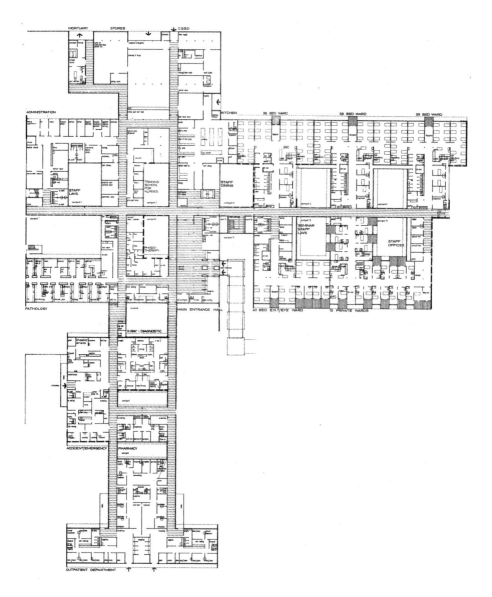

FIGURE 7.3 Ground-floor plan of Rashid Hospital's first phase, Dubai's largest and most expensive architectural project at the time. Courtesy John R. Harris Library.

be amongst the best buys of hospitals built in the last five years."[36] A British medical expert, Leslie Honeyman, under contract with the municipality described Rashid Hospital as a "one line remit" that he was tasked to spend. In an interview with the trade magazine *Building*, the Scottish-trained doctor was described as "the one and only fully trained" medical officer in Dubai. The municipality assigned him as its middleman to British goods. In this role, Honeyman sold himself as "the single representative of the client with responsibility for all important decisions."[37] The expatriate's bravado suggests that Dubai's leaders were too ignorant, or too occupied otherwise, to care about how the credit line was spent. Honeyman played the part of consultant well and was proud of his responsibility in a land that needed him.

Besides falsely denying that Dubai had other trained medical officers, he misrepresented the hospital project, inflating his own role and oversimplifying the process of creating a hospital.[38] Honeyman ignored the British economic landscape, of which his job was but a small bit. Since Dubai's oil discoveries, more banks had taken interest in financing Dubai's development projects. For Rashid Hospital, Morgan Grenfell Merchant Bankers provided the £6.5 million credit line, but not just based on the prospects of Dubai's oil.[39]

Their interest was further piqued by the British government's Export Credits Guarantee Department (ECGD) program, which guaranteed private loans for foreign projects committed to British industries. ECGD agreed to work with Dubai-based projects only once it was assured that oil companies could not back out from their extraction plans.[40] Whereas such paltry British-led projects from the Trucial States Development Office (worth tens of thousands of pounds at most) had delivered little more than a "tiny morsel" of aid a few years ago, the British government now backed private loans worth tens of millions to secure work for British companies.[41] The effort not only benefited British companies but also ensured that contracted companies were British, not the foreign competition.[42] And it was not the legitimacy or feasibility analysis of these projects that drove investment; rather it was the lender's ability to fulfill loan payments. Whether or not the projects were necessary and feasible, the British private sector was made all the wealthier by them.

Creating a hospital "along British lines" not only delivered British technology and manufactured goods; according to David Crawford, editor of a British architecture magazine, it also exported a "whole generation of experience gained in building up the postwar British welfare state." Such public projects were considered proof of a "worldwide reputation," not just in expertise but also in the experience of civic life. Crawford claimed that the British welfare-state legacy was "one of the strongest bases on which hopes for the continued and increased export of British constructional and design knowledge can be based."[43] His argument suggested that, as Dubai and other cities in the region built recognizable institutions like government agencies, schools, and hospitals, British experts appreciated the significance of these institutions, because they had also presumably lived with such state-building initiatives.

Architects who worked for John Harris recognized that a main selling point for the office was its dedication to institutional buildings. The firm's international allure had to do with its understanding of the relationship between institution building and architecture.[44] Beyond having "a lot of experience in the design and building of hospitals," British building-industry consultants were well-versed in Britain's centralization of national health care. Such experience enabled them to design and produce larger and more specialized institutions, which in turn spurred more advancements in equipment technology and larger-size orders. Such advancements and centralization of British public health care created an excellent opportunity to pursue an export bonanza.[45]

ALONG BRITISH LINES

If designing Al Maktoum Hospital had been based on templates for colonial hospitals, then Rashid Hospital materialized out of the high-end financing of advanced medical equipment. Architecture was designed to house it all. The delay until September 1969 in securing financing suited Harris's schedule, affording him time to complete work on a 1,600-bed hospital in Kuala Lumpur. By the time Harris had returned to Dubai, he had built a reputation outside Britain as an architect of hospitals, "an authority on this type of building in countries where there are extremes of climates."[46] He had also established a proficiency in managing an "almost impossibly tight programme," not because Dubai urgently needed more hospital beds but because keeping a compressed time schedule kept prices down.

Rashid Hospital was designed as a vast assemblage of precisely measured and compatible parts. The £6.5 million budget was not presided over by a governmental client but by the terms of a British merchant bank's loan papers. Responsible for maintaining the budget's strict ceiling, Harris convened in his London office the expertise hired to deliver the new hospital and every piece of medical equipment.[47] Every detail—from last-minute structural changes to the slightest furniture and "fittings down to linen, tableware etc."—was scheduled and itemized in what Harris described as an "intense co-ordination."[48] Budgetary stringency translated into an "emphasis on straightforward rapid construction."[49] Each ounce of steel, hardwood, and Formica paneling was accounted for. Even a portrait of Sheikh Rashid to hang in the lobby was a line in the budget.

In contrast to Honeyman's supposedly single-sourced project, Harris's plan demanded a synchronized network of suppliers, engineers, medical experts, and surveyors who produced according to systematized schedules. One Essex door manufacturer secured a contract for all 850 doors; Norris Air Conditioning (a newly formed subsidiary of Norris Warming for the purpose of the contract) earned almost 15 percent of the project's budget; a manufacturer with a reputation for supplying "complete planning services" for large European ships was hired to install "a complete kitchen and food service system." In similar fashion, the Leeds-based manufacturer Thackrays supplied the hospital's "built-in theatre systems."[50]

Having agreed to an eighteen-month development schedule, Harris and the consultant teams were motivated by the tight timetable, not frustrated by it. They treated the project as a chance to design an efficient delivery system for a high-standard hospital. Harris had once been wrongly criticized for causing delay at Al Maktoum Hospital, simply by being an architect on another continent. Now he coordinated a London-based team and set out to prove that, with only a three-person site team in Dubai, it could realize a medical "superstructure" on time and under budget.

As construction proceeded on schedule if not ahead of it, Harris wrote to his cohorts at Widnell & Trollope (the quantity surveyor for Rashid Hospital as well as the Doha hospital) to report on his search for subsequent opportunities to build other fast and programmatically complete hospitals.[51] Beyond just a hospital, Harris designed a format to sell to future clients. It was a system his company would implement in other projects in Dubai and one that others would quickly replicate.

Rashid Hospital's British contractor, Sunley & Sons, advertised its work on the hospital as a "turnkey project," a term previously used to refer to the development and transfer of completed factories and power plants to foreign governments. By the time of Rashid Hospital's completion, "turnkey" had taken on a broader meaning to include projects with more sophisticated suites of technologies that also diversified the ways British industries entered foreign markets. British exports to Dubai had started with used Land Rovers, packaged foodstuffs, and secondhand medical equipment, but now Dubai's development demanded

FIGURE 7.4 The Pakistani and Indian construction team assembling the upper floor of Rashid Hospital. Workers lived on site in tents. Courtesy John R. Harris Library.

more advanced, and more lucrative, deliveries. With Rashid Hospital, "turnkey" delivered an entire living complex, replete with advanced medical technology, industrial equipment, cooling systems, and household furnishings.[52]

In Harris's records of the hospital's construction, one major component is conspicuously absent: labor. Despite the project's centralized organization, each contracted party managed its own labor requirements. This made recruiting processes difficult to summarize.[53] At the time, Sheikh Rashid's Bahraini advisor, Mahdi Al Tajir, used his offices at Dubai's port to run a labor recruitment agency for Dubai-based companies and for his own personal profit.[54] Because he was already associated with this project as Harris's direct government contact, it is conceivable that he also supplied the contractor's labor force. By 1968, the men building the hospital belonged to a significant demographic; as builders, they were part of the city's third-largest employment sector.[55] Specifically at the hospital site and throughout the city, they came mostly from Pakistan and India.[56] The project's predominately concrete construction matched the migrant laborers' assumed skill sets. While structures included steel columns and beams manufactured in Britain, the bulk of the campus was made out of concrete block, manufactured on site and taking advantage of Dubai's low labor costs. A familiar sight in Dubai at this time was the "brickwork," a building site's own concrete block-making unit that disappeared once the building was completed.

Labor concerns also determined Rashid Hospital's building schedule. The first buildings to go up on site were the "bungalows" for the hospitals' future doctors and executive staff. The project's "senior construction staff" subsequently moved into these houses. John R. Harris Architects ran their first Dubai office out of one of these houses.[57] Meanwhile, the rest of the construction staff lived in tents issued on site. The turnkey agreement was considered complete once the contractors cleared the British men out of the houses and swept up the complex's tent city.

HEALTH CITY

For the site of Dubai's second phase in health care, John Harris had advised years earlier to look "outside the limits of the town."[58] Al Maktoum Hospital, once on the outskirts of Deira, was already in the midst of Dubai's speculative real estate market, and land around it was unobtainable. To amass enough uncontested land that Rashid could legally claim without the burden of compensating payments, a site was demarcated well beyond both major districts of the city. This time, the project, assured proper funding and a firmer grasp on supply chains, would be for a total hospital.

The large and unimpeded site allowed for the project's conceptual clarity, though it remained unclear on what needs the new hospital was based. One bed was scheduled for every 200 persons living in Dubai (to be doubled in later phases), and outpatient facilities could handle 700 patients daily. As with Dubai's overarching economic policy, there were no filed policy statements or population studies to argue for such a surge in available health care. Nevertheless, no city with such advanced medical care could claim a similar per capita bed count. Statistics, in this way, were less about analysis than an existential assertion.

Located beyond most of the city, the new hospital was carefully sited in relation to a recently installed piece of infrastructure. In 1963, Halcrow delivered Al Maktoum Bridge.[59] Completed in less than a year for £194,000, the bridge transformed Dubai by uniting it. Before the bridge's opening, neither brute force nor political persuasion had brought Dubai Creek's two districts closer together, physically or socially. Infrastructure, just as the harbor project had done previously, linked the two sides. Improving upon the flurrying fleet of abras and the marshy crossing at the furthest edge of the creek, the bridge promised quickness and smoothness. For the five-cent roundtrip toll charge, one could drive across the bridge and experience both a political and transportation solution.[60] Exemplifying the unifying potential of infrastructure, Al Maktoum Bridge made Rashid Hospital just as easy to approach by car from either district. Between Deira and Bur Dubai, it was its own district, its own Health City.[61]

When it opened in 1973, Rashid Hospital was one of Dubai's first major drive-to destinations. If one approached it from Deira after crossing the Al Maktoum Bridge, the entrance was off the first roundabout whose only other exit led you toward Port Rashid and the outskirts of Bur Dubai. There, a guardhouse greeted arriving traffic, signaling as much the entrance to Health City as the exit from the rest of Dubai. Once the stationed guard signaled a driver through, the road continued like one of the tertiary roadways in Harris's town plan, trimmed with high curbs and decked with fountains and islands of green landscaping. The hospital's large tract of land was nearly as big as that designated for London's Wexham Park Hospital.[62] The campus comprised its own road network, supported by its own roundabouts and traffic signs, woven through the complex's various departments and living quarters. Signs at drop-off areas at the building entrance guided traffic to seemingly endless rows of paved and partially shaded parking, then still a novelty in Dubai.

FIGURE 7.5 Overview of Rashid Hospital, sometimes referred to as Health City. The hospital was one of Dubai's first drive-to destinations. Courtesy John R. Harris Library.

Even before the plethora of "city-in-a-city" developments that have characterized Dubai's twenty-first century growth, Rashid's Health City was a district where doctors, nurses, and other service providers lived and worked.[63] The hospital was designed to power itself. Electricity, still sometimes an erratic provision in Dubai, was to be generated by an on-site power plant "with boilers, incinerators, three transformers and a unit to re-circulate the laundry water."[64] The campus included its own mosque shaded by a fashionable concrete shell.[65] Staff took their meals from the hospital's canteens, and not just during work shifts. There were dormitory-style accommodations for nursing and technical staff in the campus's three-story buildings. Doctors and medical executives were issued the two- and three-bedroom bungalows. Future phases added villas for management staff, making the campus even more like one of Harris's proposed neighborhood units.

The campus managed its own population. "Four or five" Zanzibari women, trained as nurses in England before the hospital's completion, worked with the British staff to constitute the hospital's first residents.[66] Through the 1970s, technicians and nurses were recruited largely from South Asia, often through classifieds in the English-language *Times of India*. Advertisements placed for "unmarried female nurses" promised free housing on site with a "nominal charge for food only."[67] Rashid Hospital was a city in itself, an encapsulated life set apart from the rest of Dubai. For these employees, Dubai was a hospital.

Clearly demarcated and set apart from the existing built city, Rashid Hospital was legible and coherent. If the new port offered global trade connections and if the new airport offered global travel connections, then Rashid Hospital offered free, international-standard health care, an assurance to local residents in a city growing to accommodate even more foreigners.[68] One could drive slowly around the hospital premises and measure what Dubai had compared to what neighboring cities did not. It was evident that Dubai was an "an ideal type of developing country for a doctor," unmatched in the region, even by Abu Dhabi with its seven-year head start on oil revenues and profits nearly 500 times Dubai's in 1969.[69] In contrast to the coherence that Rashid Hospital's campus promised, Abu Dhabi was "being transformed pell mell," its hospital reportedly "structurally unsatisfactory."[70] As foundation work began on Dubai's new hospital, the municipal magazine *Akhbar Dubai* announced that, "After having first become the region's commercial center, Dubai is transforming to be become its health center."[71] The British Royal College of Surgeons named it "a bright sparkle in the Middle East."[72]

To highlight Dubai's noticeable upgrade, Sheikh Rashid specified "grass and mature plants being round the hospital."[73] And there were to be fountains. The effect was certainly to set an oasis-like campus against the desert that lay outside it, but it was also part of a more dramatic strategy. Anthony Lodge, Harris's lead architect at the hospital, was instructed to coordinate with Dubai's municipal gardener, Mr. Saari, on how the hospital's landscaping linked with the larger city. Saari's job was to make Dubai's newest spaces its most verdant, a directive one could easily trace back to Harris's 1965 planning guidelines.[74] Landscaping and water elements maintained a visual connection, at least for car passengers, from one new distinct site of urban development to the next.

By 1971, Harris noted in the follow-up development plan, the city was "proudly [transforming] itself into a city of trees and flowers."[75] According to Harris, ribbons of green landscaping, along roadsides and on traffic islands, stitched a fractured city together, visually attaching outlying developments to the city along the roads that brought one to them. One of the most cared-for streets was the road almost solely used by heavy-load trucks delivering rock to Port Rashid's construction site. Closed off to the general public, the road could at least be beautified to signal its importance to the rest of the city. Green functioned as a visual cue to the lines of Dubai's new utilities (water lines, electrical and telephone wires, and asphalt roads) that supplied an ease of life to Dubai's growing number of districts.

ARCHITECTURE INTERIORIZED

Rashid's Health City needed its own map: three operating theater suites on the top floor, with one on the ground floor for emergencies; a maternity department with special baby care unit; wards for general and acute medical cases ranging in size from one to thirty-nine beds; ENT and ophthalmology departments; advanced pediatrics facilities; an intensive care unit; private wards; a central sterile services department; and a pharmaceutical and pathology department.

As sprawling as Rashid Hospital was, its purpose resided in its isolation—from those "special climatic conditions" deemed menacing to health care.[76] International standards were not adjusted to local climatic conditions. Instead, the climate was negated. Whereas Harris's Doha hospital had been praised for its attention to solar positioning and the use of reflective light to minimize interior temperatures, Rashid Hospital was sequestered from its surroundings. Solar techniques were replaced with a faith in air conditioning. Facades of most buildings were barely punctured by fenestration, further emphasizing the hospital's reliance on its interiors. Fewer and sparser windows minimized the exterior architectural detailing needed to provide shade and decreased interior cooling loads. Inner courtyards were also shrunk to minimize exterior surface. Designed not just to control temperature, the British-built air exchange system was itself a protective seal against the outside, devised to prevent "sand and grit particles [from] entering the system."[77] The result was a "severely functional," muscular expression of air-conditioned interiority.[78]

FIGURE 7.6 Laboratory inside Rashid Hospital. Courtesy John R. Harris Library and Henk Snoek / RIBA Collections.

> FIGURE 7.7 Rashid Hospital's pediatric unit.
Courtesy John R. Harris Library and Henk Snoek / RIBA Collections.

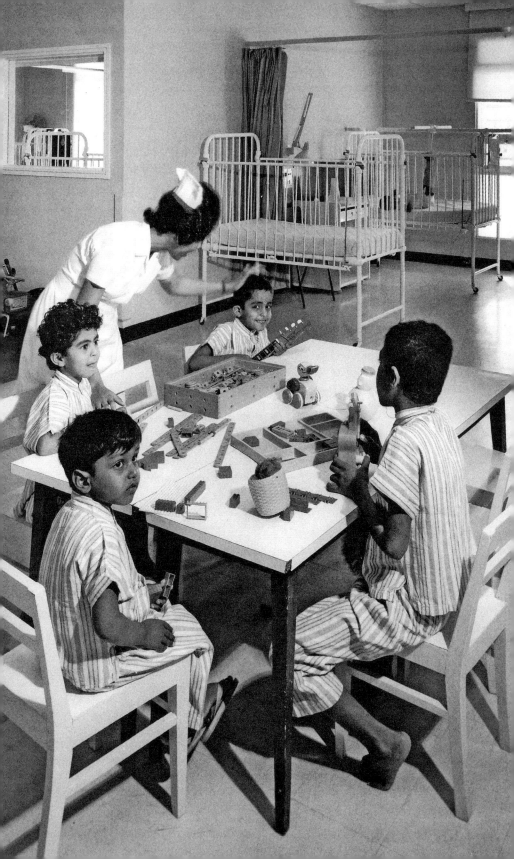

The London *Times*'s architecture correspondent complimented Harris's results as "elegant."[79] The assessment might have had to do with the complex's economical moves that provided unifying measures, like the shell-concrete domes that marked the entrance and the dark metallic fasciae that crowned each building. In general, though, architecture recedes to the background. It functions as a frame for climate control and medical technologies. It enables perfunctory interiors to be assembled within a reliably sealed container, sheathed in patented membranes, in which lives are improved and protected.

In promotional materials, mostly South Asian and Arab patients are treated by nurses (perhaps the early Zanzibari hires). In comparison to what was achieved at Al Maktoum Hospital, Rashid Hospital's interiors are less perfunctory, as much about providing protected, comfortable environments as about fighting illness and disease. Staged photographs capture mundane institutional activities like a man folding sheets taken out of industrial-size dryers, technicians inspecting high-tech laboratory equipment, and children playing with a supply of clean toys. The photographed scenes demonstrate that interiors exhibited modern living standards not yet achievable in the city beyond. Before hotel lobbies and shopping malls, for Dubai's residents, it was a hospital that demonstrated how central air conditioning could transform urban living.

Rashid Hospital was "the largest single building in the region," "the largest and best-equipped [hospital] between Bahrain and Karachi."[80] Sheikh Rashid allegedly reveled—not in inspecting the advanced machinery, but in wandering the seemingly endless hallways and opening double doors leading to more hallways. Corridors stretched longer than some of Dubai's existing roads and could be traversed even faster. Metal carts with rubber-coated wheels moved effortlessly over polished tile floors, even while most of Dubai's roads had yet to be smoothed over with asphalt. Extensive, seemingly infinitely expandable space reinforced the concept of a fortified zone for healthy living in Dubai, where technology enhanced human life. Western newspapers might have found the outside city still a "sultry backwater" at the time of the hospital's opening, but life in its sprawling Health City moved smoothly and efficiently.

> **FIGURE 7.8** Entrance to Rashid Hospital marked with its signature monolithic domes
>   on slender columns. The dome became the health department's logo.
>   Courtesy John R. Harris Library and Henk Snoek / RIBA Collections.

A BOUNTEOUS HARBOR, NOT A BRITISH HARBOR

Harris and the rest of the development team delivered 393 beds to Dubai's emergent health department in March 1973, with a gratifying few British pounds under budget. The pamphlet created for the opening ceremony praised the complex as a "show-piece." On show was as much the Dubai government's latest facilities as British industries' capability to provide them.[81]

Both the city and the consultant team had much to gain from a publicity campaign. Dubai achieved an operable and advanced hospital "along British lines" without even having a fully operable health department in place to regulate it; the health department's first offices would in fact open on the campus. The hospital set Dubai on a par with Qatar and Kuwait, two states in the Gulf region known for their exemplary medical facilities and targeted as competitors to Dubai's regional ascendency. The expertise hired by Dubai's "skeleton government" walked away with a profit and an improved résumé for their next potential projects. For the hospital's consultants and purveyors, Rashid Hospital was a proved record to present to other government clients who needed efficient, quickly built health care facilities. As Sunley stated in advertisements placed in the *Financial Times* to celebrate the hospital's completion, it was "keen to execute further substantial overseas projects."[82]

The hospital's completion wrapped up what were in the end more than £60 million of post–oil discovery projects: In 1970, the new airport had opened; in 1972, six months before the hospital's delivery, Port Rashid became fully operable. Another round of British-led projects had already been announced, even before the first tranche was completed: Al Shindagha Tunnel to connect Deira and Bur Dubai at the creek's mouth and a dry-docks project adjacent to Port Rashid. In 1973, Dubai's champions boasted another £117 million in new projects guided by three British firms: Halcrow, Costain, and Taylor Woodward.[83] The following year, Costain alone claimed involvement in £100 million worth of new projects.[84] There seemed to be an endless appetite for construction contracts, and, from them, British firms carved out a "profitable field for British commercial enterprise."[85]

In the process of earning a profit for themselves and for the British economy, the building-industry experts were creating a city ready for business. Port Rashid's early completed berths were a boon to Rashid Hospital's on-time delivery. Equipment from Britain and cement from East Africa could be quickly offloaded, transferred in trucks that could speed along Dubai's most cared-for stretches of asphalt that skirted around the edges of the built-up city. Labor from South Asia came this way as well. Goods, and people, were delivered from one of Dubai's separate development zones to another, without ever having to enter the existing city. British designers, engineers, and contractors were creating the means by which Dubai could access more goods, more people, more wealth. All three were helping grow Dubai into a city with increasing access to opportunity.

FIGURE 7.9 New Dubai Hospital, early 1980s. Courtesy John R. Harris Library.

The successes that British industries helped realize also made it all the more difficult for them to protect the British "built-in advantage." The British political agency reported that while Dubai residents might associate British companies

> vaguely with what they know of British power and have grown accustomed to do what we ask, . . . nowadays there are other sources of influence: Ambassadors from all over the Middle East, messengers from [Iran's] Shah in special jet aircraft, bankers with black leather briefcases.[86]

The political agent also mentioned French interests, "with their roving Ambassador applying unscrupulous support."[87]

By 1971, Dubai's "European and American community" well exceeded 1,000, living off the handsome figures of infrastructure and oil-producing projects and representing a web of professionals in competition with one another.[88] Dubai's consumer market was also being further overtaken, especially by Japanese manufacturers. One *Economist* article's conclusion was that British companies would "have to work at it much harder."[89]

Rashid's visits to London kept Dubai linked to British industry, but the ruler reached out to other destinations as well during his summer travels. His first trip to London in 1959 concluded with a flight to Cairo. Several others included stops in Iran, where according to Donald Hawley, he was "very lavishly entertained."[90] In his reporting to the political agents over the years, Rashid often downplayed these other trips. His 1961 itinerary in Tehran included tours of the city's factories, after a trip to London when he failed to enlist British industry to open manufacturing sites in his city.[91] In response to British government inquiries about his visits to Iran, Rashid usually conceded that many kinds of aid had been offered, but he had declined them. While telling the political agent that he rejected the offers, Rashid reiterated his choice to rely on British advisors, but he also made it clear that he had options. For the time being, Iran's help might have been less appealing than potential British sources, but Rashid nevertheless enjoyed an expanding world of opportunities.

There was an exception to Rashid's pass on Iranian aid. In 1969, the Red Lion and Sun Society, an Iranian humanitarian and medical aid organization, donated a hospital to Dubai, which still operates today in Dubai's Jumeirah district. If reviews of Rashid Hospital described it as "severe," the political agency dismissed the Iranian hospital as "lavish." The political agent Julian Bullard noted the attention paid to mosaic-bearing facades, marbled entryways, and vinyl wallpaper. For the gardens, "not only the flowers but the earth" was imported from Iran.[92] The hospital offered comfort and advanced technologies, and even more comfort for its "visiting VIPs."[93] Iranian craftsmen delivered Iranian architectural ornament, perhaps just as demonstratively as when the wind-tower houses were introduced on Dubai Creek. The aid society purchased medical equipment "of the highest quality and . . . selected with great care from a number of countries," including Great Britain and Japan.[94]

The Iranian gift was not mentioned in promotional materials in British and American papers about Dubai, and it was not feted in the local *Akhbar Dubai* magazine. Still, the transaction did speak clearly to the raft of investors and purveyors, British and otherwise, negotiating with Sheikh Rashid's government: There were other influences besides British ones at work on Dubai's changing landscapes. Iranians, after all, had been major contributors to Dubai's harbor before British parties found any interest in it. At least for the time being, health care would continue predominantly "along British lines." At Rashid Hospital's official opening, the commemorative booklet stated that Rashid Hospital had transformed Dubai into a "healthy place." It also included a map of Dubai on which was marked the location for the city's next health care project: New Dubai Hospital. John Harris won the commission for that one too.[95]

FIGURE 8.1 A khazzan under construction at Chicago Beach. Photo by Michael Hamilton-Clark ©2014.

CHAPTER 8

FUTURE FLYOVERS

1971 Dubai Development Plan

IN 1969, an unremarkable stretch of Dubai's coastline had an economic purpose and therefore a name—Chicago Beach. A ceremony was scheduled there on August 6. Heavy winds delayed the event until the following day, when engineers in charge expressed "no doubt" that conditions were satisfactory for the planned spectacle.[1] Four years of calculations, they insisted, would hold. The event remained invitation only and "unpublicized," in case it proved a magnificent failure.

Invited guests driving along the unvarying shoreline that led to Chicago Beach had enough cues for where they should veer from the asphalt road toward the beach. A tenuous pier, not built to last long, stretched into the shallow sea. It defined the edge of a pool dug out of the beach and filled with seawater. Around the inland lake sprawled a makeshift village for workers who reporters called locals but were really migrants from South Asia. They had built the site's most visible element—the towering behemoth of blackened steel. It was as imposing as it was inelegant, a fabrication of steel parts welded together to create a shape more than once described as a giant inverted champagne glass.

Those who had built it and those who had been invited to witness it had never seen anything so large on Dubai land. It reached as high as a twenty-story building, "half the size of the Great Pyramid," and its 270-foot diameter made it nearly as vast as an American football field.[2] Weighing 15,000 tons, it was Dubai's greatest icon even though few people had seen it. Engineers had made it levitate above the shallow lake, but they had designed it to disappear.

The August event was to commemorate the gigantic vessel's departure. Chicago Bridge and Iron Company, after which Chicago Beach was named, had pitched their invention as a "cost cutter" to store Dubai's offshore oil. The inventors called it a "big, submerged tank." English-language newspapers usually referred to it as a *khazzan*, Arabic for "storage tank." One trade magazine claimed that, for "the cheerful residents of Dubai," *khazzan* meant "treasure house."[3]

In order to store oil, the khazzan took its shape based on simple physics: the water displacement principle. A corporate film described how it worked:

> It hasn't got a bottom. And when it is submerged, it will fill with water. As the oil is pumped into the top, it floats on the water inside, and the pressure of the oil will push the water out of the bottom, which is open. When a tanker draws off the oil, water comes in again to fill the space the oil left behind.[4]

The idea solved the new petroleum industry's "biggest challenge": oil storage. "There is no need to build long (and costly) pipelines to shore. Or to build onshore storage tanks." The first khazzan cost about $7 million, roughly $11 million less than a traditional piping and onshore storage system, according to one source.

The khazzan's 500,000-barrel capacity was small, if Dubai hoped to produce 300,000 barrels a day. Two more tanks were therefore planned. The Chicago company's scheme might have saved in upfront development costs and helped accelerate the start of oil-extraction efforts, but it also enabled the foreign-controlled oil company to export crude as quickly as possible, without any of the revenue-adding processing ever landing in Dubai.

Those invited to the ceremony were people who stood to profit from the plan. Oil company families, local dignitaries, engineers, some bagpipe players, and lots of curious Dubai children joined the site's workers who had nowhere to go on their day off. The *New York Times* reported on an "Arab tradition of the Gulf" to "blood" the khazzan with four slain camels. An Indian municipal worker named Oscar Mandoody, however, claimed years later that the tradition was his invention for dedicating a new seafaring vessel without a bottle of champagne.[5] Other "dramatics" included Rashid using a "dagger or knife" to cut the rope that symbolically kept the vessel ashore.[6] Tugboats then hauled the "bottomless wonder," filled with compressed air to keep it afloat for the ninety-six-kilometer journey to Fateh Field, the offshore area where Continental Oil Company had found enough oil to begin exports. As it merged with the horizon, the khazzan became officially "part of an invisible industry."[7]

With the khazzan now beyond the horizon, there was nothing else for onshore guests to witness, but much still had to happen offshore. By night, the tugboats, with the floating khazzan in tow, reached Fateh Field. Those aboard the tugboats watched as air was released from the khazzan's abdomen, and the engineers' calculations were put to the test. "About the best way I can describe it," one Chicago Bridge engineer recalled of the moment, "is a noise like a thunderous belch."[8] The khazzan tilted to its side as its cavern filled with water. The whole thing teetered nervously but held to engineers' expectations, straightening up and slowly descending into the water. By morning the following day, what remained to be seen of the khazzan was its fifteen-meter-high bright-yellow tip, a beacon for oil tankers approaching their subterranean harvest.

The khazzan—its bounty of oil, its bathtub-science ingenuity, and its recognizable shape—was embraced for its conducive role in Dubai's wealthmaking. It was also deployed to signify Dubai's resourcefulness and inventiveness. This khazzan, and the subsequent two, were the "three Pyramids of Dubai."[9] A water tower in Dubai was later fashioned to resemble one, though upside-down, as if the oil were being put back into the ground. The khazzan was also featured on a postage stamp. Sheikh Rashid displayed a dynamic model of it in his office. Oil company families received "personalized" models as Christmas gifts. The innovative and cost-saving icon buoyed the narrative that petroleum profits, this time, were going to be spent differently, and innovatively.

The khazzan was named Majmaa I. From Arabic, *majmaa* can be translated to "group" or "collection" or, yet again, "storage container." In Arabic and Urdu, likely a language spoken by at least some of the khazzans' builders, *majmaa* can also refer to a large crowd or assembly. It seems a fittingly elastic word: Majmaa I was sent to sea to collect oil so that crowds would continue to work on, profit from, and deliver a new city financed by oil.

NEW DUBAI

When guests left the ceremony, sealed in their air-conditioned cars, they might have had the impression that the village for Chicago Beach workers was surrounded by *nothing*: no buildings, no "future development" signage, no municipal services, no roads, no lighting, no history, no culture. They had probably been blind to subtle gestures of settlement or slight artifacts of history—a cluster of cultivated palms, a frond house or two, impressions left behind by an abandoned fishing settlement, a sandpit brimming with used tires and discarded materials. The day's events had focused on the sea and the uninflected haze concealing the horizon; it had been crafted as a meditation on the abstraction of oil, on the calculations of geology, physics, and economics. Witnesses had gazed out toward something they ultimately could not see, the invisible industry. With nothing to be seen, there was no obstruction to entrepreneurial imagination. Horizons were limitless, solutions were at hand.

From the same indeterminate horizon appeared money, people, technologies, and building materials, riding on a mounting current toward nearby Port Rashid. Imports were not intended to erase history; they arrived under the assumption that *no history existed.* "A virgin coastline will become a concrete plane," said one engineer about the ongoing work at Port Rashid.[10] His description suited a whole new city in the making, a vast site marketed as unhindered potential, expansion, and newness.

The guests returned to their homes, for the time being still attached to the old city. In the last year, a new asphalt road had converted a seaside collection of villas beyond the limits of Bur Dubai into a posh suburb that kept the old settlement's name, Jumeirah. Without television stations, the neighborhood could sustain its own cinema. The area started to get its own schools and shops. In 1969, the city's European, or white, population had tripled in the three years since the discovery of oil. Their salaries—earned from oil companies, bank branches, and engineering firms—made them part of the force that moved Dubai's field of ambition outward, away from Dubai Creek toward seemingly boundless horizons.

Through its proposal for the giant new port, Halcrow introduced Sheikh Rashid to the profit potential of mapping large ambitions onto uncharted realms, where his only restriction was his lending capacity.[11] An early drawing for Port Rashid revealed that a canal was intended to connect its berths to Dubai Creek. The waterway would have combined the two ports, but this plan was later canceled. The new port was designed instead to be severed from the old city. Its bounds marked a new city. A proclaimed blankness, starting at Port Rashid and stretching toward the Abu Dhabi border, defined Dubai's expansive potential. No planner drew a town plan for this new city. It materialized out of a patchwork of ad hoc municipal surveys and the ruler's ongoing deal-making. Dubai Creek no longer provided the allure for newcomers; it was Port Rashid and other major efforts on the city's outskirts offering jobs to legions of workers.

In this new city, white and affluent residents rented houses as they were built within land grants secured by developers in Jumeirah. Al Satwa and Al Karama districts, intended mainly for middle- and lower-income families, were built out according to prescribed grids; the barastis in the area known as Al Safa obeyed fire lanes and exterior boundaries enforced by municipal workers, but within those bounds its residents were left on their own. Around these delineated outer districts was little constructed evidence of the new city. Unpaved swaths of desert kept the rich separated from the poor. In between their gates and walls was little more than an abstraction of ambitions and an open-ended promise of profits that Rashid and his advisors promoted. Rashid declared the new port and the surrounding area a "free zone," where there was an "openness to all who would be given full freedom to start businesses there."[12]

In 1968, John Harris began to draw a new plan for Dubai, one that sought to bring this new city into a relationship with the existing city. The political agent Donald Hawley had urged the original town plan upon

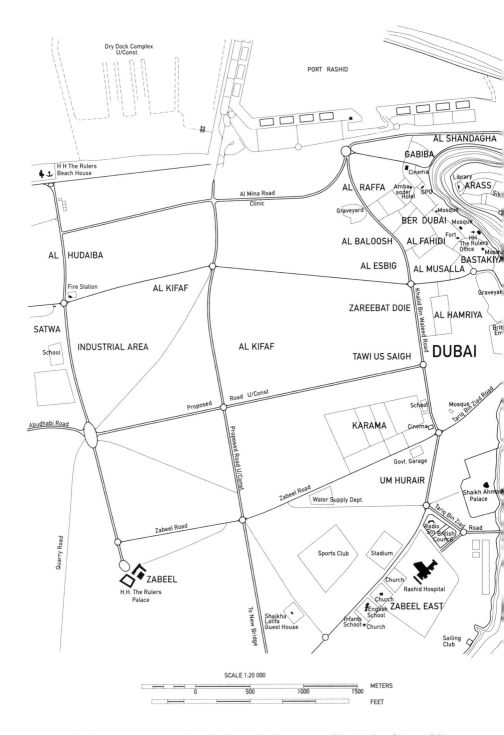

FIGURE 8.2 Dubai, circa 1973. The political agency has been renamed the British Embassy, and the major roads from Harris's 1960 town plan are evident. Rashid Hospital, Port Rashid, and the proposed dry docks are connected by wide asphalt roads that circumvented the built-up districts of the city. Redrawn by Azza Aboualam. Courtesy John R. Harris Library.

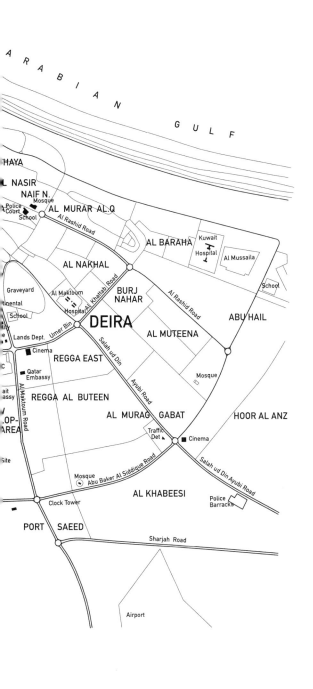

Parachute Club

A R A B I A N   G U L F

HAYA

NASIR

NAIF N.
Mosque

Police
Court   AL MURAR AL Q
School   Al Rashid Road

AL BARAHA   Kuwait
               Hospital
AL NAKHAL   Al Mussaila

Graveyard   Al Maktoum   School
tinental   BURJ   Al Rashid Road
School   Hospital   NAHAR
                            ABU HAIL
Lands Dept.   DEIRA
               AL MUTEENA
Cinema
               REGGA EAST
Qatar
Embassy   Mosque
ait
assy   REGGA AL BUTEEN
OP-   AL MURAG GABAT   HOOR AL ANZ
AREA
                            Traffic
site   Det   Cinema

               Mosque
               Abu Baker Al Siddique Road
                            AL KHABEESI   Police
Clock Tower   Barracks

PORT   SAEED
               Sharjah Road

Airport

To Hatta

Sheikh Rashid. This time, Harris urged Dubai Municipality to commission the reappraisal. The 1960 town plan had been part of an infrastructural ploy to unite Deira and Bur Dubai, a strategy that had started to work just as this new schism began. Like Rashid Hospital, a new master plan was to demonstrate how Dubai's landscape responded harmoniously to new oil wealth. It was supposed to reveal how Dubai would grow efficiently, how new roads would connect Dubai's new districts, and where arriving populations would reside.

FIGURE 8.3 Port Rashid, originally contracted in 1967 for £9 million, would be fully operational in 1972 with a final cost two-and-a-half times the original price. The road headed toward the bottom of the image leads to quarries inland. It was also the road that connected the port to Dubai's largest construction sites without crossing through the old city. By the time it was completed, the neighboring dry docks to the left were already proposed. Courtesy John R. Harris Library.

A master plan is typically commissioned to convey a sense of stability and to plot a city's bounded form. It gives geographical and spatial expression to administrative order and signals additional services to come (ring roads, public transit, financial districts, marinas, public parks). John Harris's 1960 town plan fit this description. The year 1968 seemed a logical time to reassess the plan, when oil sales were expected to push the city even further from the bounds of the first town plan. However, when the new plan was eventually issued in 1971, Dubai's financial and political landscape hardly proved amenable to a planner's temperament. A plan lays out how a city will grow, with legible stages and units. In the years leading up to 1971, Rashid and his advisors believed that Dubai's financial survival could not afford such legibility.

ONE NATION, ONE CAPITAL

The Chicago Beach ceremony was publicized only after it had been a success. According to one Lebanese magazine, residents were "dancing and singing in the streets of Dubai" to celebrate when "the Merchants Paradise joined the oil world," but not everyone was so jubilant.[13] Between the time when Dubai's oil wealth was confirmed and when the first exports were made ready, the British government delivered news that dampened the optimism in Dubai. On January 16, 1968, Prime Minister Harold Wilson announced that all British political officers and military personnel would withdraw from the Middle East and Asia by 1971.[14] Just as oil was about to flow from Dubai, just as oil was to launch a tax-free, bureaucracy-free city of limitless business opportunity, the British government fixed a unilateral end date to its supposedly bilateral relationship with Dubai and the other Trucial States. The announcement on what became known as Black Tuesday rattled Sheikh Rashid's plans to create a new oil-subsidized city. As constricting as the supposed truces had been, they had been essential in creating the Dubai that existed and was planned to be. Wilson's news threatened the boom his government had helped instigate. David Roberts, the political agent at the time, conceded the announcement was "a blow" to Sheikh Rashid's ambitions.[15]

Within a month, British officers stationed in Dubai and Abu Dhabi were focused only on withdrawal. They hastily arranged for Sheikh Zayed bin Sultan Al Nahyan of Abu Dhabi and Sheikh Rashid to meet and agree to "the formation of a Union of the two countries under one flag."[16] British officials urged the two leaders to invite the other Trucial sheikhdoms to join. The meeting was a historic but nominal gesture to the rest of the region and to the rest of the world that a new United Nations–recognized nation was taking shape. Even though some observers considered Dubai the logical future capital, the British Foreign Office, which saw itself as the author of this new nation, eventually and resolutely backed Abu Dhabi for the role, with Sheikh Zayed as the first president.[17]

In 1969, Dubai earned $376,114 in petroleum profits; Abu Dhabi earned nearly $180 million.[18] Two days after the two rulers met, the British Bank of the Middle East made an unethical disclosure, in "strict confidence," to the political agent in Abu Dhabi: Sheikh Zayed had transferred £1.5 million to Sheikh Rashid's account. Two days later, Zayed forwarded more money to Dubai's electric company, which was then struggling with blackouts and considering an increase to its subsidized rates. By bailing Rashid out of a potential embarrassment, Zayed let him know who would lead the new nation.[19] In creating this new nation, wealth constituted political power.

In a seeming paradox, Dubai's indeterminate status—neither state nor colony, an urban port unbeholden to ideas and laws of nations—had determined its physical forms and financial strategies. Nondefinition as an entrepôt had ultimately worked to Dubai's advantage. The city's contentious gold trade, and most of its re-export trade for that matter, ran in defiance of international trade norms. More than simply benefiting Dubai's economy, its in-betweenness had benefited the economies of the British and others too. The entrepôt trade both *made* the city cosmopolitan and exploited the profits from the city's *being* cosmopolitan. Nationhood, especially with Abu Dhabi as the capital, would not accommodate a port that flouted all regulations outside of its own. A nation-state must instead fulfill outside expectations. It is limited to one capital, one leader, one anthem. In becoming part of the United Arab Emirates, Dubai was summoned to harden into a recognizable form that the British government had staved off for a century and a half.

From the day he agreed to swift federation with Sheikh Zayed, Dubai's Sheikh Rashid outwardly claimed to embrace the idea of a new nation, but his actions proved only otherwise. One political agent referred to Rashid's "wickedness" in trying to bribe people from the five Northern Trucial states to emigrate from their own Shaikhdoms to Dubai where, he promised them, they would have free house, free water, free electricity and a present of RS. 25,000.[20]

Rashid's incentives, the British officer claimed, threatened to depopulate the sheikhdoms north of Dubai in order to concentrate the region's merchant wealth and manpower in Dubai. These tactics were nothing new for Rashid; he had incessantly devised ways to keep trade activity, and wealth, not only in Dubai but out of Sharjah and Abu Dhabi. He had been known, for example, to threaten any Dubai merchant who might consider conducting business from a lesser port on the coast.[21] Rashid's laissez-faire policy therefore had its limits when it came to protecting Dubai's regional preeminence. The political agency had at least tacitly condoned Rashid's protectionist tactics because concentrating trade in Dubai also matched their "Dubai model," but now that model no longer supported the British exit strategy.

ETERNAL FLAME, BOUNDLESS SEA

Besides corralling regional trade to its port, the leaders of Dubai tried to insulate their independence by getting petroleum quickly to global markets. They saw their city-state status quickly slipping away and therefore put their fate in the hands of oilmen and engineers. The more oil produced, the more wealth Dubai's leadership could claim and therefore the more independence it could assert. Oil companies were pushed to find more oil, but findings did not come close to Abu Dhabi's.

Another strategy was to announce Dubai's arrival into the oil market. By the late 1960s, oil companies had a practiced run-up for how to commemorate a new petroleum state: photo ops, VIP events, corporate films, newspaper supplements, monuments, and imported fireworks. For Dubai, these events added up to a campaign to protect its professed role as a singular port in the world. A celebration was planned.

Continental Oil Company delegated the ceremonies to a company that already had a formula for announcing oil states: British Petroleum. On October 12, 1969, Dubai's first luxury hotel, the Carlton, was booked for VIPs. Festivities weren't for the general public; instead, they were planned for oil-industry

FIGURE 8.4 The clock tower, once a symbol of British imposition, was by the 1960s a necessary component of many Gulf cities as an expression of modernization. In 1963, Syrian engineer Zaki Al Homsi designed one for Dubai, allegedly as a gift from the ruler of Qatar. Residents reported that the four clock faces gave four different times. Courtesy John R. Harris Library.

experts, representatives from associated industries, their spouses, and important local leaders. That evening Sheikh Rashid hosted a dinner with British-import fireworks but no "social entertainment."[22]

The next morning, guests were escorted by motorcade beyond the city's busiest intersection, the Clock Tower Roundabout, to what was supposed to be its next monumental space: the Flame Roundabout. Police closed the roundabout so that guests could gather under a flag-draped canopy for a reading from the Koran, a speech by Rashid's son Hamdan, a band playing Dubai's "national anthem," and the unveiling of Dubai's monument to oil. It was a four-meter-high steel abstraction, described by one witness as "buff pink," something reminiscent of two Moorish arches intersecting at ninety-degree angles. In the vestibule underneath created by the two arches, Sheikh Rashid lit what was billed as an eternal flame symbolically fed by Dubai's bountiful oil supply.[23] The entire party then made the short drive back toward town to the air-conditioned Deira Cinema.

There they sat for a screening of *Dubai*, an English-language industrial film commissioned by British Petroleum. The British director Rodney Giesler was hired to document how oil profits were delivering a modern city.[24] Having made a similar film for Kuwait's oil company, Giesler had only a few months to produce this one. In his treatment, he imagines capturing a vibrant city with a "furious montage"—morning rush hour, people "swarming" off water taxis, phones "being snatched up," letters "torn open," "teleprinters chattering into life." He describes Dubai as a "miniature united nations" of people, where the Pepsi Cola factory keeps thirsts quenched, and an old house collapses to make way for "a piece of modern Mediterranean architecture." Dubai on the go.

Not as "furious" at Giesler promised, and at times even lethargic, the film splits Dubai's history into two parts, with oil's discovery as the pivot between them. The first act presents a pre-engineered Dubai, harsh and unlivable, where a man could die "in a matter of hours." Dubai was "utterly neglected by nature." Its residents relied on ingenuity to survive. The Gulf's waters are established as the film's guiding metaphor: "The desert offered Dubai nothing, so it had to turn to the sea." First the Gulf waters provided fish, then pearls, then maritime trade. In this way, according to the film, Dubai developed "by its own efforts."

Dubai's residents had improved their lives by gradual steps of improvement. Solving water scarcity, for example, was achieved by merely digging a hole. The film praises Sheikh Rashid for taking larger steps, for example, in saving Dubai Creek. The Canadian narrator's North American accent skirts any hint of British colonial history and proposes a revised history. Just as the US State Department's report had done before it, the film scrubs out the British political agency's role in first hampering Dubai's trade growth and then later pushing its urban development. According to George Curzon in 1903, British ships had once "found strife and . . . created order," but now that role was reinvented for petroleum engineers.[25] With the profits from trade, Dubai's merchants were able to "buy skills to develop Dubai further." And those purchases made more purchases possible. Dubai's history, as the film tells it, is a gradual subjection to expertise; the more bought, the greater the profits and the larger the "sophisticated and cosmopolitan community," including "engineers, accountants, surveyors, teachers, architects, doctors."

After supplying fish, pearls, and trade routes in the first act, the sea delivers offshore fields of oil in the film's second act. Oil and post-oil development subsequently require the ingenuity of more engineers. Giesler was able to film the Chicago Beach ceremony; he set the scene to a soundtrack of trumpets. The trumpets are one example of the director struggling and stumbling to present engineers and oil development photogenically. Instead of impressive construction sites, the film captures a tedious meeting where Mahdi Al Tajir translates a British engineer's presentation to the ruler. Similar air-conditioned interiors further define the second act. A heavy-eyed man smokes a cigarette while he waits for a telex to finish printing. A couple dines on too much food at an awkwardly staged table on a club's dance floor. The interiors are climate-controlled; they are not the "swarming" and "furious" ambience Giesler had pitched in his treatment. The film searches for the photogenic in a city where the principal attraction is the selling of abstracted emptiness, the chance to cut a profit from making something out of nothing.

Dubai is pitched as "a challenge for engineers." The film's narrative, not unlike the Foreign Office's film *These Are the Trucial States*, is about how a hostile environment is made habitable by work ethic. This time, it is the work of engineers and financers who deplane at Dubai's airport. Now that "the oil industry has arrived," there needed to be new rules of order and systemization.

The film does not conclude by discovering the new city made possible by oil profits, primarily because there is hardly anything to film in the new city, at least not yet. The film celebrates more of what does not exist: "taxes and form-filling" and "red tape." The film's ending is the city's beginning as an unimpeded post-petroleum metropolis, free from "a bureaucracy that most of the outside world is saddled with." In the future, solutions are not political by nature; they are a marriage of engineering and financing. The film's final words are a warning, composed as a question, to Rashid and his tight circle of advisors: "Now that the oil industry has arrived," would Rashid "still be able to attend to the smallest detail of government?" The film's advocacy for updating Dubai's one-person rule is the planeloads of arriving experts: "The many foreigners who have come to work here have been accepted by Dubai with characteristic ease and goodwill."

The audience at Deira Cinema applauded the film, but they were more than just passive viewers: They helped to write the plot. As the film's protagonists, they were "bringing their skills and presenting their advice" to a place portrayed as defective and hopeless: They were the ones delivering, and profiting from, Dubai's modernization; not only did they create Dubai's current success, but they also dictated its next steps.

After the film, lunch was served at the home of Mahdi Al Tajir in high-end Jumeirah, but it was hurried. Soon enough they were back with the motorcade, moving along the stream of posh new villas overtaking Jumeirah's waterfront. The motorcade veered off the main road and onto sand roads for the next event.

The day's final performance was scheduled to take place in the glare of an open, unadorned shoreline, not far from Chicago Beach, at the peak of the afternoon sun. Guests had been more comfortable in the air-conditioned cinema. Now their dress shoes filled with sand, and salty air stung their perfumed necks. Hats weren't really in fashion, so bald spots were exposed to the sun. As the invited guests found their balance in the sand, each of the motorcade's drivers stood next to his car, ready to take guests back to the hotel rooms as soon as the event was over. Participants were instructed to wait and keep focused on the Gulf waters that hardly moved, a low leaden stratum that extended to the indiscernible horizon. They tried to block the sun's glare with slightly cupped hands over their brows, like limp salutes.

The approaching climax was heard before it was seen. Two DC-3 airplanes materialized from the north along the coast, over the construction site of Port Rashid, and headed toward the assembly. When they were nearly overhead, the aircrafts veered right, out toward the sea and the source of the afternoon glare. From under their shaded eyes, the guests watched the planes grow smaller, maybe wondering whether they would come back or drop some parachutists or release some colored smoke. None of these happened. The planes had been hired as pointers, simply to direct the guests to look outward in the direction of Fateh Field and its submerged khazzan. With little else to be seen, there was only the diminishing effect of the low-flying DC-3s. Guests gazed at the same uninflected haze witnessed by the khazzan's celebrants a few months earlier at Chicago Beach. If there was much to be imagined, there was little to be seen. Oil executives were nevertheless satisfied with the "splendour" of the day.[26]

Giesler's celebratory film captured a storyline being gathered and made real in British newspapers, one that failed to dim in response to the political inevitability of the British departure and the imminent creation of the United Arab Emirates. Referring to the recurring blend of advertisements, cheerful reporting, and "advertorials," the political agent Julian Bullard called Dubai a "magnet" for good-news business stories in British newspapers like the *Financial Times* and the London *Times*.[27] Rashid's advisors and marketing consultants helped organize special supplements to the dailies that heralded Dubai's successes. Advertisements by companies with contracts in Dubai sponsored the supplements and claimed Dubai's achievements as their own.

With interviews of the very people profiting from a good-news story, the attending articles were also helping to draw attention away from a growing current of warnings. Disappointments could be spun with optimism: With Dubai's oil reserves failing to match Abu Dhabi's levels, they were relabeled as a "welcome asset." Dubai's economy, it was reported, "enjoys more sober hopes."[28] "Oil," it was claimed as if with relief, "will not wrest [Dubai's regional] entrepôt status."[29]

Rashid had once gone to London with a rather naive brochure about his city; within a couple of years' time, Dubai was the subject of sophisticated public relations efforts. English-language media readily exalted a "swinging little emirate," whose pluck and flexibility sustained a prospering enterprise in global trade.[30] The news articles were quick to supply readers with impressive statistics about Dubai's growth, but Bullard challenged the legitimacy of these numbers likely sourced from Mahdi Al Tajir's office. Conflicting or questionable financial figures, however, did not stop stories that praised Dubai as an "outstanding example of self-help" that was "[lifting] itself up by its boot-straps."[31]

MORE LIKE ANY OTHER ARAB CITY

The political agent Julian Bullard read Dubai differently. As he saw it, the city's threadbare bureaucracy could hardly manage its day-to-day business, let alone its oil wealth. Financial management, overseen by a single British advisor, barely existed. Management of the city, in general, was no better. The water sources tapped thirty kilometers outside the city would not be able to sustain residents for much longer. Sewage and drainage systems regularly overflowed.[32] Garbage collection was still considered at a "crude stage," performed "by laborers using push carts." Millions were being spent on delivering electricity in slipshod ways to the city's older districts, producing "overhead spaghetti" looming over narrow streets. With the demand for electricity ever increasing, there were regular blackouts in a city once touted for avoiding them.[33] Dubai, according to Bullard, was becoming "more like any other Arab city."[34]

Even as Port Rashid's berths became available, the steel-and-concrete edges of Dubai Creek were still attracting large numbers of ships, and the municipality steadily increased storage surcharges to make sure that cargo moved out fast.[35] But it didn't happen fast enough: Shipowners were automatically slapping a 15-percent surcharge on all shipments to Dubai because of notorious offloading delays. Quick-build warehouses and Quonset huts squeezed in where they could to absorb arriving cargo.

The harbor and the road infrastructure around the creek were not just pressed by Dubai's demands. Just as the British agency MEDD had predicted in response to the 1960 town plan, access to the harbor was strangled by mounting traffic. The single bridge and all roads out of Dubai were clogged with trucks also supplying the petroleum-fueled boom in Abu Dhabi, whose port was "unworkable for all practical purposes."[36] New expectations of city life—schools, cinemas, fire stations, a public library, a museum, and a printing press—were being wedged into the urban fabric around the creek.[37] They followed no plan, just expedience.

Dubai was "fast losing the simplicity and harmony which used to be one of its main attractions."[38] Expansion also brought vice. By 1974, Dubai reached scales not seen before: 2,917 reported crimes, of which 462 were drug

FIGURE 8.5 Congestion in Dubai exposed the difficulty of keeping older districts up-to-date and accessible for car traffic. Increasing amounts of the city's proposed developments were for this reason planned beyond the built-up city. Courtesy John R. Harris Library.

and alcohol related; three murders; eight rapes; and twenty-one "unnatural offences"; 974 people went to jail.[39] New roads led not only to more traffic jams but also to more deadly pile-ups.

There was also grave economic disparity. "Ragged urchins" were a common presence in Dubai's streets, and, while

> the economy of Dubai . . . rests on the lean backs of illegal immigrant laborers from Iran, Pakistan and Baluchistan who shovel sand and carry bags of cement for seven riyals a day, . . . [there] are hundreds of businessmen, many of them quite young, most of them from Europe or the Levant, who think nothing of spending £20 or £30 on a night's entertainment.[40]

One world toiled in the heat; the other handled phone lines to London and Beirut in air-controlled environments.

A decade before, in the early 1960s, Dubai's leadership had collaborated with British officials and their stock of consulting experts to found a municipal bureaucracy and to establish a land registry; a road network; a reliable port; and lines for water, electricity, and telecommunications. In 1969, Dubai's municipal government counted 1,500 employees, of which more than 1,000 worked for the police and customs. The municipality itself counted no more than 150 employees, the bulk of whom were menial laborers. The municipal advisory council had been shut down without major consequences. About a quarter of the municipality's leadership was British but now paid a salary by Dubai's government.

By the 1970s, British newspapers celebrated Dubai's "skeleton administration," though it could not keep up with demands for municipal services.[41] For a city quickly approaching 100,000 residents, the state of municipal management should have been alarming. Bullard alerted his superiors that the laissez-faire domain that Rashid's champions praised

> is rapidly outgrowing him, or rather outgrowing his methods. . . . Can this form of government continue much longer, as Dubai expands and problems multiply? I fear not. Is there not a need already for a more systematic administration, depending less on personalities and more on delegated authority? I think there is. But will Rashid agree to changes of this kind? Again, I fear not, or at least if he does, the changes will tend to be too few, too small and too late.[42]

Oil was not going to solve Dubai's administrative problems. In 1969, a British merchant banker consulted Bullard on whether Sheikh Rashid was good for a $20 million loan. The political agent extended "an encouraging answer," claiming that at the time he could safely estimate that Dubai's oil reserves would keep Dubai solvent for another couple of years. By 1970, Bullard's report makes clear that he would not be as confident if asked the same question again.

Bullard regularly warned his superiors that the city was at financial risk: "Money is pretty short in Dubai." Trade fell in recession, and costs for major infrastructure projects like Port Rashid continued to mount. Halcrow, the main consultant for Port Rashid, was owed £150,000, and its resident representative Neville Allen threatened to leave town.[43] It would take the oil company's tripling its oil production that year to keep Sheikh Rashid solvent.[44]

Despite the cash problem, new projects were pursued with abandon. Bullard reported that much of the havoc was the work of Rashid's closest advisor Mahdi Al Tajir, who was suspected of pocketing under-the-table commissions for new projects and preparing to "decamp to Europe or the United States" with his "vast fortune."[45] J. C. Kelly, the Dubai manager for British Bank of the Middle East, warned Bullard that he found Rashid "woefully ignorant" of his current and projected oil revenues. It was intimated that Tajir was the only person in Dubai who knew Dubai's income status. Bullard reported that if there were not clearer income and expenditure sheets, Rashid's projects would start to run into trouble with uneasy lenders. Within the span of a few years, opinion of Rashid's approach to his finances had gone from trustworthy to troubled to perilous.

Bullard's superior in Bahrain issued a grimmer report: The group of emirates headed for federation was "unlikely to survive, but no one is willing to be responsible for killing it."[46] The political agent no longer had informal access to the ring of advisors around Rashid; his advice was not sought. To prepare his cohorts for Sheikh Rashid's visit to London in 1969, Bullard provided talking points so that they might encourage Rashid toward a more "systematic basis" for administering Dubai. "We do not want to seem to be trying to interfere," he suggests, "but we wonder whether Your Highness would consider setting aside either one day a week, or perhaps better certain hours every day, perhaps until 10 a.m., for receiving the heads of your own government departments?"[47] He points also to "social problems" and the reemergence of "subversive elements" as a result of Dubai's lax immigration policies. None of these issues were brought up in meetings with Sheikh Rashid.

The Foreign Office had historically considered Dubai's economic viability as a key to the region's stability, but the city's prosperity had sunk to a lower priority by 1968. Britain's focus remained on the creation of the United Arab Emirates. Rashid, as a result, was a free man in his rush to secure Dubai's regional economic dominance, however riskily he chose to do that.

A NEW PLAN

If Bullard's concerns were administrative, John Harris's were spatial. The latter observed a city losing its bearings and sought to restructure "the continuing development of Dubai along reasonable lines."[48] He petitioned for the opportunity to update Dubai's town plan. The 1960 plan had been called "elaborate" and "utterly unrealistic."[49] It was now unrealistic for an entirely different set of reasons.

The town plan had envisaged a city of one-story buildings, an idea being contradicted on the ground before the plan was even issued. At best, the plan had provided the roadways along which the vigor of a feverish real estate market was supposed to align. Instead of neighborhood units of one-story villas, there were residential blocks that reached four stories and higher. Building was limited less by municipal control than by available financing and construction team experience. The absence of elevators also restricted building heights.[50] The spaces that the plan designated for schools, parks, and community centers had been consumed in the real estate frenzy. They held too much financial potential to be left for a municipal government with no money to fund public amenities. The wide buffer zones designed to isolate neighborhood units from fast-moving traffic were also real estate too valuable to give up. If they didn't supply much-needed parking, then they were converted into development sites.

Cleared, delineated plots were the deal sweeteners for the ruler's stream of curious foreign investors. They were also the free subsidy that the municipality wielded to coax people off of their properties so that new roads could be laid.[51] Usually, only people deemed nationals were eligible for such deals. Real estate development, either in older districts or on land provided in the new planned districts, was an easy way for Dubai's less-wealthy nationals to participate in Dubai's real estate bonanza. Construction materials arriving at the port fused into their new, and often inferior, concrete buildings that housed shops and leasable apartments. Dubai's other residents sought shelter in the new apartment blocks, if not in the informal districts beyond.

Municipal workers did their best to enforce a building code written by Harris's office.[52] Still, most results were nondescript shells hidden behind

FIGURE 8.6 After vacating its first Dubai office at the Rashid Hospital construction site, John R. Harris & Partners moved to this building on Deira's Cinema Square. The office is an example of how Dubai's apartment buildings were necessarily functioning as offices. Courtesy John R. Harris Library.

signage and air conditioning window units; their life expectancies counted in months, not years. High rents helped buildings amortize quickly. Beyond the fact that new districts lost the coherence of a neighborhood unit, the buildings themselves blurred the line between office space and residential space. It was all too common to find company representatives transforming their personal apartments into business offices the next morning.

When Harris delivered the first town plan, he communicated directly with Sheikh Rashid. The two drove together around the city's unbuilt outskirts to explore how Harris's plan would be realized. This time Harris addressed overworked bureaucrats in Deira's municipal offices. Despite the municipality's small staff, it managed to create a bureaucratic hierarchy that stood between Harris and the ruler. John Darby, whom Harris claimed to have recommended for the position, directed the minimal planning staff in the recently established Engineering Office. Darby's planning staff counted one town planner, one surveyor, and two draftsmen, whose workload of reviewing development proposals allowed them scarce time for planning and analysis. They mostly responded to urgency, giving rash sign-offs to new development proposals and fending off accusations that their review processes thwarted Dubai's progress. Nevertheless, in May 1971, Harris put before the Engineering Office his new master plan, a document that asked them to slow down when they were under chronic pressure to speed up. It is a wonder that a new town plan could have even been considered.

The previous plan had been criticized for not having been based on any analysis or calculated forecasts about Dubai's future population and needs. There had, for example, been no assessment of future car-ownership rates or projections about the city's employment sectors. The 1971 development plan attempted a quantified lay of the land, though with no new analysis to back it up. It admitted there were no accurate population numbers available (three years after the first census) but estimated that the total population was "approaching 100,000." It published a nearly even male–female ratio, 51–49, likely inaccurate. And it projected a population of 200,000 by 1981 (closer to 300,000 by then).[53]

As if informed by Bullard's skepticism about municipal statistics, the plan gave little attention to them either. Without reliable demographic, traffic, and economic statistics, the plan could hardly assert a bold position. It noted that imminent nationhood, seven months away from when the plan was published, "will undoubtedly have considerable effects on the planning and development of Dubai." Those "considerable effects" remain unspecified in the plan, because there was little way for the architect to know what would happen. Oft-used oil-production figures—including the forecast of reaching a daily production quota of 300,000 barrels—were not referenced to ascertain how much income the city would be generating or how many migrants the work opportunities would attract. The plan mostly referred to Dubai as a town, but twice it defiantly called Dubai "Capital City," just as the 1960 plan had. Named both a town and a capital city, Dubai harbored a future once again beyond analysis.

One certainty was that the city had surrendered to the automobile. In 1965 Harris had observed that Dubai was still a city where "the main form of movement" was pedestrian, but in the new plan he noted the

"impressive" unfurling of new roads that dominated the city. Harris expressed no concern with replicating roundabouts and stretching build-outs
of major roads. This time, the buffer zones around districts were not to
protect precious neighborhood units from the ills of automobile traffic.
Rather, they were retained for the city's next growth surge. They were the
rights-of-way for the city's "future flyovers."[54] While the plan nominally
recognized the city's "limited" bus service, a possible monorail, and the
creek's abra ferries, Harris advised that building and maintaining roadways
were the sufficient means by which Dubai could manage growth, both as
circulation and as access to future development sites. As opposed to the
political agent, Harris expressed little concern about traffic congestion.
Roads would continue to expand, according to Harris, not just to alleviate
traffic but also to stimulate more development. Extending roadways and
increasing car ownership might eventually lead to necessary measures
to "restrict" car use, but for the time being, Dubai functioned just fine,
pursuing its ongoing roll-out of asphalt, roundabouts, and flared entries
to accommodate the city's increasing number of cars.

Harris accepted Dubai's expanding roadways. He just wanted to manage
the direction in which they were drawn. By hardening roads with asphalt
at the lowest of standards, the municipality maintained the fast pace of
roadbuilding that stretched Dubai's urban boundaries.[55] Dubai no longer
kept a coherent shape. It leapt forward as quickly as the roads let it. Cars
were accumulating on new blacktop roads at congestion-inducing rates. And
they were parked on the sandy surfaces Harris had intended as green spaces.

To counter those tendencies, Harris endorsed ring roads around the creek
as the "foundations of a proper start." Restricting Dubai's major roadways
to a series of ring roads would provide Dubai a course toward "safe development." The limits would also help coordinate the utility infrastructure,
such as water and electricity lines, that extended along the roads. If Dubai
maintained a commitment to ring roads, then municipal services could more
easily respond to development along predictable and coordinated geom-
etries. Being able to accurately predict the locations of future development,
the municipality could more readily supply the needed utility connections,
thereby "continuing development of Dubai along reasonable lines."

Without discouraging the use of cars, Harris still wanted to rein the city in, back to where it had started. The plan maintained Dubai Creek as the city's enduring "focal point" and "centre of activity," "both from a functional and an aesthetic viewpoint." While development was already conspicuously spreading beyond the creek and while more than half of Port Rashid's berths were operational, the document asserts that Dubai Creek was still "where marine activity continues to flourish."[56]

In an interview for the local weekly *Akhbar Dubai* a few years after the plan's issuance, Harris referred to "the development ring of Dubai" as the city's central organizing factor.[57] From Harris's point of view, the 1960 town plan had defined the first ring road by connecting main circulation routes of the new town areas by means of Al Maktoum Bridge. Further outlying roads, linked by bridges and a tunnel, would keep the two sides stitched together and maintain Dubai Creek as the city's geographic and symbolic center. The 1971 plan suggested three new links further inland and confirmed the tunnel that Halcrow had proposed at the creek's mouth.

Circling ring roads around Dubai Creek allowed Harris to stress that Dubai had a city center, particularly one with valuable historical heritage. No fewer than five pages of the document's sixty pages were dedicated to preserving Dubai's buildings that predated 1960. These historical buildings had "an intrinsic value, an undeniable attraction, an unquestioned harmony: none of which are measurable but all of which contribute to the fascination exerted by Dubai and its Creek." Harris recommended a registry for historical buildings, and Al Fahidi Fort was designated to become a museum. These buildings, the plan asserted, would be the historic core of the city and, lucratively, an attraction for the thousands coming into Dubai's airport.

In addition to historic preservation, Harris insisted on correcting an omission that he'd been forced to defer during Hawley's term as political agent—a civic center. Harris argued for "a prestige area" at the creek, on the Deira side, that would keep the city's focus at its origins. The civic center's architectural features were a theater, an assembly hall, and a public library with a verdant courtyard garden. A "prestigious quay for ceremonial occasions" was proposed along an "inlet of water from the Creek." A bus terminal

and a pedestrian ferry terminal were to further emphasize the centripetal role the center should have on Dubai. Within the "development ring," all transit led to Harris's proposed civic center.

Although the plan recognized the emergence of new districts that reached beyond Harris's proposed development rings, it insisted that the city's future expansion would continue in concentric circles around the old harbor. Jumeirah's "high-class residential accommodation," even if it was interrupted by the cranes and bulldozers of Port Rashid, attracted Dubai's wealthiest and most influential to live apart from the active city.[58] Their choice threatened Harris's idea of a city centered around the creek. As a counterbalance to this pull of the upper-end market to the margins, Harris's plan proposed other sites for housing Dubai's wealthiest expatriates, including around his proposed civic center and near the British political agency. Further inland, where the creek was "widening out more as a lake," Harris's plan proposed marina-themed residences, even artificial islands. None of these, including the civic center complex, was realized in the end.

Bur Dubai and Deira were already becoming what they are largely today: mixed-use districts for middle-class apartment blocks and very compact accommodations for workers. Those who could not afford Bur Dubai and Deira had the "self-built" districts further out. The "third-class" housing district designated in the 1960 plan had by now been cleared and designated for local residents and rental-market housing. The 1971 plan identified three recent areas for Dubai's most indigent residents' "temporary housing": Al Safa, inland from the Chicago Beach site, and Al Qsais and Kartun, both located near the Sharjah border.[59] All of these were located on the outermost reaches of Dubai's development, demonstrating how planned districts for Dubai's poorest migrant workers would continue to be situated in relation to the city—outside it.[60]

< **FIGURE 8.7** More than once, John Harris urged the municipality to pursue a commercial and civic center. This design, proposed in 1965, may have been incorporated into Harris's 1971 master plan, with the civic center located at Dubai Creek. It included shopping, restaurants, offices, and elevated pedestrian paths. Courtesy John R. Harris Library and Henk Snoek / RIBA Collections.

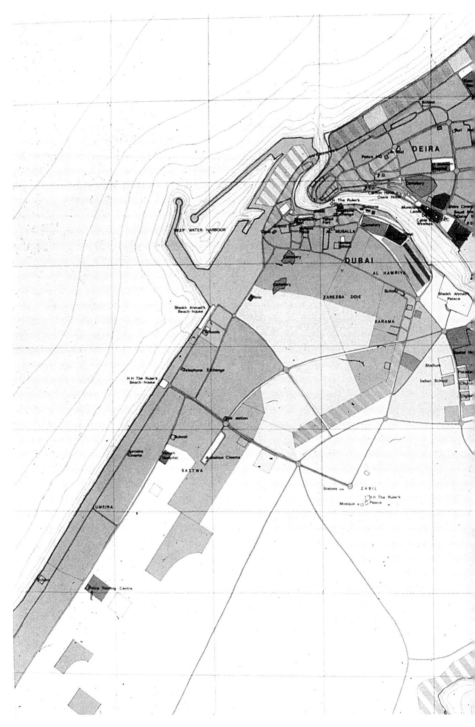

FIGURE 8.8 The 1971 illustrative Dubai Development Plan, John R. Harris & Partners. The illustrative plan seems to contradict the plan's written component. Courtesy John R. Harris Library.

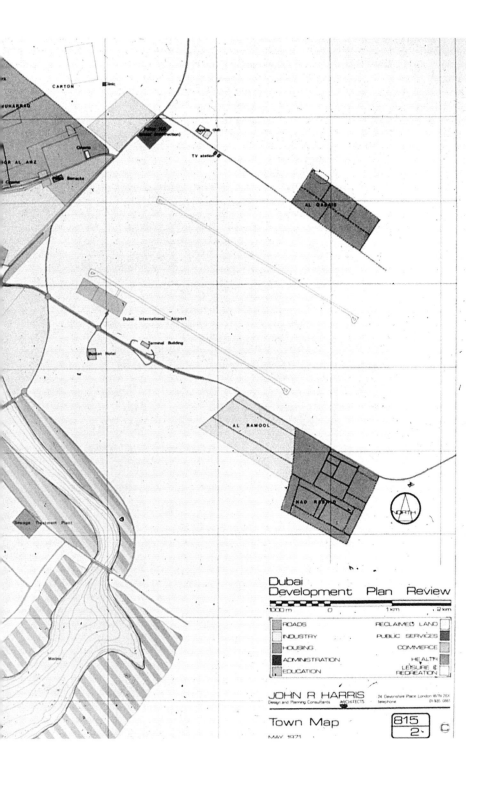

CARTON

MUHARRAQ

GR AL ARZ

AL GARAIS

TV station

Dubai International Airport

Terminal Building

Hotel

AL RAMOOL

HAD REBHO

NORTH

Sewage Treatment Plant

Marina

Dubai
Development Plan Review

1000 m   0   1 km   2 km

ROADS   RECLAIMED LAND
INDUSTRY   PUBLIC SERVICES
HOUSING   COMMERCE
ADMINISTRATION   HEALTH
EDUCATION   LEISURE &
                         RECREATION

JOHN R HARRIS   24 Devonshire Place London W1N 2DX
Design and Planning Consultants ARCHITECTS   telephone   01-935 0861

Town Map

815
2

C

MAY 1971

COGNITIVE DISSONANCE

There was an intrinsic contradiction in Harris's 1971 plan. On one hand, the plan proposed a responsible and legible urbanism, centered around the creek; and on the other hand, it acquiesced to the investment-driven survival strategy it could not counter. The 1971 plan's written component conveys the pursuit of organization and of gathering the city around Dubai Creek. In stark contrast, the illustrative plan outlines the undeniable direction of Dubai's sprawl that reached southwesterly toward where the khazzan had been launched and further. In the written version, Harris described the city he wanted. In the illustrative plan, he presented the city of unstoppable financial forces. If the written version represented Harris's moderate calls for appreciating Dubai's historical character and regulating how the new and necessary interacted with that character, and if it was focused on distributing Dubai's population growth and urban expansion into legible, car-friendly districts encircling Dubai Creek, then the illustrative plan succumbed to the fervent clambering for new and unobstructed terrain away from Dubai Creek.

Instead of demonstrating how a creek-centered city might grow, the illustrative plan drew the eye toward the new city's blank spaces, toward areas of easy expansion unrestrained by municipal orders and tight, expensive development plots. The illustrative plan was simple, providing broad-stroke land-use designations and identifying an expanded road network much of which had already been paved through Halcrow's road construction contracts. The land-use designations provided included industry, housing, administration, and commerce. Some new and proposed designations were marked on the plan, but Harris laid out mostly what was already existing or planned.

More noteworthy were those parts where there was no designation—the white blankness—where land flanking the extended roadways was unburdened by the planner's swatches of color. The blankness was Dubai's future. This was the terrain of Rashid's new city, attached to the hopes of the launched khazzan. This would be where Dubai's most memorable development would occur, isolated from the planner's restraints. Well beyond Dubai Creek, blankness signaled boundlessness, an avowed freedom from history and expectations, where "the desert yields to the tarmac."[61]

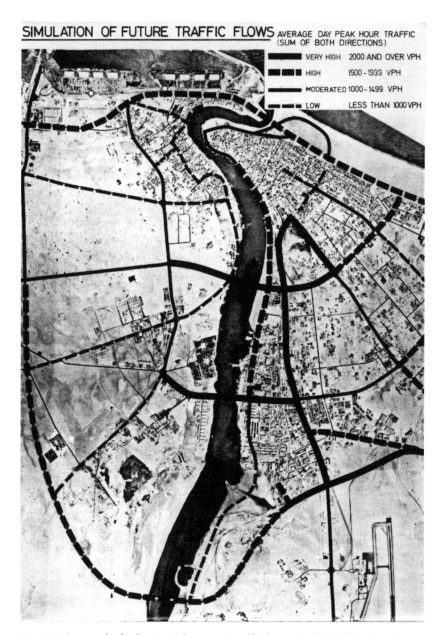

SIMULATION OF FUTURE TRAFFIC FLOWS AVERAGE DAY PEAK HOUR TRAFFIC
(SUM OF BOTH DIRECTIONS)

VERY HIGH 2000 AND OVER VPH
HIGH 1500 - 1999 VPH
MODERATED 1000 - 1499 VPH
LOW LESS THAN 1000 VPH

FIGURE 8.9 An example of a planning study commissioned by the municipality. Well into the 1980s, Dubai's municipal planners continued to envision a city that remained anchored around Dubai Creek, based on Harris's "development of rings." At the same time, the city's built form defiantly reached south in the direction of Abu Dhabi, as a result of Sheikh Rashid and his advisors' investment negotiations. Courtesy Anastase Emmanuel.

The illustrative plan compressed the city's existing center—its density in high contrast to the blankness—into a barely legible portion of the drawing. The roads of the "development ring" were hardly traceable. The plan did not even locate Harris's proposed civic center on Dubai Creek. Blankness prevailed, traversed by the tendrils of roadways that edge—lower left—in the direction of Abu Dhabi. Such graphical handling, or mishandling, made no effort to negate Dubai's surrender to the seemingly open terrain Harris, in words, tried to resist.

Harris believed that a city of ring roads around the creek could accommodate an increasing reliance on cars. It turned out that the automobile had no difficulty in following the roads that seemed to dangle outwardly from the city's core toward Abu Dhabi. Harris's plan, as expansive as it was beyond the creek, still only captured a fraction of just how far Dubai could go. The plan's edges did not frame the city; instead they cut it off, suggesting that the new extended roads continued to unfurl beyond the page's edges. One line led gingerly toward the bottom of the plan's frame, parallel to the coast. It is what Harris referred to in the plan as "the Abu Dhabi road." At the time, it was a two-lane road for most of its stretches. Mentioned only once in the plan, its near absence betrayed the plan's dissonance with an imminent reality. The road would soon become the city's organizational spine—Sheikh Zayed Road.

SCATTERED

In 1977, a report from the United States Agency for International Development (USAID) criticized Dubai's development as "scattered in such a manner as to leave large areas of land undeveloped."[62] The lines of roadways of the 1971 master plan that stretched to the margins had by then performed as conduits, like skeletal vertebrae, onto which newer and larger projects could attach. And Rashid was prepared to dole out land for new investment proposals, ignoring any limits his municipal planning unit tried to create. Rashid's brokering of new sites was another cause of stress for the municipality's planners, who constantly had to respond to the ruler's uncoordinated negotiations with investors and developers.[63] Since new roads inevitably attracted new development, the city had to line them with the expected utility

FIGURE 8.10 The Dubai Metropolitan Hotel, John R. Harris & Partners' contribution to Dubai's new city being developed on the orders of Sheikh Rashid along the Abu Dhabi road, which later became Sheikh Zayed Road. In 1984, a British engineering office was contracted to give the hotel a £2 million face-lift, which included red pitched roofs. Courtesy John R. Harris Library.

lines for electricity, water, and telephone. Dubai's growth, unhinged from Harris's "base for sound development," burdened an understaffed administration unable to guess at the city's next primary growth corridors because there were too many possibilities to follow.

Harris's office succumbed to the idea of the new city, agreeing to design a hotel for a site well beyond the "development of rings," on the future Sheikh Zayed Road. Around the time of USAID's "scattered" comment, the Dubai-based developer Khalaf Al Habtoor, with whom Harris's firm had worked on later phases of Rashid Hospital, commissioned Harris to design a new resort hotel. The site had little more than the two-lane Abu Dhabi road with which to orient itself. Habtoor's hotel would stand where the only visible signs of occupation were a shed and a dumpsite of tread-worn tires. The Metropolitan Hotel was designed to be self-sustaining, replete with restaurants, shops, gardens, and its own cinema. Its pool was wrapped in a wall to separate it from the desert, its only context being the desert sky. The basement housed

Dubai's first "members only" night club. By the 1980s, however, additional construction sprawled toward Al Habtoor's location, and the hotel was no longer so distant from the city.

Khalaf Al Habtoor is often hailed for his grasp of the direction in which Dubai's development was heading, aided by his own telling in his 2012 autobiography. His decision to place a hotel along the Abu Dhabi road, fifteen kilometers away from Dubai Creek, is the often-cited evidence of his foresight. When asked in 2016 about how he selected the site, though, he shrugged his shoulders and kept his answer short: "Because Sheikh Rashid told me to build a hotel there."[64] According to him, Dubai's ruler selected not only the site but also the kind of development. Al Habtoor's answer seemed less deferential to a deceased leader than simply matter-of-fact, about a site whose soaring value convinced him to eventually demolish the hotel for an exponentially larger scheme. By following Rashid's direction toward the blankness rather than Harris's direction toward Dubai Creek, Al Habtoor landed a profitable enterprise as a real estate magnate.

After Harris's submission, the city planners determined a no-build line for the city just beyond the limits of Harris's plan and the Metropolitan Hotel. For the hotel project and others after it, the suggestion of a no-build line proved too restrictive for Rashid's ambitions. Not long thereafter, sometime after 1972, the mark was superseded. Dubai's ruler claimed a development site just beyond it, where his guests in 1969 had gathered at the Chicago Bridge and Iron staging site. The vacated construction zone for the khazzans was transformed into a seven-story resort hotel with vacation-style expatriate housing attended by tennis courts, swimming pools, restaurants, and ample parking. It was called Chicago Beach Hotel.[65] It seemed Rashid wanted to demonstrate that, if oil was not the way to make Dubai wealthy, other pursuits—like real estate and tourism—could.

The bounty of opportunity that a vast real estate domain promised was too great for Harris's 1971 master plan. Land use would be designated not by decree but by financial brokering. The 1971 plan was not so much misguided as it was inapplicable to the terms of engagement formulated by Rashid and his set of key consultants. Urban planning was not replaced by economic or any other kind of planning, nor by any other kind of deliberate analysis of global and regional indicators. In the new city, Port Rashid was the first of many projects that neared and surpassed the £100 million mark. Contracts for similarly sized projects were based on assessments made by the consultants who proposed them, the loans secured on "luck [that] never deserts Sheikh Rashid for long," and the lasting impression that there was always more space for things to come.[66]

As his commission for the Metropolitan Hotel revealed, Harris was also willing to suppress his urban-planning principles for architectural work, but he would not so easily give up what he thought was his designated role as Dubai's urban planner. As more urban planners began to join the Engineering Office's staff, Harris tried to secure a third attempt at a master plan. His requests for meetings with municipal officials were met with their regrets at not having time. However, in September 1977, the Engineering Office reached out to Harris to ask for a copy of the master plan. They had misplaced theirs.[67]

FIGURE 9.1 Dubai World Trade Centre (*left*) and apartments along the Abu Dhabi road, as Jonathan Raban would have seen them in 1978. Courtesy John R. Harris Library.

CHAPTER 9

ALL IN ALL

Dubai World Trade Centre

ONE DAY IN 1978, the British travel writer Jonathan Raban sat in a taxi that barreled toward Dubai. Speed was the driver's way, and Raban agreed, to shut out the desert. Sand dunes strewn with garbage and bygone car wrecks blocked any expansive views on either side of the tarmac, at least until they approached the construction site of Dubai's World Trade Centre. As the driver slowed down to take a roundabout, Raban grappled with the sight of buildings he disdained. First, three mid-rise concrete buildings aligned to the Abu Dhabi road and then a pair of squat, box-like buildings at the base of Dubai's tallest tower, 150 meters high. Raban called the tower "smug" and dismissed it for its "slab-sided cliffs of glass and concrete."[1]

His description was less than accurate. Even if the unfinished tower was already the highest in the Middle East, the trade complex gathered into itself, concise in execution, to the point of seeming a miniature of something much larger somewhere else. What glass that had been installed by then was tucked out of view in the tower's deep concrete facade. Of the same hues as the sand around it, the buildings stood like crystalized versions of the flurrying sand surrounding them. The tower might have embodied brazen aspirations Raban resented, and it might have loomed

ominously over items no larger than a shed or a bulldozer, but it could still
be lost in a sandstorm.

TWO CITIES

Raban forgot about the trade center after he dismissed it. Soon the taxi ascended Al Maktoum Bridge, where the writer caught a glimpse below of
Dubai Creek and its choreography of wooden ships. The nearly empty roadways before the bridge became busier on the Deira side, where side streets
melded pedestrian traffic with pushcarts, bicycles, cars, and trucks. Raban
relished the old city. Dreary desert sand, Raban observed, was superseded
by an "acrid, chocolate coloured dust" that gave the city "the instantly-rec-
ognizable gravity of a place with a history."[2]

Raban instructed his driver to take him to the recently opened Intercontinental Hotel, where his room's balcony gave him "a hawk's-eye view" of the
creek's goings-on. Below, his history-infused dust mixed with diesel fumes,
sunburned cargo, and port debris. The harbor still worked, more or less, the
way it did in 1958. Halcrow's modernization scheme had extended land into
water, providing the boatmen a sandy platform for their work on land. Facilities were spartan and worn. Without the aid of machines, men still unloaded
cargo from ships into heaving piles and readied carts for deliveries to Deira
across the shoreline road. Those not on duty "crouched in pools of lamplight,
cooking things on stoves." Raban "decided that I was going to like Dubai."[3]

The Dubai Raban liked was pleasantly antiquated and seemingly un-
affected by petroleum wealth—more, as Julian Bullard had described it a
decade earlier, "like any other Arab city."[4] In fact, the Dubai that Raban portrayed hardly differed from the depictions of a bustling port in the 1950s,
when British observers admired Dubai's harbor as a tableaux for their visual
pleasure. The writer claimed Dubai's residents unwittingly enacted daily ritu-
als that rendered Dubai "picturesque." Raban's previous stop in his travels,
Abu Dhabi, was "disconcertingly brand-new" and trembled with construction
projects and infrastructural transformation. Dubai, in contrast, was "like eas-
ing oneself into a well-worn tweed jacket." He appreciated the city's golden
sunsets, the ruins of pre-concrete buildings, the crowds, and the untroubled
cafés serving sweet chai. He mixed with Iranians, Pakistanis, Palestinians,

and forlorn Brits. He wrote that Dubai Creek preserved a "beauty a kind of which European cities have lost."[5]

Raban's impression of Dubai was both perceptive and inaccurate. The year before he arrived, the *Financial Times* reported that only 16 percent of Dubai's major bank loans funded property development, compared to 42 percent in Abu Dhabi.[6] An anonymous advisor to Dubai's ruler gave the economic downturn a positive spin, "We are spending up to the hilt, but not over it."[7] In contrast, Abu Dhabi's building schedule was so out of hand that, by April 1978, the government tried banning new construction projects.[8] Abu Dhabi might have surpassed Dubai in construction frenzy, but the relative quiet that Raban perceived in Dubai followed years of accelerated growth.

In the years prior, Dubai had enjoyed a jolt of economic fervor to clear the doldrums surrounding the city's diminished role in the new United Arab Emirates. Local oil earnings quadrupled in 1974 to a half-billion dollars, a gift of the 1973 oil crisis.[9] They regalvanized not only Sheikh Rashid's personal ambitions but also those of private developers. In 1975, Dubai counted twenty-eight banks; Abu Dhabi, sixteen. The bank inflow caused unmanageable inflation, described by one journalist as a "virus" infecting all sectors. Building materials quadrupled in price within a year's time. The rental price for a three-bedroom apartment doubled in a matter of a few years.[10]

Also by the mid-1970s, a number of infrastructure projects neared completion, especially road-network extensions to which Dubai Municipality claimed to dedicate more than 90 percent of its public works budget.[11] Roads extended well beyond the old city—longer, wider, and adorned with water fountains and flower beds that "[transformed] this desert into green nurseries."[12] Halcrow had overseen the widening of Al Maktoum Bridge as well as the completion of a $10 million tunnel, which together eased traffic crossing Dubai Creek.[13] Had Raban entered Dubai just a few years earlier, he would have likely sat in a traffic jam on the bridge.

Raban entered a city where projects, like his hotel, had been initiated in a boom and now were opening in a lull. Seven years earlier, Dubai counted five hotels with a total of 252 rooms. The limited supply resulted in businessmen allegedly arriving in Dubai to discover that what they had reserved was not a room, but a bed in a shared room with strangers. Less fortunate businessmen slept on stoops and freshened up in a public restroom before making their sales pitch the next day. By 1978, there were more than 1,800 hotel beds available in the city, six times the count in 1971.[14] One result of that oversupply was that a luxury room with a "a hawk's-eye view" became affordable on a writer's budget.[15]

It was not just that Raban entered Dubai after a boom time; he also, whether or not he realized it, was enjoying a city scheduled to be left behind for new Dubai. From his hotel balcony, Raban could have looked out and scanned, from left to right, the extent of the new city where Rashid's government was spending all of its money and more. To his left, the new city's furthest inland reach was the World Trade Centre, designed in John Harris's London office. To his right, on the coastal waters, was Port Rashid, "jammed with cargo-boats disgorging the latest technological marvels" to Dubai's markets.[16]

In between the tower and the port, the new city was to emerge on land that for now was a jumble of staging sites and workers' housing and, further out, was readily available for new development to attach itself to Port Rashid's trade networks. For this realm, released from old Dubai, Sheikh Rashid had once declared an "openness to all who would like to start businesses there with full freedom."[17] Mahdi Al Tajir, one of Rashid's most flamboyant advisors, announced on local television in 1974 that Dubai had set aside a billion dollars for a free zone—for what exactly was not made clear. Whereas cities like Beirut and Singapore had already announced free zones, Tajir expressed the vastness of land Dubai had to offer. More than the entire island of Singapore could fit in the area Dubai promised as a free zone.[18] "Free zone," Tajir knew already, was a slippery term without an actual meaning, always more fitting for a sales pitch than for a contract.

Raban ignored the World Trade Centre that was at least twice the height of any building in Abu Dhabi—a place he labeled a "sunny, miniature Manhattan"—but not because he rejected expensive comfort; after all, he was staying at an Intercontinental. Raban eschewed the unabashed financial motives behind the new city and its skyscraper. He scorned how every square meter was "vetted as a good investment." The surfaces of Dubai's most current developments were to him banal manifestations of the experts' and bankers' self-serving calculations. He sensed a fixation on "the biggest, most expensive, most modern thing of its kind." In Abu Dhabi, he had accepted that stance. But in Dubai, he had a choice, and he preferred an old city where he encountered "substance and experience." His romanticizing of Deira's old ways may not have been unlike the work of British Arabists Wilfred Thesiger and T. E. Lawrence, both of whom he criticized for having a "love affair" with the region. Raban portrayed Deira as "an alternative kingdom; a tough utopia without either money or machines."[19] Like his forebears, Raban took comfort in old Dubai's discomforts.

He did not realize that the old city was also made of consciously indexed parts. It too had resulted from a fixation on appearances and impressions. Even if Halcrow's harbor project had seemed quaint to Raban in 1978, it had been intended as much as a financial gambit as an optical fix. Subsequent arrivals of international banks, elevator-served apartment buildings, a Jashanmal department store, even the hotel where Raban stayed were calculated investments that banked on the appearances they projected. The British "shop window" aid of the 1960s had focused on foundational and easily justifiable goals and messages: hospitals, workers' housing, governmental offices, bank branches, and land surveys. Building codes, which John Harris's office helped write, assured a basic level of protection against harm and catastrophe. The necessity of all these efforts, however, did not isolate them from mercantile motives.

By the time Raban arrived, Dubai's major projects had pivoted from the old districts to Rashid's new city; and from merely installing essential services, like roads and apartment blocks, to meeting less essential expectations, like business-class comfort and services. So-called international standards might have been met with hospital facilities and public hygiene codes, but there was now the matter of offering *world-class* facilities. To compete with Abu Dhabi's exorbitant wealth, Dubai had to be projected as something more than sufficient; it had to be comfortable. World class facilities—the "vetted" investments Raban disdained—might seem to be calculated by a financial team, but Rashid's office presented no evidence that the new city was carefully analyzed or based on established projections. Promises of business-class environments professed in the corporate-speak of "free zones" and "global trade" were more storytelling tactics than actually calculated investments. New Dubai was instead a performance of calculations and analyses. If not based on a vetted business plan, then the resulting urban landscape was made at least to resemble where a business plan is made.

In preferring the old and renouncing Dubai's new city, Raban validated the government's constructed narrative—namely, that a new city *did* exist. And its newness was being defined as separate from the worn fabric hemmed to Dubai Creek. For a time during its construction, the last ten-meter segment of road leading from the creek to the roundabout at the World Trade Centre was unpaved. The sand in between was a rite of passage for drivers arriving at a new location set apart from the rest. Desert sands around the construction site marked its distance from the old ways of Dubai Creek. During construction, the tower was often photographed as a defiant, engineered, and unchanging obelisk amid sinuous and mercurial sand dunes. Its presence was designed to be unaccountable to existing rules and expectations. Its 150-meter height and its compact, vertical form signaled its inward-focused plan marketed to an idealized demographic, "the international company and businessman."[20]

Never before in Dubai had so much explicit messaging to the outside world been concentrated into a single building project. The trade center's champions called it "an unmistakable signpost," broadcasting advanced technology and luxury to the world. The World Trade Centre was made for vast exhibitions and marketplaces, but, at a more visceral level, the complex was itself the exhibit. Claiming the Middle East's first skyscraper allowed Dubai to appear exceptional, beyond the basic improvements sought in past decades. Reproduced images of the tower could "attract much publicity" and announce the city as the "trade centre of the Arab World."[21] It was to be a showpiece "of such excellent quality" that it prompted "spin-off" development after it.[22]

The tower's owner, its tenants, its marketing and management teams, the dozens of participating experts, and even the British head of state all contributed to the tower's broadcasted messaging, which was as much about Dubai's achievements as their own. Topped with a twenty-five-meter television mast, the tower was more than a signpost for Dubai; it was meant to be a mark of prestige for any company that contributed to its construction and for any company that could afford its lease terms. Their self-promotion only enriched the signpost.

Sheikh Rashid owned the tower and its management company and commissioned both to signify his new city.[23] Before "icon" was an overused term to

FIGURE 9.2 Dubai World Trade Centre tower photographed in a favored context—surrounded by *nothing*. Photo by Gordon Heald.

describe architecture, Dubai's World Trade Centre tower made for easy stock photography in advertisements promoting Dubai or its luxury hotel and exhibition events. It signified how "a deserted spot in the city, like any other" could be transfixed with meaning.[24] As an emblem of Dubai in the pages of the *Financial Times*, it filled in for the city still incomplete and needing new investors. The message was manifested in the brawn of the tower's steel and concrete but also in the plushness of a luxury hotel's wall-to-wall carpeting. It was displayed in a restaurant's iced trays of Maine lobsters and spoken through the most advanced telecommunications wiring. Inside, the World Trade Centre was an index of the businessman's perks for sale. Encapsulated in its vertical shell visible for miles around, the tower was a "symbol of the city."[25] John Harris called the tower the "culmination" of his work in Dubai.[26]

FIGURE 9.3 (NEXT SPREAD) Dubai World Trade Centre, looking north, with a cricket match underway on land reserved for the project's future expansion. Courtesy John R. Harris Library.

DISPLAY FOR EXHIBITION

The idea of a World Trade Centre originated in a meeting that allegedly occurred late one night in the new airport's main concourse. Designed by the British partnership Page & Broughton and opened the same year as the British political departure in 1971, the terminal offered "state of the art" experiences in Dubai—automated systems, expansive sheets of glass, and lofty and sweeping interiors. *Akhbar Dubai* described the terminal as "the destination for businesses for its cleanliness and smoothness of operations." It was designed to receive jumbo and supersonic jets.[27] Every day about a thousand people streamed through the airport, including arrivals from the UK, Lebanon, Bahrain, Egypt, Iran, and Sudan. Its opening attracted "delegates from all over the Arab world"; in March 1974, its £4 million main hall was draped in Union Jack flags to celebrate the British Building and Construction Equipment Exhibition.[28]

Designed by Harris's firm, the exhibition gridded Dubai's largest interior space with aluminum stands filled to capacity with British building-industry exhibitors: engineers, architects, contractors, and vendors. Booths displayed world maps punctured with colored pins to mark where the companies were under contract, mostly in places once controlled by the British empire. Models presented dams and desalination plants like purchasable, ready-made items. Floor samples too big for the hall, like earth movers and large-haul trucks, were exhibited in the brand-new parking lot. Travelers were greeted at once by Dubai's sophisticated airport and a display of British expertise that helped realize the airport and the city beyond. Participants in the one-week exhibition reported a total of £350,000 in "off-the-counter sales," and nearly all the displayed equipment in the parking lot was sold.[29]

On March 14, 1974, a jet carrying Queen Elizabeth II of Great Britain landed in Dubai. En route to Indonesia, the monarch allegedly asked to move a planned refueling stop from Bahrain to Dubai.[30] Alerted to her arrival, Sheikh Rashid, John Harris, and a handful of advisors were said to have welcomed her at the airport and given her a tour of the exhibition. Harris later recalled that, hours after the queen had departed, he returned to the airport to catch his own flight. As he set his luggage on the check-in conveyor, noticing that the airport had updated its conveyor systems, he felt a hand on his shoulder. An assistant to Sheikh Rashid had come to summon him to the ruler's office for another meeting. At the customs building, Mahdi Al Tajir translated for Harris as Sheikh Rashid explained his new idea. The queen's brief visit, Harris later noted, had convinced the ruler that Dubai needed dedicated exhibition facilities. By the end of that meeting, Harris may have missed his flight, but he had gained his largest and most prominent commission in Dubai.[31]

FIGURE 9.4 The first design proposal for an exhibition center in Dubai. Courtesy John R. Harris Library and Henk Snoek / RIBA Collections.

Harris returned to London and entrusted Gordon Heald, an architect on his staff, with designing Dubai's exhibition center. With only a vague idea to guide him, Heald produced a proposal more comprehensive than an exhibition center, based on what he understood as a recent ingredient in revitalizing cities in North America and Europe—a complex that in addition to exhibition spaces offered conference facilities, a hotel, office space, and retail. Heald had less than three months to develop the scheme, including producing a model and sending the drawings out for a price quote. While Harris at first embraced Heald's enhanced proposal, the £25 million cost estimate unsettled him. With no time to trim the scheme down, Heald quickly produced a drawing that demonstrated how the project could be built in separately financed phases, and then he boxed the presentation materials for Harris's flight back to Dubai.[32]

Not as confidently as he had hoped, Harris presented Heald's scheme of "two interlocking six-story pyramids."[33] One pyramid included the hotel; the other housed the convention spaces and offices. The interwoven buildings were alabaster and smooth, each with a tiled interior courtyard. All of it was encompassed by a vast parking lot. Presenting a building he thought too extravagant to Rashid and his advisors, Harris heard from some who agreed. One majlis regular, for example, argued that Dubai needed only a "trade village."[34] Rashid turned down the proposal but for the opposite reason: He thought it too understated. Rashid, bolstered by his recent $500 million windfall in oil sales, insisted on a skyscraper.[35]

The municipality ran a publicity campaign about the proposed exhibition center. Interviewed for *Akhbar Dubai*, Harris described the building as an "exhibition and conference centre" to complement Dubai's industrial developments, offering "a location where deals can be made and ideas discussed."[36] He articulated the complex's ambitious plan: exhibition halls that could accommodate up to 3,500 people, entertainment facilities, venues to conduct conferences with up to 400 people, and a 300-room hotel. The municipal director Kamal Hamza arranged for a photograph of Harris and Rashid, as if they were engaged in the conversation that had already happened. The interview was featured in the magazine's next issue, with the photograph as the cover image. Rejected for being too small, the proposed

FIGURE 9.5 John Harris and Sheikh Rashid pose with the rejected low-rise proposal for what would become the Dubai World Trade Centre. Courtesy John R. Harris Library.

international exhibition center could still be celebrated as Dubai's largest ongoing architectural project.

Harris and Heald's model parted ways: The model was shipped to Beijing to promote Dubai's development ambitions, and Harris returned to London to prepare something more spectacular.

Harris came upon a template for what Rashid wanted: a world trade center. He subsequently traveled "round the world assessing the present state of the trade centre movement," visiting both the World Trade Center in Tokyo and the one in New York City, both designed by Minoru Yamasaki. The New York project was dominated by the world's two tallest towers.

FIGURE 9.6 New York City's World Trade Center, still largely a construction site, during John Harris's visit, 1974. Courtesy John R. Harris Library.

Leasing officers in New York provided Harris with marketing materials that described the kinds of interior spaces being pitched to trade commissions and global executives. Interiors were presented as a matrix of options, with "complete flexibility" for bespoke handling of a client's wishes. Office units were catalogued like luxury apartments: "duplex units" with lounge areas, interior gardens, marble-top tables, executive offices, and roomy closets for suit jackets and overcoats.

Beyond individual offices, the marketing pamphlets promised a $350 million "new international marketplace" that was the "first stop for overseas businessmen." There were also "ancillary conveniences for businessmen," including "fine shops and restaurants, other essential consumer services, on-site parking facilities and a 350-room hotel."[37] On the outside, New York City's World Trade Center was an expression of financial might. Inside, it was a combinational structure of exhibition concourses, high-end office spaces, and conventions halls. The World Trade Center, soon a global brand of corporate property management, packaged interiors as pampering hospitality and cushy privileges.[38]

SITE

During the initial design phase, Dubai's largest architectural project had no site. The earliest existing site drawing locates the future complex on the Bur Dubai side of Dubai Creek, above Al Shindagha Tunnel then under construction on land historically controlled by the Maktoum family. Wedged between the northern end of Port Rashid and the piers of Dubai Creek, the new complex would have connected the old and new harbors as a continuous field of trade and business, much as the canceled canal would have done.[39] Flight trajectories were said to have been the reason for the site's rejection, but probably a more determinative factor was the old city's notorious traffic.

Better positioned in terms of traffic was another option. In the same *Akhbar Dubai* issue with Harris's interview about the initial proposal, Dubai Municipality's city planning engineer Saadullah Noori identified a site inland from Deira and near the airport, free of "adjacent developments [that might] restrict the architects and engineers."[40] If Noori's site had been chosen,

Dubai's two most noteworthy architectural projects—the airport and the towering trade center—would have been bundled together to create Dubai's future business district. However, this second site lies in the district today known as Al Qsais, near the border with Sharjah, and the inter-sheikhdom tension probably doomed this option. By 1974, there had already been more than a decade of antagonism between Dubai and Sharjah, a rivalry that was fueled by the British government's historical preference for Dubai over Sharjah.

The complex needed its own city, separated from both the old ways of Dubai Creek and the rivalry of Sharjah. It was finally sited on the other side of Dubai Creek, directly inland from Port Rashid. Often referred to as "out in the desert," Dubai's World Trade Centre was going to be the anchor of the new city. Sheikh Rashid had already bought out any ownership claims to the land, likely an easy task.[41] "Flies were like smoke," recalled municipal director Kamal Hamza about the site, which was also plagued by prickly bushes, uneven grading, and regular flooding. It was, however, no random choice.

Architecture was to provide the inhabitable component of Port Rashid. On the outskirts of the port's staging areas, laborer housing, and warehouses, it was anchored at the large roundabout that served the heavy trucks bringing quarried rock to Port Rashid and the new dry-docks project. It both defined the southern edge of the port's development site and suggested that the new city would expand from there. It marked a point from which new Dubai's development would extend southward, between the Abu Dhabi road and the coastline where the khazzan-gazers had stood.

Sheikh Rashid, following his advisors' recommendation, cordoned off a location "as large as possible" for the project.[42] The trade center's designated site reached southward, along the Abu Dhabi road, for a kilometer and further inland for almost another kilometer. Excepting the port and the airport and its runway, it was the largest development site in Dubai. As with Al Maktoum Hospital, the boundaries outlined more than what was currently deemed necessary; they made for a down payment on intended expansions that eventually included more convention spaces and even the city's largest shopping mall.

FIGURE 9.7 John Harris presents the exhibition center's tower proposal to Sheikh Rashid in October 1974. Easa Al Gurg, a skeptic of the tower proposal, is kneeling on the left. Financial advisor William Duff is seated behind him. Courtesy John R. Harris Library.

THE TOWER TAKES SHAPE

In October 1974, Harris returned to Dubai with a tower proposal whose facade evoked the New York twin towers' threadlike columns. In fact, earlier tower schemes even included twin towers, a concept that Harris reportedly had difficulty abandoning, even when the design team could not fit the project's various program requirements into two uniform towers.[43] In the end, Rashid approved a plan with a single tower and two adjacent block buildings that offered larger floor plates for exhibition spaces and hotel layouts. Even the low-rise buildings had precedents in the New York scheme. The revised proposal was also featured on the cover of *Akhbar Dubai* as the "tallest building in the Arab world."[44] The tower's height was locked in at thirty-three stories.

One later design revision borrowed another element from the New York scheme—a dais connecting the three buildings five meters above ground level. An invented terra firma was intended to keep sand and other irritants out of the new interiors of carpeted and polished surfaces. It also

FIGURE 9.8 The initial tower design included a facade that recalled the twin towers of New York City's World Trade Center. Courtesy John R. Harris Library and Henk Snoek / RIBA Collections.

emphasized that Dubai's World Trade Centre was lifted from the old ways in pursuit of its own rules on a stage crafted for its own purposes. Service and utility access were pressed into the levels below the platform. Ramps circulated cars to and from the new urban level above the hidden service areas. On the new concrete plane, architects designated the access point to the trade center's three buildings: the tower, the exhibition center, and a luxury hotel. The dais's vacant edges implied that additional buildings could be plugged in to this new ground plane via elevated passages and air-conditioned concourses.

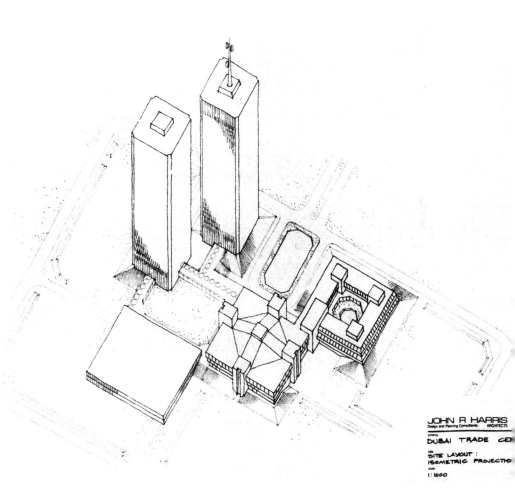

FIGURE 9.9 An early tower proposal included twin towers, calling to mind the original World Trade Center in New York City. Courtesy John R. Harris Library.

FIGURE 9.10 The six-story Hilton Hotel along the departure ramp from the dais at the World Trade Centre. Courtesy John R. Harris Library and Courtesy Henk Snoek / RIBA Collections

The hotel building opened in 1978. Its below-dais floor accommodated the hotel's plant and services. Above were five stories of hospitality. In line with Harris's professional concern about solar gain, the building was described as "a concrete box six stories high." Fenestration was limited to narrow insets, sixty centimeters wide. The design tried to compensate for the sparse use of glass with pristinely finished concrete panels—to a degree not achieved before in Dubai—that protected what was described inside as "an oasis of coolness in the noonday heat."[45]

In the final year of the hotel's construction, once Hilton signed a management contract, Boston-based Graham-Solano Interiors chose "a translation of traditional Arab forms and materials" for the interior's theme.[46] The lobby was trimmed with hardwoods and succulent plants. Its cocktail bar looked out onto an oasis-inspired fountain arrangement in the courtyard. The 350 hotel rooms (the same number proposed in New York City's original scheme) were each allotted only one of the slender windows. The rooms therefore could not offer expansive views. Instead, luxury had to be expressed in wall-to-wall carpeting, wooden *mashrabiya*-like screens over the windows, and expected accoutrements like touch-tone telephones and minibars. After the opening, an aboveground swimming pool was hastily added, in response to a marketing study.

The center's second low-rise building was designed to be even more closed off from the environment; its bunker-like appearance conveyed its purpose as an exhibition center. With hardly a shred of fenestration specified, the hall was designed for its interior. A tubular-steel space-frame structure freed the 2,500-square-meter floor from intermediate columns and housed the electrical and cooling systems.[47] An upper-level mezzanine offered VIP spaces and views over the large open hall below. Selecting the building's finishes was not as important as ensuring the space's flexibility so that, depending on the arrangement, it could accommodate up to 2,000 spectators. The dais-level floor was designed to host "an ice rink, boxing or wrestling matches, national or cultural events, and many other sporting or commercial spectacles."[48] Its systems were to ensure the "best air-conditioned display space in the Gulf" and the "most modern exhibition lighting systems."[49] Even before the hall opened, it was deemed too small

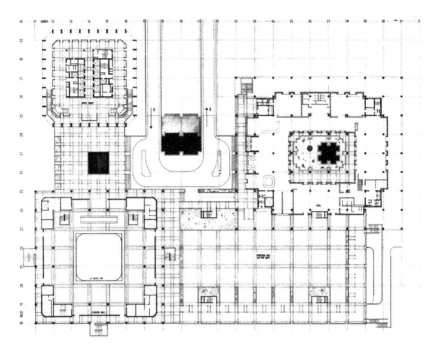

FIGURE 9.11 Site plan for Dubai World Trade Centre. The raised platform is approached by the ramp (*above center*). On the right is the Hilton Hotel designed around an inner courtyard; bottom left is the exhibition hall; top left is the tower. The edges of the "pedestrian deck" (*bottom right*) were left open for future expansions. Courtesy Stephen Finch, John R. Harris Library.

for Dubai's exhibition programming. Supplemental tents often had to be assembled on the ground below.

The plans for the center's most remarkable building, the tower, included more intimate display venues just above the marble and chrome lobby. Occupying the tower's first seven floors were spaces dedicated to a "wholesale mart," where "buyers and sellers [could] maintain personal contact and . . . discuss trends and changes."[50] A 200-seat stepped theater was designed for the third and fourth floors to host trade conferences, film screenings, and concerts. Four of the lower floors were at first dedicated to "commercial delegations, embassies, consulates, foreign government trade and tourist offices."[51] The rest of the tower floors were laid out as flexible office space leasable to companies needing proximity to the center's market and exhibition halls and, of course, Port Rashid.[52]

Inside Dubai's most expensive real estate, promoters pitched the concept that executive leaseholders would create a new city of executive deal-making and networking. At the World Trade Centre an idealized business community would come to life, pressed into the tower's stacking of 1,225-square-meter floor plates. While most offices in Dubai occupied spaces laid out as residential apartments, the World Trade Centre concentrated Dubai's purpose-built office space into a single tower.

Like the New York City twin towers, Dubai's tower maintained its original square plan through the design process, but the originally proposed facade that recalled New York's was replaced with one more attuned to Dubai's climate. As his previous work demonstrated, Harris continued to distrust using glass in hot climates, especially before the availability of solar reflective glass that reduced at least some internal heat absorption.[53] "There have been some disasters," Harris once recalled, noting that he had been asked twice to advise

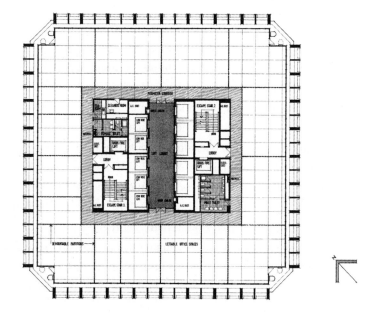

FIGURE 9.12 Typical plan of upper floors of Dubai World Trade Centre tower. The tower's sides were 40 meters in length. Courtesy Stephen Finch, John R. Harris Library.

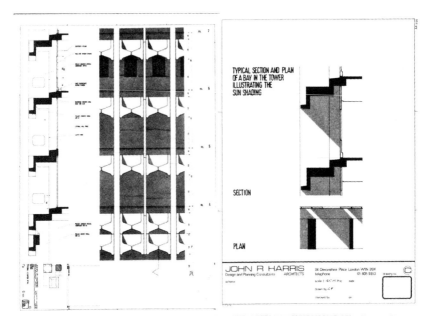

FIGURE 9.13 Section and elevation studies of the tower's double facade and its shading capacity. Courtesy Stephen Finch, John R. Harris Library.

on glazed buildings gone awry.[54] To ameliorate the effects of glazing, Gordon Heald, continuing as the project's lead designer, configured a modular facade that ensured a well-shaded interior. His design split the building's facade into two layers or, as Harris described it, created a "building within a building." The result is still one of Dubai's most remarkable towers, though its double-facade has unfortunately only scarcely been replicated.

Heald specified the inner facade to be outfitted with panels manufactured by and shipped from a single British company. Each composite-aluminum framed panel comprised a window pane and an insulated wall.[55] Heald conceived the outer facade as a composition of fastened concrete components, fit together like a puzzle, that simultaneously provided some of the building's structure as well as shading to the glazing installed in the panels behind it. Fabricated on site and "developed by the architects into a translation of a traditional Arabic arch," the assemblage of prefabricated parts was to be bolted into the inner facade through to the floor plates.[56] The space in between the two facades was to be just enough for a "very thin man" to clean windows and perform maintenance.[57]

Harris referred to the design as a grid of "sunshading units." The repeated "Arabic arch" was shaped by the architects' studies not of architectural styles but of sun-path diagrams, which determined the angle that provided maximum shading to the greatest number of windows throughout the year. The resulting grid of shadow-giving portals bestowed a Chiroco-esque effect to the building. Such an effect meant the building "[avoided] the flat quality so often associated with buildings of this type."[58] Other solar-minded maneuvers in the building's design included its solar orientation, which anchored the tower's corners to the four cardinal directions. The result was that no side of the tower suffered from direct solar exposure. There was also a marketing advantage: The orientation maximized the number of windows with a view over the new city.

IMPERMEABILITY

As much as the World Trade Centre was to be the materialization of Dubai's economic freedom, it was also a site of bounded control and isolation. In a graduation of projects—from Al Maktoum Hospital, to Rashid Hospital, and most definitively through the creation of the World Trade Centre—John Harris helped shape and take part in Dubai's development through the establishment of demarcated sites. The trade center's nearly one-square-kilometer site was defined by autocratic decree and the cash contract that continued to rise in value as the project grew in scale. Consultants and subcontractors, as many as several hundred, operated within geographical as well as contractual bounds. Among the vast patchwork of Dubai's land claims that materialized from Rashid's ongoing business dealings, the site was not part of a larger whole or of a predetermined land-use zone in a master plan. Rather, it was a piece carved out of the 1971 development plan's white blankness, a cultivated swath that dangled in a vast territory of even more opportunity. Inside its perimeter, contracted experts determined the project's logistical rationality. Outside it, the project could be read as a designed totality.

The site's excised demarcation also plumbed twenty-five meters below ground. The engineers, preparing for construction to begin in April 1975, encountered subgrade conditions, somewhere between those of a desert and

FIGURES 9.14A–9.14F Stages of Dubai World Trade Centre's construction: (A) December 31, 1975; (B) May 31, 1976; (C) August 31, 1976; (D) November 30, 1976; (E) January 31, 1977; (F) May 31, 1977. Courtesy Stephen Finch, James Sunley.

> **FIGURE 9.15** Construction photograph of Dubai World Trade Centre, April 30, 1979. Courtesy Stephen Finch, James Sunley.

a swampy sinkhole. With the subsurface water table regularly threatening from just a meter below ground surface, the site flooded often. Inspectors for the future building's foundations—the contracting company was Bernard Sunley & Sons; the lead engineers were R. J. Crocker—needed to address not only the water but also a "sub-strata high in sulphates and chlorides."[59] Such a chemical composition could destroy any concrete and steel bored into its depths. Once the site's first 760 pilings were driven down to a rock base, a hole was dug around them to pump out the noxious ground material.[60] A giant concrete square tub was subsequently built around the pilings and "tanked" with the bituthene entrusted to seal the foundation off from moisture and irritants.[61]

On top of the pilings came the base on which the tower would rise: a plate, two-and-a-half meters thick, of solid, sulphate-resistant concrete. The "superstructure" that rose from the concrete plate was a reinforced-concrete building system. In addition to the problems of corrosive soils, engineers were also plagued by fears of "concrete cancer," an effective but inexact term for how "an aggressive environment" could cause chemical reactions capable of inducing structural failure.[62] This dangerous prospect often condemned Dubai's early reinforced-concrete buildings to a short life. The World Trade Centre tower's decay—daresay its collapse—would have been a compounded disaster for Dubai's image as well as for the British companies involved.

These concerns might have driven Sunley & Sons to stress that the project was just like any it had built in the UK. They assured that the project abided by British codes and production quality. With such statements, Sunley further cut the site off from the rest of Dubai, re-imagining it as if it were on British land. The contractor's public statements made it seem, for example, that the hundreds of workers manning the on-site casting stations for the tower's concrete parts were British. The project's on-site British management, in reality, was kept to a minimum, with no more than a few dozen. Sunley also stressed that its Dubai-based personnel were supported by a "large back-up team in the UK," but in actuality communication was limited by the available technology. Gordon Heald recalls that international calls had to be arranged twenty-four hours in advance. There were telex

FIGURE 9.16 What became known as the World Trade Centre Roundabout was originally designed to deliver quarried rock to Port Rashid (*top left*). The road leading to the port was one of the original roads lined with trees and greenery. The road along the right leads north to the creek. The road headed toward the bottom of the frame is the Abu Dhabi road, later named Sheikh Zayed Road. Courtesy John R. Harris Library.

and the mail, but the latter required days, if not weeks, for response. Heald, who was Harris's only permanent on-site representative, made countless decisions on his own because of these hindrances. Despite the marketing statements, these British companies were only as good as their on-site representatives.[63]

To consider the World Trade Centre a British construction site requires looking past the hundreds, eventually thousands, of construction workers who actually manned the casting stations, built the complex, and installed its building systems. They both lived and worked inside the World Trade Centre construction site. Six kilometers beyond Dubai Creek along roads driven at dangerously fast speeds, they had no easy access to anywhere else. That made the construction site the only place they knew in Dubai. At the start of construction, austere villas and barracks were built for staff. Eventually, laborers brought in at the peak of construction were being housed

FIGURE 9.17 Workers' housing at the World Trade Centre construction site included larger villas for British contractors (*bottom right corner*) and barracks-style housing and tents for builders. Courtesy Stephen Finch.

in on-site tents. One might question whether the tents satisfied the British regulations Sunley cited. And in terms of safety standards, while there is no official source or count, there were rumors of unreported on-site deaths and casualties of South Asian workers during construction.

The South Asian workers, sometimes described as Bernard Sunley staff, were deleted from the construction narrative in order to project a truly British-built undertaking. In this way, their labor was calculated into the companies' logistical computations, handled similarly to daily temperature forecasts and shipping schedules and housed on site with other construction supplies. The number of South Asian laborers—an "army of trades-men"—varied between a few hundred and a couple thousand, depending on Sunley's construction schedules.[64] Building schedules were reliant upon competent builders, mostly Pakistanis, who maintained a quality of concrete pours never previously achieved in Dubai, including the final "rendered" surface to the tower's exterior.[65]

Once the tower's base was completed, contractors divided the tower's construction into a three-team effort.[66] One team built the core's "rigid reinforced
concrete backbone," cast with openings for the building's eventual twelve
elevators, vertical ducts, two fireproof stairwells, and each floor's kitchens and
toilets.[67] Three levels below, another team assembled the outer columns and
the beams that were attached to the core. Then three levels below that team,
the final team cast the floor slabs. Sunley reported that this regimentation of
labor added a floor to the tower every ten days. *Akhbar Dubai* claimed that
construction kept a twenty-four hour per day schedule.[68]

Every ten days, the workers, development team, and municipal officials
enjoyed a new unique view of Sheikh Rashid's new city from a higher floor.
The builders at the tower could observe their counterpart, Port Rashid, which,
despite its incessant congestion, managed to make consistent on-time deliveries to Sheikh Rashid's most cherished architectural project. Port Rashid's
own army of South Asian men, invisible from the World Trade Centre but
as many as 3,000, operated the huge port not much differently than others
had run Dubai Creek—in loosely fitting clothes and sandals and hardly any
advancements in transfer technologies. Their daily work delivered supplies
to the World Trade Centre and other projects realizing the new city. And like
the World Trade Centre's workers, their site was their home.

In between the tower and the port was the low-slung, uneven blanket of
construction detritus, the generator of Dubai's new city: Quonset huts and
temporary warehouses; mounds of earth; forgotten debris from earlier phases
of construction; silos; expired dredging equipment; and residential blocks,
barracks, and tents—all kept at a safe distance from the manicured, tree-
trimmed road that connected one site of exclusivity, Port Rashid, to the next,
the World Trade Centre. Above it all, in Dubai's heavy humid air, loomed a
human-induced cloud made up of truck soot, kicked-up sand, and the plumes
from rocks being crushed into aggregate to extend the port further. While the
new city was kept isolated from the old, "the constant buzz of the machinery
made it to the city centre."[69] According to the port's engineers, cranes and
workers worked constantly, more than twenty-two hours a day, stopping only
for prayers five times a day. "The builders pitted themselves against two ad-
versaries: the intractable desert and the hostile sun ... and won."[70]

FIGURE 9.18 Advisors and consultants follow Sheikh Rashid during a site tour, late 1970s. Architect Gordon Heald is on the left. Courtesy John R. Harris Library.

During the trade center's construction, Sheikh Rashid no longer invited his important guests to view Dubai from his creekside veranda. Instead, he drove them out in his Mercedes-Benz, seats covered in clear plastic to protect them from construction-site grit, and then urged his guests into the rickety construction elevator that clung to the unfinished tower's facade and hoisted them up to the highest floor possible.[71] From up high, Rashid could look down directly below him and assess the trade center's measurable progress since his last visit. Reaching as far as the Gulf waters, the disheveled Port Rashid staging area came to a stop at the edges of the trade center's clear intentions and contracted deadlines. As the tower rose, more similarly demarcated sites could be seen, inserted into the new city: new resorts, office towers, and living complexes. "The unchanging face of Arabia," according to an engineer at Port Rashid, was now finally being changed, project by project, development site by development site.[72]

When the tower had reached eight stories, midway through 1976, the design and construction teams received news from Sheikh Rashid: He wanted it to be taller. Rashid's sudden request might have resulted from news that Abu Dhabi planned an even taller building. An article in the British *Guardian* reported an exaggerated and "unkind rumour" that the trade tower had "exceeded the architect's extra-generous specifications because the ruler kept insisting on extra stories to ensure his building was the tallest in the Gulf."[73] The project's engineers begrudgingly heightened the building based on what the foundation could carry, but added only diminished floor plates at the top. Press releases announced a thirty-nine-floor tower, but that counted the accessible rooftop as a floor. An added television mast helped the building top out at 175 meters, qualifying it to reign as Dubai's tallest building for at least twenty years. Three years after the World Trade Centre's official opening, Abu Dhabi's "offshore tourist tower," planned to be "exactly twice the height" of Dubai's tower, was canceled.[74] Once again, competition, or the threat of it, helped shape Dubai, if only by some eighteen meters.

INSIDE CITY

Several years after the tower's completion, during a public talk in which he recounted building the World Trade Centre in the desert, Harris was asked by an audience member about "whether we [British experts] should be going this far down the line" in delivering more advanced buildings in Dubai. Rather than addressing the height and audacity of the structure, the question referred to the installation of "sophisticated" interior building systems and whether local companies could maintain them. In his response, Harris emphasized that the trade center was the materialization of a business transaction between consultants and well-traveled clients who knew what kinds of amenities they needed to be internationally competitive. Whether anyone *should* provide them was, in Harris's opinion, misplaced moral pondering. Building technologies were being purchased on the private market, Harris implied, not through British-led development aid. In regard to the questioner's distinction between installation and maintenance, Harris referred to the trade center's twenty-five on-site engineers who kept the systems running.[75]

What Harris didn't clarify in his answer was that, ever since his earliest projects in Dubai, his proposals had consistently considered installation *and* maintenance. This is one reason why his work was often considered "severe" or not formally pronounced. Budgets certainly limited Harris's design options, but so did his realization that each building needed to function properly and be maintained in a "very strong, fierce climate."[76] The climate was also financially unstable. Harris's buildings were designed to function along the technologies and maintenance levels that Dubai could confidently provide at a given time.

In the late 1960s, for example, during the design phase of the National Bank of Dubai, glass was a building material already associated with financial headquarters; Harris had ignored the trend for the sake of creating a building that could be properly maintained in Dubai. Additionally, glazing, cooling equipment, and other building systems had to be assessed before causing "a great many heart-breaks" from a lack of maintenance. [77] Glass surfaces also required additional cleaning, in a city whose water supply was continually at risk. Further, until the late 1970s, Harris's buildings for Dubai remained low rise, since, as he noted, "the nearest lift engineers were in Beirut."[78] Stories circulated of new buildings whose elevators, jammed with dust and sand, had never worked, leaving owners with upper floors unleased.

Operating under the guaranteed maintenance regimes available, Harris's buildings expressed Dubai's technological advancement and were often later deemed obsolete, not because of their poor state and wear, but because of their reliance on eventually outdated technologies. Working within the limits of their bounded sites, each of Harris's projects was designed with its maintenance team in mind. The World Trade Centre was no different.

When completed, the Dubai World Trade Centre was run by a regiment that maintained controlled environments, climatic and social. While Harris counted twenty-five maintenance engineers, the *Financial Times* reported fifty. Staff, at least at first, was scheduled to live on site. The center's managerial structure was just as important as its physical one in selling the complex as a counterpoint to the city's poorly maintained office blocks.[79] Leases included a substantial maintenance surcharge (£2 per square foot of leased space) that financed the flow of an effortless interior city. Every space inside—not to mention the "oasis" gardens, shaded parking, and the flood-lit exterior tennis courts—was a site of serviced maintenance calculated into management fees.[80]

Owned by Sheikh Rashid, the in-house management company was led by an "English-born" director and stressed that it hired British employees who "were not absentee landlords—we're on the fourth floor."[81] The team worked out of the same air-conditioned interiors that it marketed as sealed luxury hovering over harsh desert. They ensured that plants were watered, lobbies were vacuumed, trash was collected, leaky taps were repaired, and worn carpet and stained dropped-ceiling tiles were replaced. They also assisted global companies whose staff might not always be in town to supervise a furniture delivery or the installation of a new telephone system.

Maintenance involved room service, and not just in the Hilton's rooms. After construction on the complex had begun, another component was added to the project: one fourteen-story and two fifteen-story slab buildings with a total of 492 apartments. In similar fashion to the neighboring tower's management services, the apartments were managed "to top hotel standards" by Hilton staff. Tenants were promised luxury quarters, "lavishly furnished" and appointed with "washing machines, cooking utensils and even cutlery, including sets of teaspoons." Residents had access to hotel-like amenities—gyms, rooftop multipurpose rooms, tennis courts, and daily room-cleaning service. Rent, paid by the month, was considerably higher than in the rest of Dubai, but it was all-inclusive, like a hotel's rates, capturing utilities, management, recreational fees, and cleaning service in one bill.[82] Whether in an office on the thirtieth floor, or a furnished apartment, or a Hilton suite, guests could calculate how their spent wealth was channeled into their exclusive environment.

Sheikh Rashid's advisors stressed to Harris "the importance of amenity and recreation . . . in the interest of trade."[83] At the World Trade Centre, opportunities to combine business and air-conditioned personal comfort were spread out over more than 40,000 square meters of nearly continuous well-appointed interior spaces. According to the *Financial Times*, the center was designed "to offer the international company and businessman a complete business service."[84] Services included a businessman's club; car rental and travel agencies; a post office; a cinema and theater; "a quick service restaurant" and more formal dining; stores; a stationery shop; and "limitless free parking." The lobby's mezzanine was supposed to offer language courses,

"desks, local telephones, news service tickers, and notice boards . . . [to] help visitors adjust to unfamiliar surroundings."[85] The World Trade Centre promised obliging customer care in an environment of business-class accoutrements like telex machines, ashtrays, complimentary financial newspapers, and conference-call telephones. For a calculated per-square-foot price, you could live, work, and play inside the vast complex. According to one advertisement, the complex was "all in all."[86]

More than any other component, central air conditioning sealed the center off from its surroundings and contrived a boundlessly cool interior space. The exhibition center could be chilled for an ice rink, and the tower was "fully air-conditioned to an ambient temperature of 72°F" thanks to seven kilometers of concealed coils.

Elsewhere, other development projects were bringing the city inside. Perhaps the development that most directly competed with the World Trade Centre was the Galadari Galleria, which, at thirty-two stories, was noticeably one story lower than the trade center tower's original height. The Galleria's expansive interiors comprised 2,500 square meters of office space, 6,000 square meters of commercial space, a permanent ice rink, and an 800-seat cinema.

The World Trade Centre was scheduled to surpass any competition with a sprawling shopping mall as the center's commercial plug-in. After Harris's preliminary designs were completed, the expansion was canceled, to the great disappointment of the consultant teams. It is said that the Ruler's Office decided to focus instead on infrastructure in a deal that left Dubai's wealthiest merchants to develop the city's commercial potential.

Another aspect of the trade center that seemed to set it off from the rest of the city was its need for singular fire-safety measures. Its occupants could not rely on the city to save them in the event of a fire. As late as 1977, according to a USAID report, the city had no fire regulations and no fire hydrants. While there were "pumpers" that attached to water supply systems, firefighters could not gain enough water pressure to reach the heights of Dubai's tallest

‹ FIGURE 9.19 A later model of the World Trade Centre demonstrates how interior spaces were to be extended in future phases. To the right of the expanded exhibition space was to be Dubai's largest mall. This project was canceled. Courtesy John R. Harris Library and Henk Snoek / RIBA Collections.

FIGURE 9.20 Fastened to the building by wire, construction workers install the inner layer of the Dubai World Trade Centre tower's double facade. Photograph taken from the construction crane's bucket, 1978. Photo by Gordon Heald.

buildings.[87] The tower rose to more than twice the height of Dubai's tallest buildings at the time. Projections estimated 2,000 to 3,000 building occupants at any one time, a terrific concentration of people, especially for Dubai. A well-known advisor to Sheikh Rashid and an early detractor of the tower proposal, Easa Al Gurg claimed to have "nightmares about what might happen in the event of a fire" and reported that he "unknowingly anticipated" the movie *Towering Inferno*. The city's fire chief had also allegedly watched the film, which came out in 1974, the same year Harris began conceptual designs. In the movie, a devouring fire breaks out in a newly opened skyscraper. Neither a throng of firefighters nor a fleet of helicopters can save the well-heeled attendees trapped at the opening gala. Only the architect, played by Paul Newman, can save them, if he gains access to the tower's mainframe room.

The Dubai World Trade Centre had no mainframe room, but the architect filled the tower with fire egresses. In addition to a sprinkler system and the expected pair of fire-protected stairwells in the core, the tower's exterior corners were outfitted with submarine-like steel ladders that brought one to the ground. Fleeing occupants could access them through the windows of the inner facade: Every fourth window was operable and offered access to the narrow exterior gallery. Harris claimed the exterior escape routes were an architectural innovation and asserted that the tower, designed without extant local fire codes, met both British and American fire regulations. The tower's fire-safety measures were the foundations for the city's own future regulations.[88]

ANOTHER BRITISH PORT

In the local *Akhbar Dubai*, Harris described the World Trade Centre project as "a challenge to engineering companies worldwide," but British newspapers treated the project as primarily a challenge to British companies.[89] Not dissimilar from the work on Rashid Hospital, the center's HVAC equipment, glazing, aluminum fittings, kitchen appliances, and more were shipped to Port Rashid from the UK. The project was a boon for consulting services too. At the end of World War II, engineering emerged as the largest sector and employer in London's economy.[90] Development contracts in the Gulf region sustained London's predominance through the 1970s. In 1977, 20 percent of Great Britain's £2 billion in foreign construction contracts were signed in the United Arab Emirates.[91]

About 10,000 British citizens lived in Dubai in 1978, a sign of a solid local tradition in "buying British."[92] Trade magazines and daily papers wrote positively of "Dubai's thriving British community" that kept the British advantage anchored.[93] For Hal Smith, the New Zealander running Harris's Dubai office throughout the 1970s, it seemed most of these people were engineers, architects, and contractors working on "key infrastructure work e.g. hospitals, ports, airports, roads, water, drainage, schools, etc." and were "well aware that they were involved in something special."[94]

A feature in the October 1977 issue of *Middle East Construction* featured thirty-six-year-old engineer John Currie living with his "symmetrical family" in Dubai's upmarket Jumeirah district.[95] Here he had "a chance for real change," a vague term likely referring to his own economic standing and the transformation of a landscape according to his profession's rules. Currie, according to the article, was a "typical expatriate," enjoying tax-free income and working hard and enjoying a safe adventure in Dubai. Upon arrival, he and his family "were expecting to find a desert wilderness and were pleasantly surprised to find a comfortable villa—provided with furnishings by the company—a company car, good shops and social facilities, and a first-class school for the children." Currie's position at Halcrow was described as "one of the toughest" with eleven-hour days and six-day work weeks. In addition, the "social life is equally hectic with dinner parties, barbecues and . . . the local rugby club." Currie's wife "sews, reads, writes letters" and did secretarial work for a British company. They are "guests in another country," Currie observed, but in Britain "you cannot save anything, and the cost-of-living continues to go up." He estimated that his salary was twice as much as he would earn in the UK: "Ultimately it is the newly acquired thatched cottage in Devizes which makes those long working hours worthwhile."[96]

The Currie family feature fed a narrative that sold Dubai as a profitable workplace for British expatriates. British building-industry companies enticed employees with wealth and opportunity, and, in turn, the experts presented Dubai as a frictionless and untaxed place of advancement—a portrayal that attracted even more to come.

Currie worked on Halcrow's road contracts, but a year before the feature, his British employer became even more deeply entrenched in determining Dubai's future. The legend around the project reaches further back to one early morning in 1972, when Sheikh Rashid allegedly called Halcrow's engineer (and Dubai's "resident engineer") Neville Allen and asked to meet him at Jebel Ali, an elevated rock formation above Dubai's otherwise monotonous flatness and near the recently negotiated border with Abu Dhabi.[97] The legend casts two visionaries—one political and the other technical—gazing across unbuilt land toward the Gulf waters. Sheikh Rashid is said to have told Allen he wanted to build an even bigger port there. Allen supposedly gave an on-the-spot cost estimate.[98] Some thirty-five kilometers beyond the World Trade Centre, Port Jebel Ali was officially announced in 1976, and whispers spread of yet another new city Rashid was planning.

Though cast in terms of myth and vision, Port Jebel Ali was a political and economic move, terribly risky for Dubai's finances and terribly beneficial to Halcrow and the British economy. The colossal new port was meant to fasten Dubai's furthest possible claim at the Abu Dhabi border. Rashid not only wanted to lay claim to territory; he also wanted to secure a port that profited from Abu Dhabi's market as well.

The London *Times* framed the chosen site as evidence of intra-UAE rivalry:

> Jebel Ali's closeness to the border can mean only one thing: the hope that [Dubai] may exceed the city of Abu Dhabi in importance and become the natural capital of the Emirates.[99]

A "flavour of theatre" engulfed the Port Jebel Ali project, before and after its official groundbreaking in August 1976.[100] Halcrow admitted that Port Jebel Ali's initial planning was "short and secret," even within its own company. A site model was "kept under guard," and the site was fenced and posted with deceptive signage announcing the "Jumeirah Sand Company."[101] The *Financial Times* called the idea "the biggest risk of all."[102]

Whether Dubai could sustain an office tower seemed a trivial question in the face of Halcrow's plan for Jebel Ali: a port that quadrupled Dubai's trade capacity, a monorail, a new international airport, and a whole new city of 500,000 people. The figures were astronomical. In 1976 the port was priced at $765 million, and estimates continued to rise. In 1978 it was reported that 1 million cubic meters of earth were "being dug, blasted or dredged" to create a fifteen-meter-deep basin; 5,000 tons of cement were imported from Mombasa by then, and 30,000 tons of gravel and crushed rock had been swept up across a 100-mile radius to contribute to the site.[103] A special dredging machine was ordered from Japan, while organizers had to "scour the world for suitable dredgers," going as far as the Bahamas to find them.[104] By 1978, the number of berths at the port was increased to seventy-four, and the price rose to $1.6 billion (about $6 billion today), about 1,600 times the price of the project that originally brought the company to the region twenty years earlier.

When estimated costs for the project doubled in two years, alarmed advisors urged Rashid to scale back. In response, Rashid asked Halcrow to

consider cutting the project by half. Halcrow's negotiator, Bill Briggs, opposed the idea with the claim—unexplained by the news source—that
such a drastic cut would only save 10 percent. Briggs told the ruler that the
project was "at the point of no return."[105] He assured the ruler that a recent
downturn in trade markets should not concern him. More than just a port,
Briggs reminded him, Jebel Ali was designed as a bold industrial complex—
"oil-refining, steel-making and rolling, vehicle-assembling, chemicals, cable-
manufacturing, rubber products, industrial gases, and other manufacturing
industries."[106] Rashid remained committed to his long-term consultants and
"went very firm on it being large"; the ruler unceremoniously signed the
papers one evening after dark in the confines of Halcrow's Dubai offices.[107]

Almost a year later, Sheikh Rashid visited the site to initiate a new
180-megawatt power plant, doubling Dubai's power generation. Between
the energy needs of the port's new desalination plant, aluminum smelter,
and construction sites, there was no extra energy to share with the inhabited
city.[108] Port Jebel Ali, with hardly a resident soul, was consuming as much
energy as the rest of Dubai.

In 1979, Halcrow, whose Middle East subsidiary was now registered in
Switzerland, controlled commissions totaling $3.6 billion in the UAE, in no
small part thanks to Port Jebel Ali.[109] Such a large figure, however, did not
overcome a looming threat of global competition. In the October 19, 1978,
issue of the *Times*, two articles written by the same person gave divergent
assessments of Great Britain's command of the region's building industry.
The more optimistic article, "British Engineering Still Dominates," insists that
British contractors, architects, and consulting engineers maintained an edge
over the increasing presence of "more advanced Arab-controlled firms." The
other article, however, takes a gloomier perspective on the "stiff competition"
that forebodes "hard times ahead . . . in this heartland of Arabia."[110]

Elsewhere, British financial reporting bemoaned the British loss to Japanese export markets, but there was still an estimated $4 billion worth of ex-
ports per year to protect.[111] To maintain any lead, the writer urged the British
government to take "a close interest in these huge industrial opportunities"
and "back up" British companies vying for work in the region.[112] Halcrow's
contractual brinkmanship to keep the immense Port Jebel Ali project alive

revealed what a sustaining boon such a project could have on the British economy. One tally in the late 1970s counted fifty British companies involved in Jebel Ali: "cranes from Lincolnshire, trucks from Cheshire, rock crushers from Leicester, navigational equipment from Kent." The Foden trucks from Cheshire were said to run on Rolls-Royce engines to keep them moving twenty-four hours a day, six days a week.[113]

The London *Times* published its conflicting articles just after the announcement that Queen Elizabeth II was to visit the Arabian Peninsula. A little more than seven years after the British government withdrew its political officers from the region, the queen's "part-royal, part-business" visit was planned to shore up political and economic ties in the region.[114] A proposed "British Weeks" sales campaign was found to suggest too much "flag-waving," but according to one British export agent, the announced visit made it the "time to start pushing and shoving in the souk."[115]

Besides just trade, there was the matter of securing sources to petroleum. With the recent Iranian revolution having wiped Iran's sources off the books, there was an added urgency for sustaining ties to the Arab side of the Gulf.[116] A Reuters article, published in one of Dubai's local dailies, described the visit as "the most delicate foreign mission by a British monarch in modern times."[117] After more than a hundred of such similar visits by the British monarch around the world, "none will have seemed so exotic, nor so fraught with anxieties both of protocol and global strategy."[118]

CORDS AND SCISSORS

On February 12, 1979, Queen Elizabeth II was scheduled to initiate her nineteen-day tour of Saudi Arabia, Kuwait, Bahrain, Qatar, Oman, and the United Arab Emirates with a "supersonic four hours" aboard the Concorde airplane now on the market, making her arrival the trip's first sales pitch.[119] She would arrive in Dubai on February 26, 1979, and there was much to arrange beforehand. Less than two decades earlier, the British political agency was grappling with potential insurgency; now the British monarch was going to be feted. The city was to be "covered in decoration."[120] Anyone involved in planning her thirty-hour stay felt the pressure exerted by Dubai's government and the queen's organizers. Though it would not be completed for almost another year, the trade center—through its clear narrative, its steady rise, and its apparent compliance with British building standards—was an exemplar of Dubai's having already "bought British," in the form of what was soon estimated to be a $275 million cash contract. Its design and construction had proceeded without controversy. It was on schedule, if not ahead of it. Organizers found it a perfect backdrop for the day's "carnival feeling."[121] Rashid decided that the queen would officially open his prized project.

The queen's final itinerary included exactly an hour at the trade center. Buckingham Palace administrators relied on Harris as their point person for that single hour, which was planned down to the minute. In the weeks prior, Harris and his partner at the time, Hal Smith, were in regular communication with the queen's organizers, embassy officials in Dubai, other major British consultants seeking the monarch's attention, Dubai's Chamber of Commerce, and what was by then named the Ruler's Office. Among the various parties, it was agreed that the trade center's raised platform would perform as the meeting point for the tour, where 140 invited guests could watch the queen cross the raised platform to enter each of the complex's three buildings.

Harris coordinated the invite list, assessed the signage on and around the site, and tried to arrange for the still-operating construction site to appear less like one. The World Trade Centre management, which Buckingham Palace kept distanced from the event planning, beseeched Harris to encourage "all sub-contractors and suppliers" to take out ads in special issues of the *Financial Times* and the local *Khaleej Times*.[122]

Harris took care of even the smallest details, such as ordering the cord and curtains that would reveal the commemorative plaque in the tower lobby. One detail that greatly concerned Harris was a pair of golden scissors. They had to come from the right London goldsmith, Garrard. Securing those led to other unresolved details that highlighted the unorthodoxy of Rashid's decision to have a foreign head of state open his architectural achievement. First, who would cut the ribbon to open the tower—the ruler or the queen? Eventually, it was decided that the queen would cut the ribbon, but then who would hand her the scissors? One option was for Harris to hand the scissors to Sheikh Rashid, who in turn would give them to the queen, thus involving both heads of state but placing Dubai's ruler in the inferior position. The second option was that Harris, instead of the ruler, would hand the scissors to the queen. This option, however, cut Rashid out of the ceremony. Harris sought counsel from the British Embassy on the matter. The embassy alerted Buckingham Palace. Even for the queen's organizers, "this was a unique occasion and not even Buckingham Palace knew the answer."[123]

The golden scissors were more than a ceremonial detail: They embodied the very question of what the visit signified. Before Dubai, the queen's stops elsewhere in the Gulf mostly kept to cultural events. In Saudi Arabia, she visited the new university in Dhahran and enjoyed a dinner under the stars outside Riyadh. In Bahrain, she watched "schoolgirls pretending to be pearls . . . [leaping] out of mock-up oyster shells" and attended a race track's opening.[124] In contrast, Dubai's government maximized her thirty hours in the city to emphasize the city's British-sourced modernization. Whereas elsewhere in the region the queen had mostly observed completed projects, in Dubai she visited projects to launch them as British achievements. She visited an aluminum smelter under construction by a British company and pressed a button that started a desalination plant built by a Scottish firm. She later pressed another button that opened the sluices to Dubai's new dry docks next to Port Rashid. Pulling cords and pressing buttons, the queen switched on a modern city made by British expertise. And, as both spokesperson and salesperson, she could ask her host to continue his preference for British expertise.

To commemorate the queen's visit, British companies Costain and Taylor Woodrow, both working on the dry docks, took out a half-page advertisement in the *Financial Times*, situated just below reporting on their project. In giant letters that went across the page, the companies made clear: "WE BUILT IT."[125] "WE" referred to both the companies and their home economy.

DREAM INTO REALITY

The queen's first day in Dubai included a leisurely boat ride on Dubai Creek and a ceremony at the Dubai Municipality. After a night's sleep aboard her yacht in Port Rashid, Queen Elizabeth II sailed the next morning to Port Jebel Ali, where she witnessed the realization of British designs for an aluminum smelter, a desalination plant, and the massive terrain of the port project. Giant-wheeled trucks and earth movers lined up to create a path for the queen's motorcade along the port's excavated bed, soon to be immersed in Gulf waters. She pulled a cord to unveil a plaque scripted by British consultants. Sheikh Hamdan, Rashid's son, spoke in Arabic, and then the queen addressed the assembly:

> I'm very glad today to be able to pay my tribute to a bold and imaginative industrial venture in which a major contribution has been and is being made by British industry.[126]

Referring to the nearby British-designed desalination plant, the queen pronounced, "One of man's oldest dreams is to turn the desert green." The desalination plant, among other ventures was "[converting] that dream into reality."[127]

FIGURE 9.21 Dubai residents gathered below the World Trade Centre's raised platform to welcome the British monarch. Construction workers had transformed scraps of rebar into flagpoles for British and UAE flags. Courtesy John R. Harris Library.

Leaving the Port Jebel Ali ceremony and headed to the World Trade Centre, the queen traversed the entirety of Rashid's empty new city along the Abu
Dhabi road. As the motorcade approached the World Trade Centre, crowds
of people waved British flags and cut-out portraits of the queen and squinted
to see her white-gloved hand waving from inside the limousine. Along the
construction site's edge, the construction crew had painted leftover rebar
rods white and adorned them with British and UAE flags in an attempt to
conceal what was still a construction site. Local women, clapping and singing,
wore colorful dresses usually reserved for weddings, groups of girls and lines
of men performed dances, and boys played drums. A hot air balloon drifted
by as it struggled to rise higher than the tower's 150 meters.

As the motorcade approached the roundabout, Harris held on to the
golden scissors in his suit pocket, still wondering what he should do. He
waited as the motorcade seamlessly engaged the trade center's entry ramp
up to the raised plaza. One hundred forty people had been invited, but thousands stood wherever they could. When the queen stepped out of the limousine, the scheduled hour began.

Sheikh Rashid's son introduced the monarch to John Harris, who in turn
introduced her to representatives of some of the participating British companies. Sunley's director, John Fryer, did the same for the Duke of Edinburgh.
Keeping one hand on the scissors in his coat pocket, Harris read brief remarks
in honor of the queen. And Fryer did the same in honor of Sheikh Rashid.
It then came time for the scissors. Harris had not sought Rashid's advice on
the matter, but at the last moment he sought the queen's:

> Whispering to Her Majesty, "Who should I give the scissors, Ma'am?" The Queen
> replied under her breath, "Me." I followed Her Majesty's instructions, bowing
> low and turning the hand of the gold scissors towards her. The tape was cut.[128]

After the ribbon fell, Harris turned to look at Sheikh Rashid and noted that
he looked delighted.

Queen Elizabeth stepped into the tower's double-height marble lobby.
Cameras followed her as she crossed the lobby's still new-smelling carpet
to pull a cord that revealed yet another plaque for the day. The core's two
operating elevators delivered the queen and her retinue to the completed

viewing platform. The weather forecast had promised that an early morning fog would eventually clear, but it hadn't quite. Looking out over the city, the queen could probably spot her yacht returning from Port Jebel Ali to Port Rashid. When it was first sited at the large roundabout, the World Trade Centre was meant to create an axis with Port Rashid, the two showpiece projects bookending the new city to materialize between them. The tower had been designed to render "profound structural changes in Dubai's physiognomy" by "[wresting] the commercial hub of Dubai away from" the creek.[129]

In the time between when the tower was proposed and when Queen Elizabeth II officially opened it, "profound structural changes" had happened again, with the pursuit of Port Jebel Ali thirty-five kilometers away. Designed for one purpose, the World Trade Centre opened for another: to signal that the Abu Dhabi road functioned as the organizational spine of a new Dubai, reaching toward the outermost limit. Dubai's potential now stretched beyond Dubai Creek, beyond Port Rashid. The new city reached further than the site of the khazzans at Chicago Beach, to a distant horizon not perceptible from the tower's viewing platform.

Today the tower is regarded as the opening act of Sheikh Zayed Road. From the viewing platform that day, the queen could see that there were already three other towers under construction along Dubai's soon-to-be central axis. The Metropolitan Hotel, further out, could probably be spotted too. It would still be another few decades before there were dueling rows of skyscrapers on either side of a twelve-lane highway. Swept for the day's events, the pitch-black asphalt of the Abu Dhabi road might have been that day's clearest indication of Dubai's future. It appeared crisp and indelible just beneath the tower, but as it stretched beyond the trade center apartments, toward Port Jebel Ali in the midday haze, it disappeared.

Twenty minutes had been allotted for the ribbon cutting, two elevator rides, and a rooftop viewing, the same amount of time reserved for the queen's visit to the complex's other two buildings: first, a quick glimpse at the exhibition center's health care show (with strong representation by British suppliers) and then poolside refreshments at the Hilton. The queen thereafter returned to Port Rashid, where she pushed one final button that caused a concrete basin to flood with water, officially opening the $500 million dry docks, a huge new facility still without a management team and crippled by a structurally flawed British-engineered crane. From the floodgates, she might have looked up and caught a glimpse of the World Trade Centre in the distance. The tower she had just opened resumed "its normal hectic routine" toward its actual completion.[130] There were still several months of necessary work, and then came the "daunting task in quickly filling it" during a downturn in commercial real estate.[131] It would be several years before the tower's leasable space was close to fully occupied.[132]

Just as much as a hospital or a functioning port, the ambitions behind the trade center added up to increasing Dubai's chances at permanence and stability. It might seem paradoxical to associate a business-center complex with a city's lasting stability. Its completion at a downturn in real estate markets especially challenges that argument, but the tower was not designed to make a profit. Instead, it was meant to direct attention, and outside wealth, toward Dubai—at least until the next project was announced. Even if thirty-two floors of office space did not materialize into the enterprising "trade centre of the Arab world," marketers could still plant an image of the tower in a newspaper advertisement and state as much.

That being said, the tower's physicality did matter: Its hundreds of pilings driven deep into the ground, its thousands of tons of concrete cast into recognizable shapes, assured its buyers that it would not blow away. The tower was earthquake resistant. More essential ideas of permanence, however, were in the stories the tower could be used to tell. Rashid offered its inauguration to another head of state, not out of deference but out of a strategy that allowed his investment to be read in any useful way—at that moment as a mark of British quality. And the British building industry needed the photo op just as badly as Rashid did.

During her carefully coordinated time in Dubai, the queen acknowledged projects whose contracts were nearly settled; there were no new deals. In his critical review of the queen's visit, the Indian writer Rafiq Zakaria

FIGURE 9.22 (NEXT SPREAD) Queen Elizabeth II's view looking from the World Trade Centre's observation deck, toward Jebel Ali. The Abu Dhabi road, to be named Sheikh Zayed Road, heads in that direction. Courtesy John R. Harris Library.

contextualized the events within the 350 years of British history in the Gulf region: "not only strategic; it was also commercial." He quotes a British executive who noted that the local economy appreciates the British as "an efficient and responsible people," who had an advantage of "being here for a long time." The British queen's stay didn't directly produce any new contracts, and, moving forward, Zakaria predicted that British companies faced "fierce competition" from Pakistan, India, and South Korea for new high-stakes contracts. He also noted that while Britain earned billions annually in development contracts in the Gulf, India collected an annual $6 million in foreign exchange "through the supply of mostly semi-skilled labour; one British firm alone earns much more than that." Zakaria characterized the royal visit as evidence that British domination snuffed out possibilities for Asian economies and that the visit was an active measure to reinforce that domination.[133] Zakaria may have been correct, but he did not challenge another narrative—namely that, for many outsiders, Dubai and other Gulf cities were little more than signatories of lucrative development contracts.

The strategy of Dubai's leadership, up to this point, did not counter that mercenary view. Announcements of the World Trade Centre and Port Jebel Ali, and the heady talk of their price tags, were declarations of Dubai's existence in the language of business deals. The projects were obviously not based on the "immediate needs of the community."[134] Nevertheless, it might also be too simple to say they were based on the idea of a future. The future was not written in a plan or a vision. There was no composed idea of what Dubai would become, only that it needed to continue becoming.

Motivations behind the World Trade Centre and Port Jebel Ali were in fact less about making a future than about maintaining a present, a present on which many needed to stay focused in order to keep it remaining true. Whether draping the airport in Union Jack flags or inviting the British head of state to inaugurate his highest-risk development projects, Sheikh Rashid revealed he was ready to deal in the currency of optics in order to keep the story going. The World Trade Centre professed financial success, but its profits mattered less than its cache of meanings. Its tower delivered a prismatic scheme of messages. It allowed people to see, and claim, what they wanted. It offered comfort to those who could afford its interiors, and it extended views out over the parts of Dubai still open to manipulation and financial investment. With such a photogenic tower, Sheikh Rashid and his advisors followed an existential drive to find permanence through the sales of investment opportunity. It was not foresight—the against-all-odds commitment to a plan—on which Dubai survived into the twenty-first century. It was the acting out of audacious scenarios, the talk of them, the space in between "dream into reality," that made Dubai remain. Only in the future was Dubai made to last.

STORYLINES

"Success is a very elusive thing."

Advertisement for World Trade Centre in *Gulf News* (16 Nov. 1980)

DUBAI CREEK, 2016: A dozen American retirees, snug in expensive comfort shoes, step out of a chartered minibus into Dubai's muggy heat. They follow an unshaded gravel path to a show tent. It houses the sales center for a new development project in Dubai. Inside is machine cold and cave dark. Their scheduled host, his rugby-build profile barely discernible in the darkness, welcomes the group in a Scottish accent. Around him spotlights cast attention on presentation panels and candy-colored models. Text displays explain how this development, one of Dubai's largest ongoing projects, will refashion timeworn Dubai Creek into "creekside living," replete with landscaped walkways, food carts, recreational boats, an "urban beach," and waterfront real estate.[1] Slogans promise "a new heart for our city" at "the cradle of our heritage and the lifeline that steered Dubai's growth."[2] *"Our* city" and *"our* heritage" suggest that certain people belong there, are from there. The guide compares the project in size to a Scottish town. One retiree tells him his analogy means little to an American.

Without entertaining the remark, the guide enters the spotlight cast on a blown-up black-and-white photo: a blurry image of Dubai Creek, circa 1950. Perhaps he thinks old people like old pictures. Using his arms to frame the photo, he says, "Our project won't look anything like the old Dubai Creek." It is a promise, not a lament. He turns to another station where he touches screens to start animations, and he invites his audience to survey the rest of the tent's models that are indeed not anything like old Dubai. There are no Iranian wind towers or sand roads or fascinating interplays of old and new. Instead there will be a hoarding of up-to-date urban expectations, including outdoor shopping malls, terrace restaurants, and a sky-high icon designed by a celebrity architect. Like the first transfiguration of the creek, this one needs foreign money. It won't come from Kuwait or Qatar this time but, according to the host, from speculative homebuyers in India and China.

DEPARTURE

This high-stakes return to Dubai's "cradle" defies the city's development pattern since John Harris's 1960 town plan. Since then, Dubai's urban development has been mostly expansionary. New did not replace old; instead, space—like time—moved forward, unfurling beyond the old city's tangle of coral and concrete buildings toward a more compliant terrain of fallow desert, sparse palm groves, and fishing settlements—first, inland along Dubai Creek, then toward Port Rashid, then the World Trade Centre, and then toward the Abu Dhabi border. This development principle left earlier districts to perform as they had been intended and to adapt at a more gradual pace. Like the rings of a tree, one could pretty much travel back to the center and find traces of a city that had once been.

By the early 1980s, a yawning stasis crept over Dubai Creek. Halcrow's series of contracts had produced little more than an industrial canal. Much of the creek's edges had not been finished beyond the planting of steel pilings to keep the dredged-up land from falling back into the water.[3] Halcrow had devised the new land as a financial gift to Sheikh Rashid. A great deal of it though was left unbuilt, used for little more than dusty car parks and loading areas. Interest in the land's development dissipated when Rashid's plans moved toward Port Rashid and beyond. Neglect and decay settled in. For the people still there, Deira's most popular place was now a shopping mall, Al Ghurair Centre.

In 1981, the London *Times* architecture critic reported that Dubai's older districts were now in "as shanty a condition as can be seen in, say, Jamaica."[4]

Waterfront storage houses, once feverishly built to house incoming cargo, deteriorated from disuse. As the commercial value of the creek's edges declined, the municipality cleared them out. A "face-lift" was planned.[5] Beautifying competitions were organized. The municipality peppered the creek's coastline with patterned walking paths and shopping-mall planters—as if leisure could fill the void once filled by hard labor. In addition to the museum inside Al Fahidi Fort, the city attempted to create other museums and tourist sites and to fill the once-essential souks with goods tourists buy.

The new city was not so lively either. After decades of being defined by its growth, Dubai was settling into the infrastructural shell that had been built for it. In 1984, the *Financial Times* reported that British building-sector consultants scored their highest overseas yields ever in 1982, greatly driven by work in Dubai. The future, however, looked dimmer. That year's contracts were half as much. International competition increased while the prices of contracts shrank. The writer warned contract-conscious readers, "Be prepared for a hard slog."[6] Imports decreased by 14 percent in the first half of 1984, with every category of trade, except for cement and pipes, in decline.[7] Having lured away much of Dubai Creek's earlier traffic, Port Rashid, the dry docks, and now Port Jebel Ali stared at a slump.

Dubai Creek was also losing the smaller-scale shipping it had held onto, to the gain of ports in Zanzibar, Pakistan, and India. The "stampede" of banks exposed the city to financial collapses and face-saving government buy-outs.[8] "Briefcase bankers," a term that would resurface during the financial fever of the early 2000s, had once streamed into Dubai but now found their attachés filled with defaulted loans.[9] Dubai's traders, previously known for constantly expanding their emporiums, were "belt-tightening."[10] Moreover, they were interested in protective measures similar to Abu Dhabi's, which required businesses to be locally owned—a blow to Dubai's "free port" credo. "In the future," one British journalist forewarned, "Dubai will become more like Abu Dhabi."[11]

A major reason for Dubai's trade troubles was its loss of its largest client: Iran and its 36 million people. The post-1979 American sanctions against the country had at first boosted Dubai's contraband trade numbers—Iranians were said to favor American cosmetics and Winston cigarettes, which Dubai could deliver. But, as the Iran-Iraq War dragged on, Iran's consumers lost access to the petroleum profits to pay for nonessential goods from Dubai's port.

For Dubai, the war was a mixed blessing. It pinched Dubai's trade numbers, but it reportedly sent ships wrecked by both Iranian and Iraqi offenses to the dry docks.[12] Repair orders, however, were not enough to pay back immense loans. A lack of port traffic was matched with a lag in the completion of the dry docks, tarnishing the city's reputation as a place where projects were finished on schedule. Further out in Port Jebel Ali, the talk of a new city deflated with population projections scaled back from 500,000 to 300,000 and then to 67,000. By 1984, it had settled for being a "village."

Finance pundits favorable to Dubai blamed the slowdown on Dubai's success at meeting its development targets.[13] But what would Dubai be like without the major development contracts that had defined its existence for the past twenty years? The absence of good-news stories left room in the English-language press for more negative takes on what were once considered Dubai's advantages. British news sources had narrated the profit-fueled campaign to build a city, but they now offered warnings about its consequences. The city, previously described as open to foreigners, now was a threatening place "swamped with immigrants of all kinds out to make a fast buck."[14] Hygienic and standardized building codes were interpreted to mean "old traditions are swept away beneath all the bulldozers and ugly concrete buildings."[15] Dubai no longer seemed the *Financial Times* "magnet" it had once been.[16]

RETURN

The economic slump gave Dubai's government the time to consider a new headquarters for the Ruler's Office: Sheikh Rashid's administrative unit and body of advisors, separate from the Deira-based municipality. In 1984, the ruler's administration still officially occupied the offices that Donald Hawley visited exactly twenty-five years prior. In 1959, the offices were brand new and constructed out of imported prefabricated parts. From the balcony, Dubai's two most powerful people had scanned Dubai Creek, looking toward Deira. A meeting there resulted in Rashid's hiring John Harris. A modern city had transformed that view into a skyline of privately financed mixed-use blocks topped with bright neon signs.

Deira was Dubai's urbanity, its dense streets housing the city's cosmo-politan demographics. In contrast, the city's more concerted, government-led development occurred in the direction that Rashid and Hawley could not see that day—away from Dubai Creek. For the past fifteen years Rashid's multimillion dollar schemes had willfully focused on that latter direction. It would have seemed logical had Rashid moved his nucleus of organization outward as well. Administrative offices for Sheikh Rashid could have, for example, been sited at the World Trade Centre, or at Port Rashid overlooking the freshly opened dry docks, or at the proposed new city at Port Jebel Ali.

The new offices were to remain on Dubai Creek, linked to the older build-ings that had been the nerve center of Dubai's transformation. For the last twenty-five years, this complex had housed Rashid's large majlis—the hall where residents, bankers, and consultants waited to see him—the site of what Kamal Hamza called Dubai's "Arab democracy." It was, for example, where powerful residents had had their say in the World Trade Centre's size and ambi-tions. Hallways and stairways were said to have been perpetually inhabited by those waiting to see the ruler and to listen in on majlis discussions. Adjoining the larger room was the ruler's private office, where he received special guests and signed contracts. The Ruler's Office had also been the customs office, its high-ceilinged ground floor functioning as dusty storage and its creekside grounds populated with cranes and port debris.

Rooms were lit with bare bulbs; desk furniture was nothing more than functional. The modesty of the Ruler's Office once demonstrated that Sheikh Rashid invested Dubai's wealth into urban infrastructure, not his own of-fices. But modesty had become dilapidated. His private office, once deemed stylish for its humble indulgences of wood veneer and aluminum blinds, felt dated.[17] The sills along the long ribbon windows were lined with dusty models of completed and forgotten projects. Interior surfaces throughout the building were warped by humidity and scarred by slipshod renovations to accommodate ever-changing telephone and lighting systems. Indoor air conditioning units were paired with bright plastic buckets, bought in the souk, to catch leaking water. The hospital-green paint in the offices was peeling from the walls. Swing doors to various departments creaked from age and rot.[18]

The municipality scheduled an expansion for these offices, even though the ruler no longer presided over them. Sheikh Rashid had by then stepped back from leadership responsibility, having suffered a stroke in 1981. He deferred to his children and advisors and disappeared from public life. Emptied of its purpose, the Ruler's Office sought new meaning.

THE BRIEF

Assigned to the project, Dubai Municipality proposed to keep the original buildings and supplement them with new, meaningful architecture. The proposed addition was referred to as the *diwan*, or ruler's court. John Harris sought the project not as a direct commission from the ruler but through his winning entry for an invited design competition organized by the municipality in early 1984.[19]

The World Trade Centre had once been a topic of energetic discussions at the ruler's majlis meetings and in Rashid's private office. For the diwan project, Harris no longer had such access to the ruler. Architecture now answered to bureaucratic review, still under Kamal Hamza's direction at the municipality.[20] Harris, like other candidates, learned about the project through a published brief: The new building would extend the current facilities into Bur Dubai's built fabric, specifically into the most pronounced Bur Dubai district, Bastakiya, distinguished by its old grand houses built out of coral and topped with the distinct *barajeel*, or wind towers. Its architectural innovation had been replicated in other creekside districts, with interiors ventilated by the captured wind. Bastakiya had been built by Iranian traders, mostly in the 1920s. Its lofty houses established the setting that had made Donald Hawley murmur "Canaletto."

Like other competition entrants, Harris and his staff were left to parse the brief's wording. One sentence caused much deliberation among the team in London: "The design should reflect the local Islamic Architectural features (e.g. Wind Towers) and present the building as one of Dubai's modern buildings."[21] The call for "Islamic Architectural features" was no surprise; there was a growing interest, expressed at majlis meetings, in seeing local or Islamic characteristics reflected in architecture. The way to execute this sensibility remained unresolved. Wind towers were explicitly specified in the brief, but

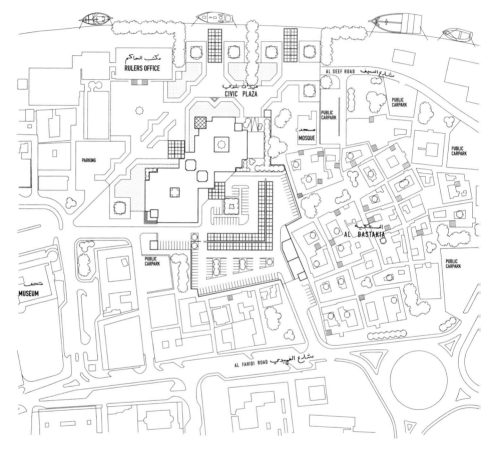

الشرم
CREEK

مكتب الحاكم
RULERS OFFICE

ديوان الحاكم
CIVIC PLAZA

AL SEEF ROAD شارع السيف

PUBLIC CARPARK

PUBLIC CARPARK

مسجد
MOSQUE

PUBLIC CARPARK

PARKING

البستكية
AL BASTAKIA

PUBLIC CARPARK

PUBLIC CARPARK

تحف
MUSEUM

AL FAHIDI ROAD شارع الفهيدي

FIGURE E.1 Competition submission site plan for the ruler's diwan demonstrates how the project's large spatial requirements, including parking and security, were carved into Bastakiya's composition of houses and alleys. Redrawn by Azza Aboualam. Courtesy Stephen Finch, John R. Harris Library.

there was an ingrained paradox in the brief's design guidelines: How could a design for a "modern" building that "[emphasized] its self-sufficiency and integrity" incorporate wind towers, which were ultimately a technology retired upon the arrival of air conditioning?

Harris acknowledged throughout his career the need to ground new buildings in their environment. For him, this concern was usually expressed in terms of climate and economy. At the trade center, the profile of the facade's concrete arches, for example, were foremost designed to maximize shade cast on windows behind them, but they were also secondarily intended to evoke an "Arab arch," to use Harris's term. For the diwan project, application of Arab or Islamic architectural features was a formal demand, instituting ornament as a standard like any quantifiable one.

After Harris's firm won the competition, Hamza's staff urged even more application of Islamic architectural features.[22] And applied they were, generating an even more emphatic gap between referential ornament and the modern construction techniques to which they were fastened. Oversize replicas of Bastakiya's wind towers encased the diwan's HVAC and elevator equipment; cast aluminum lattices, referencing wooden screens, or *mashrabiya*, functioned as security and shading measures as well as balustrades for balconies. And similar to those at the World Trade Centre, the facade's repeating

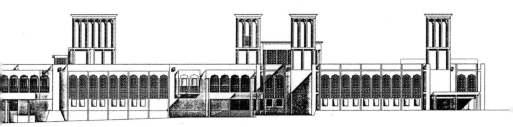

DIWAN FOR HH THE RULER OF DUBAI
WEST ELEVATION

FIGURE E.2 Revised elevation for the ruler's diwan, after the municipality's request for more features of Islamic design. Courtesy Stephen Finch, John R. Harris Library.

bays were crowned with pointed arches that both architect and design committee associated with Islamic architecture.

The municipality's interest in such historical details might suggest an
interest in historic preservation. Such a sentiment would have been in con-
gruence with Harris's master plans. However, the design brief presaged the
opposite. In the years leading up to the competition and continuing through
its site preparation, more of the surviving coral buildings were demolished; a
large number were destroyed specifically for the diwan. Shortly after Harris's
firm secured the commission, a design team member scurried to Dubai to
photograph the Bastakiya district before it disappeared entirely.[23]

FIGURE E.3 Aerial of Bastakiya, Bur Dubai, before construction of the ruler's diwan. The two connected
buildings on Dubai Creek (*top right*) are the functioning Ruler's Office. The old houses inland from
them were demolished for the new project. Courtesy John R. Harris Library.

FIGURE E.4 Overview of houses in the Bastakiya district, which were adapting to newly available technologies. These houses would be demolished for the ruler's new diwan. The ruler's existing offices can be seen in the background. Courtesy John R. Harris Library.

Stephen Finch, an architect on Harris's design team, later recalled that the diwan project coincided with the London architecture scene's increasing interest in designing with historical context in mind. The shift away from a modernist tendency to replace the old with the new was also configuring how British architects approached their work abroad. Before the diwan project was announced, two people close to Harris were working on documenting Bastakiya and the older commercial districts around it. Harris supported the work of architect Peter Jackson, who had once worked in his Dubai office, to document Bastakiya's architecture. In the process, Jackson met the young Bastakiya resident Rashad Bukhash, who recorded measurements of his family home for the scaled drawings used in future publications on the district. It was an act of archival preservation just before the house's demolition.[24] Additionally, Harris's son Mark, also an architect, documented Bastakiya and Bur Dubai's souks for his master's thesis at Harvard. Work of this nature helped capture the district's final days, though it seemed destined to have little influence beyond how some new buildings borrowed from disappearing ones.[25]

A major task for the diwan's design team was to figure out how a project—with 16,000 square meters of high-ceilinged office space, chandelier-adorned assembly rooms, a plant compound, more than 300 parking spaces, all surrounded by the surveillance of at least three guardhouses—could fit contextually among what remained of the crumbling Bastakiya district.

Harris's proposal imagined a fantastical possibility. It might have been influenced by a decision made three years prior regarding the World Trade Centre tower. After the tower's completion, Rashid allegedly returned from a fishing expedition, claiming he could not locate the tower from twenty kilometers offshore.[26] Forty men subsequently spent twenty-eight weeks applying 65,000 kilograms of white paint to make the tower "stand out for miles around."[27] Similarly, the revised designs for the Ruler's Office proposed a gleaming white diwan as an idealized version of the twenty or so earthen-colored buildings demolished to make way for it. Once completed at the end of 1987, the diwan complex rose beyond the last of Bastakiya's coral-and-earth wind towers, as an elevated abstraction of Bastakiya's building arts, more Iranian than Arab. The diwan's fanciful contrivances attempted a new history, not because there was no history but because a real history was not preferred.

Ever since Iranian traders had landed there in the 1920s, Bastakiya had been a site of change and transition.[28] By the late 1960s, exposed electrical wiring laced its buildings together and activated the TV antennae perched a notch lower than wind towers. Air conditioning units were carved into the coral and mud of masonry walls or were pressed into structures of concrete brick. Quick-setting concrete mix and polycarbonate siding filled cracks in coral walls.

Since its founding, Bastakiya was a mix of cultures and time periods. One house was known for screening Hindi films from its rooftop so that neighbors on their roofs could watch along. A few houses were still inhabited by Iranian families, until few were inhabited at all. Through the late 1970s, Bastakiya was being vacated as its families accepted land plots or apartments in new districts like Al Satwa. Their departures were followed by bulldozers and

FIGURE E.5 A street in Bastakiya reveals the neighborhood's incorporation of contemporary needs and comforts into older building systems, 1974. Photo by Peter Jackson.

earth movers that effortlessly leveled the old homes, their foundations only as deep as the walls were wide.[29]

The Bastakiya buildings not razed for new development projects were eventually converted into ersatz versions of themselves, minus the visible evidence that old buildings were once reinforced with new materials and technologies. A designated heritage site was to host new manifestations of old homes to complement the new diwan. Jackson and Bukhash's drawings, intended to preserve the diminishing district, also contributed to building the heritage site.

The heritage site was not a project for the Harris office, but it proved to be the diwan's necessary accompaniment. Seeming to complement the new diwan's white paint, the heritage buildings were given a monotone brown wash, a stand-in for the hues and tones that accumulated over generations of residents. Looming over the historical reenactment, the diwan was an exaggerated telling of its surroundings. It was arguably Dubai's first building to explicitly apply Dubai's past in modern architecture. Its wind-tower encasements were probably the first in Dubai to reproduce the forms divorced from their original purpose.

Prior to the diwan, Harris's buildings for Dubai strove to combine a commitment to modern architecture with a tempered expression of Dubai's aspirations—assessing what kind of facilities a hospital could offer or how much opulence a national bank could display. Under a new regime of expectations, the diwan's design sought to combine modern with an expression of history, so literal that it was fictional.

MEANING

The diwan project is susceptible to the criticism that the city's architecture often receives today: A limited and overused index of symbols—including Islamic patterning, wind towers, falcons, dhows, the sinuous curves of dunes, and camels—bind contemporary buildings to reduced conceptions of history and context. The anthropologist Ahmed Kanna has described how Dubai's contemporary architecture can be caught in a predicament: on the one hand, signaling a fictive ancient city—what he calls the "vanished village"—through references to a simple set of symbols and, on the other hand, sustaining the proliferation of shiny, steel-and-glass assertions of a bold dedication to the future.[30]

In between a glorified past and a prewritten future, John Harris's firm produced most of its work for the city. Through the 1970s, Dubai's architecture, much like the other infrastructural development of the city, relied on the delivery and accommodation of industrial technologies and the achievement of measurable standards. It was not architecture without meaning; technology-induced service *was* the meaning—for example, medical care supplied from a hospital's interiors or a savings account protected in a bank. By the end of the 1970s, the city had amassed decipherable and quantitative attributes—the kilometers of asphalt, the counts of hospital beds and hotel rooms, the daily flight arrivals, and the number of port berths. These fulfilled a modern city's checklist.

More expectations were revealed, like the municipality's formulation of "Islamic design." No longer merely a casual topic in the majlis, it was now formalized in public documents and in the majlis's very architecture.

FIGURE E.6 Aerial of Bastakiya with the diwan on the left. On the right are the remaining wind-tower houses not yet demolished. Courtesy John R. Harris Library.

Aesthetics—design criteria—were to be approached as a quantifiable task. The diwan project revealed that design could do more than merely supply controlled environments; it could now affirm narratives about history and place, however inaccurate those tellings might be. No longer sufficient to offer "a concrete plane" of seemingly straightforward infrastructure, architecture now had to offer more kinds of stories.

Dubai's leadership might have been responding to outside criticism. In 1979, a drawing of the World Trade Centre tower made the front page of the Bahraini paper *Akhbar Al Khaleej*. Titled "Our Arab Cities Lost Their Identities," the article argued that Arab cities had been harmed by recent development projects. Foreign investors and architects were blamed for extracting profits without considering heritage and culture.[31] An image of the Yemeni city Sanaa's skyline illustrated what was being lost, alongside an early rendering for the World Trade Centre captioned with this warning: "Foreign Western architecture is replacing our Islamic one." While one might argue the tower later incorporated the "Arab arch," the article asserted that Western architects could not produce Islamic architecture.

Although there were discussions about local architectural identity and how Dubai's new architecture responded to it, the debate was largely shaped by Western voices, most often from architects outside the Gulf. In 1989, ten years after the British monarch had visited Dubai, Prince Charles and Princess Diana arrived in the city, interested in visiting heritage sites. Upon hearing of the pending visit, British architect and Dubai resident Rayner Otter had allegedly written a letter to invite the prince to visit the home he had made inside one of the threatened Bastakiya houses. Charles subsequently visited the dilapidated and shrinking district. Simply by visiting Bastakiya, he is credited for personally intervening to preserve Bastakiya, after dozens of houses had already been demolished, many of them for the diwan project.[32] Charles also visited the new diwan, which "really encouraged" him. His assistant wrote to Harris that the prince was "so pleased that you took so much trouble to design it in context." More than just for Dubai, the complex was "a splendid example to set to other Gulf countries, where so much has been ruined by inappropriate design and construction."[33] In 1979, Queen Elizabeth had arrived in Dubai to marvel at "a bold and imaginative industrial venture" achieved with British expertise; her successor-in-waiting arrived to warn of too much transformation, or at least the appearance of it.

SCRIPTS

Toward the end of the queen's 1979 tour, her husband Prince Philip was asked for his takeaway thoughts. He reminisced on his visit to Port Jebel Ali:

> British industry tends to get a bit run down at home. It's incredible to see what they've achieved here. . . . It makes one wonder what happens at home sometimes.[34]

Like others before him, the British consort imagined Dubai as a place of frictionless work opportunities. He seemed convinced that Britain's accumulated expertise in engineering, design, and contracting could perform spectacularly if "what happens at home" did not get in the way. He might have been referring to unions, democratic institutions, or land-use restrictions that thwarted new development proposals. In Dubai, government did not hinder expertise but instead hired it. Through almost two decades of engagement, the British building industry and countless suppliers had helped realize more than the city's expansion; they had also constructed the mythology of a land that awed Prince Philip.

Central to that mythology was the image of Dubai's ruler, "a full-scale entrepreneur" and "a merchant prince."[35] Before his stroke, Sheikh Rashid was regularly portrayed in the English-language press as lean, fit, and quick to his feet. In an issue of *Middle East Construction* (which also featured the Currie family in their Jumeirah villa), a profile of Sheikh Rashid presented a sensible, mindfully miserly, and early-rising leader.[36] He was the ideal client, who embodied the reason to invest in Dubai despite any downturn. Financial papers molded the ruler into a "small-government" champion with "no taste for politics or diplomacy" and an administrator of a government handled like a "vast holding company."[37] The axiom credited to him—"what is good for the businessman is good for Dubai"—dovetailed with his consultants' professed apolitical worldview, one where profit margins and growth statistics led to human welfare. The experts presented a mastermind in control, and, in return, he presented a city built to their specifications.

The experts amassed their labors into built narratives as much for themselves as for their client, but the storyline had one major flaw: It was not prepared for the moment when the charismatic leader, once distrusted by local British officers, would no longer be there to craft the storyline. In late 1988, the diwan opened, set against the ghosts of its earthen forebears and the creek's dusty commercial skyline. Sheikh Rashid may not have ever occupied the building. He died in October 1990. An empty diwan was left bedecked with symbols never enacted.

SUPERFICIAL

An early scriptwriter for Dubai was the British political agent Peter Tripp, whose scenario and film treatment for *These Are the Trucial States* imagined a productive role for Great Britain in the region. By the 1960s, the scriptwriters

FIGURE E.7 Dubai residents on an abra headed across Dubai Creek, with the diwan on the opposite side in Bur Dubai. Courtesy Richard Turpin, John R. Harris Library.

were no longer political agents; they were the private-sector experts whom the British government had delivered and whose motivations were explicitly transactional. Based upon their own designs and pitches, the new scriptwriters' concrete planes and hygienic surfaces were installed. They took out ads in international papers celebrating their feats in Dubai, they gave quotable quips to journalists, and they made corporate films. The outlines of John Harris's 1960 town plan configured the demarcated spaces in which they could create what *they* thought Dubai should be. Within those lines, Dubai's investors produced a city that assuredly retreated indoors into building systems that isolated sand, dust, humidity, and heat to the other side of new membranes. The diwan project added an extra quantifiable layer: the design criteria for the appearance of those membranes.

Many have dismissed Dubai as a city of deceptive surfaces that obscure lurking truths behind them. Dubai-based British officials once stressed the importance of image, or the photogenic, to argue for the most basic efforts of modern advancement in Dubai. Even when the city's infrastructural development (including residential blocks, power stations, piers, roads, bridges, water tanks, pylons) were at their most unadorned, the evidence of their existence—the image or the statistic—was intended to project a modern and competent city. Beginning in the 1950s, the British government endorsed infrastructure building as a measure to protect its own standing in the region and its own image, by making life in the city appear bearable. It is therefore difficult to argue that even Dubai's most basic modernization projects were not about installing surfaces. While it might be necessary and fruitful to search beyond surfaces—to investigate the "dark" or secret side— of any city, it is also essential to read carefully the broadcasted messages and signs that beg for our attention. Many of the buildings Harris produced for Dubai were the perceptible frames of a loosely knit campaign to legitimize Dubai as city. And most of them have been demolished or made unrecognizable. That makes their appearances more difficult to read and therefore more important to recall.

Prior to his visit to Dubai in 1978, Jonathan Raban wrote *Soft City*, a pensive work about how urban dwellers cope with daily life in cities. He observed that, "We still find it very hard to face the elementary truth of life in big cities: that in them we are necessarily dependent on surfaces and appearances."[38] Rather than ignoring or disdaining surfaces, Raban urges the reader "to attend [to them] with greater sympathy and seriousness."[39] Considering how often surfaces are so quickly spurned as disingenuous and untrustworthy, it can seem a shocking recommendation to deploy "sympathy and seriousness" for what might ultimately be an attempt at spectacle and illusion.

In *Soft City*, Raban approaches the city as a venue of performance: stagecraft, acting, window dressing, even melodrama. All of these things create a city, and, in the process, we as city residents are complicit in creating and sustaining the stages. If Raban is correct, rejecting certain surfaces in Dubai as false or deceptive may not necessarily bring us any closer to truths. The false wind towers implanted onto the diwan, for one, were not meant to trick the viewer into thinking that Dubai's most powerful were still keeping cool by ancient ways. They were placed there to tell a story that we might not believe but we do listen to.

The latest return to Dubai Creek—the project that promises to look nothing like old Dubai—is another message that architecture delivers. It is a story meant to replace earlier ones, since stories grow stale if they are not rewoven. This time the story is about sustainability, luxury, sidewalk shopping, and Asian speculative markets. While we listen to the pitch, we are called to marvel at the new project's enormous transformation of land into "human environment." Veracity is substantiated in the nine-figure budget, the registry of experts, and the legion of investors from the world over. The new story at the creek is still written by consultancies, some of which helped craft the earliest scenarios at the edges of Dubai Creek. Dubai's audience—whether it is retirees in a show tent, observers from their laptops, investors from Azerbaijan, or work seekers in South Africa and Bangladesh—has been essential to the making of Dubai. Given that other cities today also rely, so emphatically, on stagecraft for how they are beheld by the world, that is not surprising. What makes Dubai stand out, the next round of scriptwriters will have to tell us.

INDEBTED

Like many architects, my job sent me to Dubai. Unlike many architects, however, I got paid to examine a city closely. In 2006, research for the architecture firm OMA supported a presentation at the tenth International Architecture Exhibition in Venice. For the first time at the biennial, Dubai and other Gulf cities got substantial attention. A team of researchers and I visualized an indexing of major projects overlaid with urban histories available at the time. I have Rem Koolhaas, Kayoko Ota, and others at OMA to thank for putting me on to the initial questions. After the exhibition, we produced two publications: *Al Manakh* and *Al Manakh 2: Gulf Continued*. Both sought to provide much needed insight to the Gulf region's changing landscapes, not only in boom times but in bust ones too. With these projects, my field of indebtedness expanded rapidly, to include Lilet Breddels, Arjen Oosterman, Daniel Camara, Mitra Khoubrou, Daniel Rabin, Guillaume Yersin, Irma Boom, Rory Hyde, Timothy Moore, Sandra Bsat, Sonja Haller, Stephen Ramos, Shajahan Madampat, Katrin Greiling, Alamira Reem Al Ayedrous, Reda Sijiny, and Sahil Latheef.

While working on the exhibition, the OMA team put together that the firm of one British architect, John Harris, produced Dubai's first town plan and the city's first skyscraper. It was a connection only made in small print before *Al Manakh*. Sorting through photographs with John Harris's son Mark, I realized there was much more of a story to tell. Mark offered me access to John's work spaces and his photographs and documents. In every year of this project, Mark uncovered more founts of material. His help and patience have been considerable. Before she died in 2016, John's wife and first business partner, Jill Harris, suggested that a book about John Harris should be more a book about Dubai. I took her advice.

With the *Al Manakh* projects completed, I quit my job and focused on this book, written and researched in between working stints and teaching contracts. The book has been enriched by countless people I've met. Not only did they make sure that I saw more of Dubai than I thought possible, but I've come to rely on them to comprehend Dubai's global reach and its elusive history. These include Joumana Al Jabri and her whole family, Mishaal Al Gergawi, Sultan Sooud Al Qassemi, Hind Mezaina, Antonia Carver, Simeon Kerr, Butheina Kazim, Huda Smitshuijzen Abifarés, Ammar Al Attar, and Khaled Adham. Sara Kassa and Natalie Al Shami, two contributors to the initial exhibition, were my first guides to the city, translators in many ways. Countless people helped me meet the right people and shared invaluable resources and perspectives, including Kamal Hamza, Farrokh Derakhshani, Abdullah Saleh, Tassos Emmanuel, Rashad Bukhash, Margaret Bullard, Oscar Mandoody, Linda Pearson, Heli Allen, Riad Kamal, Yasser Mahgoub, Saadudin AbdulHamed Mohamed, Hooky Walker, James Craig, Kenn Dalley, Nuha Ansari, Michael Hamilton-Clark, Abdulkhaleq Abdulla, Diana Barnardiston, Guy Guillemard, Jonathan Makepeace, James Linton, Patrick Michael, Charles Tripp, Hal Smith, Gordon Heald, and Peter Jackson. Stephen Finch, an architect formerly at Harris's firm, provided important perspective and documents in the final years of this project.

As a student at Yale, three instructors helped me find my way to express architecture in writing: Kevis Goodman, Lauren Kogod, and Vincent Scully. As a faculty member at Yale, two deans of the architecture school, Robert A. M. Stern and Deborah Berke, gave me the invaluable opportunity to work with graduate and undergraduate students. Conversations with those students have strengthened the arguments in this book. Faculty members Joyce Hsiang, Bimal Mendis, Eeva-Liisa Pelkonen, Keller Easterling, Alan

Plattus, and Kishwar Rizvi have been supportive throughout this project. The community of Yale librarians—including Robin Dougherty, Lindsay King, and Richard Richie—is incomparable. At Yale, I also had the terrific backup of assistants and researchers, including Mahdi Sabbagh, Azza Aboualam, Dima Srouji, Dina Taha, Maggie Tsang, and Hiba Bhatty. At Harvard Graduate School of Design, Rosetta Elkin, Pierre Bélanger, Gareth Doherty, and Diane Davis sought ways to incorporate my work into productive on-campus discussions. Naomi Woods, Ghazal Jafari, and Reem Khorshid also gathered helpful leads.

Beyond the campus setting, Janna Wagner was a great support in New Haven. And George Zdru too, offering a plush urban garden where I finished the manuscript. Han Malinverno hosted me in the Alps so that I could complete an early draft. During my countless research visits to London, Malu Halasa, Andy Cox, Frank Gallacher, and Omar Kholeif gave me a homelife and vital encouragement.

Colleagues and friends have read the entire manuscript or parts of it. They did more than keep me sharp; they kept me going: Anna Shefelbine, Shomon Shamsuddin, Hashim Sarkis, Nicholas de Monchaux, Sultan Sooud Al Qassemi, Khaled Adham, Tabitha Decker, Rory Hyde, Mary Tobler, Omar Kholeif, Joel Beinin, and Rosie Bsheer. Neha Vora and Attiya Ahmad gave me insightful commentary on Chapter 7 at a workshop organized by Rosie Bsheer in Yale's history department. Laleh Khalili and Steven Caton also provided helpful feedback. While many looked closely at the text, only Edo Smitshuijzen volunteered to improve the manifold archival images. Elizabeth Reisz answered all my questions about finance.

I've had wonderful opportunities to share and test my work with larger publics through events and publications. People who have helped me in this regard are Nasser Rabbat, Farah Al-Nakib, Shumon Basar, Rachaporn Choochuey, David Goldfield, Harvard Arab Students Association, Adina Hempel, Adrian Lahoud, Fadi Tofeili, Nathalie Elmir, Christine Tohmé, Mahdi Sabbagh, Meghan McAllister, Lukasz Stanek, Marieke Rietbergen, Michelle Provoost, Wouter Vanstiphout, Kevin Mitchell, George Katodrytis, Oliver Wainwright, Chris Michael, Muneerah Alrabe, Hussam Dakkak, Basmah Kaki, Hessa AlBader, Abdurahman Medallah, Neil Brenner, and Eyad Houssami.

Thank you to Stanford University Press for taking a chance on this book. My faithful editor Kate Wahl could tell me, with uncanny skill, exactly what I needed to do. Leah Pennywark gave me much-appreciated editorial advice. Caroline McKusick, Emily Smith, and Faith Wilson Stein have been a great support team. As copyeditor, Jennifer Gordon ushered this project beautifully around the final bend. Thank you to Kevin Barrett Kane for the careful layout of images with text.

Thank you to the Graham Foundation for Advanced Studies in the Fine Arts for supporting this book's publication.

Thank you to the Stimuleringsfonds Creative Industrie (Netherlands) for supporting this book's publication. I especially valued the thoughtful feedback from the selection committee. I also received an instrumental research grant from the former Netherlands Foundation for Visual Arts, Design and Architecture (FBKVB) at the start of this project.

Writing down all these names makes me realize just how rich and collaborative this project has been. Yet it often felt lonely because, in the end, I had to write the book and take responsibility for it. For me to do that, Anna was there the whole way. Without Sander, there'd be no book. I'm grateful to my parents and to my family in the Netherlands who accepted me with open arms from day one.

The book is dedicated to Dubai and to the people who build it, because I'm indebted to them for all I've learned.

NOTES

PROLOGUE

1. "Career High Points," *Gulf Business* 2, no. 1 (May 1997).

2. Oliver Lindsay, *The Battle for Hong Kong 1941–1945: Hostage to Fortune* (Stroud, UK: Spellmount, 2007), 157–236.

3. Ibid.

4. The Trucial States was the collective name British-authored documents gave to the sheikhdoms of Abu Dhabi, Dubai, Sharjah, Ajman, Umm Al Quwain, Ras Al Khaimah, and Fujairah. The invention of this terminology is further defined in Chapter 1.

5. Donald Hawley, *The Emirates: Witness to a Metamorphosis* (Norwich, UK: Michael Russell, 2007), 171.

6. Ibid., 29.

7. James Onley, *The Arabian Frontier of the British Raj: Merchants, Rulers, and the British in the Nineteenth-Century Gulf* (New York: Oxford University Press, 2007), 45. Prior to the political agency, an Arab agent paid by the British government, and sometimes a British agent, were stationed in a rented house in Sharjah.

8. Today, Dubai is an emirate and a city of the United Arab Emirates (and before that it was one of the seven sheikhdoms that the British government referred to as the Trucial States; see note 4 above). Since this book is about urbanism, Dubai will be addressed as a city. Its former status as a city-state will be touched upon, as well as its gradual loss of that designation.

9. Minutes of discussions regarding Halcrow's survey of Dubai and Sharjah Creeks (28 Jan. 1955), National Archives, United Kingdom (NA), FO 371:114696.

10. See, for example, Paul deGive and Thomas A. Roberts, "Rashid—Merchant Prince of the Persian Gulf," *Christian Science Monitor* (9 Aug. 1973); and Hawley, *The Emirates,* 145.

11. See, for example, Graeme H. Wilson, *Rashid's Legacy: The Genesis of the Maktoum Family and the History of Dubai* (London: Media Prima, 2006), 25.

12. In *Dubai: The City as Corporation* (Minneapolis: University of Minnesota Press, 2011), an important study of contemporary Dubai, Ahmed Kanna analyzes this two-pronged mythology as a living paradox in the chapter titled "The Vanished Village."

13. Donald Hawley, *Desert Wind and Tropic Storm: An Autobiography* (Wilby, UK: Michael Russell, 2000), 55.

14. John Darwin, *The Empire Project: The Rise and Fall of the British World-System, 1830–1970* (Cambridge, UK: Cambridge University Press, 2009), 580.

15. Hawley, *The Emirates*, 19.

16. Adrian Hanna, "Royal Antediluvian Order of Buffaloes Aero Trucial Lodge 9147." http://www.sixgolds.com/sharjah.htm

17. Kanna, *Dubai: The City as Corporation*, 174.

18. Address by Robert Gibbons given at the Thanksgiving Service for John R. Harris (12 May 2008), John R. Harris Library.

19. At the time of writing, two of the twenty-three pavilions planned for Dubai's Al Shindagha Museum have opened, one focused on Dubai Creek and the other on the perfume industry. For several years, foreign consultants have scrambled to find documentation to fill and narrate these museums.

20. Hawley, *The Emirates*, 223.

21. Nelida Fuccaro, "Review of *Ruling Shaikhs and Her Majesty's Government: 1960–1969* by Miriam Joyce," *International Journal of Middle East Studies* 39, no. 3 (August 2007): 480–482.

22. Onley, *Arabian Frontier of the British Raj*, 1–54.

23. Email (26 June 2008), World Architecture Congress at Cityscape Dubai 2008.

24. See, for example, Johann Hari, "The Dark Side of Dubai," *The Independent* (7 April 2009).

CHAPTER 1

1. John Gordon Lorimer and Richard Lockington Birdwood, *Gazetteer of the Persian Gulf, Oman, and Central Arabia* (Shannon: Irish University Press, 1970, republished), vol. I, pt. 2, 2638. The Persian Gulf is sometimes referred to as the Arabian Gulf. In this book, it will be referred to as the Gulf.

2. Muhammad Morsy Abdullah, *The United Arab Emirates: A Modern History* (Abu Dhabi: Makarem, 2007), 27.

3. Lorimer and Birdwood, *Gazetteer*, vol. I, pt. 2, 2638. Even before the Maktoum family's predecessors arrived in Dubai in 1833 from Abu Dhabi, Dubai was represented in these treaty signings. In 1820, the sheikhdom's nine-year-old ruler was represented by his uncle at a signing in Sharjah.

4. Lorimer and Birdwood, *Gazetteer*, vol. I, pt. 1, 198; J. B. Kelly, *Britain and the Persian Gulf: 1795–1880* (Oxford: Clarendon Press, 1968), 139–160, 211.

5. One example of proscribed imports was German diving equipment that could have lessened the toil of pearl divers enduring brutal seasons of harvesting pearls from the seabed. A British official argued for the ban's benevolent impact: If the technology had been made available to the coast's pearl divers, fewer people would have been needed to work in the pearl industry, thus making more men available for pursuing less favorable pursuits, like "gun-running, slaving and piracy." However, the technology could have also brought about a more diverse economy. With fewer people dedicated to the pearl industry, a more varied and resilient economy might have evolved to withstand Japan's artificial cultivation of pearls in the 1930s. See Abdullah, *United Arab Emirates*, 103–104.

6. Aqil Kazim, *The United Arab Emirates A.D. 600 to the Present: A Socio-Discursive Transformation in the Arabian Gulf* (Dubai: Gulf Book Centre, 2000), 152.

7. Donald Hawley, *The Trucial States* (London: Allen & Unwin, 1970), 164.

8. Lorimer and Birdwood, *Gazetteer*, vol. I, pt. 2, 2637. Curzon's visit to the region was described as such: "The memorable cruise made by Lord Curzon in the Persian Gulf at the end of 1903 was undertaken for the purpose of inspecting the Indian establishments maintained there, of visiting the Arab Shaikhs in treaty relations with the British Government, and of testifying to the paramount political and commercial ascendance exercised by Great Britain in Persian Gulf waters."

9. Ibid., vol. I, pt. 2, 2632, 2638; John Hayhurst, "Curzon's Durbars and the Alqabnamah: The Persian Gulf as Part of the Indian Empire," in *British Library Asian and African Studies Blog* (30 Dec. 2014). https://blogs.bl.uk/asian-and-african/2014/12/curzons-durbars-and-the-alqabnamah-the-persian-gulf-as-part-of-the-indian-empire.html

10. By 1949, Dubai and the other sheikhdoms had been given the appellation British Protected States, which did little to clarify the political relationship. In *Bagpipes in Babylon: A Lifetime in the Arab World and Beyond* (London: I. B. Tauris, 2006), Glencairn Balfour-Paul, once the political agent in Dubai, described the British as "keep[ing] the precise status of the sheikhdoms undefined" (p. 190).

11. Abdullah, *United Arab Emirates*, 66. The holding company of PDTC was Petroleum Concessions Limited.

12. Marshall to Hird (16 May 1957), National Archives, United Kingdom (NA), FO 371:127013; Abdullah, *United Arab Emirates,* 67; Frauke Heard-Bey, *From Trucial States to United Arab Emirates: A Society in Transition* (London: Motivate, 2005), 258.

13. Pelly to Secretary of State (26 June 1950), National Archives, United Kingdom (NA), FO 371:82047.

14. "A Note on the Wealth of Dubai" (24 June 1950), National Archives, United Kingdom (NA), FO 371:82047. Upon India's independence in 1947, British administration of the Trucial States transferred from the colonial government of India to the Foreign Office in London.

15. Ibid.

16. Julian Walker, *Tyro on the Trucial Coast* (Durham, UK: Memoir Club, 1999), 58. The site is roughly where the British consulate is today. British scouts actually selected, and preferred, the site. In preparing the grounds for the political agent, an official contemplated on what life would be like for the future agents: "I hope you will agree with me that any British officer or a clerk, who is posted to such a dreary place, and such a climate, without any amenities, or even his fellow Europeans . . . to meet for recreation, will need the very best of accommodations for himself and his wife if he is to maintain his health, or even his mental balance, throughout the summer" (Jackson to Walters [4 Nov. 1947], National Archives, United Kingdom [NA], WORK 10:124).

17. Sir William Halcrow & Partners to Pirie-Gordon (12 Jan. 1955), National Archives, United Kingdom (NA), FO 371:114696. In British government files up until 1971, Sir William Halcrow & Partners is often referred to as Halcrows. Later, before it was acquired by the larger conglomerate CH2M and then by Jacobs Engineering Group, it was known as Halcrow, the name that will be used throughout this book.

18. Heard-Bey, *From Trucial States,* 249.

19. The Arabic word "bur" suggests something like territory. By the time Bur Deira was definitively part of the city Dubai, it was referred to as Deira, a recognized district of the city. In this book Bur Deira is used when discussing the separate, other town, the one still contentiously independent of Bur Dubai. Bur Dubai is still used today to refer to a district of Dubai that roughly corresponds to the bounds of the old town.

20. H. D. G. Law, "Romance of the Persian Gulf," *Edinburgh Review* 246, no. 502 (1927): 210.

21. Rupert Hay, "Persian Gulf States and Boundary Problems," *Geographical Journal* 120, no. 4 (1954): 439. Tabitha Decker referred me to this excerpt.

22. Donald Hawley, *The Emirates: Witness to a Metamorphosis* (Norwich, UK: Michael Russell, 2007), 199.

23. "A Note on the Wealth of Dubai" (24 June 1950), National Archives, United Kingdom (NA), FO 371:82047.

24. Ibid.

25. Burrows to Riches (27 Sept. 1957), National Archives, United Kingdom (NA), FO 1016:591.

26. Hay, "Person Gulf States," 437.

27. Tripp to Lamb (23 Aug. 1961), National Archives, United Kingdom (NA), FO 957:231.

28. Dubai Harbour (7 Jan. 1956), National Archives, United Kingdom (NA), FO 371:120633.

29. James Onley, "Britain's Informal Empire," *Journal of Social Affairs* 22, no. 87 (Fall 2005): 37.

30. Heard-Bey, *From Trucial States*, 250–251.

31. "entrepôt, n." *OED Online* (Sept. 2019). Oxford University Press.

32. Lindsay to Pelly (8 Oct. 1949), British Library, Indian Office Records, R/15/2/385. Holloway eventually built Dubai's first hospital building, little more than a concrete-block barracks (Christopher Meyer, "Visit to Dubai, August 1957," John R. Harris Library).

33. Tripp to Richards (17 Aug. 1955), National Archives, United Kingdom (NA), FO 1016:401.

34. Ibid.

35. "British quality" was a term often used to describe British experts and services. It was an entry in the "Glossary of Awaiting Encounters" in the pamphlet "Hints to Business Men Visiting the Persian Gulf," Board of Trade, London (1960).

36. Donald Hawley, *The Emirates*, 53.

37. Annual Review for 1970 (10 Dec. 1970), National Archives, United Kingdom (NA), FCO 8:1510.

38. Confidential report, "Trucial States" (24 April 1957), National Archives, United Kingdom (NA), FO 371:126900.

39. Heard-Bey, *From Trucial States*, 310.

40. John Darwin, *The Empire Project: The Rise and Fall of the British World-System, 1830–1970* (Cambridge, UK: Cambridge University Press, 2009), 580.

41. Jan Morris, "In Quest of the Imperial Style," in Robert Fermor-Kesketh, ed., *Architecture of the British Empire* (New York: Vendome Press, 1986), 17.

42. Stephen Ramos, *Dubai Amplified: The Engineering of a Port Geography*, Design and the Built Environment Series (Burlington, VT: Ashgate, 2010), 10.

43. Kamal Hamza in discussion with author, Dubai (7 Dec. 2010).

44. Extract from *Al Meezan*, English translation (28 Sept. 1956), National Archives, United Kingdom (NA), FO 1016:507.

45. Burrows to Riches (17 Oct. 1956), National Archives, United Kingdom (NA), FO 371:120611.

46. Anita Burdett, *Records of the Emirates: 1961–1965* (Slough, UK: Archive Editions, 1997), vol. I, 212.

47. Walmsley to Wigmore (12 Jan. 1960), National Archives, United Kingdom (NA), FO 371:140144. Italics added.

48. Burrows to Riches (17 Oct. 1956), National Archives, United Kingdom (NA), FO 371:120611.

49. Walmsley to Wigmore (12 Jan. 1960), National Archives, United Kingdom (NA), FO 371:140144.

50. "The Next Five Year's Plan" (8 Sept. 1959), National Archives, United Kingdom (NA), FO 371:140143.

51. Tripp to Walmsley (17 Aug. 1961), National Archives, United Kingdom (NA), FO 957:231.

52. James Onley, *The Arabian Frontier of the British Raj: Merchants, Rulers, and the British in the Nineteenth-Century Gulf* (New York: Oxford University Press, 2007), 12, 48, 54.

53. Fatma Al-Sayegh, "Merchants' Role in Changing Society," *Middle Eastern Studies* 34, no. 1 (January 1998): 90–91.

54. Ibid.; Kazim, *United Arab Emirates*, 202–204.

55. Abdullah, *United Arab Emirates*, 223–233.

56. "Appendix A: An Estimate of the Political Situation in the Town of Dubai" (9 Oct. 1956), National Archives, United Kingdom (NA), FO 1016:507.

57. Burrows to Riches (10 Jan. 1957), National Archives, United Kingdom (NA), FO 371:126871.

58. Confidential Annex (10 Dec. 1956), National Archives, United Kingdom (NA), FO 371:120553.

59. Burrows to Lloyd (9 April 1957), National Archives, United Kingdom (NA), FO 371:126900.

60. Pirie-Gordon to Burrows (11 May 1955), National Archives, United Kingdom (NA), FO 1016:401.

61. Burrows to Macmillan (31 May 1955), National Archives, United Kingdom (NA), FO 1016:401.

62. Tripp to Burrows (21 May 1955), National Archives, United Kingdom (NA), FO 1016:401.

63. Burrows to Macmillan (31 May 1955), National Archives, United Kingdom (NA), FO 1016:401.

64. Tripp to Richards (2 June 1955), National Archives, United Kingdom (NA), FO 1016:401. Italics added.

65. Quote from Tripp in Simon C. Smith, *Britain's Revival and Fall in the Gulf: Kuwait, Bahrain, Qatar, and the Trucial States, 1950–71* (London, New York: RoutledgeCurzon, 2004), 52.

66. "The Next Five Year's Plan" (8 Sept. 1959), National Archives, United Kingdom (NA), FO 371:140143.

CHAPTER 2

1. Gault to Riches (23 June 1956), National Archives, United Kingdom (NA), FO 371:120541.

2. Tripp to Gault (1 July 1957), National Archives, United Kingdom (NA), FO 1016:591.

3. "Appendix A: An Estimate of the Political Situation in the Town of Dubai" (10 Sept. 1956), National Archives, United Kingdom (NA), FO 1016:507.

4. Tripp to Richards (21 Dec. 1956), National Archives, United Kingdom (NA), FO 1016:507.

5. Tripp to Gault (1 July 1957), National Archives, United Kingdom (NA), FO 1016:591.

6. Various correspondence (1956), National Archives, United Kingdom (NA), FO 371:120611.

7. Burrows to Lloyd (9 April 1957), National Archives, United Kingdom (NA), FO 371:126900.

8. Tripp to Gault (1 July 1957), National Archives, United Kingdom (NA), FO 1016:591.

9. Burrows to Lloyd (2 April 1957), National Archives, United Kingdom (NA), FO 371:126900.

10. Tripp to Burrows (30 Oct. 1957), National Archives, United Kingdom (NA), FO 1016:591.

11. Tripp to Given (3 Sept. 1957), National Archives, United Kingdom (NA), FO 1016:507. In 1939, Sheikh Rashid exploited his own wedding celebrations to assert his family's political power over Deira, the other side of Dubai Creek that had historically resisted Maktoum rule. Under the guise of the celebrations, Rashid and a

party of horsemen executed an attack on Deira when they arrived on the way to the family home of his future wife. Catching Deira's defenders off guard, Rashid and his cavalry conducted a violent and, at least for a time, effective seizure of political control. In addition to maintaining Maktoum claims at Dubai Creek, Rashid had also led Bedouin troops to protect Dubai from Abu Dhabi's claims. The Rashid of these stories knew how to be "firm." But he soon realized that these undertakings did not offer lasting resolution. An account of this wedding attack has been redacted from the British public files.

12. "Appendix A: An Estimate of the Political Situation in the Town of Dubai" (10 Sept. 1956), National Archives, United Kingdom (NA), FO 1016:507.

13. Tripp to Burrows (30 Oct. 1957), National Archives, United Kingdom (NA), FO 1016:591.

14. Tripp to Given (20 Dec. 1957), National Archives, United Kingdom (NA), FO 1016:591.

15. Tripp to Rashid (17 June 1958), National Archives, United Kingdom (NA), FO 1016:625.

16. "Appendix A: An Estimate of the Political Situation in the Town of Dubai" (10 Sept. 1956), National Archives, United Kingdom (NA), FO 1016:507.

17. "Trucial States Diary No. 11 for the Period November 1–30" (n.d.), National Archives, United Kingdom (NA), FO 371:120553.

18. Burrows to Riches (17 Oct. 1956), National Archives, United Kingdom (NA), FO 371:120611.

19. Minutes from Ali Bustani (16 Feb. 1957), National Archives, United Kingdom (NA), FO 1016:591. Er Raouf arrived the day after Colonel Hennessey, "a water diviner," departed. Hennessey had "discovered a number of sites where he claimed potable water in considerable quantities existed at varying depths. [Sheikh Rashid] is reported to have been dissatisfied with the colonel's final report" ("Trucial States Diary No. 11 for the Period November 1–30" [n.d.], National Archives, United Kingdom [NA], FO 371:120553). Engineers from Halcrow were already in Dubai working on infrastructural schemes, but they were being paid by the British government for their initial analysis work.

20. Stanley John Habermann, "Iraq Development Board: Administration and Program," *Middle East Journal* 9, no. 2 (1955): 179–186.

21. Burrows to Riches (17 Oct. 1956), National Archives, United Kingdom (NA), FO 371:120611.

22. Tripp to Burrows (20 April 1957), National Archives, United Kingdom (NA), FO 371:126900.

23. "Trucial States Diary No. 11 for the Period November 1–30" (n.d.), National Archives, United Kingdom (NA), FO 371:120553.

24. Tripp to Burrows (20 April 1957), National Archives, United Kingdom (NA), FO 371:126900.

25. "Trucial States Diary No. 12 for the Period December 1–31" (n.d.), National Archives, United Kingdom (NA), FO 371:126871.

26. Frauke Heard-Bey, *From Trucial States to United Arab Emirates: A Society in Transition* (London: Motivate, 2005), 246.

27. Denson to Mackay (21 Feb. 1957), National Archives, United Kingdom (NA), FO 371:126900. Er Raouf conveyed the story of an apparently less wealthy resident giving up part of his home so that a road could be straightened.

28. Tripp to Burrows (20 April 1957), National Archives, United Kingdom (NA), FO 371:126900.

29. G. G. Fitzmaurice, "The Trucial States (Dubai Municipal Regulations) Regulation, 1958" (5 Feb. 1958), National Archives, United Kingdom (NA), FO 371:132859.

30. Tripp to Burrows (20 April 1957), National Archives, United Kingdom (NA), FO 371:126900.

31. A likely reason that Er Raouf did not return was the military coup in 1958, which led to the dissolution of the IDB and ejected the British from their role in Iraq's governance. Prior to the coup, Iraq's British-friendly development program might have had the potential to be a model for Dubai's development, though significantly downsized in terms of money and ambition. Another possible reason was that Er Raouf had become increasingly less "disinterested." A report from a clerk for the municipality, who was also an employee of the political agency, suggested that Er Raouf had started to represent the Arab merchants' interests in obtaining more control over the harbor from the city's Iranian merchants (Minutes from Ali Bustani [16 Feb. 1957], National Archives, United Kingdom [NA], FO 1016:591).

32. Burrows to Lloyd (1 Feb. 1957), National Archives, United Kingdom (NA), FO 371:126900.

33. Tripp to Burrows (20 April 1957), National Archives, United Kingdom (NA), FO 371:126900. Italics added.

34. Tripp to Lamb (14 Aug. 1961), National Archives, United Kingdom (NA), FO 371:157071.

35. Abu Dhabi's oil exports began in 1962. See Heard-Bey, *From Trucial States*, 109.

36. Wells to Mayne (2 Dec. 1957), National Archives, United Kingdom (NA), INF 12:673.

37. Charles Ambler, "Projecting the Modern Colonial State: The Mobile Cinema in Kenya," in Lee Grieveson and Colin MacCabe, eds., *Film and the End of Empire* (Basingstoke, UK: Palgrave Macmillan, 2011), 208.

38. Note from J. Bourne, Reference FM1/1730 (11 Dec. 1957), National Archives, United Kingdom (NA), INF 12:673.

39. Tripp to Fletcher (15 Nov. 1957), National Archives, United Kingdom (NA), INF 12:673. *Barasti* is a Hindi word often used by British officials to describe simple huts made from palm fronds and salvaged materials from the port.

40. Tripp to Burrows (25 Oct. 1955), National Archives, United Kingdom (NA), FO 371:114656.

41. Wells to Mayne (2 Dec. 1957), National Archives, United Kingdom (NA), INF 12:673.

42. During Tripp's earlier appointment at the Sudanese Political Service, a another, better-funded propaganda film was produced about Sudan. For more information about *These Are the Trucial States* and its relationship with a British history of propaganda filmmaking, see Todd Reisz, "Landscapes of Production," *Journal of Urban History* 44, no. 2 (2017).

43. Wells to Mayne (10 June 1958), National Archives, United Kingdom (NA), INF 12:673.

44. The film World Wide Pictures made for British Petroleum (BP) was titled *ADMA for Short* and was released in 1958. The title refers to the oil consortium Abu Dhabi Marina Areas Limited. The only apparent copy is stored at the British Film Institute, which will not release the reels for viewing.

45. Note from J. Bourne, Reference FM1/1730 (11 Dec. 1957), National Archives, United Kingdom (NA), INF 12:673.

46. Richard Misek, *Chromatic Cinema: A History of Screen Color* (Oxford: Wiley-Blackwell, 2010), 111–116.

47. *These Are the Trucial States*, Imperial War Museum (IWM), COI 764. Voiceover texts translated by Mahdi Sabbagh.

48. Tripp's superior, political resident Bernard Burrows, described the predicament regarding Arab educators, mostly Egyptian and Palestinian, in the region as such: "But the only available teachers are Arabs from the north who are already

proving themselves the spearhead of pan-Arabism, and doing their best to involve the Trucial States in outside political events and indirectly at least preparing the ground for internal political change" (Burrows to Lloyd [9 April 1957], National Archives, United Kingdom [NA], FO 371:126900).

49. Tripp to Burrows (30 Oct. 1957), National Archives, United Kingdom (NA), FO 1016:591. The term "Dubai model" has more recently taken on a different meaning. Today it can refer to a simplistic understanding of Dubai's development strategies as an exportable template to other cities, or even nations.

50. "Trucial States, Production 208" (n.d.), National Archives, United Kingdom (NA), INF 12:673.

51. Ibid.

52. Ibid.

53. Tripp to Fletcher (15 Nov. 1957), National Archives, United Kingdom (NA), INF 12:673.

54. Ibid.

55. Ibid.

56. *These Are the Trucial States.*

57. "Trucial States, Production 208" (n.d.), National Archives, United Kingdom (NA), INF 12:673.

58. Wells to Bourne (14 Aug. 1958), National Archives, United Kingdom (NA), INF 12:673.

59. Carr to Langston (8 Oct. 1958), National Archives, United Kingdom (NA), INF 12:673.

60. MEDD to Dudley (26 June 1963), National Archives, United Kingdom (NA), FO 371:175565.

61. Hawley, *Trucial States*, 224.

62. In 2019, the Dubai government opened a new museum about Dubai Creek, which samples the fifteen-minute film throughout the permanent exhibition.

63. Foreign Office officials planned to submit the film to BBC's *Panorama* television program.

CHAPTER 3

1. "Extract from Trucial States Diary No. 5 for the Period May 1–31" (7 June 1957), National Archives, United Kingdom (NA), FO 371:126999. The Trucial Oman Levies were renamed the Trucial Oman Scouts in 1956. British records do not state whether the officers who saved the travelers were British, Arab, or a combination of both.

2. Gault to Lloyd (7 June 1957), National Archives, United Kingdom (NA), FO 371:126999.

3. "Extract from Trucial States Diary No. 5 for the Period May 1–31" (7 June 1957), National Archives, United Kingdom (NA), FO 371:126999.

4. Gault to Lloyd (7 June 1957), National Archives, United Kingdom (NA), FO 371:126999.

5. Telegram from Burrows (2 June 1957), National Archives, United Kingdom (NA), FO 371:126999. One Foreign Office official questioned why the British officials in Abu Dhabi had assumed responsibility. Without passports, his reasoning went, the foreignness of the stranded could not be proved, and therefore, according to HMG's own laws, the British government was not obliged to intervene. Others disagreed (Notes from F. F. Garner [28 May 1957], National Archives, United Kingdom [NA], FO 371:126999).

6. Foreign Office to Bahrain (17 June 1957), National Archives, United Kingdom (NA), FO 371:126999.

7. "Extract from Trucial States Diary No. 5 for the Period May 1–31" (7 June 1957), National Archives, United Kingdom (NA), FO 371:126999.

8. Minutes from Pearn (25 June 1957), National Archives, United Kingdom (NA), FO 371:126999.

9. Gault to Lloyd (7 June 1957), National Archives, United Kingdom (NA), FO 371:126999.

10. Consular Section, Rangoon to Chancery, Bahrain (1 June 1957), National Archives, United Kingdom (NA), FO 371:126999.

11. The Burmese home the pilgrims claimed was in the Rakhine region of current-day Myanmar from where the Rohingya fled in 2017. It was not until the late 1950s that a community of Muslims in that region began to identify more widely with the term "Rohingya." The pilgrims might have been part of this community, or, as the diplomat suggested, they could have recently migrated to that region for work. See Jacques Leider, "Rohingya: The History of a Muslim Identity in Myanmar," *Oxford Research Encyclopedias* (24 May 2018). https://oxfordre.com/asianhistory/view/10.1093/acrefore/9780190277727.001.0001/acrefore-9780190277727-e-115

12. Rangoon to Foreign Office (21 June 1957), National Archives, United Kingdom (NA), FO 371:126999.

13. Dubai to Foreign Office (28 June 1957), National Archives, United Kingdom (NA), FO 371:126999.

14. Gault to Foreign Office (24 June 1957), National Archives, United Kingdom (NA), FO 371:126999.

15. Notes from Jones (28 Aug. 1957), National Archives, United Kingdom (NA), FO 371:126999.

16. Notes from Saunders (4 Sept. 1957), National Archives, United Kingdom (NA), FO 371:126999.

17. Dubai to Foreign Office (8 Sept. 1957), National Archives, United Kingdom (NA), FO 371:126999.

18. Dubai to Foreign Office (23 Sept. 1957), National Archives, United Kingdom (NA), FO 371:126999.

19. Dubai to Foreign Office (8 Sept. 1957), National Archives, United Kingdom (NA), FO 371:126999.

20. Andrea Wright, "Migratory Pipelines: Labor and Oil in the Arabian Sea," PhD dissertation, University of Michigan (2015). http://hdl.handle.net/2027.42/113653

21. Christopher Meyer, "Visit to Dubai, August 1957," John R. Harris Library.

22. Adams to Given (6 Sept. 1957), National Archives, United Kingdom (NA), FO 371:126999; "Sharjah Harbour Report on Proposed Improvements" (12 Jan. 1955), National Archives, United Kingdom (NA), FO 371:114696.

23. "A Report on the Current Developments of Dubai" (Nov. 1960), National Archives, United Kingdom (NA), FO 957:231.

24. "Sir William Halcrow & Partners Consulting Engineers," company portfolio (1964). Until its acquisition by the US-based conglomerate CH2M, the British firm Halcrow was synonymous with growth and development in the Gulf. In the last decades it was referred to as Halcrow; in the early years of the company's presence in Dubai, it was referred to as Halcrows. At least until 2011, Halcrow had a significant part in large-scale planning in Dubai. In 2017, CH2M was acquired by US-based Jacobs Engineering Group.

25. In March 1958, when Halcrow signed a contract to execute its plan for Dubai Creek, the company's close relationship with the British government was quickly revealed. Halcrow needed to gather additional geographical data about the coast, and the Foreign Office was content to allow the engineers to communicate directly with the naval fleets assigned to Gulf waters. Such granted access demonstrates the Foreign Office's developing managerial approach in Dubai: Limit government responsibility by increasing private-sector opportunity.

26. "Sir William Halcrow & Partners Consulting Engineers," company portfolio (1964).

27. Bell to Riches (20 Dec. 1956), National Archives, United Kingdom (NA), FO 1016:514.

28. "Report on Proposed Improvements by Sir William Halcrow & Partners" (12 Jan. 1955), National Archives, United Kingdom (NA), FO 371:114696.

29. Minutes of discussions regarding Halcrow's survey of Dubai and Sharjah Creeks (28 Jan. 1955), National Archives, United Kingdom (NA), FO 371:114696.

30. Scott to Morgan (13 Dec. 1956), National Archives, United Kingdom (NA), FO 371:120633.

31. "Sir William Halcrow & Partners Consulting Engineers," company portfolio (1964); "Report on Proposed Improvements by Sir William Halcrow & Partners" (12 Jan. 1955), National Archives, United Kingdom (NA), FO 371:114696.

32. Tripp to Gale (4 Nov. 1955), National Archives, United Kingdom (NA), FO 371:114696.

33. Tripp to Maclaren (22 Sept. 1955), National Archives, United Kingdom (NA), FO 371:114696.

34. Maclaren to Tripp (2 Oct. 1955), National Archives, United Kingdom (NA), FO 371:114696.

35. Tripp to Gale (4 Nov. 1955), National Archives, United Kingdom (NA), FO 371:114696.

36. A British official in Bahrain referred to a "hurried" report being made by the Copenhagen-based firm Christiani and Nielsen around the same time as Halcrow's investigations. It could not be located in the British archives. The British construction company Taylor Woodrow was also approached to assess whether its Kuwait-based operation could execute Halcrow's proposal without them. They said they could but would in any case need to hire another consultant to produce necessary drawings already produced by Halcrow (Reilly to Ewart-Biggs [6 Sept. 1956], National Archives, United Kingdom [NA], 371:114696).

37. Adams to Reilly (31 Jan. 1955), National Archives, United Kingdom (NA), FO 371:114696.

38. Notes from Jones (6 Dec. 1956), National Archives, United Kingdom (NA), FO 371:120633.

39. Tripp to Adams (16 Aug. 1955), National Archives, United Kingdom (NA), FO 371:114696.

40. Burrows to Riches (25 Jan. 1957), National Archives, United Kingdom (NA), FO 371:126871. The British contracting company Wimpeys executed the trial borings.

41. Minutes of discussions regarding Halcrow's survey of Dubai and Sharjah Creeks (28 Jan. 1955), National Archives, United Kingdom (NA), FO 371:114696.

42. Notes from Buckmaster (26 Aug. 1955), National Archives, United Kingdom (NA), FO 371:114696.

43. Geoffrey Jones, *Banking and Oil: The History of the British Bank of the Middle East* (Cambridge, UK: Cambridge University Press, 1987), vol. II, 150.

44. Minutes of discussions regarding Halcrow's survey of Dubai and Sharjah Creeks (28 Jan. 1955), National Archives, United Kingdom (NA), FO 371:114696.

45. Tripp to Adams (27 June 1955), National Archives, United Kingdom (NA), FO 371:114696.

46. Minutes of discussions regarding Halcrow's survey of Dubai and Sharjah Creeks (28 Jan. 1955), National Archives, United Kingdom (NA), FO 371:114696.

47. Notes from Buckmaster (26 Aug 1955), National Archives, United Kingdom (NA), FO 371:114696.

48. Notes from Denson (30 Sept. 1955), National Archives, United Kingdom (NA), FO 371:114696.

49. BBME to Director of Finance, Kuwait (4 Dec. 1958), National Archives, United Kingdom (NA), FO 371:157407.

50. In a telegram from February 1957, Tripp alludes to a "large money gift" from Qatar's Sheikh Ali, who would marry Rashid's daughter eight months after the loan signing.

51. "Sharjah Harbour Report on Proposed Improvements" (12 Jan. 1955), National Archives, United Kingdom (NA), FO 371:114696.

52. "A Note on the Finances of Sharjah" (12 Aug. 1950), National Archives, United Kingdom (NA), FO 371:82047.

53. "Sharjah Harbour Report on Proposed Improvements" (12 Jan. 1955), National Archives, United Kingdom (NA), FO 371:114696.

54. Ibid.

55. Minutes of discussions regarding Halcrow's survey of Dubai and Sharjah Creeks (28 Jan. 1955), National Archives, United Kingdom (NA), FO 371:114696.

56. Tripp to Gale (4 Nov. 1955), National Archives, United Kingdom (NA), FO 371:114696.

57. Craig to Tripp (29 Oct. 1961), National Archives, United Kingdom (NA), FO 957:231.

58. Griffith to Craig (23 Sept. 1961), National Archives, United Kingdom (NA), 957:231.

59. Craig to Acting Political Resident (20 Sept. 1964), National Archives, United Kingdom (NA), FO 371:174711.

60. Ibid.

61. For example, in 1983, the *Financial Times* used the same wording—that Sharjah "allowed their harbour to silt up." Stephanie Gray, "Dubai—Merchants Make Art of Brinkmanship," *Financial Times* (30 Nov. 1983).

62. Heli Allen, in discussion with author, Dubai (12 Sept. 2010).

63. With some British-supported fanfare, Sheikh Rashid officially became Dubai's ruler on September 11, 1958. William Duff arrived in Dubai in 1960 and quickly graduated from managing Rashid's private accounts to overseeing Dubai government finances. Foreign Office officials had originally sent Duff to meet Sheikh Shakhbut in Abu Dhabi. After the ruler rejected his services, Sheikh Rashid hired him.

64. Anita Burdett, *Records of the Emirates: 1961–1965* (Slough, UK: Archive Editions, 1997), vol. II, 368.

65. Hawley to Lamb (12 March 1961), National Archives, United Kingdom (NA), FO 957:231.

66. Hawley to Middleton (6 Dec. 1959), National Archives, United Kingdom (NA), FO 1016:668. Sheikh Ahmad's $1.2 million palace was already under construction in Dubai. Many of his contributions to Dubai's development (including to the airport and to water lines) were driven by his own comforts. It is also possible that Sheikh Ahmad's funding had enable Sheikh Rashid to pay off his loan to Kuwait early.

67. "Sir William Halcrow & Partners Consulting Engineers," company portfolio (1964).

68. Notes from A. T. Lamb (19 June 1961), National Archives, United Kingdom (NA), FO 371:157025; Lamb to Hawley (June 1961), National Archives, United Kingdom (NA), FO 371:157025.

69. Notes from Wyatt (24 May 1961), National Archives, United Kingdom (NA), FO 371:157047.

70. Griffith to Hawley (11 May 1961), National Archives, United Kingdom (NA), FO 957:231.

71. Hawley to Griffith (23 May 1961), National Archives, United Kingdom (NA), FO 957:231.

72. Notes from Lamb (26 June 1961), National Archives, United Kingdom (NA), FO 371:157025.

73. "Instruction to All Government Departments, Public Companies, or Private Individuals Wishing to Lay Pipelines and Cables, or Erect Overhead Lines in Dubai" (1960–1961), *The Official Gazette of the Government of Dubai and Its Dependencies.*

74. "Report on Proposed Improvements by Sir William Halcrow & Partners" (12 Jan. 1955), National Archives, United Kingdom (NA), FO 371:114696.

75. Trucial States' Visit July 10–16 (25 July 1961), National Archives, United Kingdom (NA), FO 957:231.

76. Hawley to Walmsley (10 April 1961), National Archives, United Kingdom (NA), FO 371:157019.

77. Heli Allen, in discussion with author, Dubai (12 Sept. 2010).

78. "Dubai and the Northern Trucial States Review of the Year 1969" (30 Dec. 1969), National Archives, United Kingdom, FCO 8:1509. The Austrian-Kuwaiti Engineering Company was hired as the project's contractor. The Austrian company was also working on shaping the creek in 2018 for the new development project, Dubai Creek Harbor.

CHAPTER 4

1. Donald Hawley, *Desert Wind and Tropic Storm: An Autobiography* (Wilby, UK: Michael Russell, 2000), 40.

2. Julian Walker, *Tyro on the Trucial Coast* (Durham, UK: Memoir Club, 1999), 29.

3. Leila Hadley, *Give Me the World* (London: The Traveler Book Club, 1958), 257.

4. Donald Hawley, *The Emirates: Witness to a Metamorphosis* (Norwich, UK: Michael Russell, 2007), 68.

5. Donald Hawley, interview by Malcolm McBain (7 Aug. 2007), transcript, British Diplomatic Oral History Programme, Churchill College, Cambridge University.

6. Hawley, *The Emirates*, 18.

7. "The Trucial States (Dubai Municipal Regulations) Regulation, 1958" (5 Feb. 1958), National Archives, United Kingdom (NA), FO 371:132859.

8. Lamb to Beaumont (17 Nov. 1959), National Archives, United Kingdom (NA), FO 371:140144.

9. Annex: Dubai Airport (circa 9 May 1959), National Archives, United Kingdom (NA), FO 371:140205.

10. "Dubai Lands" (28 Sept. 1959), National Archives, United Kingdom (NA), FO 371:140222.

11. Oscar Mandoody, in discussion with author, Dubai (27 Nov. 2011). To the chagrin of many Dubaians, Rashid conceded to the customs-building welcome routine that Hawley demanded, but he was often known to irk Hawley with frequent unannounced arrivals at the political agency's compound.

12. Hawley, *The Emirates*, 166.

13. Ibid., 181.

14. Walker to Marshall (3 Sept. 1959), National Archives, United Kingdom (NA), FO 371:140143.

15. Annex A: Dubai (25 July 1961), National Archives, United Kingdom (NA), FO 957:231.

16. Anita Burdett, *Records of Dubai: 1761–1960* (Slough, UK: Archive Editions, 2000), vol. VIII, 70.

17. Hawley to Foreign Office (23 Sept. 1959), National Archives, United Kingdom (NA), FO 371:140143.

18. Hawley to Foreign Office (5 Oct. 1959), National Archives, United Kingdom (NA), FO 371:140143.

19. "Dubai Lands" (28 Sept. 1959), National Archives, United Kingdom (NA), FO 371:140222.

20. Todd Reisz, "'Along Sound Lines': Drawing Up Dubai's Labor Camps from 1950 to 2008," *Perspecta 50* (Sept. 2017).

21. Hawley, *Desert Wind*, 55.

22. Hawley, *The Emirates*, 147, footnote 241.

23. Ibid., 163.

24. Hawley to Foreign Office (3 Oct. 1959), National Archives, United Kingdom (NA), FO 371:140143.

25. "Hospital, Doha, Qatar on the Persian Gulf," *Builder* (5 April 1957), 623. Jill and John Harris submitted their proposal in 1952. The RIBA library claims no record of the Doha competition. Later the Doha State Hospital was renamed Rumailah Hospital. See "Men of the Year, 1953: John Harris," *Architects' Journal* (21 Jan. 1954), 73. Other "men of the year" for 1953 included Alison and Peter Smithson. By that time, Jill Harris was no longer listed with the project.

26. Hawley, *The Emirates*, 175, footnote 290.

27. Patrick Abercrombie, *Greater London Plan 1944* (London: His Majesty's Stationary Office, 1945), iii.

28. Marshall to Hawley (2 Oct. 1959), National Archives, United Kingdom (NA), FO 371:140143.

29. Hawley to Foreign Office (3 Oct. 1959), National Archives, United Kingdom (NA), FO 371:140143.

30. Farah Al-Nakib, *Kuwait Transformed: A History of Oil and Urban Life* (Stanford, CA: Stanford University Press, 2016), 99, 110.

31. Sargeant, "Development in Kuwait. Progress Report" (18 Feb. 1956), National Archives, United Kingdom (NA), FO 1016:514.

32. Panayiota Pyla, "Back to the Future: Doxiadis's Plans for Baghdad," *Journal of Planning History* 7, no. 1 (Feb. 2008): 7–8.

33. Notes from Marshall (5 Oct. 1959), National Archives, United Kingdom (NA), FO 371:140143.

34. Notes on Dubai town planning (2 Nov. 1959), National Archives, United Kingdom (NA), FO 371:140143.

35. Marshall to Hawley (30 Oct. 1959), National Archives, United Kingdom (NA), FO 371:140143.

36. Notes from A. R. Walmsley (3 Nov. 1959), National Archives, United Kingdom (NA), FO 371:140143.

37. Farah Al-Nakib, "Kuwait's Modern Spectacle Oil Wealth and the Making of a New Capital City, 1950–90," *Comparative Studies of South Asia, Africa and the Middle East* 33, no. 1 (2013): 7–25.

38. Foreign Office to Dubai (4 Nov. 1959), National Archives, United Kingdom (NA), FO 371:140143.

39. Ibid.

40. P. W. Macfarlane, "Planning an Arab Town," *Town Planning Institute Journal* (April 1954): 110–112; Minoprio & Spencely and Macfarlane, "Master Plan for Dacca," Dacca Improvement Trust, London (1959); P. W. Macfarlane, "The Plan for Baghdad," *Housing Review* 5 (1956): 193–195.

41. Macfarlane, "Planning an Arab Town," 113.

42. Al-Nakib, "Kuwait's Modern Spectacle," 7–25.

43. Hawley to Foreign Office (5 Nov. 1959), National Archives, United Kingdom (NA), FO 371:140143.

44. Marshall to Harris (6 Nov. 1959), National Archives, United Kingdom (NA), FO 371:140143.

45. Harris to Undersecretary of State (12 Nov. 1959), National Archives, United Kingdom (NA), FO 371:140143.

46. Hawley, *The Emirates*, 176.

47. "Impressions of Sheikh Rashid" (3 Jan. 2006), John R. Harris Library.

48. By this time, Ali Bustani worked only half his workday at the political agency, clocking in as Dubai's town clerk in the afternoons. His presence in both offices allowed the political agent to keep informed about "further ambitious schemes for town improvement." Split between two governments, Bustani represented how British "gentle encouragement" was gradually building bureaucracy (Hawley, *The Emirates,* 75).

49. Ibid., 176.

50. Tripp to Burrows (15 Feb. 1957), National Archives, United Kingdom (NA), FO 371:126900.

51. Hawley, *Desert Wind*, 55.

52. Heli Allen, in discussion with author, Dubai (12 Sept. 2010).

53. Weatherhead to Halcrow (10 March 1960), National Archives, United Kingdom (NA), FO 371:148973.

54. John R. Harris papers (n.d.), John R. Harris Library.

55. Hawley, *The Emirates*, 179.

56. Notes made during visit to Dubai in May 1960 (12 July 1960), John R. Harris Library.

57. Ibid.

58. A. E. J. Morris, *John R. Harris Architects.* (Westerham, UK: Hurtwood), 1984.

59. Hawley, *Desert Wind*, 55.

60. Ibid., 40.

61. Urban planning for French colonies typically left the older city centers intact, subsequently referred to in English as the *medina*, the Arabic word for "city."

62. In 2008, at the Association of Siamese Architects, architectural historian Davis Robson observed that the time-intensive reproduction processes might have been a reason for why Harris's plan merged old and new.

63. John R. Harris, "Town Plan for Dubai," 1965. Harris reissued the plan in 1965 with written guidelines.

64. Margaret Luce, *From Aden to the Gulf: Personal Diaries 1956–1966* (Salisbury, UK: Michael Russell, 1987), 121.

65. Recently, Dubai officials claimed there are more than 13,500 kilometers of paved roads in the city. See Dubai Media Office @DXBMediaOffice, "In the 1960s, #Dubai got its first paved road . . . Today it has one of the world's best road network that spans over 13500 KM," Twitter (9 Nov. 2017), 9:38 a.m. https://twitter.com/DXBMediaOffice/status/928678118012981248

66. Robert L. Jarman, *Political Diaries of the Arab World, Persian Gulf 1904–65* (Slough, UK: Archive Editions, 1998), vol. 23, 686; Kamal Hamza, in discussion with author, Dubai (7 Dec. 2010).

67. "Economic and Commercial Report for the Quarter Ending June 30, 1964" (29 June 1964), National Archives, United Kingdom (NA), FO 371:174711.

68. Notes from Weston (5 March 1966), National Archives, United Kingdom (NA), FO 371:185524.

69. Salim Zabbal, "Dubai: The Venice of the Gulf," *Al Arabi* (22 Sept. 1960): 82. Translation by Dima Srouji; "Trucial States Diary No. 11 for the Period November 1–30" (n.d.), National Archives, United Kingdom (NA), FO 371:120553.

70. The three-tiered road system characterized British New Towns, although it is also credited to Scotland Yard, specifically to an assistant commissioner for the metropolitan police force named Alker Tripp, who described such a system as early as 1938. In the 1944 "Plan for Greater London," credit is given to Tripp, "whose art of traffic jurisdiction covers part of the Region, but whose ideas on planning for traffic know no artificial boundary." While a driver's destination might be quite close, road rules would require a longer, if smoother, approach in the name of continuous and risk-free traffic. For Scotland Yard, the road hierarchy provided a means of securing traffic safety. In introducing the system, Tripp's had two main goals: to minimize intersections and to separate major arteries, and therefore cars, from where people live and work.

71. Robert Vitalis, *America's Kingdom: Mythmaking on the Saudi Oil Frontier* (Stanford, CA: Stanford University Press, 2006) chronicles how racist planning underpinned American companies' design and building of company towns in Saudi Arabia's Eastern Province; see also Reem Alissa, "The Oil Town of Ahmadi Since 1946: From Colonial Town to Nostalgic City," *Comparative Studies of South Asia, Africa and the Middle East* 33, no. 1 (2013): 41–58.

72. Lewis Mumford, "The Neighborhood and the Neighborhood Unit," *Town Planning Review* 24, no. 4 (1954): 256.

73. American Consult Dhahran to Department of State, "Dubai Seeks an American International Airline" (9 June 1965), file AF 2/4–4, NARA 649, National Archives (US). Access via National Archives (UAE).

74. Minoprio & Spencely, with Macfarlane, had also employed neighborhood units in their master plan for Kuwait. Their scheme for Kuwait is often characterized as establishing in urban form a means by which a developing welfare state could evenly, and visibly, disburse accumulated oil wealth among local residents.

75. Harris, "Town Plan for Dubai."

76. Summary of Dubai Despatch No. 7 (20 Sept. 1964), National Archives, United Kingdom (NA), FO 371:174711.

77. Dubai's first water distribution system was paid for by Sheikh Rashid's son-in-law Sheikh Ahmad bin Ali Al Thani of Qatar. Having built his palace further inland along the creek, the emir wanted running water. He therefore paid for a twenty-one–mile pipeline from a water source at Tawi Awir. The first stop for the pipeline, however, was for his palace and gardens.

78. "A Report on the Current Developments in Dubai" (Nov. 1960), National Archives, United Kingdom (NA), FO 371:157025.

79. Ibid.

80. Ibid.

81. Hawley to Lamb (21 Feb. 1961), National Archives, United Kingdom (NA), FO 371:157025; Wyatt to Hawley (10 May 1961), National Archives, United Kingdom (NA), FO 371:157047.

82. Record of a meeting (28 Nov. 1960), National Archives, United Kingdom (NA), FO 371:157025.

83. Jarman, *Political Diaries,* vol. 22, 684.

84. "Record of a meeting" (28 Nov. 1960), National Archives, United Kingdom (NA), FO 371:157025.

85. Kamal Hamza, in discussion with author, Dubai (7 Dec. 2010).

86. Howell to Luce (10 May 1961), National Archives, United Kingdom (NA), FO 371:157399.

87. Griffith to Howell (1 May 1961), National Archives, United Kingdom, (NA), FO 957:231.

88. Annex A: Dubai (25 July 1961), National Archives, United Kingdom (NA), FO 371:157026.

89. Ibid.

90. Ibid.

CHAPTER 5

1. A British map from 1822 represents Dubai as protected by ramparts, but it might have been a dramatic representation of what really existed at the time. In any case, the twentieth century found no wall around either of Dubai Creek's two towns.

2. "Remarks Sheets: Public Health" (26 Nov. 1958), National Archives, United Kingdom (NA): FO 1016:651. Al Maktoum Hospital comprised two fenced enclosures: The smaller enclosure included the hospital director's house and buildings for hospital staff, a cook, and the guards; the larger one was for the hospital's two buildings and other structures including the generator house.

3. Salim Zabbal, "Dubai: The Venice of the Gulf," *Al Arabi* (22 Sept. 1960): 82. Translation by Dima Srouji.

4. "Annual Report—Al Maktum Hospital, 1959" (Feb. 1960), National Archives, United Kingdom (NA), FO 371:149150.

5. "Al Makhtum Hospital, Dubai, Annual Report & Returns, 1960" (19 Jan. 1961), National Archives, United Kingdom (NA), FO 371:157067.

6. Rosemarie Said Zahlan, *Origins of the United Arab Emirates: A Political and Social History of the Trucial States* (London: Macmillan, 1978), 31–32.

7. Christopher Meyer, "Visit to Dubai, August 1957," John R. Harris Library.

8. "Recollections of the Early Development of Dubai" (n.d.), John R. Harris Library.

9. Minutes of the Tenth Meeting of the Trucial Council (18 May 1958), National Archives, United Kingdom (NA), FO 371:126900.

10. According to John R. Harris site photographs.

11. Foreign Office to Bahrain (26 March 1959), National Archives, United Kingdom (NA), FO 1016:651.

12. Minutes of the Tenth Meeting of the Trucial Council (18 May 1958), National Archives, United Kingdom (NA), FO 371:126900.

13. "Al Makhtum Hospital, Dubai, Annual Report & Returns, 1960" (19 Jan. 1961), National Archives, United Kingdom (NA), FO 371:157067.

14. Zabbal, "Dubai: Venice of the Gulf," 85.

15. Minutes of the Tenth Meeting of the Trucial Council (18 May 1958), National Archives, United Kingdom (NA), FO 371:126900.

16. Craig to Lamb (21 Aug. 1962), National Archives, United Kingdom (NA), FO 371:163037.

17. "Report on Al Maktoum Hospital" (circa 5 May 1960), National Archives, United Kingdom (NA), FO 371:149150.

18. "Al Makhtum Hospital, Dubai, Annual Report & Returns, 1960" (19 Jan. 1961), National Archives, United Kingdom (NA), FO 371:157067.

19. "Report on Al Maktoum Hospital" (circa 5 May 1960), National Archives, United Kingdom (NA), FO 371:149150. At one point during his Dubai posting, Hawley had to be evacuated from Dubai to Bahrain and eventually to London because of a foot condition. During his three-year appointment, he spent a number of weeks convalescing in a London hospital.

20. Hawley to Middleton (31 March 1959), National Archives, United Kingdom (NA), FO 371:140087.

21. Zabbal, "Dubai: Venice of the Gulf," 86.

22. Hawley to Middleton (31 March 1959), National Archives, United Kingdom (NA), FO 371:140087.

23. Zabbal, "Dubai: Venice of the Gulf," 88.

24. There would eventually be a Kuwait Hospital in Dubai, paid for by the Kuwaiti government.

25. Robert L. Jarman, *Political Diaries of the Arab World, Persian Gulf 1904–65* (Slough, UK: Archive Editions, 1998), vol. 22, 702.

26. Thomson to Marshall (circa 18 July 1960), National Archives, United Kingdom (NA), FO 371:149150.

27. "Report on Al Maktoum Hospital" (circa 5 May 1960), National Archives, United Kingdom (NA), FO 371:149150.

28. Rae to Thomson (29 April 1960), National Archives, United Kingdom (NA), FO 371:149150. One of John Harris's earliest commissions was for a small building for the British Building Research Institute in Kuwait.

29. "Al Maktoum Hospital" (5 Sept. 1960), National Archives, United Kingdom (NA), FO 371:149150.

30. "The British Bank of the Middle East," *Times* (London) (10 July 1957).

31. The British officer residing in Abu Dhabi, Edward Henderson, wrote that he "had heard a lot of adverse criticism" of the Doha State Hospital, but he did not mention his sources and expressed he might be "badly informed" (Anita Burdett, *Records of Dubai: 1761–1960* [Slough, UK: Archive Editions, 2000], vol. VIII, 535).

32. Meyer, "Visit to Dubai, August 1957."

33. Confidential Annex (5 Dec. 1956), National Archives, United Kingdom (NA), FO 371:120553.

34. Dubai Airport (circa 9 May 1959), National Archives, United Kingdom (NA), FO 371:140205. Comment was made in regard to the prospect of an airport in Dubai.

35. "Al Maktum Hospital Dubai Arabian Gulf," *British Hospitals Home and Overseas* (1968–1969), John R. Harris Library.

36. "New Hospital for Kuwait Designed by Briton," *Times* (London) (2 Feb. 1961).

37. Whatever Harris's reasoning, it turned out to be opportune. Dubai continued to be a source of new work for his firm, while Kuwait gained a reputation for its growing disdain for British expertise. In 1977, the *Times* reported that there was "not a single British contractor at work in Kuwait, despite its . . . projected expenditure of $1,300m over the next four years" (David Crawford, "Results Justify Faith of Emirates," *Times* [London] [17 Oct. 1977], xiv).

38. Tripp to Fletcher (15 Nov. 1957), National Archives, United Kingdom (NA), INF 12:673.

39. "Al Makhtum Hospital, Dubai, Annual Report & Returns, 1960" (19 Jan. 1961), National Archives, United Kingdom (NA), FO 371:157067.

40. Ibid.

41. "Trucial States Diary No. 1 for the Period January 1–31" (1 Feb. 1959), National Archives, United Kingdom (NA), FO 371:126871.

42. Jarman, *Political Diaries*, vol. 22, 704.

43. Ibid., vol. 22, 708. Craig went on to list the negative consequences: "but in return we have to suffer advertisement hoardings, illicit distilling, plastic lamp shades and—worst of all—tinned pineapple chunks with every Arab meal."

44. "A Guide: The Municipality of Dubai 1961–1963," (Al Bayan, reprinted 1998), 8, 46. Translation provided by Dima Srouji.

45. Ibid.

46. Local Order No. 3, Government of Dubai, Dubai Municipality (20 May 1961); *The Official Gazette of the Government of Dubai and Its Dependencies* (1961).

47. *Official Gazette of Government of Dubai*, 10, 14, 77.

48. Donald Hawley, *The Emirates: Witness to a Metamorphosis* (Norwich, UK: Michael Russell, 2007), 256–258.

49. Tripp to Craig (30 Dec. 1961), National Archives, United Kingdom (NA), FO 371:163071.

50. Craig to Tripp (9 Jan. 1962), National Archives, United Kingdom (NA), FO 371:163071.

51. Ibid.

52. Ibid.

53. The work that was eventually completed for the job was one of the first expressions of Dubai Municipality oversight. Dubai's electrical company (a private concern) reported to the municipality that it deemed the work unsafe (Craig to Tripp [10 July 1962], National Archives, United Kingdom [NA], FO 371:163071).

54. Craig to Lamb (21 Aug. 1962), National Archives, United Kingdom (NA), FO 371:163037.

55. "Al Makhtum Hospital, Dubai, Annual Report & Returns, 1960" (19 Jan. 1961), National Archives, United Kingdom (NA), FO 371:157067.

56. Craig to Brown (23 Oct. 1962), National Archives, United Kingdom (NA), FO 371:163071. Despite Craig's report that foundation work was begun, there is no apparent evidence that this hospital was ever completed. As of 1969, British records list two hospitals in Sharjah, totaling fifty beds ("Trucial States Intelligence Report" [3 Dec. 1968], National Archives, United Kingdom [NA], FCO 8:1255).

57. Walker, Confidential Annex (circa 5 Aug. 1958), National Archives, United Kingdom (NA), FO 371:132784.

58. "Al Maktum Hospital Dubai Arabian Gulf."

59. Kamal Hamza, "Dubai: Pearl of the Coast," produced by Dubai Municipality, 30.

60. The original Holloway building has been preserved as part of a shopping center's fantastical recreation of traditional architecture. The rest was demolished.

CHAPTER 6

1. Horner to Department of State, "The Boom in Dubai" (1 April 1964), file AF 3/2–5, NARA 772, National Archives (US). Access via National Archives (UAE).

2. Ibid.

3. Allen to Department of State, "Economic Summary of Dubai: 1964" (1 Feb. 1965), file AF 3/2–5, NARA 772, National Archives (US). Access via National Archives (UAE).

4. Allen to Department of State, "Dubai's Foreign Trade During First Half Calendar Year 1965" (28 Sept. 1965), file AF 2/4–4, NARA 761, National Archives (US). Access via National Archives (UAE).

5. Ibid.

6. Christopher M. Davidson, *Dubai: The Vulnerability of Success* (London: Hurst and Company, 2008), 98.

7. Bullard to Weir (18 May 1970), National Archives, United Kingdom (NA), FCO 8:1510.

8. Roberts to Balfour-Paul (10 Dec. 1966), National Archives, United Kingdom (NA), FO 1016:832.

9. Abdullah Al Saleh, in discussion with author, Dubai (30 Oct. 2016).

10. K. G. Fenelon, *United Arab Emirates: An Economic and Social Survey*, 2nd ed. (London: Longman, 1976), 84–85.

11. Charles McKean, "In Glitter and Style New Buildings Are Better Than Old Ones," *Times* (London) (23 Feb. 1981).

12. Michael Tomkinson, *The United Arab Emirates* (London: Michael Tomkinson Publishing, 1975), 144.

13. Ibid.

14. Talking points for use with the ruler of Dubai (1 July 1969), National Archives, United Kingdom (NA), FCO 8:999.

15. Andrea Wright, "Migratory Pipelines: Labor and Oil in the Arabian Sea," PhD dissertation, University of Michigan (2015). http://hdl.handle.net/2027.42/113653

16. Esmond Bradley Martin, "Geography of Present-Day Smuggling in the Western Indian Ocean: The Case of the Dhow," *Australian Association for Maritime History* 1, no. 2 (Oct. 1979): 19.

17. Talking points for use with the ruler of Dubai (1 July 1969), National Archives, United Kingdom (NA), FCO 8:999.

18. Robert L. Jarman, *Political Diaries of the Arab World, Persian Gulf 1904–65* (Slough, UK: Archive Editions, 1998), vol. 24, 423.

19. Tomkinson, *United Arab Emirates*, 58.

20. Roberts to Crawford (25 Jan. 1968), National Archives, United Kingdom (NA), FCO 8:840. Importing labor was also a profitable venture. One of Sheikh Rashid's closest advisors, Mahdi Al Tajir, is said to have controlled a "monopoly of the labour force supplied to foreign contractors and firms."

21. Jarman, *Political Diaries*, vol. 23, 670.

22. "Trucial States Census" (circa 6 June 1968), National Archives, United Kingdom (NA), FCO 8:863.

23. "First Population Census of the Trucial States: Methods Report," Middle East Development Division (March–April 1968), 11. The Bahraini government, having recently completed its own census, directed the project.

24. Ibid. Abu Dhabi's census took place on a single day in the spring of 1968, when all residents were required to remain home between 5 a.m. and 4 p.m. to answer the census takers.

25. A later report notes that because some people were not reported, especially the women of some households, this number might have been low. It estimates that the city's population was between 60,000 and 70,000 ("Dubai [Trucial States]: Report on Labour, Industrial and Social Developments" [20 Dec. 1968], National Archives, United Kingdom [NA], LAB 13:2165).

26. "First Population Census of the Trucial States."

27. "Dubai (Trucial States): Report on Labour, Industrial and Social Developments" (20 Dec. 1968), National Archives, United Kingdom (NA), LAB 13:2165.

28. Craig to Acting Political Resident (20 Sept. 1964), National Archives, United Kingdom (NA), FO 371:174711.

29. "Dubai and the Northern Trucial States Review of the Year 1969" (30 Dec. 1969), National Archives, United Kingdom (NA), FCO 8:1509.

30. Summary of Dubai Despatch No. 7 (20 Sept. 1964), National Archives, United Kingdom (NA), FO 371:174711.

31. "Report on Social, Industrial and Labour Developments in Abu Dhabi" (13 June 1966), National Archives, United Kingdom (NA), LAB 13:2165. By 1968, the category "Dubai national" included people who had been naturalized, including Iranians and also Yemenis. See Sultan Sooud Al Qassemi, "United Arab Emigrants: Stories of

Pioneer Arab Migrants Who Became Emirati" (26 July 2016). https://medium.com/@SultanAlQassemi/united-arab-emigrants-92314e7f3eca

32. Bullard to Everard (1 July 1969), National Archives, United Kingdom (NA), FCO 8:999.

33. Foreign and Commonwealth Office to Bahrain Residency (22 March 1970), National Archives, United Kingdom (NA), FCO 8:1540; Everard to Edes (7 July 1969), National Archives, United Kingdom (NA), FCO 8:999.

34. "The Trucial States Control of Illegal Immigration Regulation 1970 (Queen's Regulation No. 2 of 1970)" (signed 8 July 1970), *Persian Gulf Gazette*, Bahrain (15 Oct. 1970).

35. Bullard to Weir (15 Oct. 1970), National Archives, United Kingdom (NA), FCO 8:1540. According to the documentation, it is not clear in which language(s) this announcement was issued.

36. "Report on Labour, Industrial and Social Developments" (20 Dec. 1968), National Archives, United Kingdom (NA), LAB 13:2165.

37. Ibid.

38. Margaret Bullard, in discussion with author, Oxford (5 March 2011).

39. Ibid.

40. William Tuohy, "Dubai: Where Gold Smuggling Is Way of Life," *Los Angeles Times* (13 Jan. 1971).

41. Timothy Green, *The New World of Gold: The Inside Story of the Mines, the Markets, the Politics, the Investors*, rev. ed. (London: Weidenfeld & Nicolson, 1985), 176.

42. Ray Vicker, "The Gold Hustlers," *Wall Street Journal* (26 Feb. 1968).

43. Horner to Department of State (12 Feb. 1964), file AF 3/2–5, NARA 905, National Archives (US). Access via National Archives (UAE).

44. A US consulate official in Dhahran reported that the manager of First National City Bank, who was a source of information on Dubai, claimed that British passports were being provided for "well-known leading smugglers in order to protect them when they travel to India to look after their gold smuggling business" (Memorandum of a conversation [29 June 1964], file AF 3/4–5, NARA 2745, National Archives [US]. Access via National Archives [UAE], 1614).

45. Arabian Department to Political Residency (3 July 1959), National Archives, United Kingdom (NA), FO 371:140293.

46. "Talks in Washington on the Middle East: Persian Gulf and Arabia" (27 Jan. 1969), National Archives, United Kingdom (NA), FCO 8:934.

47. Vicker, "The Gold Hustlers."

48. Ibid.

49. R. T. Naylor, *Wages of Crime: Black Markets, Illegal Finance, and the Under-world Economy*, rev. ed. (Ithaca: Cornell University Press, 2004), 234.

50. Patrick Eyers, "Report" (27 April 1962), National Archives, United Kingdom (NA), FO 371:163042.

51. Ibid.

52. Note from Crawford (26 Nov. 1962), National Archives, United Kingdom (NA), FO 371:163042.

53. Walmsley to Luce (4 Dec. 1962), National Archives, United Kingdom (NA), FO 371:163042.

54. Note from Crawford (26 Nov. 1962), National Archives, United Kingdom (NA), FO 371:163042.

55. Luce to Walmsley (15 Nov. 1962), National Archives, United Kingdom (NA), FO 371:163042.

56. Note from Given (30 Nov. 1962), National Archives, United Kingdom (NA), FO 371:163042; Note from Crawford (26 Nov. 1962), National Archives, United Kingdom (NA), FO 371:163042.

57. Dubai Airport (circa 9 May 1959), National Archives, United Kingdom (NA), FO 371:140205.

58. Graeme H. Wilson, *Rashid's Legacy: The Genesis of the Maktoum Family and the History of Dubai* (London: Media Prima, 2006), 180–184.

59. Ali Bustani, "Dubai/Sharjah Relations" (11 June 1957), National Archives, United Kingdom (NA), FO 1016:591.

60. Anita Burdett, *Records of the Emirates: 1961–1965* (Slough, UK: Archive Editions, 1997), vol. I, 69.

61. See, for example, "Economic Report No. 3 of 1961" (circa 25 Oct. 1961), National Archives, United Kingdom (NA), FO 371:157023.

62. Naylor, *Wages of Crime*, 196–197.

63. Tuohy, "Dubai: Where Gold Smuggling Is Way of Life."

64. Anthony Thomas, "When Statistics Lie," *Times* (London) (30 May 1969).

65. Peter Fox, "Brisk Trade in Gold," *Times* (London) (21 Dec. 1971).

66. George Beardsley, "Illegal Gold Trade Pinched," *Chicago Tribune* (8 Aug. 1971).

67. "Illegal Currency Manipulations Affecting South Vietnam, Fraud and Corruption in Management of Military Club Systems, Part 8" (16–17 March 1969), Hearings Before the Permanent Subcommittee on Investigations, US Senate, 2048.

68. "Illegal Currency Manipulations Affecting South Vietnam, Fraud and Corruption in Management of Military Club Systems, Part 3" (6 March and 18–21 Nov. 1969), Hearings Before the Permanent Subcommittee on Investigations, US Senate, 600.

69. Ibid., 640.

70. There must have been other similar rings, since the money connected to Rahman was less than 20 percent of the total $250 million Ribicoff's team suspected to be caught up in similar transactions.

71. "Illegal Currency Manipulations Affecting South Vietnam, Fraud and Corruption in Management of Military Club Systems, Part 8" (16–17 March 1969), 2048.

72. "Illegal Currency Manipulations Affecting South Vietnam, Fraud and Corruption in Management of Military Club Systems, Part 3" (6 March and 18–21 Nov. 1969), 639.

73. Ibid., 538.

74. Martin, "Geography of Present-Day Smuggling," 25.

75. Press Trust of India, "Tragic End to Quest," *Times of India* (5 June 1969); Henchman to Roberts (15 April 1968), National Archives, United Kingdom (NA), FCO 8:911.

76. Fenelon, *United Arab Emirates*, 84–85.

77. "Banking Follows Trade Pattern," *Financial Times* (2 Dec. 1970).

78. Richard Johns, "Bankers' Agreement Ends Free-for-All," *Financial Times* (16 Dec. 1971).

79. Mack to Harris (10 Oct. 1967), John R. Harris Library. Halcrow was hired as the building's consultant engineer.

80. Harris to Halcrow (7 Sept. 1967), John R. Harris Library.

81. Anastase Emmanuel, in discussion with author, Kingston upon Thames (4 March 2011).

82. David Docherty, "British Contractors' Prominent Role," *Times* (London) (21 Dec. 1971).

83. While drawings of the NBD headquarters reveal that there was a central air conditioning plant in the building, there were also openings made for window units in the building's creekside offices.

84. Farah Al-Nakib, *Kuwait Transformed: A History of Oil and Urban Life* (Stanford, CA: Stanford University Press, 2016), 151.

85. Harris had to allot part of the building's budget to procure the architect Victor Heal, a London architect in ongoing service to the Bank of England. Heal's

firm was commissioned as "consulting architects for the security areas of the Bank" (Mack to Harris [10 Oct. 1967], John R. Harris Library).

86. The price of gold reached $160 per ounce in 1975, a rate too high to appeal to Indian markets, especially calculating the risk of possibly having to dump a shipment overboard (John Bonar, "Why Gold Is Too Hot," *Times* [London] [10 Aug. 1975]).

87. Roberts to Crawford (30 Dec. 1968), National Archives, United Kingdom (NA), FCO 8:829.

88. Geoffrey Jones, "No White Elephants in Dubai," *Financial Times* (6 March 1968).

89. Richard Johns, "Dubai: Outstanding Example," *Financial Times* (2 Dec. 1970).

90. In 2006, Rahman was described in a local Dubai paper as the "vice chairman of Emirates Trading Agency LLC and Associated Construction and Investments Co. LLC (ETA-ASCON), the Dubai-based $2 billion industrial behemoth," which he helped to start with the Galadari family, a local Dubai family that had also been active in the gold trade. See "Mr. B. S. Abdur Rahman—One Man, Many Missions," *Gulf Today* (29 July 2006). http://www.nellaieruvadi.com/article/article.asp?aid=454

91. Bonar, "Why Gold Is Too Hot."

92. See, for example, "Bangladesh Customs Hit Gold Bonanza in Unlikely Places," *Arab News* (28 May 2017). http://www.arabnews.com/node/1106356/world

93. "Banks Expand with Growth of Commerce," *Financial Times* (5 June 1969); Johns, "Bankers' Agreement Ends."

94. Financial Times, *Behind Closed Doors: BCCI: The Biggest Bank Fraud in History* (FT Business Information, 1991). *Time* magazine put the bank on its cover (29 July 1991) with the title "The World's Sleaziest Bank." BCCI's dramatic downfall has left the building an empty shell for most its life.

95. Conversation between Rem Koolhaas and Carlos Ott, Rotterdam (January 2007).

CHAPTER 7

1. "Fun," *Daily Mirror* (11 July 1961), National Archives, United Kingdom (NA), FO 371:157071.

2. In 1969, the Rover Company still touted that it furnished Dubai and the region with its most popular vehicle. An advertisement in the *Financial Times* (5 June 1969) described the Land Rover as "The Nation Builder."

3. Anita Burdett, *Records of Dubai: 1761–1960* (Slough, UK: Archive Editions, 2000), vol. VIII, 42.

4. Arabian Department to Political Residency (3 July 1959), National Archives, United Kingdom (NA), FO 371:140293.

5. Roberts to Moore (19 May 1966), National Archives (NA), FO 371:185581.

6. "Ruler of Dubai Drives 'Tube' Train on London's Underground Railway," D.97096 (June 1959), National Archives, United Kingdom, CO 1069:826.

7. Visit of the ruler of Dubai (27 May 1969), National Archives, United Kingdom (NA), FCO 8:999.

8. Arabian Department to Political Residency (3 July 1959), National Archives, United Kingdom (NA), FO 371:140293.

9. Michael Webb, "A Hospital on an Expansive Plan," *Country Life* (9 Feb. 1967): 276–278.

10. "Wexham Park Hospital—2," *Architects' Journal* (3 Feb. 1967).

11. "Sheikh Rashid's UK Visit 1969" (n.d.), National Archives, United Kingdom (NA), FCO 8:999.

12. The legend sometimes includes the detail that a jar filled with oil was given to the ruler. Harris recalls a "jam jar," but beyond his recollection, the story remains unverified. The government of Dubai's 1974 annual report records June 6, 1966, as the date of oil's discovery. The exact day of this event may have been a day or two later (Duff, *Statistics Report 1974*, Dubai, Central Accounts Section, Statistics Office, Government of Dubai).

13. "Recollections of the Early Development of Dubai," speech notes (n.d.), John R. Harris Library.

14. See, for example, Stephen J. Ramos, "Boom," in *Dubai Amplified: The Engineering of a Port Geography*, Design and the Built Environment Series (Burlington, VT: Ashgate, 2010).

15. Richard Johns, "Dubai: Outstanding Example of Self-Help," *Financial Times* (2 Dec. 1970).

16. "Wide Range of Partners in a Free-for-All Market-Place," *Financial Times* (2 Oct. 1972). The consultant engineer for Port Rashid was Halcrow. The airport was designed by British architecture firm Page & Broughton with Costain as the contractor. The sewerage system was designed by British consultants J. D. and D. M. Watson.

17. Brian Broughton, in discussion with author (21 June 2018).

18. Kamal Hamza, "Dubai: Pearl of Arabian Coast" (1968), 3. Translation by Mahdi Sabbagh.

19. Kamal Hamza, in discussion with author, Dubai (7 Dec. 2010).

20. Hamza, "Dubai: Pearl of Arabian Coast," 6.

21. Hamza, "Dubai: Pearl of Arabian Coast" (Beirut: 1969).

22. For example, see "Ruler of Dubai" (23 July 1963), National Archives, United Kingdom (NA), FO 371:168955.

23. "Commercial Capital of the Lower Gulf," *Financial Times* (5 Nov. 1968).

24. "Welcome to Dubai," advertisement, *Times* (London) (3 March 1969).

25. Geoff Dunlop, "All to Share Port Boon," *Times* (London) (3 March 1969).

26. Joe Roeber, "Better Off Than the Fabulously Rich," *Times* (London) (30 May 1969).

27. Horner to Department of State, "The Boom in Dubai" (1 April 1964), file AF 3/2–5, NARA 772, National Archives (US). Access via National Archives (UAE).

28. Roberts to Balfour-Paul (20 April 1967), National Archives, United Kingdom (NA), FCO 8:858.

29. Howell to Bullock (3 Feb. 1967), National Archives, United Kingdom (NA), FCO 8:858.

30. Draft brief regarding Sheikh Rashid's visit (19 July 1969), National Archives, United Kingdom (NA), FCO 8:999.

31. "Increase in Exports to Trucial States," *Guardian* (11 Jan. 1966).

32. "Wide Range of Partners," *Financial Times* (2 Oct. 1972).

33. Robin Mead, "Equipment Firms Plan to Step Up Their Exports," *Times* (London) (26 April 1972).

34. Harris to Al Tajir (4 Sept. 1969), John R. Harris Library.

35. "£3m Design by UK Architect," *Times* (London) (20 May 1968).

36. "Hospitals and Clinics: The Rashid Hospital," *Annals of the Royal College of Surgeons of England* 58 (1976).

37. "Project Close-Up: Rashid Hospital Dubai," *Building* (21 Jan. 1977): 107, 108.

38. Meeting notes (13 Feb. 1969), John R. Harris Library. Both Sheikh Rashid and his trusted deputy, Mahdi Al Tajir, kept close tabs on the project's array of consultants. Construction of Rashid Hospital also offered an opportunity for local companies to acquire development skills to match those of British counterparts. For example, Khalaf Al Habtoor, who founded a Dubai-based engineering company during the time of the hospital's construction and later a development company, took on a larger role in the latter phases of the Rashid Hospital project. There was also Hillal Ahmed Al Lootah of Dubai who was hired "to furnish all furniture and equipment for our 398–bed Rashid Hospital." The Lootah family now runs companies ranging in interests from manufacturing to real estate development (Public statement, government of Dubai [4 Aug. 1971], John R. Harris Library).

39. Giles Merritt, "Morgan Grenfell to Finance £6.5m. Dubai Hospital," *Financial Times* (30 Sept. 1969).

40. David Docherty, "British Contractors' Prominent Role," *Times* (London) (21 Dec. 19710; Cotterill to Weston (26 July 1967), National Archives, United Kingdom (NA), FO 1016:839.

41. ECGD, the Export Credits Guarantee Department, is the UK's official export credit agency. In 2008, the ECGD's website described its mission "to help UK exporters of capital equipment and project-related goods and services win business and complete overseas contracts with confidence" ("Export Credits Guarantee Department" [9 June 2008]. http://webarchive.nationalarchives.gov.uk/20061023210202/ ecgd.gov.uk/print/index.htm).

42. West Germany and the United States were two countries that supplied local private companies with financial guarantees. See National Archives, United Kingdom (NA), FO 371:168933 for British Foreign Office correspondence discussing public financing provided to promote a West German engineering company.

43. David Crawford, "Welfare State Forms Planning Basis," *Times* (London) (17 Oct. 1977).

44. Stephen Finch, in discussion with author, London (30 Aug. 2018).

45. Mead, "Equipment Firms Plan to Step Up Their Exports."

46. Speech notes (13 Dec. 1974); "Draft Press Release: Rashid Hospital, Dubai" (n.d.), John R. Harris Library.

47. "Recollections of the Early Development of Dubai" (n.d.), John R. Harris Library.

48. Ibid.

49. Draft press release (n.d.), John R. Harris library; "Project Close-Up: Rashid Hospital Dubai," 108.

50. David Curry, "Gulf Hospital," *Financial Times* (19 Nov. 1971).

51. Harris to Meyer (2 Aug. 1971), John R. Harris Library.

52. "Sunley Gets £6.5m. Hospital Contract," *Financial Times* (13 Oct. 1969).

53. Andrea Wright, "Migratory Pipelines: Labor and Oil in the Arabian Sea," PhD dissertation, University of Michigan (2015). http://hdl.handle.net/2027.42/113653

54. Oscar Mandoody, in discussion with author, Dubai (27 Nov. 2011).

55. "First Population Census of the Trucial States: Methods Report" (Sept. 1968), Middle East Development Division.

56. "Project Close-Up: Rashid Hospital Dubai," 110.

57. Peter Jackson, in discussion with the author, Sharjah (13 March 2009).

58. Record of a meeting (Nov. 1960), National Archives, United Kingdom (NA), FO 371:157025.

59. Robert L. Jarman, *Political Diaries of the Arab World, Persian Gulf 1904–65* (Slough, UK: Archive Editions, 1998), vol. 23, 682.

60. Allen to Department of State, "Economic Summary of Dubai: 1964" (1 Feb. 1965), file AF 3/2–5, NARA 772, National Archives (US). Access via National Archives (UAE).

61. "Dubai," *An-Nahar* (Beirut) (15 June 1971). Translation by Dima Srouji.

62. This site also designated space for other projects deemed necessary to appeal to outsiders' impressions of Dubai, including Dubai's first sports stadium, first Christian churches, and non–Arabic-language schools. Al Nasr Stadium, later renamed Al Maktoum Stadium, opened in 1978 with an exhibition match between a home team and Liverpool, which accepted the $130,000 invitation to play. John Harris made a design proposal for this stadium ("Rashid Opens New Stadium," *Khaleej Times* [Dubai] [27 May 1978]).

63. By 1963, the Qatari developer with the airport contract had also built a "compound with homes and all facilities for Darwish airport workers" (Horner to Department of State [24 July 1963], file AF 1/3–3, US NARA 3502, National Archives [US]. Access via National Archives [UAE]).

64. "Dubai: Era of the Quality Conscious Client," *Middle East Construction* (Oct. 1977): 96.

65. The mosque, whose design is credited as Arenco, still stands but now is on the other side of six-lane Al Ittihad Street and no longer part of the Rashid Hospital complex ("Dubai: Era of the Quality Conscious Client," 96).

66. "Political Agency Report" (n.d.), John R. Harris Library.

67. Classified Ad 5, *Times of India* (6 Jan. 1977).

68. Tim Edgar, "Improving Medical Services Free for All," *Times* (London) (21 June 1971).

69. David Docherty, "Medical Services Expanding," *Times* (London) (21 Dec. 1971).

70. "Brief No. 1: Visit of the Ruler of Abu Dhabi" (6 June 1969), National Archives, United Kingdom (NA), PREM 13:2774; "Report on Social, Industrial and Labour Developments in Abu Dhabi" (13 June 1966), National Archives, United Kingdom (NA), LAB 13:2165; Lamb to Balfour-Paul (11 Jan. 1967), National Archives, United Kingdom (NA), FCO 8:858. In 1978, Abu Dhabi leadership took a pass on a $12 million hospital proposal by Harris.

71. "Dubai Transforming to Become Health Center," *Akhbar Dubai* (10 Sept. 1969). Translation by Sandra Bsat.

72. "Hospitals and Clinics: The Rashid Hospital," *Annals of the Royal College of Surgeons of England* 58 (1976).

73. Meeting notes (18 June 1971), John R. Harris Library.

74. Ibid.

75. Ibid.

76. "Project Close-Up: Rashid Hospital Dubai," 110.

77. "The Rashid Hospital Dubai 1973," commemorative booklet for opening of Rashid Hospital, John R. Harris Library.

78. "Project Close-Up: Rashid Hospital Dubai," 108.

79. Charles McKean, "In Glitter and Style New Buildings," *Times* (London) (23 Feb. 1981).

80. "Rashid Hospital Dubai 1973"; "Dubai Development Plan Review" (May 1971): 23, John R. Harris Library.

81. "Rashid Hospital Dubai 1973."

82. "Sunley in Dubai," advertisement, *Financial Times* (29 March 1973).

83. Ramos, *Dubai Amplified*, 98.

84. Ralph Izzard, "Sights Set on Making Dubai," *Times* (London) (23 May 1974).

85. Griffith to Howell (1 May 1961), National Archives, United Kingdom, (NA), FO 957:231.

86. "Dubai and the Northern Trucial States 1970 and After" (10 Dec. 1970), National Archives, United Kingdom (NA), FCO 8:1510.

87. "Persian Gulf: Annual Review for 1970" (1 Jan. 1970), National Archives, United Kingdom (NA), FCO 8:1570.

88. "Dubai and the Northern Trucial States Review of the Year 1969" (30 Dec. 1969), National Archives, United Kingdom (NA), FCO 8:1509.

89. "British Trade: The Fool You Know," *Economist* (6 June 1970).

90. Burdett, *Records of Dubai*, vol. VIII, 70.

91. Craig to Tripp (11 Oct. 1961), National Archives, United Kingdom (NA), FO 371:157071.

92. "Dubai and the Northern Trucial States Review of the Year 1969" (30 Dec. 1969), National Archives, United Kingdom (NA), FCO 8:1509.

93. Trucial States Development Office papers (n.d.), John R. Harris Library.

94. Rashid Hospital papers (n.d.), John R. Harris Library.

95. The design was selected through a competition, perhaps the second design competition for an institutional building in Dubai. The first was for the Dubai Municipality's new building, which Harris's firm lost to the Japanese firm Pacific Consultants International.

CHAPTER 8

1. Dana Adams Schmidt, "World's Largest Oil Tank Installed," *New York Times* (10 Aug. 1969).

2. Tad Harvey, "Bottomless Wonder," *Popular Science* 196, no. 1 (Jan. 1970), 80; Schmidt, "World's Largest Oil Tank Installed." In a Chicago Bridge and Iron Company advertisement that ran months before the launch, the company describes itself as having "the design ingenuity and construction skill needed to 'build big'—anywhere in the world!" ("Cost Cutter Under the Sea," advertisement, *Times* [London] [30 May 1969]).

3. Harvey, "Bottomless Wonder," 83.

4. Quoted in *Dubai* (film), directed by Rodney Giesler (United Kingdom: Spectator Films, 1970).

5. Schmidt, "World's Largest Oil Tank Installed"; Oscar Mandoody, in discussion with author, Dubai (27 Nov. 2011).

6. Washington to Willcocks (15 July 1969), file 48743, British Petroleum Archive, University of Warwick.

7. *Dubai* (film).

8. Harvey, "Bottomless Wonder," 82.

9. Note from W. L. Dolan (4 Nov. 1970), file 48743, British Petroleum Archive, University of Warwick; "The Three Pyramids of Dubai," advertisement, *Financial Times* (16 Dec. 1971).

10. *Port Rashid* (film), directed by Ted Davis and Derick Williams (United Kingdom: Richard Costain Film Unit, 1971).

11. Frauke Heard-Bey, *From Trucial States to United Arab Emirates: A Society in Transition* (London: Motivate, 2005), 261.

12. "Reception at Airport for Dubai's Ruler," *Akhbar Dubai* (10 Sept. 1969). Translation by Sandra Bsat.

13. Translation of an article published in *Al Hawadeth Magazine* (29 Oct. 1969), British Petroleum Archive, University of Warwick.

14. See Aqil Kazim, *The United Arab Emirates A.D. 600 to the Present: A Socio-Discursive Transformation in the Arabian Gulf* (Dubai: Gulf Book Centre, 2000), 302–305. Bahrain and Qatar were originally proposed to be part of the new nation-state.

15. Roberts to Crawford (25 Jan. 1968), National Archives, United Kingdom (NA), FCO 8:840.

16. Anita Burdett, *Records of the Emirates: 1961–1965* (Slough, UK: Archive Editions, 1997), vol. III, 3, 46–55. By this time, there were two political agents in the Trucial States, with one dedicated specifically to Abu Dhabi. The political agent in Dubai remained focused on Dubai and the other Trucial States.

17. Sheikh Saqr of Sharjah, at least for a while, backed Dubai as the nation's capital (see National Archives, United Kingdom [NA], FCO 8:1211). The United Arab Emirates' original constitution referred to Abu Dhabi as the capital until a new one could be built. This clause was eventually removed, and Abu Dhabi assumed the permanent location of the nation's capital. It became customary that the presidency would be held by the ruler of Abu Dhabi.

18. Stephen J. Ramos, *Dubai Amplified: The Engineering of a Port Geography*, Design and the Built Environment Series (Burlington, VT: Ashgate, 2010), 91; Richard Johns, "Abu Dhabi Faces £13m. Budgetary Deficit," *Financial Times* (6 Feb. 1970).

19. Burdett, *Records of the Emirates*, vol. III, 52–54.

20. Lamb to Balfour-Paul (17 Aug. 1966), National Archives, United Kingdom (NA), FO 371:185528. The cash gift was about $3,300, or $24,200 today.

21. In September 1964, the political agency reported that Sheikh Rashid "has indicated that he intends to bring pressure to bear on Dubai merchants trading in a manner which may result in Ras Al Khaimah becoming less dependent commercially on Dubai" (Robert L. Jarman, *Political Diaries of the Arab World, Persian Gulf 1904–65* [Slough, UK: Archive Editions, 1998], vol. 24, 438).

22. British Petroleum, whose archives have provided the details about this event, had a small share in the Dubai Marine Areas oil company but did not "participate" in the commemoration. The fireworks, imported from the British company Brock's Fireworks Ltd., had been difficult to get through Dubai customs, a sign that customs regulations were in place.

23. The roundabout came to be known as the Flame Roundabout. The sculpture was eventually moved to another roundabout, where it was the first monument to welcome new arrivals from the airport. Eventually, it was removed from this roundabout as well and put at the side of the road to Sharjah, at the tip of a park. The flame has been replaced by an electric lamp.

24. BP Papers claim that the film "took gold" at the British Industrial Film Festival in Brighton (Telegram [6 Aug. 1970], file 48743, British Petroleum Archive, University of Warwick).

25. John Gordon Lorimer and Richard Lockington Birdwood, *Gazetteer of the Persian Gulf, Oman, and Central Arabia* (Shannon: Irish University Press, 1970, republished), vol. I, pt. 2, 2638.

26. Letter from Dolan (11 Dec. 1969), file 48743, British Petroleum Archive, University of Warwick.

27. "Dubai and the Northern Trucial States 1970 and After" (10 Dec. 1970), National Archives, United Kingdom (NA), FCO 8:1510.

28. John K. Cooley, "Persian Gulf Is Yawning Awake," *Christian Science Monitor* (7 June 1971); "Economy Enjoys More Sober Hopes," *Financial Times* (16 Dec. 1971).

29. "Dubai: Oil Will Not Wrest Entrepôt Status," *Times* (London) (19 June 1975).

30. Richard Johns, "Emphasis Stays on Trading," *Financial Times* (16 Dec. 1971).

31. Richard Johns, "Dubai: Outstanding Example of Self-Help," *Financial Times* (2 Dec. 1970); K. G. Fenelon, "Continuing on the Road to Prosperity," *Financial Times* (2 Dec. 1970).

32. Kenn Dalley, "New Buildings in Dubai," *RIBA Journal* (Nov. 1978), 471.

33. "Dubai Municipality; International Planning Competition for the Preparation of a Comprehensive Plan and Planning Program," United States Agency for International Development (USAID), Washington, DC (1977), 60–63.

34. "Dubai and the Northern Trucial States Review of the Year 1969" (30 Dec. 1969), National Archives, United Kingdom (NA), FCO 8:1509.

35. Oscar Mandoody, in discussion with author, Dubai (27 Nov. 2011).

36. David Ledger, "Boomtown Growing Pains," *Times* (London) (30 May 1969).

37. "Proposed Projects for Next Year's Budget," *Akhbar Dubai* (26 Nov. 1973), 48. Translation by Sara Kassa.

38. "Dubai and the Northern Trucial States Review of the Year 1969" (30 Dec. 1969), National Archives, United Kingdom (NA), FCO 8:1509.

39. William Duff, *Statistic Report 1974*, 23–24.

40. Though critical of the widening "gap between rich and poor," Bullard still approved the absence of "any nonsense about welfare" ("Dubai and the Northern Trucial States Review of the Year 1969" [30 Dec. 1969], National Archives, United Kingdom [NA], FCO 8:1509).

41. David Housego, "Transforming Dubai," *Financial Times* (3 Jan. 1974).

42. "Dubai and the Northern Trucial States Review of the Year 1968" (5 Jan. 1969), National Archives, United Kingdom (NA), FCO 8:1210.

43. Bullard to Weir (18 May 1970), National Archives, United Kingdom (NA), FCO 8:1510.

44. "Persian Gulf: Annual Review for 1970" (1 Jan. 1971), National Archives, United Kingdom (NA), FCO 8:1570.

45. In 1975 Tajir bought the notorious Keir House in Scotland for £2 million. For a time, he was known as Scotland's richest person.

46. "Persian Gulf: Annual Review for 1970" (1 Jan. 1971), National Archives, United Kingdom (NA), FCO 8:1570.

47. Talking points for use with the ruler of Dubai (1 July 1969), National Archives, United Kingdom (NA), FCO 8:999.

48. "Dubai Development Plan Review" (May 1971), 30, John R. Harris Library.

49. "A Report on the Current Developments in Dubai" (Nov. 1960), National Archives, United Kingdom (NA), FO 371:157025.

50. Anastase Emmanuel, in discussion with author, Kingston upon Thames (4 March 2011).

51. Kamal Hamza, in discussion with author, Dubai (7 Dec. 2010).

52. Gordon Heald, in discussion with author, London (18 Oct. 2018).

53. "Dubai Development Plan Review" (May 1971), John R. Harris Library.

54. Ibid. Even though these road reservations were recommended in the 1971 plan, the flyover would be considered an unnecessary idea, well into the 1980s, as the municipal planner Anastase Emmanuel learned when he suggested inserting one on the Abu Dhabi road, where the web of overpasses today lead to Burj Khalifa (Anastase Emmanuel, in discussion with author, Kingston upon Thames [4 March 2011]).

55. Michael Hamilton-Clark, in discussion with author (4 April 2012).

56. "Dubai Development Plan Review" (May 1971), 25, John R. Harris Library.

57. "20 Million Sterling Pounds to Construct Dubai International Exhibition Centre," *Akhbar Dubai* (6 June 1974). Translation by Sara Kassa. Harris's words were translated into Arabic and have been translated here back to English.

58. Jumeirah's ongoing development did maintain a road system similar to that used in the new Deira districts. While Sheikh Rashid had these districts laid out, mostly by Halcrow, outside the purview of the Harris plan, he did urge the municipality to maintain certain aspects of Harris's neighborhood-unit concept, avoiding the simple grid and preferring smaller districts that remained focused inward away from major roads (Anastase Emmanuel, in discussion with author, Kingston upon Thames [March 4, 2011]).

59. Only Kartun—Arabic for cardboard—is marked on the illustrative plan. A step up from these districts were "self-built low-cost" housing built by residents in the areas of Port Saeed and Al Safa, both in proximity to Dubai's two ports. Al Safa would eventually be cleared of its informal housing, sometime between 1973 and 1977, and landscaped into Al Safa Park, which has now been incorporated into the Dubai Canal project.

60. See Todd Reisz, "'Along Sound Lines': Drawing Up Dubai's Labor Camps from 1950 to 2008," *Perspecta 50* (Sept. 2017).

61. "Dubai and the Northern Trucial States 1970 and After" (10 Dec. 1970), National Archives, United Kingdom (NA), FCO 8:1510.

62. "Dubai Municipality; International Planning Competition for the Preparation of a Comprehensive Plan and Planning Program," USAID, Washington, DC (1977), 65.

63. Kamal Hamza, in discussion with author, Dubai (7 Dec. 2010).

64. Khalaf Al Habtoor, in discussion with author, Dubai (9 Nov. 2016).

65. Anastase Emmanuel, in discussion with author, Dubai (17 March 2014).

66. "Persian Gulf: Annual Review for 1970" (1 Jan. 1970), National Archives, United Kingdom (NA), FCO 8:1570.

67. Darby to Harris (21 Sept. 1977), John R. Harris Library.

CHAPTER 9

1. Jonathan Raban, *Arabia: Through the Looking Glass* (London: Picador, 1987), 163. Raban mistakes the Hilton Hotel for the World Trade Centre tower.

2. Ibid., 163–164.

3. Ibid.

4. "Dubai and the Northern Trucial States Review of the Year 1969" (30 Dec. 1969), National Archives, United Kingdom (NA), FCO 8:1509.

5. Raban, *Arabia*, 164–165.

6. "Banking," *Financial Times* (4 April 1977).

7. John Andrews, "Spending Spree Scaled Down," *Guardian* (5 June 1978).

8. "Abu Dhabi Bans New Projects," *Khaleej Times* (Dubai) (25 April 1978).

9. Stephen J. Ramos, *Dubai Amplified: The Engineering of a Port Geography*, Design and the Built Environment Series (Burlington, VT: Ashgate, 2010), 74.

10. "Dubai: Oil Will Not Wrest Entrepôt Status," *Times* (London) (19 June 1975); Peter Hopkirk, "United Arab Emirates," *Times* (London) (19 June 1975).

11. "Proposed Projects for Next Year's Budget," *Akhbar Dubai* (26 Nov. 1973), 48. Translation by Sara Kassa.

12. "15 Million Dirham for Dubai Municipality Projects," *Akhbar Dubai* (26 Nov. 1973), 50. Translation by Sara Kassa.

13. "In Brief," *Middle East Economic Digest* (2 Jan. 1976).

14. "Dubai Municipality; International Planning Competition for the Preparation of a Comprehensive Plan and Planning Program," United States Agency for International Development (USAID), Washington, DC (1977).

15. The hotel is currently a Radisson Blu Hotel.

16. Hopkirk, "United Arab Emirates."

17. "Reception at Airport for Dubai's Ruler," *Akhbar Dubai* (10 Sept. 1969). Translation by Sandra Bsat.

18. "1000 Million Dollars for Establishment of Free Zone in Dubai," *Akhbar Dubai* (17 Jan. 1974). Translation by Sandra Bsat.

19. Raban, *Arabia*, 15, 191.

20. Kathleen Bishtawi, "Dubai Trade Center," *Financial Times* (25 April 1979).

21. "The Trade Centre of the Arab World," advertisement, *Financial Times* (25 April 1979).

22. "Rough Notes Taken at Ruler's Majlis in Dubai on 30th July 1974" (30 July 1974), John R. Harris Library.

23. The complex has gone by different names, including Dubai International Trade and Exhibition Centre (DITEC). In local Arabic, the complex's tower is often referred to as Burj Rashid, or Rashid Tower. For the sake of clarity, the project is consistently referred to as the World Trade Centre.

24. Al Barri, "Burj Rashid: An Emirati Icon," *Akhbar Dubai* (4 June 1977). Translated by Azza Aboualam.

25. "Dubai International Trade Centre—A Response and a Stimulus to World Trade" (n.d.), John R. Harris Library.

26. "Thirty-Three Floors: The Tallest Building in the Arab World," *Akhbar Dubai* (24 Oct. 1974). Translation by Sandra Bsat.

27. "Dubai International Airport," *Akhbar Dubai* (28 Nov. 1974). Translation by Dima Srouji.

28. David Docherty, "British Contractors' Prominent Role," *Times* (London) (21 Dec. 1971); Ghassan S. Amhaz, *From the Creek to the Skies: Civil Aviation in Dubai* (Dubai: Printwell, 2011), 118.

29. "Dubai International Airport," *Akhbar Dubai* (24 Oct. 1974), 64–65. Translation by Dima Srouji.

30. There is limited documentation of the meeting or of the queen's response to the exhibition, but much is said about its outcomes. According to a representative at Buckingham Palace, the queen made several stops in Dubai in the early and mid-1970s to refuel on her way to Southeast Asia and Oceania, including March 14, 1974. Buckingham Palace cannot confirm that the queen deboarded in Dubai on that date or any other of her brief stops (Conversation, [23 March 2016]). In one telling of the event, Harris recalls that Prince Philip also attended the tour of the exhibition (Speech notes, "Thirty Years in the Arabian Gulf" [Nov. 1985], John R. Harris Library). The meeting is also described in a promotional brochure produced by Dubai World

Trade Centre; however, the story is largely based on Harris's recollections. It includes his misdating the event to 1972. The brochure is titled "Dubai World Trade Centre: 20 Years of Success."

31. Speech notes, "Thirty Years in the Arabian Gulf." There is evidence that an exhibition center had already been considered before the alleged meeting.

32. Gordon Heald, in discussion with author, London (18 Oct. 2018).

33. Anthony R. Davis, "New Business Focus for the Gulf," *Middle East Architectural Design* (Oct. 1978): 28.

34. Easa Saleh Al Gurg and James Craig, *The Wells of Memory: An Autobiography* (London: John Murray, 1998), 109.

35. Ramos, *Dubai Amplified,* 74.

36. "£20 Million to Construct Dubai International Exhibition Centre," *Akhbar Dubai* (6 June 1974). Translation by Sara Kassa.

37. World Trade Center, Port Authority of New York, marketing binder, John R. Harris Library.

38. According to its website, the World Trade Centers Association was incorporated in 1969. https://www.wtca.org/about

39. Halcrow's canceled plan to connect Port Rashid to Dubai Creek is discussed in Chapter 8.

40. "£20 Million to Construct Dubai International Exhibition Centre."

41. Dubai Municipality, "Notes on Material for Dubai Report" (5 Dec. 1970), John R. Harris Library.

42. Meeting notes, "Trade Centre Complex-Dubai" (30 July 1974), John R. Harris Library.

43. Gordon Heald, in discussion with author, London (18 Oct. 2018).

44. "Thirty-Three Floors: The Tallest Building in the Arab World," *Akhbar Dubai* (24 Oct. 1974). Translation by Sandra Bsat.

45. John D. Allen, "British Engineering Still Dominates," *Times* (London) (19 Oct. 1978).

46. Draft press release (n.d.), John R. Harris Library.

47. Davis, "New Business Focus for the Gulf," 27–38.

48. "Dubai International Trade and Exhibition Center" (16 Sept. 1983), John R. Harris Library.

49. "The Trade Centre of the Arab World."

50. "Notes to Editors," prepared for press coverage of visit by Queen Elizabeth II to Dubai (n.d.), John R. Harris Library.

51. Ibid.

52. Advance press information (Feb. 1979), John R. Harris Library.

53. "Interview: John R. Harris. HH Sheikh Rashid and Dubai World Trade Centre" (n.d.), John R. Harris Library.

54. Speech notes (23 March 2000), John R. Harris Library.

55. Gordon Heald, in correspondence with author (29 Nov. 2018).

56. DITEC draft press release (n.d.), John R. Harris Library.

57. Speech notes, "Thirty Years in the Arabian Gulf."

58. DITEC draft press release.

59. "High Water Table Problems Overcome," *Khaleej Times* (Dubai) (26 Feb. 1979).

60. Speech notes, "Thirty Years in the Arabian Gulf."

61. "High Water Table Problems Overcome."

62. "Haunted by Ghost Buildings," *Construction Week Online* (12 June 2010). https://www.constructionweekonline.com/article-8628-haunted-by-ghost-buildings

63. Gordon Heald, in correspondence with author (26 Oct. 2018).

64. Allen, "British Engineering Still Dominates."

65. Ibid.; Gordon Heald, in discussion with author, London (18 Oct. 2018). The tower was designed to maintain its natural concrete color; therefore, special attention had been paid to the exterior's final finish.

66. "High Water Table Problems Overcome."

67. Speech notes (23 March 2000).

68. Khalil Al Barri, "Burj Rashid: An Emirati Icon," *Akhbar Dubai* (4 June 1977). Translated by Azza Aboualam.

69. *Port Rashid* (film), directed by Ted Davis and Derick Williams (United Kingdom: Richard Costain Film Unit, 1971).

70. Ibid.

71. During the planning for the tower, one floor was scheduled to be Sheikh Rashid's offices, but that plan was canceled. Plans courtesy Stephen Finch, John R. Harris Library.

72. *Port Rashid* (film).

73. John Andrews, "Spending Spree Scaled Down," *Guardian* (5 June 1978).

74. Geoffrey Weston, "Focus on the United Arab Emirates," *Times* (London) (19 April 1982).

75. Speech notes, "Thirty Years in the Arabian Gulf."

76. "Recollections of the Early Development of Dubai" (n.d.), John R. Harris Library.

77. Ibid.

78. Ibid.

79. Bishtawi, "Dubai Trade Center"; Speech notes, "Thirty Years in the Arabian Gulf."

80. In his investigation of interior lobbies in Manhattan, David Gissen explores how architectural, even urban, spaces are delineated by their regimens of cleaning and upkeep. There is an evident financialized aspect to the experience of these spaces, which communicates that these spaces are part of larger economic structures (David Gissen, *Manhattan Atmospheres: Architecture, the Interior Environment, and Urban Crisis* [Minneapolis: University of Minnesota Press, 2014], 23–28).

81. Bishtawi, "Dubai Trade Center."

82. Ibid.

83. "Rough Notes Taken at Ruler's Majlis."

84. Bishtawi, "Dubai Trade Center."

85. Dubai International Trade and Exhibition Center, study prepared by Trizec Corporation Ltd. (Dec. 1976), John R. Harris Library.

86. "The Trade Centre of the Arab World."

87. "Dubai Municipality; International Planning Competition for the Preparation of a Comprehensive Plan and Planning Program," USAID, Washington, DC (1977).

88. Gordon Heald, in discussion with author, London (18 Oct. 2017).

89. "Dubai International Expo," *Akhbar Dubai* (24 Oct. 1974). Translation by Sandra Bsat.

90. John Henry Forshaw and Patrick Abercrombie, *County of London Plan* (London: Macmillan, 1944), 84, 87.

91. "Lion's Share of British Business," *Khaleej Times* (Dubai) (26 Feb. 1979).

92. Kenn Dalley, "New Buildings in Dubai," *RIBA Journal* (Nov. 1978), 472.

93. Martin Routh, "Middle East's Biggest Port," *Financial Times* (16 Dec. 1971).

94. Hal Smith, in correspondence with author (5 July 2016).

95. "An Expatriate in Dubai," *Middle East Construction* (Oct. 1977), 100–101.

96. Ibid. Devizes is a town in England, built around an ancient castle.

97. The site had been a candidate location for Dubai's airport in the 1960s (Hadfield to Lowe [3 Feb. 1959], National Archives, United Kingdom [NA], FO 371:140205).

98. Graeme H. Wilson, *Rashid's Legacy: The Genesis of the Maktoum Family and the History of Dubai* (London: Media Prima, 2006), 368.

99. Kenneth Brown, "Dream of Dubai's Ruler Takes Shape," *Times* (London) (19 Oct. 1978).

100. "Dubai's Second Port Will Cost $1,600 Million," *Middle East Economic Digest*, special report (Dec. 1978), 31.

101. John Whelan, "Dubai Stands Firm on Size," *Middle East Economic Digest* (26 May 1978), 8–10.

102. David Saxby, "Critical Time for Sheikh Rashid," *Financial Times* (17 Oct. 1979).

103. Brown, "Dream of Dubai's Ruler Takes Shape."

104. Whelan, "Dubai Stands Firm on Size."

105. Ibid.

106. Ibid.

107. Ibid.

108. "Dubai Continues to Trade in Expansion at All Levels," *Emirates* (July–August 1979), 14–15.

109. Rafiq Zakaria, "British Queen's Visit to Gulf Consolidating Gains," *Times of India* (24 Feb. 1979); "Halcrow Middle East Makes Changes," *Middle East Economic Digest* (21 July 1978): 38.

110. Allen, "British Engineering Still Dominates"; John D. Allen, "Western Contractors Face Stiff Competition," *Times* (London) (19 Oct. 1978).

111. Zakaria, "British Queen's Visit to Gulf Consolidating Gains."

112. Allen, "Western Contractors Face Stiff Competition."

113. "Queen Inaugurates Jebel Ali" (n.d.), Halcrow archives (viewed 3 March 2011).

114. "Dubai International Trade Centre—A Response and a Stimulus to World Trade."

115. "The Royal Visit to Arabia and Iran," notes from June meeting (1978), Burry House, Middle East Association, John R. Harris Library.

116. "UAE Key Market for Britain," *Khaleej Times* (Dubai) (4 Feb. 1979).

117. "Anxieties Behind Queen's Tour," *Khaleej Times* (Dubai) (9 Feb. 1979).

118. Ibid.

119. "Queen Inaugurates Jebel Ali."

120. "Crowded Official and Popular Receptions for Queen Elizabeth," *Akhbar Dubai* (3 March 1979). Translation by Dima Srouji.

121. "Dubai International Trade Centre—A Response and a Stimulus to World Trade."

122. Memo from M. L. (24 January 1979), John R. Harris Library.

123. "Recollections of the Early Development of Dubai."

124. Colin Smith, "Best Royal Double Act," *Observer* (London) (18 Feb. 1979).

125. "We Built It," advertisement, *Financial Times* (26 Feb. 1979).

126. "Queen Inaugurates Jebel Ali."

127. Ibid.

128. "Recollections of the Early Development of Dubai."

129. "Dubai: Oil Will Not Wrest Entrepôt Status."

130. "Dubai International Trade Centre—A Response and a Stimulus to World Trade."

131. Bishtawi, "Dubai Trade Center."

132. Anne Fyfe, "Ruler's Indelible Stamp," *Times* (London) (23 Feb. 1981).

133. Zakaria, "British Queen's Visit to Gulf Consolidating Gains."

134. Frauke Heard-Bey, *From Trucial States to United Arab Emirates: A Society in Transition* (London: Motivate, 2005), 261.

EPILOGUE

1. "Discover creekside living with spectacular views at Dubai Creek Harbour's new 'Address Harbour Point'" *Property Watch* (25 Sept. 2017). http://www.property-watch.ae/discover-creekside-living-spectacular-views-dubai-creek-harbours-new-address-harbour-point/; "'The city meets the beach' at the new 'Creek Beach' district," press release (10 Oct. 2018). https://dubaiholding.com/en/media-hub/press-releases/live-dream-dubai-creek-harbours-creek-beach-district-next-door-dubai-creek-tower-dubai-square-historic-creek-creek-marina-urban-beach/

2. Amna Khaishgi, "Sheikh Mohammed Hails Future Dubai Tower as 'A New Heart for Our City,'" *The National* (Abu Dhabi), (10 Oct. 2016); "Emaar and Dubai Holding Unveil First Luxury Residential Project in Dubai Creek Harbour at The Lagoons," press release (27 Oct. 2014). https://dubaiholding.com/en/media-hub/press-releases/emaar-and-dubai-holding-unveil-first-luxury-residential-project-in-dubai-creek-harbour-at-the-lagoons/

3. Riad Kamal, in discussion with author, Dubai (9 Nov. 2017).

4. Charles McKean, "In Glitter and Style New Buildings," *Times* (London) (23 Feb. 1981).

5. "Face-Lift Soon for Deira Creek," *Khaleej Times* (Dubai) (8 June 1978).

6. Mira Bar-Hillel, "Consultants in the UK—Competition Intensifies," *Financial Times* (5 March 1984).

7. Maggie Ford, "Family Rules Collegiate Style," *Financial Times* (7 Jan. 1985).

8. Angela Dixon, "Poor Earnings Performance of UAE Banks," *Financial Times* (4 July 1985).

9. Kathy Evans, "The Legacy of 'Briefcase Bankers,'" *Financial Times* (22 May 1985).

10. Michael Field, "Hit Hard by Fall in Oil Revenues," *Financial Times* (23 Jan. 1985).

11. Patrick Coburn, "Trade Expansion Hit by Iran–Iraq War," *Financial Times* (27 May 1982).

12. Ford, "Family Rules Collegiate Style."

13. Susannah Tarbush, "Foreign Contractors Still in Demand," *Financial Times* (5 March 1984).

14. Stewart Dalby, "Happily at Home in Gulf," *Financial Times* (4 Aug. 1984).

15. Ibid.

16. "Dubai and the Northern Trucial States 1970 and After" (10 Dec. 1970), National Archives, United Kingdom (NA), FCO 8:1510.

17. David Housego, "Transforming Dubai," *Financial Times* (3 Jan. 1974).

18. Stephanie Gray, "Merchants Make Art of Brinkmanship," *Financial Times* (30 Nov. 1983).

19. The New Dubai Hospital, designed by Harris's firm, was also commissioned after a design competition. For the diwan project, the municipality received an entry from the renowned Egyptian architect Hassan Fathy.

20. Stephen Finch, in discussion with author, London (12 Sept. 2017).

21. "Limited Architectural Design Competition for Diwan of H. H. The Ruler in Dubai: Terms of Reference" (n.d.), John R. Harris Library.

22. Stephen Finch, in discussion with author, London (12 Sept. 2017).

23. Ibid.

24. Rashad Bukhash, in discussion with author, Dubai (26 Jan. 2009); Peter Jackson, in discussion with author, Sharjah (13 March 2009).

25. See Anne Coles and Peter Jackson, *Windtower* (London: Stacey International, 2007).

26. Gordon Heald, in discussion with author, London (17 Sept. 2017).

27. "Trade Centre Skyscraper to Get New White Coat," *Gulf News* (Dubai) (21 March 1980).

28. Frauke Heard-Bey, *From Trucial States to United Arab Emirates: A Society in Transition* (London: Motivate, 2005), 245.

29. Coles and Jackson, *Windtower*, 27, 78–79.

30. See Ahmed Kanna, "The Vanished Village," in *Dubai: City as Corporation* (Minneapolis: University of Minnesota Press, 2011). Kanna observes that physical evidence of the city's history is deliberately scrubbed out of the city's contemporary urban development, so that a new, unequivocal political narrative can fill the void.

31. "Our Arab Cities Lost Their Identities," *Akhbar Al Khaleej* (Bahrain) (21 Jan. 1979). Suha Babikir Kambalawi Hasan presented the article in a workshop at the Gulf Research Centre in July 2019. Translation by Azza Aboualam.

32. "Visit by HRH Prince of Wales & HRH Duchess of Cornwall to Al Bastakiya," prepared by Peter Jackson (n.d.), John R. Harris Library.

33. Riddell to Harris, (19 April 1989), John R. Harris Library. Underline in original.

34. "Queen Inaugurates Jebel Ali" (n.d.), Halcrow archives (viewed 3 March 2011).

35. Paul DeGive and Thomas A. Roberts, "Rashid—Merchant Prince of the Persian Gulf," *Christian Science Monitor* (9 Aug. 1973).

36. "Ruler and Businessman," *Middle East Construction* (Oct. 1977). The Currie family was discussed in Chapter 9.

37. Richard Johns, "Dubai: Growing Entrepôt Centre," *Financial Times* (5 June 1969).

38. Jonathan Raban, *Soft City* (London: Hamilton, 1974), 84.

39. Ibid.

INDEX